U[illegible]
Undergraduate Mathematics Program Office
3011 Angell Hall
Ann Arbor, MI 48109-1003

Mathematics of Compound Interest

MATHEMATICS OF COMPOUND INTEREST

Marjorie V. Butcher
Associate of the Society of Actuaries
Lecturer in Mathematics, Trinity College, Connecticut

Cecil J. Nesbitt
Fellow of the Society of Actuaries
Professor of Mathematics, University of Michigan

Distributed by
ULRICH'S BOOKS, INC.
549 East University, Ann Arbor, Michigan 48104

Printed in the United States of America
by Edwards Brothers, Inc., Ann Arbor, Michigan
Reprinted July, 1972
Third Printing July, 1976
Fourth Printing July, 1979
Fifth Printing April, 1987

ISBN 0-9603000-1-5
Library of Congress Catalog Card Number: 70-157152

CONTENTS

PREFACE

Often a well-educated individual is heard to confess that he feels totally at sea in his understanding of the mathematical fundamentals of borrowing and lending, even though he has a savings account, a mortgage, bonds, a car being bought "on time," an interest in government and corporate debt, and a grasp of the economics involved. This book affords him an opportunity to overcome his confessed lack, providing he has a knowledge of calculus. It is also intended for the serious student of the subject, including the actuarial student, and as a reference on compound interest theory. It has been tested in the classroom for several years at both the University of Michigan and Trinity College; yet it has been written for individual study as well.

The purpose of the book is to give a comprehensive, precise treatment of the mathematical theory of the subject generally known as mathematics of finance or investment and, in the final chapter, a survey of recent developments which are more or less interrelated. In the development of compound interest and discount, and of annuities and their applications, as well as in illustrative examples and problem lists, we strive to enable the reader to attain a mastery of the whole unified subject and, in addition, an appreciation of its niceties and detail. Every book on mathematics of finance discusses -- to some extent at least -- business practice in the borrowing and lending of money, and this book is no exception. However, its emphasis, far from being on the commercial aspects, is on the mathematical theory.

It is this stress on the mathematics, and also the level of mathematical maturity required, which chiefly distinguish this book from the majority on this subject. That is to say, we are principally concerned with providing an understanding of the mathematical tools by means of which the individual can solve most actual problems he may ever encounter in mathematics of finance.

Careful attention is given to definitions and notation and to presenting a reasonably full mathematical development, augmented by illustrative examples. Use of fundamental principles rather than formulas alone is urged throughout the book. There is stress on time-tested techniques, including line diagrams, equations of value, checks for reasonableness and verbal reasoning. The line diagram is a device for summarizing the details of a problem and often is a convenient stepping stone to the most desirable equation of value for solving the problem. The ability to do verbal reasoning in analyzing or checking a problem -- in contrast, for example, to algebraic methods -- is valuable, and opportunity for it to grow with practice is offered here. The problem lists have been carefully compiled so as to contain considerable variety and departure from the routine, of both numerical and theoretical types; and they are of sufficient length to permit ample practice. For development of his understanding and ability to use the subject, the reader is strongly urged to work problems.

The first two chapters deal with basic rates of interest and discount, and accumulating and discounting single sums. Proceeding from general definition to specific types of rates, they emphasize compound rates, including those with continuous conversion of interest. Interrelationships are developed among equivalent rates and comparisons made. Our definition and treatment of rate of interest-in-advance are new, with advantages in annuity and actuarial theory, and are tied in with the usual interpretation of rate of discount. The reader discovers the simplicity of compound rates in comparison to simple rates, and of the continuous theory which approximates the ideal of continuous growth of money at interest. The material of these chapters is typical of actuarial mathematics in general which proceeds from certain given rates to basic functions for accumulation and discount purposes. In fact, compound interest theory can be considered as one-dimensional actuarial mathematics wherein only the interest factor is studied.

In the next three chapters appear annuity theory and some of its applications. Chapter 3 develops the full theory of annuities-certain by formal mathematics and by verbal reasoning abetted by line diagrams. Of interest are annuity identities, the several approaches to the general annuity with level payments, and alternative procedures for valuing annuities. The main applications of annuities (which are given with greater completeness than usual) are (1) the standard amortization and sinking-fund methods of debt repayment of Chapter 4 and (2) in

Chapter 5 methods of determining the price and the yield of typical bonds.

The final chapter brings together a number of recent developments in the theory and application of compound interest. These developments supplement the traditional theory and practice of the first five chapters. They include (1) consideration of the impact of computer methods on the classical theory, (2) algorithms for solving annuity, amortization, sinking-fund and bond problems by computer, (3) the interesting mathematical problem of solving for the interest rate and modern techniques for doing so, (4) mathematical aspects of Truth-in-Lending legislation in the United States and (5) immunization of a large fund against loss from future variations in interest rates.

The Appendix contains a short introduction to the calculus of finite differences, references to selected books on compound interest, a set of financial tables and references to more extensive sets of financial tables.

Illustrative examples are incorporated throughout each chapter and usually also at its end. A single, comprehensive problem list follows each chapter except the last. In such a list, the first group of problems is considered basic and has the section-by-section order of the chapter; thereafter topical order is disregarded and the problems are graded. Answers to the basic problems appear after the Appendix. Answers to the remaining problems are not appended, but they are available at cost from the authors.

The authors are deeply grateful to the many persons who have rendered assistance and encouragement during the long period of preparation of this book. Our spouses, Ethel M. Nesbitt and Robert W. Butcher, have been exceptionally helpful and patient. Our students have offered constructive criticism and shown considerable interest in the progress and completion of our work, as have several of our colleagues. In Appendix A.4 we acknowledge our debt to Professors Carl H. Fischer and Allen L. Mayerson and to Mr. Donald Gieffers for the tables there. The book is photoprinted from typescript prepared by Mrs. Earl D. Rainville. We have been most fortunate to have had the benefit of her diverse and expert skills and express to her our warmest thanks. We especially appreciate, too, the work of Mr. Alfonso P. Garcia, Jr., graduate student in actuarial mathematics at the University of Michigan, for his painstaking proofreading and checking of problems.

For any errors or ambiguities in the book, the authors take full responsibility and would greatly appreciate having them brought to their attention.

Hartford, Connecticut
Ann Arbor, Michigan

Marjorie V. Butcher
Cecil J. Nesbitt

January, 1971

CHAPTER 1

RATES OF INTEREST

1.1. Introduction. A sometimes questioned, but generally accepted, assumption underlies the subject of the mathematical theory of interest. This basic assumption is that money is always productive; that is to say, any sum of money can be invested, so as to increase in amount as time passes, however short the period. Such an idea may at first seem unrealistic in practice, but in the types of transactions with which we shall be concerned -- primarily transactions involving the lending or borrowing of capital -- this assumption is readily seen to be sound, not merely for a mathematical theory but also as a basis in practice.

Consistently using the basic assumption, then, that money is always productive, we are about to begin to build a mathematical structure. In this structure will appear a great many relations or formulas. However, since most of these expressions follow as a direct consequence of definitions and a small body of basic relations, a person who concentrates on carefully learning definitions and on developing methods and techniques can attack any problem from basic knowledge of the subject without drawing on memorized formulas. In common with many authors and teachers, we urge such an approach and will attempt to aid the reader to develop skill in solving each problem from basic principles.

1.2. First concepts. Through the medium of such familiar arrangements as savings accounts, installment purchases, personal loans, mortgage loans and bond issues, we are all aware that money which is loaned earns money for the lender. Such money, earned from a loan of money, is called interest. The amount of money which is owed and upon which interest is being earned is called the principal. The sum loaned, or the actual amount transferred by the lender to the borrower, is the original principal, usually called simply the principal. In addition to it, at any date during the period of the transaction there is the accumulated principal (unfortunately also called the principal), which is the original principal together with interest accretions to that date.

Fortunately, the ambiguity is more apparent than real, since in context the proper interpretation is usually evident. In further contrast, there is the outstanding principal, which as we shall see in Chapter 4 can be thought of as the accumulated principal on the date in question, reduced by appropriate credit (at interest) for payments previously made by the borrower. But we are now getting ahead of our needs for the present chapter; as additional definitions of phrases involving the word principal are required, we shall make them. In any case, it is clear that depending on the conditions of a transaction, the principal may increase or decrease from its original amount during the course of the transaction.

Instead of considering matters from the viewpoint of the lender, one may equally well look at them from the standpoint of the borrower. For the latter, interest is money paid for money borrowed; and the original principal is the sum borrowed, namely, the borrower's proceeds. When it is immaterial to be specific about the loaning or borrowing aspect of a transaction, we shall simply speak of money invested at interest. Unless otherwise indicated, it will always be considered that interest is credited at the ends of stated interest intervals. Further, the length of time from the start of a transaction when the principal changes hands to the time of its complete repayment (with interest) is called the term of the investment, or merely the term. It should not be confused with the interest interval of which there may be several within the term.

We now come to a vital definition, that of rate of interest. Since there are several kinds of rates of interest, it is difficult to give a brief yet precise definition which always applies. Precision will not be lost and conciseness will be gained, if for this definition and for future theory and equations one sets the convention that such expressions as "interest" and "principal" may mean "number of units (e.g., dollars) of interest" and "number of units of principal" respectively. With this understanding, we now give

The General Definition of Rate of Interest: A rate of interest applicable over a given interest interval, expressed in terms of a time unit which may differ from the interval, is the ratio of the interest, earned in the interval and credited at the end of the interval, to the product of the principal (invested from the start of that interval) and of the number of time units in the interval.

In other words, the rate of interest in a given interval is numerically equal to the interest earned in the interval on a unit of principal per unit of time.

For example, a $2 interest return in a quarter year on a $200 investment of principal implies an interest rate per quarter of

$$\frac{2}{200(1)} = .01 \quad \text{or } 1\%,$$

where the interval and the time unit are both taken as a quarter year. If, in the above illustration, a year were chosen as the time unit, then one would have

$$\frac{2}{200(1/4)} = 4\%$$

as the <u>annual</u> rate of interest applicable over a quarter-year interval. Thus, identical monetary circumstances give rise to many rates, dependent on the time unit. As this chapter develops, the reader will find that both types of rates illustrated above are very natural and useful.

Our definition of rate of interest is general in the sense that it is applicable to various kinds of compound interest rates and may also be used for rates of simple interest. As the greater portion of this book will deal with compound interest rates, we shall present them first. Hereafter, when we speak simply of "interest" or of an "interest rate" we shall imply <u>compound</u> interest or <u>compound</u> interest rate,described immediately following and developed in this chapter.

It is characteristic of <u>compound interest</u> that at the ends of prescribed intervals, called <u>interest periods</u>, interest for the period on the principal at the beginning of the period is added to that principal and thereafter earns interest. One calls this process <u>compounding</u>, or <u>conversion</u> of interest into principal. For the theory (unless specified otherwise) and in many practical instances, it may be assumed that the interest, converted into principal in this manner, earns interest on exactly the same basis as the original principal.

A major distinction in regard to compound interest rates has as its basis the relation of the interest period to the time unit. <u>If the interest period equals the time unit, so that interest is compounded at the end of each time unit, we shall call</u>

the rate of interest an effective rate. The name derives from the fact that the rate of interest is numerically equal to the actual interest earned on one unit of principal in one unit of time. Denoting an effective rate by i, and referring to the general definition of interest rate, we may recapitulate by writing

$$i = \frac{\text{The interest earned during any time unit}}{\text{The principal invested from the beginning of that time unit}}$$

and specifying that the interest for the time unit is converted into principal at the end of the time unit to earn interest thereafter on the same basis as the original principal. For most practical applications, one may choose the time unit to be the interest period such as a month, quarter, half year or year, and may then deal with the effective rate per interest period. With reference to the previous illustration, if interest is converted at the end of each quarter, the 1% rate per quarter is an effective quarterly rate, but the 4% rate per year is not an effective annual rate because the interest period, one quarter, does not coincide with the time unit, one year.

In using the notation i to mean the rate of interest per interest period, we are in agreement with a number of other authors, but we have gone further and called it an effective rate. Most of these other authors impose the additional restriction that, for an effective rate, the interest period and time unit be one year; that is, they have limited the notion to effective annual rates. In the International Actuarial Notation, i is used to denote effective rate in this restricted sense. In contrast, by our generalized definition of effective rate with notation i, we recognize it as the basic rate in the development of the theory and in the solution of problems and we are in conformity with the notation of standard tables. As mentioned before, in practical applications, the most convenient time unit is often the interest period, and by making this choice for the time unit, we may express the solution in terms of the effective rate i per interest period. Of course, our definition of effective rate includes effective annual rate as a special case.

1.3. Accumulated value. Let us consider a principal A which is invested for n interest periods, where n is a positive integer, at an effective rate of interest i per period. At the end of each period, interest is converted into principal so that the principal grows by steps throughout the n-period term. Denoting the accumulated principal at the end of k interest periods ($k = 1, 2, \cdots, n$) by S_k and considering the growth in the kth interest period, we obtain the simple difference equation

$$S_k = S_{k-1} + i\,S_{k-1} \tag{1.1}$$

or

$$S_k = (1 + i)S_{k-1}\,. \tag{1.2}$$

Since $S_0 = A$, it follows by successive applications of equation (1.2) for $k = 1, 2, \cdots, n$, or by mathematical induction, that

$$S_k = A(1 + i)^k \tag{1.3}$$

and, in particular, that S_n, to be denoted by S, is given by

$$S = A(1 + i)^n. \tag{1.4}$$

We shall refer to S as the <u>accumulated value</u> or <u>final amount</u> at the end of the investment term, and to the process involved, as "accumulating under compound interest." One notes that we have now defined the accumulated value or final amount of an original principal to be the accumulated principal at the end of the investment term.

The difference between the accumulated value and the original principal, namely

$$S - A = A\left[(1 + i)^n - 1\right]\,, \tag{1.5}$$

represents the total interest earned during the investment term. As indicated by equation (1.1), such interest includes, in each period, interest on prior interest that has been converted into principal by the beginning of the period.

If \$1,000 were invested for 5 years at 1% effective per quarter, the accumulation of the \$1,000 principal at the end of the investment term of $n = 5 \cdot 4 = 20$ interest periods would be $1{,}000(1.01)^{20} = 1{,}220.19$, according to the value of $(1 + i)^n$ in the Appendix for $i = 1\%$ and $n = 20$. (For simplicity, dollar signs will usually be omitted in solutions. Also "equals" rather than "approximately equals" symbols, = instead of $\doteq$, will usually be used when numbers are rounded, whether because of substitution of tabulated values or otherwise.) In this transaction, the investor has put up \$1,000 and after 5 years has received \$1,220.19, consisting of the return of his principal and interest of

$220.19 = 1,000[(1.01)^{20} - 1]$. Had he taken the interest quarterly as earned, he would have received in this transaction $1,000(.01) = 10$ per quarter for 20 quarters, a total of only $200 in interest. The extra $20.19 illustrates the effect of turning interest back into principal by the compound interest process. The greater the effective rate and the term, the greater is the effect of compounding.

1.4. Present value. In many instances one may wish to know how much must be invested at a given time in order to provide a given amount at some later date. This involves the concept of present or discounted value. On the assumption that interest is at the effective rate i per period, the present value of a sum S due at the end of a term of n interest periods means the principal A which, if invested at the beginning of the term at the given effective rate i per period, will accumulate to S by the end of the n periods. One may determine the present value by solving equation (1.4) for A, thus obtaining

$$A = S(1 + i)^{-n} . \tag{1.6}$$

Equation (1.6) shows what is evident from definition, namely, that accumulating under interest and finding the present value (or discounting under interest) are inverse processes.

For convenience of writing, $(1 + i)^{-1}$ is often denoted by v. In this notation, equation (1.6) becomes

$$A = Sv^n . \tag{1.7}$$

The difference $S - A$ may now be expressed as

$$S - A = S(1 - v^n) , \tag{1.8}$$

and thought of as the total discount under interest on a sum S that is due at the end of n interest periods. In the previous section, this same sum $S - A$ was called the interest on the principal A. Whether one is discounting or accumulating determines his point of view on $S - A$.

For mathematics of finance, the literal meaning of the word "present" in the phrase "present value" is too narrow. Instead, the present value of an obligation is understood to signify the discounted value of the obligation at a time prior to the due date of the obligation. This time may be the actual present moment, or a time prior or subsequent to it.

The example in Section 1.3 may now be turned around to read: If \$1,220.19 is desired at the end of 4 years from now, and if money is worth 1% per quarter, what sum should have been invested a year ago? The answer -- \$1,000 -- would be obtained from 1,220.19 v^{20} at 1%, or from 1,220.19/$(1.01)^{20}$ by use of tables of v^n or $(1 + i)^n$. Thus \$1,000 was the present value, one year ago, of \$1,220.19 due 5 years from then. The present value now of the \$1,220.19 is 1,220.19 $v^{16} = 1{,}000(1.01)^4 = \$1{,}040.60$.

<u>1.5. Tables of the functions $(1 + i)^n$, v^n.</u> Equation (1.4) and its rearrangement, equation (1.7), are basic in the theory and application of compound interest. For this reason, tables of $(1 + i)^n$ and the reciprocal function v^n have been published for various values of i and for n ranging over the integers from 1 to 100 or more. A brief reference list of some of the more extensive published tables is given in the Appendix. With modern electronic computers it would be very easy to prepare values of these accumulating and discounting functions over a wide range of values of i and n.

In the Appendix there are brief tables of $(1 + i)^n$, v^n and other compound interest functions. From these tables, or otherwise, it is clear that $(1 + i)^n$ increases from 1 with increase in i or n, and that the inverse function decreases. In fact, under an effective rate of 5% per period, the present value of \$1 due at the end of 100 periods is \$0.00760, or less than 1¢, and the accumulated value of \$1 invested for 100 periods is \$131.50, a rather remarkable growth.

<u>1.6. Nominal rates of interest.</u> In business usage it is customary to quote interest rates on an annual basis. If the interest period is one year, that is, if interest is compounded annually, the quoted annual rate is an effective rate per year and, as previously mentioned, is called an <u>effective annual rate</u> of interest; it represents the actual interest earned on one unit of principal in one year.

Often, however, the quoted rate is converted more frequently than annually. For example, the rate may be 4% per year convertible quarterly. This implies that the effective rate of interest per quarter is 1%. If a unit is invested for one year under the given rate, the actual interest earned during the year is

$$(1.01)^4 - 1 = 0.040601,$$

or approximately 4.06% of the unit principal. It is in excess of the stated 4%, since interest has been earned on interest. This comparison has led to the terminology "nominal" annual rate for such a 4% rate, since it was thought to be a rate "in name only" and, as illustrated, did not represent the actual interest earned on one unit of money invested for a year.

However, in the sense of our general definition of rate of interest such a nominal rate is truly a rate of interest. Specifically, a nominal rate of interest (per time unit) is a rate of compound interest applicable over an interest period which may be different from the time unit. If the nominal rate is j, compounded m times per time unit, we shall denote it by (j, m) and have, according to the general definition,

$$j = \frac{\text{Interest earned during any interest period}}{\text{Principal invested from beginning of that period, times } 1/m}$$

$$= m \cdot \frac{\text{Interest earned during one interest period}}{\text{Principal invested from beginning of interest period}} ;$$

the interest earned in any interest period is converted into principal at the end of that period and subsequently earns interest on the same basis as the original principal. It follows now, by reference to the definition of effective rate in Section 1.2 that j/m is the effective rate per interest period. The frequency m may be any positive real number but is usually an integer. For mathematical convenience, effective rates per time unit have been included as the special case where $m = 1$.

To illustrate the definition by means of the previous example, we have .01 interest earned on a unit of principal per quarter year, so that the annual rate of interest according to the definition above is $.01/\frac{1}{4} = 4\%$, which agrees with the nominal rate actually given at the beginning of this section. For purposes of the next section, it is convenient to note that altering the time unit merely causes a proportionate change in the nominal rate. For example, rates of (4%, 4), (2%, 2) and (1/3%, 1/3)* with time units of a year, 6 months, and one month, respectively, all have the same effect, since the same effective quarterly rate of 1% pertains to each case. Thus, the accumulation problem of Section 1.3, solved in respect to each of these rates, would yield

*That is, 1/3% per time unit, convertible at the end of 3 time units.

$1{,}000(1.01)^{20} = 1{,}220.19$, as before. This illustrates the convenience and ease of solution of a numerical example by means of the applicable effective rate.

Ordinarily, the time unit for a nominal rate will be the year, and we shall speak of the nominal annual rate. There will, however, be some occasion to have nominal rates where the time unit is not a year. Likewise, while one frequently uses effective annual rates, there will be many applications of effective rates where the time unit is not a year but, instead, is the interest period for a given nominal rate. However, if the time unit for a nominal rate is not stated, it may be assumed to be a year.

If the nominal rate of interest is (j, m) and the investment term is N time units, then the effective rate of interest per interest period is j/m and the number of interest periods in the term is mN, where mN (although not necessarily m or N) is a positive integer. In this case, equations (1.4) and (1.6) for the accumulated value and present value may be expressed as

$$S = A(1 + j/m)^{mN} \tag{1.9}$$

and

$$A = S(1 + j/m)^{-mN} , \tag{1.10}$$

respectively. In applications, however, it will usually be more convenient to use the original notations i and n, and the basic equations (1.4) and (1.6).

For deciding which of (a) an effective rate of 6% or (b) (.06, 4) or (c) (.06, 12), all with a year as time unit, is most profitable for an investor, logical argument is sufficient; because, with an annual rate of 6% in each case, the rate most frequently converting interest into principal will produce the largest accumulation. Thus, (c) is most favorable and (a) least favorable. The extent of the difference for a unit principal over a 1-year term is indicated by the accumulations: for (a), 1.06; for (b), $(1.015)^4 = 1.0614$; for (c), $(1.005)^{12} = 1.0617$. Now for other applications refer to Examples 1.1 and 1.5 (Section 1.14).

1.7. Equivalent rates of interest. As has just been observed, the effect of a nominal rate of interest depends not only on the magnitude of the rate but also on the frequency of conversion. It may then happen that two different-appearing nominal rates have the same effect and are, therefore, essentially the same. We say that two rates are equivalent over a specified term if a given principal invested for that term under each rate accumulates to the same amount. The definition of equivalent rates is general; it applies whether the rates are compound or simple or one of each, and also whether they are interest or discount rates (to be defined in Chapter 2) or one of each.

Certain simplifications occur if both rates are compound rates, say for the purpose of discussion, (j_1, m_1) and (j_2, m_2) with the same basic time unit. (If two rates do not have the same time unit, a common one may be chosen and the rates adjusted proportionately, as mentioned in the last section.) In particular, (j_1, m_1) and (j_2, m_2) are equivalent over a time unit if a unit of principal invested for the time unit under each rate provides the same accumulated value, that is, if

$$(1 + j_1/m_1)^{m_1} = (1 + j_2/m_2)^{m_2} \quad . \qquad (1.11)$$

If a principal $A \neq 1$ had been used, the resulting equation would simplify immediately to equation (1.11), and this situation prevails regardless of the kinds of rates involved. Hence, the equivalence relationship never depends on the particular principal used; if no principal is given, any convenient one may be assumed, and if an inconvenient one is given, another may be chosen.

In the instance above, where two compound rates were used, if a term of N time units had been taken, simplification would again lead to equation (1.11). Consequently, we may drop the qualification that equivalence is "over a specified term" and say that two compound rates are equivalent if a principal invested for the same term under each rate accumulates to the same amount. Moreover, if m_1 and m_2 have the greatest common factor m, and $m_1 = m\,m_1'$, $m_2 = m\,m_2'$, then equation (1.11) reduces to

$$(1 + j_1/m_1)^{m_1'} = (1 + j_2/m_2)^{m_2'} \quad . \qquad (1.12)$$

This expression compares the accumulation of a unit by both rates over the shortest term in which both rates compound an integral number of times, and often choice of such a term is convenient.

For any given nominal rate (j, m) there will be an equivalent effective rate i for the same time unit, given by the relation

$$(1 + j/m)^m = 1 + i$$

or

$$i = (1 + j/m)^m - 1. \tag{1.13}$$

If (j_1, m_1) and (j_2, m_2) are equivalent, then by subtraction of 1 from each side of (1.11), it follows that the two rates have the same equivalent effective rate per time unit. Further, since to find a present value is inverse to accumulating, if two rates of compound interest are equivalent, they yield the same present value for any given sum due in the future.

In applications, the effective rate per time unit may be given and nominal rates equivalent to the effective rate may be introduced. The notation $i^{(m)}$ is used to denote the nominal rate compounded m times per time unit which is equivalent to the effective rate i with the same time unit. From equation (1.13), or directly from the definition of equivalence, we see that the two rates are related by the equation

$$(1 + i^{(m)}/m)^m = 1 + i. \tag{1.14}$$

This relation may be solved for $i^{(m)}$ in terms of i to yield

$$i^{(m)} = m\left[(1 + i)^{1/m} - 1\right] . \tag{1.15}$$

If, for instance, $i = 4\%$, then $i^{(2)} = 3.9608\%$ and $i^{(12)} = 3.9285\%$. Whenever $m > 1$, we have $i^{(m)} < i$; for a smaller nominal rate, with its more frequent conversions of interest into interest-earning principal can accumulate a given principal to the same sum as a higher effective rate. In fact, the greater the value of m, the greater will be the spread between the two equivalent rates. (It is assumed here, as usual, that $i > 0$.)

Brief tables of $(1 + i)^{1/m}$, $i^{(m)}$ and $v^{1/m}$, for commonly used values of i and m, appear in the Appendix.

As a final observation, it should be pointed out that by now we have discussed two types of effective rates i equivalent to a given nominal rate (j, m). The first is the effective rate $i = j/m$ per interest period (with the time unit changed to equal the given interest period), and this type will be used very generally in applications. The second is the effective rate per time unit, namely, $i = (1 + j/m)^m - 1$, which has its interest period chosen to be the original time unit. A main use of this latter type is in the comparison of different nominal rates. Thus, the solution of the comparison example in the last section might have involved finding the effective annual rate equivalent to each of the given rates, with the investor desiring the greatest such rate -- that is, the one for (c) -- namely $(1.005)^{12} - 1 = 6.17\%$, since (a) and (b) yield effective annual rates of only 6% and 6.14%, respectively.

Study of Example 1.2(a) - (c) in Section 1.14 may now be helpful.

Statements in newspapers and advertisements about financial matters are sometimes a source of wonderment. A bank in Maine has advertised a savings account paying annual interest at 5.1161 8979%. Checking up on this phenomenon, one discovers that $.051161\ 8979^{(12)} = .05$, which is to say that the stated rate and (.05, 12) are equivalent. This example indicates why it is useful to have both the notations $i^{(m)}$ and (j, m) for nominal rates. The former is useful if one starts with (a usually simple) effective rate and goes to equivalent nominal rates; the latter is natural if one starts with a given nominal rate.

1.8. Force of interest. Up to now we have developed the theory on a discrete basis; that is, rates have compounded at the ends of interest periods of finite duration. If a calculus were to have been used, it would have been the calculus of finite differences. However, it seems reasonable to imagine that discrete rates have been used in business practice to approximate to the ideal of continuous growth of sums invested at compound interest. Mathematically, this ideal of interest conversions at infinitesimal intervals can be expressed by means of the infinitesimal calculus. The ideal is helpful in the theory of compound interest, but has received only limited use in practice. However, this use is growing, for instance, by banks for their savings accounts.

To develop the continuous theory of interest, let us consider a principal A which grows continuously over a term of N time units under interest that is momently converted into principal. Further let t range continuously from 0 at the start of the transaction to N and let $S(t)$ denote the accumulated principal at time t including all prior interest conversions. The nominal rate of interest operating at time t, it being assumed that interest is continuously converted into principal, is called the force of interest at time t and will be denoted by δ_t. By the general definition of rate of interest in Section 1.2, and on the assumption that $S(t)$ is a differentiable function of t, we have

$$\delta_t = \lim_{h \to 0} \frac{S(t + h) - S(t)}{S(t)h} \quad *$$

or

$$\delta_t = \frac{1}{S(t)} \frac{dS(t)}{dt} . \tag{1.16}$$

Equation (1.16) shows that δ_t is the rate of increase in the principal, per unit of principal and unit of time, at time t. It is sometimes convenient to think in terms of the differential relation resulting from (1.16), namely

$$dS(t) = S(t)\, \delta_t dt .$$

We may interpret this equation as stating that the approximate growth, $dS(t)$, in the principal in the instant at time t is brought about by the interest, $S(t)\,\delta_t dt$ earned through the operation of the nominal rate δ_t for the infinitesimal duration dt, in other words, by the effective instantaneous rate $\delta_t dt$.

From (1.16) it follows that

$$d \ln S(t) = \delta_t dt$$

which, after integration with $0 \le t \le N$, becomes

$$\ln \left[\frac{S(N)}{S(0)}\right] = \int_0^N \delta_t dt,$$

so that if we set $S(N) = S$ and $S(0) = A$,

$$S = Ae^{\int_0^N \delta_t dt} \tag{1.17}$$

and

$$A = Se^{-\int_0^N \delta_t dt} . \tag{1.18}$$

These equations, expressing accumulated and present values on a continuous basis, are analogous to equations (1.9) and (1.10) for the discrete theory, but are more general in the two senses that (1) the mathematics does not restrict the term N beyond requiring

*Observe that the numerator represents the total interest earned in the interval $(t, t + h)$, such interest being converted into principal as soon as it is earned. For δ_t a varying rate, the definition of nominal rate in Section 1.6 requires a little modification since interest when credited does not subsequently earn interest on the original basis.

it to be positive, but permits it to be <u>any</u> positive real number, and (2) the rate of interest is not necessarily a constant throughout the investment term but is allowed to vary with time. For extension of varying rates to the discrete case, rate definitions would require some revision and formulas of the type

$$S = A\prod_k (1 + j_k/m_k), \qquad A = S\prod_k (1 + j_k/m_k)^{-1}$$

would be introduced; generalizing the term in the discrete case will be discussed in Section 1.10.

If now, for the continuous theory, we assume that $\delta_t = \delta$, a constant, then equations (1.17) and (1.18) give

$$S = Ae^{\delta N} \tag{1.19}$$

and

$$A = Se^{-\delta N}. \tag{1.20}$$

In particular, a unit of principal invested for one time unit under the constant force δ, accumulates to e^{δ}. If i is the equivalent effective rate, then

$$e^{\delta} = 1 + i \tag{1.21}$$

or

$$\delta = \ln(1 + i). \tag{1.22}$$

Equations (1.21) and (1.22) link the continuous and discrete theories, since δ is convertible on a continuous basis and i on a discrete basis.

It is worthwhile to observe that equation (1.22) might have been obtained by considering

$$\begin{aligned} \delta &= \lim_{m\to\infty} i^{(m)} &&\text{, by definition,} \\ &= \lim_{m\to\infty} \frac{(1+i)^{1/m} - 1}{1/m} &&\text{, from equation (1.15),} \\ &= \lim_{h\to 0} \frac{(1+i)^h - 1}{h}^{*} &&\text{, where } h = 1/m, \end{aligned}$$

*The reader may recognize this limit to be the derivative of $(1 + i)^x$ at $x = 0$, namely, $\ln(1 + i)$. Note Section 1.10 which allows m and h to be continuous as needed here and line 1, p.15.

$$= \lim_{h \to 0} \frac{(1+i)^h \ln(1+i)}{1} \text{ , by l'Hôpital's rule,}$$

$$= \ln(1+i).$$

However, this approach to the concept of force of interest does not lend itself to the development of such formulas as equations (1.17) and (1.18) for the case of a variable force.

As with discrete nominal rates, so also with a force of interest, the year is the most common time unit and is often the only one considered. In this book, we shall specify annual force of interest where applicable and thus keep "force of interest" a more general term.

Forces of interest equivalent to commonly used effective rates are tabulated in the Appendix. One might check tabulated values or compute others from (1.22), either by means of an extensive table of logarithms or, preferably, to any desired accuracy by means of a series expansion with

$$\ln(1+i) = i - \frac{i^2}{2} + \frac{i^3}{3} - \frac{i^4}{4} + \cdots .$$

To find the constant force of interest δ equivalent to $i = .01$, we may use the series expansion to just 4 terms to obtain

$$\delta \doteq .01 - \frac{(.01)^2}{2} + \frac{(.01)^3}{3} - \frac{(.01)^4}{4} = .00995\ 0331 \ ,$$

which is the Appendix value. Examples 1.2(d) and (f) also illustrate forces of interest in equivalent rate problems.

Let us find the present value of \$100 due in 2 years if the variable annual force of interest at time t is $\delta_t = .03t^2$, $0 \le t \le 2$. We require

$$100\ e^{-\int_0^2 .03t^2 dt} = 100\ e^{-.01t^3\Big]_0^2} = 100\ e^{-.08} = 92.31,$$

with $e^{-.08}$ being available in tables of exponential functions or calculable by logarithms or series expansion.

1.9. Simple interest. In many transactions of a short-term nature interest is computed on a so-called simple interest basis. By this is meant that interest is calculated on the original principal throughout the term of the transaction and there is no periodic conversion of interest into principal; accordingly, the interest interval is the term itself. Simple interest is not practical for long-term transactions, as it penalizes the investor by not permitting the investment of accrued interest. It is useful, however, for short-term investments, in particular, those with a term less than a full interest period.

Let our simple interest notation be I, the amount of interest; A, the original invested principal; i, the rate of simple interest; and t, the investment term expressed in the time unit on which i is based (usually a year). Then referring again to the general definition of a rate of interest in Section 1.2, one has

$$i = I/(At)$$

which yields the main formula of simple interest,

$$I = Ait \ . \tag{1.23}$$

As shown by formula (1.23), simple interest varies directly with the term of the investment.

For the accumulated value S at the end of the term, we have

$$S = A + I = A(1 + it) \ . \tag{1.24}$$

Conversely, if S is due at the end of time t, then its present value, if interest is at the simple rate i, is given by

$$A = S/(1 + it) \ . \tag{1.25}$$

With simple interest, one may encounter the "time problem." Surprisingly, if the time unit is a year, t is not uniquely defined by

$$t = \frac{\text{Number of days in the term}}{\text{Number of days in a year}}$$

since in practice the numerator has been variously taken as (a) the exact number of days between the initial and terminal dates of the transaction, and as (b) the approximate number of days based on the assumption of a uniform 30-day month; and likewise the denominator is sometimes taken to be 365, and at other times 360, based on the 30-day month assumption. In practice, the Banker's Rule, inconsistently using the ratio of the exact number of days to 360, occurs most frequently; in this book its use will be assumed. The exact number of days for the numerator may be computed by a table of the number of each day of the year (Table IV in the Appendix).*

Consider the example: On August 18, A borrows \$1,200 from C and signs a note promising to pay the bearer \$1,200, plus simple interest at 8% per annum, on April 14 of the following year (which happens to be a leap year). On January 15, C needs cash and discounts A's note at Bank B, which charges a 6% simple interest rate.** What does C receive, and what rate of simple interest does he earn during the time he holds the note?

In any interest problem containing, like this one, quite a number of numerical facts, a device called a <u>line (or time) diagram</u> is very useful in summarizing these facts concisely, in suggesting procedures for solving and in reducing chance for error. The device consists of marking off, below a horizontal line, the data involving time and, above the line, of relating the data involving sums, both known and to be found, to the time scale. The interest rate is indicated and often also the date or dates on which the sums are to be valued. Thus, Figure 1.1 is a line diagram for this problem.

The number of days between dates can be found by use of Table IV with time counted from the beginning of the calendar year containing the earliest date (August 18); e.g., April 14 is treated as day 365 + 104 + 1 = 470 in the second line of time data on the line diagram. The third set of time data expresses the dates in terms of the time unit (here a year), according to the Banker's Rule, with the date August 18 denoted as time 0.

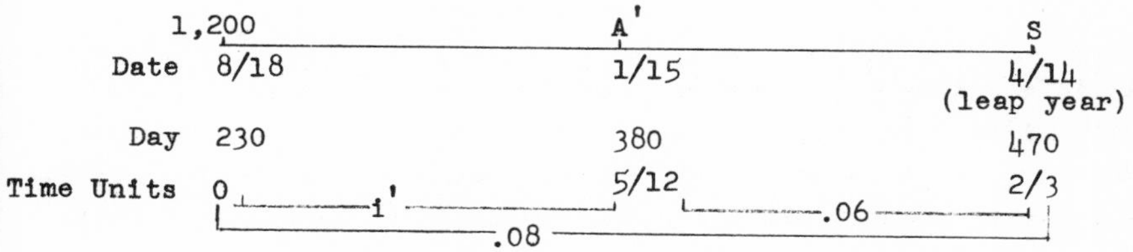

Fig. 1.1

Now the bank is buying the maturity value S, payable to it (the bearer) at maturity date, namely

$$S = 1{,}200\left[1 + .08\left(\frac{2}{3}\right)\right] = 1{,}200\left[\frac{3.16}{3}\right] = 1{,}264.00,$$

*An exception occurs when the term is an integral number of months, say May 5 to July 5 which we shall take as 2/12 year.

**Commonly, however, banks use a simple <u>discount</u> rate in such a situation (see Chapter 2).

for which it pays to C proceeds of

$$A' = \frac{1{,}264}{1 + .06(\frac{2}{3} - \frac{5}{12})} = \frac{1{,}264}{1.015} = 1{,}245.32\ .$$

Thus, C earns in interest

$$45.32 = 1{,}200\ i'\ (\tfrac{5}{12})$$

or a yield i' of 9.06%. This earnings rate exceeds the original 8% because of the favorable rate to C, relative to 8%, at which the bank discounts the maturity value.

If the approximate number of days between dates were used, leap year would be immaterial and the following subtraction system would determine the time between August 18 and April 14:

	Year	Month	Day		Year	Month	Day
4/14	2	4	14		2 - 1 = 1	12 + 4 - 1 = 15	30 + 14 = 44
				or			
8/18	1	8	18		1	8	18
					0	7	26

7(30) + 26 = 236 days.

It is quite possible to speak of a rate of compound interest (j, m) and a rate of simple interest i, with a common time unit, being <u>equivalent over a term of N time units</u>. From the definition of equivalent rates in Section 1.7, one has immediately

$$(1 + j/m)^{mN} = 1 + Ni. \qquad (1.26)$$

As in the case of equivalent compound interest rates, so here with mixed rates the equivalence is independent of the principal. However, two mixed rates equivalent over one term are <u>not</u> equivalent over another term, since formula (1.26) cannot be made independent of N; on the other hand, as we have seen, with two compound rates the term is immaterial. See Example 1.2 (e).

<u>1.10. Case where the term is not an integral number of interest periods.</u> In the establishment of formulas (1.4) and (1.6), it was assumed that the number of interest periods n is an integer. If, instead, $n = \bar{n} + t$, where $\bar{n}$ denotes the greatest integer less than n, and $0 < t < 1$, the formulas for the accumulated value and the present value are still of the familiar forms

$$S = A(1 + i)^n \tag{1.27}$$

and

$$A = S(1 + i)^{-n} , \tag{1.28}$$

respectively. For if δ is the force of interest equivalent to the effective rate i per period, then from formula (1.19), with $N = n$ being <u>any</u> positive real number

$$S = Ae^{\delta n} = A(1 + i)^n$$

since $e^{\delta} = 1 + i$. Thus, $(1 + i)^n$ is the accumulation factor and $(1 + i)^{-n}$ the present value or discount factor under compound interest, for n any positive real number, integral or not. We have just shown that compound interest is possible for a non-integral number of interest periods.

From equation (1.27), we obtain

$$S = A(1 + i)^{\overline{n}}(1 + i)^t .$$

Now if, for instance, t is a complicated fraction, $(1 + i)^t$ may be laborious to compute by means of the binomial formula or the extensive (7-place or more) logarithm tables that may be necessary to secure a desired degree of accuracy. In any situation when $n = \overline{n} + t$, a practical and useful approximation for obtaining the accumulated value is

$$S \doteq A(1 + i)^{\overline{n}}(1 + it) , \tag{1.29}$$

where accumulation is by compound interest for the $\overline{n}$ whole interest periods and thereafter by simple interest for the remaining portion t of an interest period. The approximation consists of taking just the first two terms in the series expansion for $(1 + i)^t$, which for the usual values of i and for $0 < t < 1$ is rapidly convergent, so that unless A is very large the result of formula (1.29) differs very little from the exact result.

Similarly, from equation (1.28), we have

$$A = S(1 + i)^{-\overline{n}}(1 + i)^{-t} = S(1 + i)^{1-t}(1 + i)^{-(\overline{n}+1)} .$$

Each of the forms above suggests a practical approximation for finding the present value. The second or right-hand form yields

$$A \doteq S\left[1 + i(1 - t)\right](1 + i)^{-(\overline{n}+1)}, \tag{1.30}$$

where one accumulates S by simple interest to the end of the interest period in which it is due, discounting the result by compound interest to the present. From the first form, however,

$$A \doteq [S/(1 + it)]\,(1 + i)^{-\overline{n}}, \tag{1.31}$$

where the discounting proceeds by simple interest to the beginning of the interest period in which S falls due, and then by compound interest for the remaining $\overline{n}$ periods to the present. Of the two, formula (1.30) is more frequently used, because it is usually the more convenient for computation and, besides, the result it gives can also be obtained by linear interpolation between $(1 + i)^{-\overline{n}}$ and $(1 + i)^{-(\overline{n}+1)}$, as the reader may verify. Similarly, the result of formula (1.29) may be obtained by linear interpolation between $(1 + i)^{\overline{n}}$ and $(1 + i)^{\overline{n}+1}$. In many cases, practical solutions based on linear interpolation are adequate, and obviate the extensive calculations that would be required by the pure compound interest formulas (1.27) and (1.28).

At the end of the chapter, Examples 1.3 and 1.4 illustrate cases of nonintegral term.

<u>1.11. Comparison of values under compound interest and simple interest.</u> It is informative to compare values under a compound interest rate with the corresponding values under an equal simple interest rate. Let V_0 denote a principal available at time 0. If the effective rate of compound interest is $i > 0$ per interest period (time unit) then the value V_t at time t of V_0 is, by what we have just seen,

$$V_t = V_0(1 + i)^t. \tag{1.32}$$

Here t may be any real number, integral or not, positive or negative. The graph of V_t is simply that of the exponential function $V_0(1 + i)^t$.

In the case of a simple interest rate, also of i and having the same time unit, two formulas are necessary to express the corresponding values, which will now be denoted by V_t^s. These formulas, from equations (1.24) and (1.25), are

$$V_t^s = V_0(1 + it), \qquad t \geq 0 \tag{1.33}$$

$$V_t^s = V_0/[1 + i(-t)], \qquad t \leq 0. \tag{1.34}$$

For $t \geq 0$, the graph of V_t^s is a straight line of slope V_0 i, but for $t \leq 0$, it is a portion of a hyperbola having the negative t-axis as asymptote.

To compare formulas (1.32) and (1.33), let

$$y = V_t - V_t^s = V_0\left[(1 + i)^t - (1 + it)\right], \ t \geq 0.$$

Then $y = 0$ for $t = 0$ and $t = 1$. Also,

$$y' = \frac{dy}{dt} = V_0\left[(1 + i)^t \delta - i\right]$$

$$y'' = \frac{d^2y}{dt^2} = V_0(1 + i)^t \delta^2 > 0.$$

It follows that y has a minimum value when $y' = 0$, namely, when

$$(1 + i)^t = i/\delta = (e^\delta - 1)/\delta$$

$$= 1 + \frac{\delta}{2} + \frac{\delta^2}{6} + \cdots,$$

that is, when

$$t \ln(1 + i) = t\delta = \ln(1 + \frac{\delta}{2} + \frac{\delta^2}{6} + \cdots) \doteq \delta/2,$$

by series expansion to one term. Hence, for i in its customary range and

$$t \doteq 1/2 \text{ interest period}$$

the difference function y reaches a minimum. Because $y'' > 0$, the graph of the function y, for $t \geq 0$, is concave upwards. Further, since y is continuous, vanishes only at $t = 0$ and $t = 1$, has a minimum at $t \doteq 1/2$ and has no other extremum, it now follows that $y < 0$ for $0 < t < 1$, and $y > 0$ for $t > 1$. These same conclusions regarding y may be obtained by using the binomial expansion of $(1 + i)^t$ in the definition of y and considering in turn $0 < t < 1$, $t > 1$.

When $t \leq 0$, the reciprocals, $1/V_t$ and $1/V_t^s$ have essentially the same forms as are given by formulas (1.32) and (1.33) for $t \geq 0$. It follows that for $t \leq 0$, the difference $(1/V_t - 1/V_t^s)$ has the same properties as y, with $t \geq 0$, of the preceding paragraph. Then, for $i > 0$,

$$1/V_t = 1/V_t^s \quad , \quad (-t) = 0, 1$$
$$1/V_t < 1/V_t^s \quad , \quad 0 < (-t) < 1$$
$$1/V_t > 1/V_t^s \quad , \quad (-t) > 1$$

and hence,

$$V_t = V_t^s \quad , \quad (-t) = 0, 1$$
$$V_t > V_t^s \quad , \quad 0 < (-t) < 1$$
$$V_t < V_t^s \quad , \quad (-t) > 1.$$

It can be shown that there is a maximum for $V_t - V_t^s$ when $(-t) \doteq 1/2$. In addition, from equations (1.32) and (1.34), one sees that as $t \to -\infty$, both V_t and V_t^s approach zero. Therefore, with $V_{-1} = V_{-1}^s$ and $V_t < V_t^s$ for $t < -1$, there must be a minimum for the continuous function $V_t - V_t^s$ for some $t < -1$.

Table 1.1 displays numerically the results of this discussion for the extreme example of $i = 100\%$, which was chosen in order to get demonstrable differences between V_t and V_t^s, for $|t| < 1$. In summary, we have found that accumulated values under compound interest are less than those for simple interest for terms shorter than one interest period, the greatest difference occurring near half a period, but for terms longer than one interest period, the values under compound interest increasingly exceed those provided by simple interest. As is logical, inequalities are reversed in the comparison of present values, with the present values being equal at the start and at the end of one interest period, and converging after a large number of interest periods.

Referring back to the previous section, we can now draw some conclusions as to the relative magnitudes of the results of the various formulas for instances when the term is not an integral number of interest periods (and $i > 0$). We observe that the practical approximation in equation (1.29) always gives a greater accumulated value than the exact compound interest method, since we have just established that

$$1 + it > (1 + i)^t, \quad 0 < t < 1.$$

Similarly, the approximate present value given by equation (1.30) always exceeds the true (compound) present value, which itself is always greater than the alternative approximate present value of

TABLE 1.1

Comparison of Accumulating and Discounting a Unit Sum Under Equal Compound and Simple Interest Rates (i = 100%)

t	Compound Interest V_t	Simple Interest V_t^s	y $V_t - V_t^s$
-100	0.000	0.010	-0.010
- 20	0.000	0.048	-0.048
- 10	0.001	0.091	-0.090
- 6	0.016	0.143	-0.127
- 5	0.031	0.167	-0.136
- 4	0.062	0.200	-0.138
- 3	0.125	0.250	-0.125
- 2	0.250	0.333	-0.083
- 1.0	0.500	0.500	0.000
- 0.9	0.536	0.526	0.010
- 0.7	0.616	0.588	0.028
- 0.5	0.707	0.667	0.040
- 0.4	0.758	0.714	0.044
- 0.3	0.812	0.769	0.043
- 0.1	0.933	0.909	0.024
0	1.000	1.000	0.000
0.1	1.072	1.100	-0.028
0.3	1.231	1.300	-0.069
0.4	1.320	1.400	-0.080
0.5	1.414	1.500	-0.086
0.6	1.516	1.600	-0.084
0.7	1.625	1.700	-0.075
0.9	1.866	1.900	-0.034
1.0	2.000	2.000	0.000
2	4.000	3.000	1.000
3	8.000	4.000	4.000
5	32.000	6.000	26.000
10	1,024.000	11.000	1,013.000

Note that $y = V_t - V_t^s$ has value zero for t = -1, 0, 1 and that y has its minimum at $t \doteq -4$, a local minimum at $t \doteq 0.5$ and a local maximum at $t \doteq -0.4$. As t becomes large and positive, y increases rapidly.

equation (1.31); for, from this section,

$$1 + i(1 - t) > (1 + i)^{1-t}, \quad 0 < t < 1 ,$$

but

$$(1 + i)^{-t} > 1/(1 + it) \quad , \quad 0 < t < 1 .$$

Thus, the approximate methods (1.29) and (1.31) always favor the creditor by granting him more interest than does the exact method, but the method of formula (1.30) favors the debtor. In all these cases, the maximum error occurs when t is about 1/2.

1.12. Values of dated payments. We have already seen some of the implications of the assumption that when a sum of money becomes available, by payment of interest or otherwise, it can immediately be invested to earn compound interest at some given rate. That money is productive in this sense is a basic assumption of compound interest theory and from it stems the full spread of the mathematical developments. In this and the following section, we shall see an important way in which the assumption simplifies both theory and applications. As usual, the discussion will be restricted to the case where the given rate of interest is constant, but the argument could be extended to the case of a variable rate.

In practice, with each payment of money is associated its due date. Under the given assumption, to value the payment equitably on some date other than the due date, one must accumulate or discount it (as the case may be) under the fixed rate of interest for the interval between the dates. If this rate is i per period, and time is measured in interest periods, the value at time t_0 of a payment S due at time t is precisely

$$S(1 + i)^{t_0 - t} \tag{1.35}$$

since if $t_0 < t$, this yields the present value at time t_0 of the payment S while if $t_0 > t$, it yields the appropriate accumulated value. For each time t_0, formula (1.35) assigns a value to the dated payment S due at time t. The formula, of course, is essentially the same as the right member of equation (1.32), but in different notation.

1.13. Equations of value. A basic tool in compound interest theory and applications is the equation of value. To set up such an equation, one first selects a valuation or comparison date.

An equation of value is a statement that the sum of the values on the comparison date of one set of dated payments is equal to the sum of the values on the same date of another set of dated payments, all values being in respect to a given rate of interest. The basic compound interest formulas (1.4) and (1.6) are simple equations of value.

In the case of compound interest at the effective rate i, if the comparison date is at time t_0, and payments A_h, due at times t_h, are to be equated in value to payments B_k, due at times t_k, the equation of value is

$$\sum_h A_h(1+i)^{t_0-t_h} = \sum_k B_k(1+i)^{t_0-t_k} . \tag{1.36}$$

This may be reduced to

$$\sum_h A_h\, v^{t_h} = \sum_k B_k\, v^{t_k} . \tag{1.37}$$

The absence of t_0 in equation (1.37) indicates that the equality under compound interest does not depend on the particular comparison date chosen. The equation for any other comparison date, say at time t, may be obtained by multiplying equation (1.37) by the factor $(1 + i)^t$. Thus, in a compound interest problem, one may choose any convenient common date for valuing the dated payments. Refer again to Example 1.1.

Two sets of payments which are related by an equation of value are said to be equivalent. That equivalence does not depend on the particular date of comparison is one of the characteristic features of compound interest. Payments which are equivalent (inequivalent) at any one comparison date, under compound interest are equivalent (inequivalent) at all other dates.

The situation is by no means so straightforward in the case of simple interest where equivalence at one comparison date of the two sets of dated payments does not signify their equivalence at any other date. The matter will not be pursued, but it may be realized that since two different formulas (1.33) and (1.34) are required to determine values under simple interest, and since these formulas lack the convenient exponential character of the corresponding formula (1.32) for compound interest, nothing very neat can be expected.

By altering equation (1.36) to an inequality, and proceeding as above, one sees that under compound interest, if a set of dated payments is more valuable than another set when valuation is made on a particular date, then it is more valuable on every date. This same conclusion does not follow for simple interest. For consider \$100 invested today and \$110 to be invested in 2 years, both at 6% simple interest. Two years from now, the \$100 investment has a \$112 value and is more valuable than the \$110 sum, but seven years from now the \$110 has accumulated to \$143 and the \$100 to only \$142; the crossover occurs 5 1/3 years from the present, when both investments have accumulated to \$132, and so are equivalent at that particular time.

Another aspect is given by considering a dated payment which is to be valued on one date, and the new sum revalued on another date. Under simple interest one expects a different result than would be obtained if the original payment had been valued directly on the final date, while under compound interest the results agree. From this and previous observations, one may conclude that, after all, simple interest is not so simple, so useful or so equitable as compound interest.

Suppose that a \$1,000 investment made 10 years ago has earned an effective annual rate of 5% for the past 7 years and is now worth \$1,500, and suppose that one wishes to know the nominal annual rate j, converted semiannually, which was earned during the first 3 years. In the terminology of equivalence, one must find the rate $(j, 2)$ by which 1,000 at time $t_1 = 0$ is equivalent to $1{,}500(1.05)^{-7}$ at time $t_2 = 6$, where time is measured in half-year interest periods. We may value our sums at time t_2, obtaining the equation of value

$$1{,}000(1 + j/2)^6 = 1{,}500(1.05)^{-7},$$

and then proceed to obtain j either logarithmically or by means of linear interpolation in a table of accumulated values. By the latter method, we require j in

$$(1 + j/2)^6 = 1.06602,$$

and we proceed by hunting among the Appendix values of $(1 + i)^6$ for those values which most closely bracket 1.06602. As it happens, these occur when rate i, which is our rate $j/2$, is 1 1/4% and 1%. Then we set up a table for interpolation, as follows:

	j	$j/2$	$(1 + j/2)^6$	
$\frac{1}{2}\%$	$2\frac{1}{2}\%$	$1\frac{1}{4}\%$	1.07738	.01586
$x\%$	?		1.06602	.00450
	2	1	1.06152	

$$j = (2 + x)\% = (2 + \frac{450}{1,586} \cdot \frac{1}{2})\% = 2.14\%.$$

In the interpolation method one observes that the rate $j/2$ need not be found; but in the logarithmic method, one solves first for $j/2$.

In this example, the most convenient date of all, $t = 6$, was chosen and a simple equation of value resulted. The reader should note that any other choice of valuation date would have yielded a more complicated, though algebraically equivalent, equation of value to solve; for example, valuing at $t = 0$, one has

$$1,000 = 1,500(1.05)^{-7}(1 + j/2)^{-6};$$

while valuation 6 years after the \$1,000 was invested yields

$$1,000(1 + j/2)^6(1.05)^3 = 1,500(1.05)^{-4}.$$

That interest was at rate $(j, 2)$ for the first 3 years, and at the effective annual rate of 5% for the last 7 years, makes the situation a little more complicated than the usual case where only one rate of interest is to be assumed, and also indicates that the date at which the interest rate changes is a natural choice for comparison date.

1.14. Remarks on the solution of problems in compound interest; illustrative problems. Experience has indicated that for the solution of problems students will develop more skill and accuracy if the appropriate portions of the following procedures are carried out:

(a) Determine the interest period and effective rate per period.

(b) Sketch a line diagram, with time marked off in interest periods, and indicate thereon each sum to be considered and its due date expressed in terms of interest periods. At this stage, it may be well to reread the problem to verify that the data have been correctly transcribed to the line diagram. By graphically displaying all the pertinent data of the problem, the line diagram often suggests the next steps to be taken for a simple solution.

(c) Choose a convenient comparison date and write an equation of value, the solution of which will supply part or all of the information desired. Such equations of value may make use of the various formulas for present and accumulated values that will be presented as the theory develops. However, a deeper appreciation of the underlying simplicity and coherence of the subject will be gained if formulas are not used in too direct a manner, that is merely as expressions for the substitution of numbers, but instead are treated as flexible tools for setting up equations of value.

(d) Before attempting any calculations, make whatever algebraic simplifications are possible.

(e) Be aware of what tabulated functions are available; select the best ones for the purpose at hand. As previously mentioned, in the Appendix are tabulated values of $(1 + i)^n$, v^n, $(1 + i)^{1/m}$, $v^{1/m}$ (in Table I) and δ, 100 $i^{(m)}$ (in Table II) for selected values of i, n, m. Also given are a table of number of each day of the year (Table IV) and an abbreviated table of log (1 + i) with seven decimals, for $0 \le i \le 0.1009$ (Table III). In logarithmic work in investment mathematics, this last-named table should usually be used whenever it is applicable. It is assumed that the reader has available a table of 5-place common logarithms or, preferably, of 6-place mantissas for common logarithms (published, for example, in Chemical Rubber Co., CRC Standard Mathematical Tables, 16th edition -- together with instructions as to its use in interpolation).

As to selecting the best table for a given purpose, a case in point is $A = 10^6(1.08)^{-100}$. Determined from Table I using v^{100}, A = 454.60 (accurate to nearest 10¢) but from Table I using $(1 + i)^{100}$, A = 10⁶/2199.7612 56 = 454.5947 872. The first is fast, but one would use the second if greater accuracy were needed.

Use tabulated values with care. At all stages of a solution consider whether the numbers being used are of reasonable magnitude. In use of tables numerical errors may arise from employing an incorrect function, interest rate or term. Checks for reasonableness as the work proceeds and at the finish of the problem may nip such errors and also, perhaps, mistakes in theory and computation. One should also guard against any inconsistencies in the solution, such, for example, as an effective annual rate of interest less than the equivalent annual force of interest.

(f) Unless instructed otherwise, obtain monetary answers to the nearest cent, rates to the nearest 0.01% and time to the nearest hundredth of a year or other time unit. To do so requires that a sufficient number of significant digits be carried at every stage of the calculation; usually a satisfactory rule-of-thumb is two more digits than required in the final answer. Obtaining an efficient computational form is important for both accuracy and speed in solving.

The following examples illustrate these procedures as they apply within the scope of the theory developed up to now. Reference to the first five has already been given in the text. We suggest, however, that the reader review them in the light of the complete chapter. Example 1.6, not heretofore mentioned, extends the theory by developing bounds for the error in linear interpolation.

Example 1.1

(a) Adams owes Berg the following:

(i) a non-interest-bearing debt of $10,000 due at the end of 2 years,

(ii) $20,000 (together with interest for 8 years at the effective annual rate of 6%) due 5 years from now,

(iii) a $1,000 debt just contracted and due in 6 months, together with simple interest at 10% per year.

Adams tells Berg that he would like to repay these sums by making 5 equal semiannual payments, the first due at the end of 2 years. If money is worth the nominal annual rate of 6%, compounded semiannually, what semiannual payments should Berg be willing to accept in lieu of the original obligations?

Solution: An effective semiannual compound interest rate of 3% is implied as the rate to use in valuing both the maturity values of all obligations and the semiannual payments, at a common comparison date. As a first step, we make a line diagram showing the present obligations and the proposed payments, denoted by R.

Payments					R	R	R	R	R		
Obligations		1,050			10,000						$20{,}000(1.06)^8$
Half Years	0	1	2	3	4	5	6	7	8	9	10
	3%										↑

Fig. 1.2

Next, we choose a comparison date which we believe will conveniently minimize computation; the reader should convince himself that in this case time 10 (indicated on the diagram) is the "best" comparison date. Then we write an equation of value in regard to obligations and payments, namely,

$$1{,}050(1.03)^9 + 10{,}000(1.03)^6 + 20{,}000(1.06)^8$$
$$= R\left[(1.03)^6 + (1.03)^5 + (1.03)^4 + (1.03)^3 + (1.03)^2\right].$$

This yields

$$1{,}050(1.3047732) + 10{,}000(1.1940523) + 20{,}000(1.5938481)$$
$$= R[1.1940523 + 1.1592741 + 1.1255088 + 1.0927270 + 1.0609000]$$

and finally R = \$8,022.69.

(b) Construct a table which shows the progress of the repayment of the indebtedness during the period of semiannual payments.

<u>Solution:</u> Essentially, we wish to trace the elimination, period by period, of the entire debt valued just before the first repayment. This debt is given by

$$1{,}050(1.03)^3 + 10{,}000 + 20{,}000(1.06)^8(1.03)^{-6} = \$37{,}843.82.$$

The table below convincingly shows that the series of payments of \$8,022.69 is exactly sufficient to cancel the debt in the required way.

TABLE 1.2

Showing Progress of Repayment of the Debt

(1) Half Year	(2) Value of Debt Before Payment $(4)_{-1} + (5)_{-1}$	(3) Amount Paid R	(4) Value of Debt After Payment (2) - (3)	(5) Interest on Outstanding Debt $.03 \cdot (4)$
5	\$37,843.82	\$8,022.69	\$29,821.13	\$894.63
6	30,715.76	8,022.69	22,693.07	680.79
7	23,373.86	8.022.69	15,351.17	460.54
8	15,811.71	8,022.69	7,789.02	233.67
9	8,022.69	8,022.69	0.00	

It is to be noted that the fifth half-year commences at time 4 on the line diagram and that the amounts in column (2) after the first one are the sum of the amounts in the last two columns of the previous line.

(c) If Adams will repay his obligations, instead, by 5 equal semiannual payments, the first due 6 months from now, how will these payments be related to those of (a) and how much will they be?

Solution: The line diagram depicts the old payments R and the new payments R'.

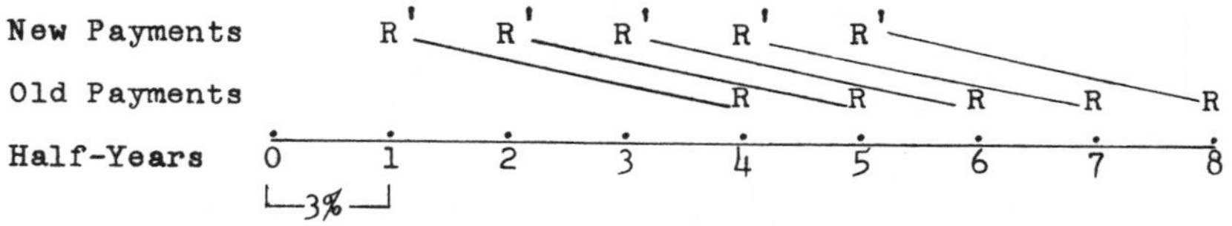

Fig. 1.3

Each new payment occurs 3 interest periods before the corresponding old payment and thus the equation of value between them is

$$R' = R\, v^3 = 8{,}022.69(.9151417) = \$7{,}341.90.$$

Because the value of R is only to cents, the accuracy of the cents in R' is in question. This method shows directly the relationship between the two sets of payments, without the labor of setting up either the type of equation in (a) or an equation of value between the entire set of new payments and of old payments.

Example 1.2

Given a 4% annual interest rate, compounded semiannually, determine to the nearest 0.001%

(a) The equivalent effective annual rate;

(b) The equivalent nominal annual rate, compounded quarterly;

(c) The equivalent nominal annual rate, compounded monthly;

(d) The equivalent annual force of interest;

(e) The equivalent annual simple interest rate;

(f) The equivalent ultimate annual force of interest if it is triple the initial force and each operates for the same length of time.

Solution: For each portion of the problem we equate the accumulated value of a unit invested for a year under the given rate of interest with the corresponding value under the rate to be found.

(a) If i is the effective annual rate, then

$$1 + i = (1.02)^2$$
$$i = (1.02)^2 - 1 = .04040.$$

(b) If $(j, 4)$ is the nominal rate requested, then

$$\begin{aligned}(1 + j/4)^4 &= (1.02)^2\\ j &= 4\left[(1.02)^{1/2} - 1\right]\\ &= 2\left\{2\left[(1.02)^{1/2} - 1\right]\right\}\\ &= 2\, i^{(2)} \quad \text{for} \quad i = 2\%\\ &= .03980.\end{aligned}$$

(c) Denoting the required rate by j, we have

$$\begin{aligned}(1 + j/12)^{12} &= (1.02)^2\\ j &= 12\left[(1.02)^{1/6} - 1\right].\end{aligned}$$

For variety, assume that neither $i^{(6)}$ nor $(1.02)^{1/6}$ is given in our tables so that $(1.02)^{1/6}$ must be calculated by squaring $(1.02)^{1/12}$, by binomial expansion, by logarithms, or by some such device. Using log 1.02 = .0086002, we obtain

$$(1.02)^{1/6} = 1.003306 \quad \text{and} \quad j = .03967,$$

which we note checks with $2\left[.02^{(6)}\right]$.

(d) In this case,

$$\begin{aligned}e^{\delta} &= (1.02)^2\\ \delta &= 2 \ln 1.02 \quad \text{(i.e., twice the force of interest when } i = 2\%)\\ &= .03961.\end{aligned}$$

(e) Since equivalence for a simple interest rate depends on the term of the transaction, there is no single simple rate equivalent to the given rate. If the term is taken as one year, the resulting equivalent simple rate would equal the effective annual rate of .04040 determined in (a). However, if the term is half a year, the equivalent simple rate i is .04000, as given by the equation

$$1 + i/2 = 1.02.$$

(f) If the term of the transaction is N years and if δ represents the ultimate force of interest, then the initial force is $\delta/3$, hence

$$e^{(\delta/3)(N/2)}\ e^{\delta(N/2)} = (1.02)^{2N}$$

or

$$e^{\delta/3} = 1.02$$

$$\delta = 3 \ln 1.02$$

$$= .05941 \ .$$

This result is altogether independent of the term of the transaction; the solution would be unchanged if N were omitted in the first equation.

In inspecting the results of the first four parts for reasonableness, we note the expected decrease in equivalent rates as the frequency m of conversions per year increases, from 4.040% when m = 1 to 3.961% as $m \to \infty$. The closeness of the rate (3.967%, 12) to the limiting rate may, however, come as a surprise to the reader.

Example 1.3

(a) In how many years will money double itself at an effective annual rate of interest of 6%?

(b) At what effective annual rate will money double itself in 10 years?

(c) How many years will it take for a unit to grow one hundred-fold at an effective annual rate of 6%?

(d) Test by (a) and (b) the validity of the commonly stated rule that the number of periods n in which money will double itself at the effective rate i per period satisfies the relations

$$n \doteq \frac{.693}{i} + .35 \doteq \frac{.70}{i}$$

and establish the first approximate result.

(e) Solve (a), (b) and (c) using an annual rate of simple interest and express the number of intervals needed for money to double at a simple rate i per interval.

Solution:

(a) If n denotes the required number of years, then

$$(1.06)^n = 2 \ .$$

Taking logarithms, we have

$$n \log 1.06 = \log 2$$
$$n = .301030/.0253059 = 11.90 \text{ years.}$$

This solution implies use of compound interest throughout the transaction. If in practice compound interest is used for just the whole number of interest periods, with simple interest thereafter, the interpolation method below would be preferable.

		n	$(1.06)^n$		
1		12	2.0122		.1139
	x		2.0000	.1017	
		11	1.8983		

$$n = 11 + x = 11 + \frac{1017}{1139} = 11.89 \text{ years.}$$

These answers differ only in the last place; that the second is slightly smaller follows from Section 1.11.

It is interesting that money invested at 6% will double in less than 12 years. One may go on to observe that in another 12 years it will double again, in a third 12 years double once more, and so on. With such rapid growth possible, it is no wonder that the level of prevailing interest rates is a matter of considerable economic importance.

(b) The required effective annual rate i is given by the equation

$$(1 + i)^{10} = 2 .$$

Solution either by interpolation (illustrated in Section 1.13) or by logarithms is possible and, of course, since an integral number of interest periods is stipulated, there is no use of simple interest as an approximation to compound interest. There result logarithmically

$$10 \log (1 + i) = \log 2$$
$$\log (1 + i) = .0301030$$
$$1 + i = 1.0718$$
$$i = 7.18\% .$$

As a quick check of reasonableness one might observe the compatibility of this result with that of (a); for surely when the term for doubling is reduced a little, the interest rate must rise somewhat.

(c) In this case, if n represents the desired number of years,

$$(1.06)^n = 100$$
$$n \log 1.06 = 2$$
$$n = 2/.0253059 = 79.03 \text{ years},$$

a remarkably short time. Yet the result is reasonable, for when money doubles in 12 years, it grows $2^7 = 128$-fold in just $7 \cdot 12 = 84$ years.

With our tables, solution by the interpolation method would be rather tedious here, since $(1.06)^{79}$ is not tabulated in them. Interpolation between $(1.06)^{70}$ and $(1.06)^{80}$ would be quite inexact and could only serve to give an estimate of what values $\bar{n}$ and $\bar{n} + 1$ would bracket the desired n. Therefore, in this case one might first calculate

$$(1.06)^{79} = (1.06)^{70}(1.06)^9$$

and observe whether $(1.06)^{79}$ and $(1.06)^{80}$ bracket the required value, 100. If not, further calculations would be required. Alternatively and preferably one could whittle down the right side of the original equation to suitable size by transforming it, for example, to

$$(1.06)^{n-50} = 100(1.06)^{-50}$$
$$= 5.4288$$

and then proceed to find $n - 50$ by interpolation.

(d) For (a), the rule $n \doteq .35 + .693/i$ gives $n \doteq 11.90$ years and for (b), $i \doteq .693/9.65 = 7.18\%$, the same results as before. The simpler rule $n \doteq .70/i$ yields $n \doteq 11.67$ years for (a) and $i \doteq 7.00\%$ for (b).

To establish the rule, we set

$$(1 + i)^n = 2$$

and take natural logarithms, obtaining

$$n \ln (1 + i) \doteq .693$$
$$n \doteq .693/\ln (1 + i)$$
$$= .693/(i - \frac{i^2}{2} + \cdots)$$
$$\doteq \frac{.693}{i}/(1 - \frac{i}{2})$$
$$\doteq \frac{.693}{i}(1 + \frac{i}{2})$$
$$\doteq \frac{.693}{i} + .35 .$$

The approximations are offsetting. Those in lines 1 and 5 in the previous display understate n; those in lines 4 and 6 overstate n.

(e) With t denoting the number of years for money to double at 6% simple interest, we have

$$2 = 1 + .06\,t$$
$$t = 1/.06 = 16.67 \text{ years.}$$

The difference between this result and the 11.90 years in (a) is a measure of the considerable effect of compounding. For a sum to double in 10 years at an annual simple interest rate i, one has

$$2 = 1 + 10\,i$$
$$i = .1000\quad ,$$

which is to be compared with the compound rate of .0718 in (b). The growth of one hundred-fold in t years is expressed by

$$100 = 1 + .06\,t$$
$$t = 99/.06 = 1{,}650 \text{ years,}$$

somewhat exceeding the 79 years of (c)! Doubling in t intervals at a rate of simple interest i per interval, given by

$$2 = 1 + i\,t\ ,$$

yields

$$t = 1/i \qquad \text{and} \qquad i = 1/t.$$

Example 1.4

Given a nominal annual rate (6%, 2), accumulate $1,000 from January 1, 1970 to November 10, 1982; then discount your result back to July 1, 1977. Would the same result be obtained by the accumulation of $1,000 from January 1, 1970 to July 1, 1977?

Solution: With a basic 6-month time unit, a line diagram for this transaction is shown in Figure 1.4.

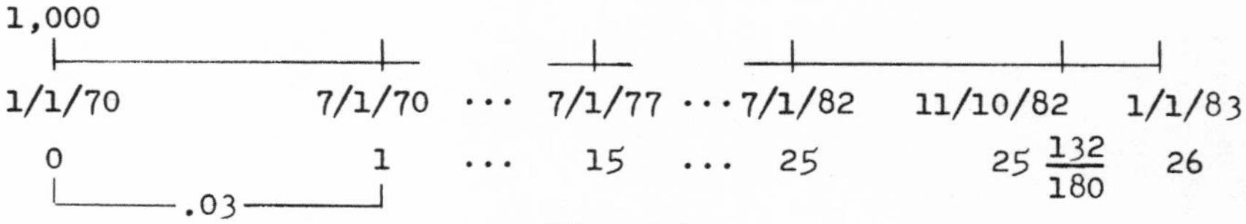

Fig. 1.4

The fraction 132/180 of a half year was obtained from Table IV and the Banker's Rule. Now

$$S = 1{,}000(1.03)^{25\ 132/180} = 1{,}000(1.03)^{25}(1.03)^{132/180}$$
$$\doteq 1{,}000(1.03)^{25}\left[1 + .03\ \left(\frac{132}{180}\right)\right] = \$2{,}139.84\ .$$

Discounting S by the usual approximation, we find

$$A \doteq 2{,}139.84\left[1 + .03\ \left(1 - \frac{132}{180}\right)\right](1.03)^{-11} = \$1{,}558.23\ ,$$

which differs by \$0.26 from the direct accumulation,

$$1{,}000(1.03)^{15} = \$1{,}557.97\ .$$

Thus, although the usual approximate methods for accumulating and discounting, given by (1.29) and (1.30), have several useful properties, they are inconsistent with each other. In fact, as each produces an error in excess, using both here is "just asking for it."

Alternatively, with the other present value approximation, we have

$$A \doteq \frac{S}{1 + .03\ \left(\frac{132}{180}\right)}(1.03)^{-10}\ ,$$

which upon algebraic substitution for S yields the exact result $1{,}000(1.03)^{15}$. Indeed, the approximations in equations (1.29) and (1.31) are always consistent with one another, the one undoing the error of the other.

Example 1.5

(a) To what will \$1,000 accumulate in 20 years if it is estimated that money will be worth

(i) an effective annual rate of 4% for the first 5 years,

(ii) a nominal annual rate of 5%, compounded semiannually, for the next 8 years, and

(iii) a nominal semiannual rate of $1\frac{1}{2}$%, converted monthly, for the final 7 years.

(b) Same problem, except that the rates operate in reverse order, each for the same length of time as it did in (a).

(c) What single effective annual rate operating for the whole 20 years would accumulate \$1,000 to the same amount as in (a)?

Solution:

(a) An initial \$1 sum accumulates as indicated on the line diagram (Figure 1.5).

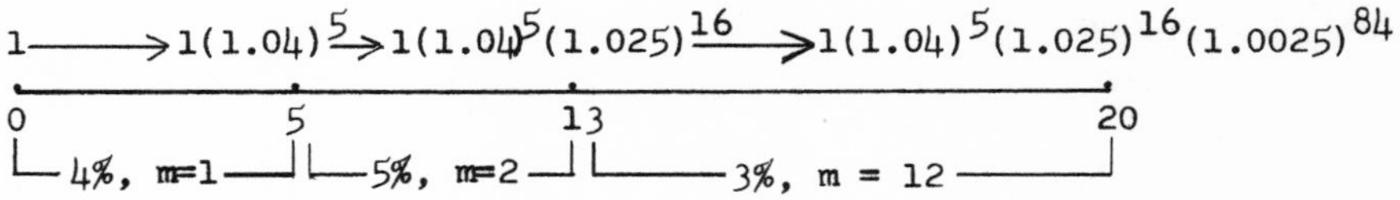

Fig. 1.5

Then calculating $(1.0025)^{84}$ by $(1.0025)^{80}(1.0025)^4$, we find

$$1{,}000\ S = 1{,}000(1.2166529)(1.4845056)(1.2333549) = \$2{,}227.60.$$

(b) The accumulation in this case is as indicated below.

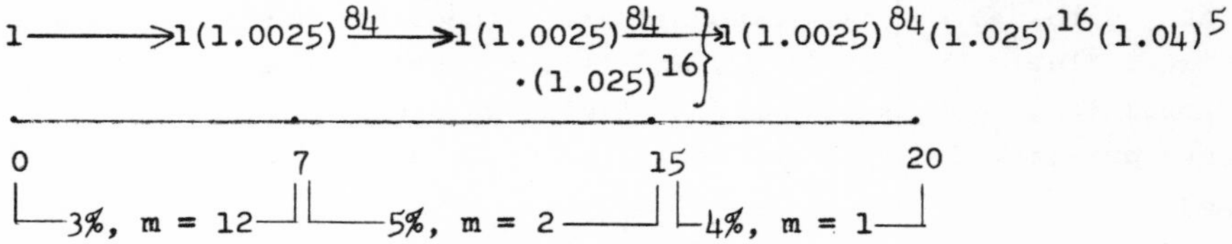

Fig. 1.6

The accumulation factors are the same as in (a), but in reverse order. Consequently, 1,000 S = \$2,227.60, as before.

(c) If i is the effective annual rate required, then

$$1{,}000(1 + i)^{20} = 1{,}000\ S = \$2{,}227.60.$$

The reader may verify that the solution for i obtained by inverse linear interpolation in Table I is $i = 4.079\%$ and by logarithms is $i = 4.086\%$. With an obvious extension of the definition of equivalent rates, we may say that the rate i is equivalent to the set of rates in (a) and in (b) for the terms specified or multiples of them.

Example 1.6

If $f(i)$ is a function of the interest rate i and has derivatives up to the second order at least, and if linear interpolation is applied in the interval $i_1 < i < i_2$ and M is the maximum value of $|f''(i)|$ in the interval $i_1 \leq i \leq i_2$, show that the theoretical error in direct linear interpolation for $f(i)$ is not greater in absolute value than

$$\frac{1}{8}(i_2 - i_1)^2 M$$

and the theoretical error in inverse linear interpolation for i, given f(i), is not greater in absolute value than

$$\frac{1}{8}(i_2 - i_1)^3 \frac{M}{|f(i_2) - f(i_1)|} .$$

(There may be additional error due to the rounding of tabular values of f(i) but the rounding error is not considered here.)

Solution: By the Newton divided difference formula with remainder term*

$$f(i) = f(i_1) + (i - i_1)\frac{f(i_2) - f(i_1)}{i_2 - i_1} + \frac{(i - i_1)(i - i_2)}{2!}f''(\tau), i_1 < \tau < i_2.$$

The first two terms on the right produce the linear interpolation approximation to f(i), while the final term is the remainder term. The quadratic $(i - i_1)(i - i_2) = i^2 - (i_1 + i_2)i + i_1 i_2$ takes on its greatest absolute value for $i_1 < i < i_2$ when $i = (i_1 + i_2)/2$, with

$$\text{Max}|(i - i_1)(i - i_2)| = (i_2 - i_1)^2/4.$$

Hence the remainder term in the above formula has absolute value not greater than

$$\frac{(i_2 - i_1)^2}{8} M .$$

For inverse interpolation the relation for f(i) may be rearranged as

$$i = i_1 + \frac{f(i) - f(i_1)}{f(i_2) - f(i_1)}(i_2 - i_1) + \frac{(i_1 - i)(i - i_2)}{2[f(i_2) - f(i_1)]}(i_2 - i_1)f''(\tau).$$

Again the first two right-hand members represent linear interpolation and the final one, the remainder term. In this case, from the preceding analysis the remainder term is seen to have absolute value not greater than

$$\frac{(i_2 - i_1)^3}{8} \frac{M}{|f(i_2) - f(i_1)|} .$$

---

*See, for example, H. Freeman, Finite Differences for Actuarial Students (Cambridge, 1960) or Mathematics for Actuarial Students, Part II (Cambridge, 1946), pp. 45, 57.

If $f(i) = (1+i)^n$, with n considered constant, then $f''(i) = n(n-1)(1+i)^{n-2}$ and is positive for $n > 1$. For such n, the remainder term for direct linear interpolation is then negative; that is, the interpolated value exceeds the true value. For inverse interpolation, however, the remainder term is positive and the interpolated value for i is less than the true value.

If $f(i) = (1+i)^{-n}$, the remainder term in inverse linear interpolation is

$$\frac{(i_1 - i)(i - i_2)(i_2 - i_1)}{2\left[(1+i_2)^{-n} - (1+i_1)^{-n}\right]} n(n+1)(1+\tau)^{-(n+2)}$$

and is negative. It follows that the true value of i lies between the results of inverse linear interpolation in regard to the functions $(1+i)^n$ and $(1+i)^{-n}$.

In Example 1.5 (c), the error in inverse linear interpolation for i is not greater than

$$\frac{1}{8}(.01)^3 \frac{20(19)(1.05)^{18}}{(1.05)^{20} - (1.04)^{20}} = 0.00025 = 0.025\%.$$

Further, if inverse linear interpolation is carried out in respect to $(1+i)^{-20} = 1/2.22760 = .448914$, we find $i = 4.094\%$ and an upper bound on the numerical error through interpolation is 0.028%. The solution by logarithms gave $i = 4.086\%$ which, bearing out the reasoning above, is intermediate to the values 4.079% and 4.094% given by the two linear interpolations and well within the intervals determined by the error bounds of 0.025% and 0.028%, respectively.

1.15. Format of the problem lists. As we mentioned in the Preface, the Problem List of a chapter is in two main parts, which are a Basic List and a Supplementary List. We believe that nearly every reader will wish to solve some problems, and we recommend that he begin with the Basic List. These basic problems are arranged by section, and answers for them are given in pages 305-315.

After working with the Basic List, the reader may then move on to the next chapter or he may turn to the Supplementary List for his present chapter. These problems are not divided by section, but are arranged, more or less, in increasing order of difficulty.

For Chapter 1, the Basic List contains 67 problems and the Supplementary List, 57 (Problems 68-124). In the latter list, the reader might be interested, say, in the equated time principle in Problems 87 and 88, the rate of return on a fund (Problem 117), and Problems 122 and 124, among others.

PROBLEM LIST 1

Basic List (Problems 1-67)

Sec. 1.1-1.5

1. A desires $800. He may obtain it by promising to pay $900 at the end of a certain period; or he may borrow $1,000 and repay $1,120 at the end of the same period. If he can invest any balance over $800 at 10% for the period, which should he choose?

2. Which sum is more valuable: $1,000 payable in 8 years, or $850 payable in 3 years, if money is worth (a) 3% effective per year, (b) 4% effective per year?

3. Find the present value of $1,000 due at the end of 25 years if interest is at (a) the effective monthly rate of 0.5%, (b) the effective annual rate of 6.1%.

4. Jamison holds Bowen's note for $5,000 due in 4 years. He offers to sell the note to Rowe for $4,400. Does the offer give Rowe any advantage over depositing in a bank paying 1.75% semi-annually?

5. A savings organization guarantees the payment of interest at the quarterly rate of 1.25%. An individual who has had $1,000 on deposit with this organization for 5 years finds that his deposit was credited with interest at the guaranteed rate for the first 1.5 years and thereafter at the quarterly rate of 1.5%. By how much has his accumulation been increased by reason of the excess interest payments?

6. At an effective annual rate of 7%, what is the difference in present value between $1,000 paid at the beginning of each year for 25 years and $1,000 paid at the end of each of those years?

7. (a) If $4 accumulates to $9 in 10 years, to what would $100 accumulate in 25 years?

(b) If A accumulates to S in n interest periods, to how much will S accumulate (i) in n interest periods? (ii) in mn interest periods?

8. A lot can be bought for $5,400 cash or for $2,500 down and $1,500 at the end of each of the next 2 years. Should a purchaser who has the cash and can invest at an effective annual rate of 6% pay cash?

9. What effective annual rate is earned on a $10,000 investment which in 10 years grows to (a) $14,000? (b) $28,000?

10. Three debts of \$1,050, \$950 and \$1,000 were due 9, 10 and 11 years ago respectively. However, they were settled by a single payment of \$3,000 ten years ago. What effective annual rate of interest was money worth in this transaction?

11. On a \$6,000 trailer, \$2,000 is paid down. The remaining unpaid balance of \$4,000 is paid off by annual payments of \$1,000 at the end of each of the next 4 years; on these same dates interest for the year on the unpaid balance outstanding during the year is paid at 6%. What is the present value of all the payments at an effective quarterly rate of .0175?

12. Given $(1.06)^{100} = 339$ and $(1.08)^{100} = 2{,}200$. Without the use of any tables, determine whether each of the following is reasonable:

(a) $(1.06)^{200} = 680$ (c) $(1.06)^{50} = 18$

(b) $(1.07)^{100} = 1{,}300$ (d) $(1.08)^{-50} = .04$.

Sec. 1.6, 1.7

13. Find the accumulated value of \$1,000 invested for 15 years at (a) a nominal annual rate of 8% compounded quarterly, (b) an effective semiannual rate of 4%, (c) an effective annual rate of 8%, (d) an effective annual rate of 8.16%.

14. Find the present value of \$1,000 due at the end of 10 years if interest is at (a) a nominal annual rate of 6% compounded monthly, (b) an effective monthly rate of 1/2%, (c) an effective quarterly rate of 1 1/2%.

15. When borrowing \$1,000 from B, A signed a note agreeing to repay the money with interest at an annual rate of (.07, 4) at the end of 5 years. One year after the date of the loan, C offered to buy the note from B at a price which would yield C 6% per year, effective. What was C's offer?

16. A man owes (i) \$1,000 due in 18 months and \$40 interest payments at the ends of the next 3 semiannual periods, and (ii) \$2,000 due in one year and \$35 interest payments at the ends of the next 4 quarters.

(a) What sum invested now at 6% per annum convertible quarterly will meet the payments above?

(b) For quarters 1, 2, ···, 6 fill in a schedule with the following column headings: (1) Quarter; (2) Fund at beginning of quarter; (3) Interest earned on fund in quarter; (4) Payments at end of quarter on (i) \$1,000 loan, (ii) \$2,000 loan; (5) Increase in fund during quarter.

17. Find m, if a unit accumulates to 1.2682418 in 4 years at (.06, m) per year.

18. (a) Calculate the nominal annual rate, convertible quarterly, equivalent to an effective annual rate of 5%.

(b) Calculate to three significant figures the effective annual rate equivalent to a nominal annual rate of 5%, convertible quarterly.

(c) Determine the effective quarterly rate of interest equivalent to (i) the rates in (a), (ii) the rates in (b).

19. Given: the present value of \$1,000 due at the end of 10 years is \$690.

(a) Without using interest tables, find the accumulated value of \$1,000 after 14 years.

(b) What is the nominal annual rate of interest, compounded quarterly?

(c) Use (b) to check (a).

(d) Find the nominal annual rate of interest, compounded monthly, that is equivalent to the rate found in (b).

20. What nominal annual rate of interest (a) compounding every 2 months is equivalent to (.06, 4)? (b) convertible every 2 years is equivalent to (.06, 2)?

21. Interest on certain funds is convertible every 3 years. Obtain to the nearest .001% (a) the nominal rate per annum equivalent to 2% effective per annum, (b) the effective rate per annum equivalent to 2% nominal per annum.

22. (a) What effective annual rate of interest is actually paid by a person who pays \$10 interest each month on a \$1,000 debt?

(b) What monthly interest should the person in (a) offer to pay if he believes (.07, 2) is fair?

23. (a) Define $i^{(m)}$ in words.

(b) Prove, other than verbally, that $i^{(m)} < i$, when $m > 1$ and $0 < i < 1$.

(c) Given that $(1.01)^6 = 1.0615\ 2015\ 0601$, find (to 4 significant figures) $.0615\ 2015\ 0601^{(m)}$, when m is 1, 2, 4, 6,12.

24. Calculate to as many significant figures as possible and compare with the tabulated value: (a) $.01^{(12)}$ using $(1.01)^{1/12}$ in Table I, (b) $(1.01)^{1/12}$ using $.01^{(12)}$ in Table II.

25. Define $i^{(1/2)}$ and find i if $i^{(1/2)} = .1050$.

26. Given $i^{(2)}/i^{(4)} = 1.01$, find i.

Sec. 1.8

27. (a) Compute to the nearest .001% the nominal annual rate of interest, convertible monthly, which is equivalent to a 3% annual force of interest.

(b) Compute to 6 significant figures the annual force of interest equivalent to a nominal annual rate of interest of 12% compounded monthly, both by series expansion and by use of interest tables.

(c) Compute the effective annual rate of interest equivalent over 1 year to a variable annual force of interest of $\delta_t = .0375 + .005\,t,\ 0 \le t \le 1$.

(d) What nominal annual rate of interest convertible once every 2 years is equivalent to a quarterly force of interest of 1%?

(e) If δ is the force of interest equivalent to (.04, 4), find the rate (j, 12) equivalent to $(3\delta, \infty)$. All the rates are annual.

28. If a unit of principal quadruples in n years under an annual force of interest δ, how large does it become in n years under a force of interest 3δ? under a force $\delta/4$?

29. If the accumulated amount at the end of t years of 1 invested at time 0 is given by the formula $1 + .05\,t$, what is (a) the annual force of interest at time 10? (b) the effective annual rate of interest earned in the 21st year?

30. (a) Accumulate a unit for 63 years under an annual force of interest which at time t is $1/[6(t + 1)]$.

(b) If the annual force of interest at time t, $0 \le t \le 10$, is

$$\delta_t = \ln 1.05 - .1\,t \ln 1.04,$$

find the present value of $1,000 due at the end of 10 years.

31. (a) Find the accumulated value of $1,000 invested for one year under an annual force of interest which is 1% for the first month and increases by 1% for each month thereafter.

(b) Find the present value of $1,000 due at the end of 10 years, if at the beginning of the term the force of interest is 4% and the force decreases uniformly to 3% at the end of 5 years, after which it remains constant.

32. One loan institution offers interest at an annual rate of 5% compounded daily on deposits, while a competitor offers interest at an annual rate of 5.1% compounded quarterly. Which offer is more favorable?

33. (a) At what level annual force of interest over 30 years will a sum accumulate to the same amount as at the varying annual forces δ_t, such that

$$\delta_t = \begin{cases} .04, & 0 \le t \le 10 \\ .06, & 10 < t < 25 \\ .05, & 25 \le t \le 30 \end{cases}$$

Express your answer exactly, as a fraction.

(b) When within the 30-year period will the accumulation at the variable rates exceed that at the level rate?

34. For how many complete years will the accumulation of $200 with interest at 3% effective per year be greater than the accumulation of $100 with interest at 6% effective per year? Given $\ln 2 = .693$ (approximately).

Sec. 1.9

35. An individual has the choice of making a 3-year investment at 8 1/2% per year simple interest or at a rate of 8% compounded annually. Which rate should he choose?

36. A fur coat, ordinarily retailing at $800, can be bought at 25% off during February. What is the highest annual simple interest rate at which an individual can afford to borrow to take advantage of the sale price, rather than delay purchase by 6 months?

37. A $500, 6-month loan bearing simple interest at 8% is discounted after 60 days at a bank charging 6% simple interest. What are the proceeds?

38. If money is worth 12% simple interest per year to a merchant, which is the best offer to him on a $1,000 invoice: (a) 4% off for cash on delivery, (b) 3% off for cash in 30 days, (c) full $1,000 in 90 days?

39. On savings accounts a bank used to pay interest at (4%, 2) on January 1 and July 1. Deposits received before the tenth of the month earned simple interest from the beginning of the month to the next interest date; on all other deposits interest accrued from the beginning of the month following receipt. Find the total accumulation on January 1, 1963 of \$100 deposits made January 9, 1960; February 1, 1960; March 12, 1960; April 8, 1960; and May 29, 1960.

Sec. 1.10, 1.11

40. A bill for \$100 is purchased for \$96 three months before it is due. Find (a) the annual simple interest rate earned by the purchaser, (b) the annual rate (j, 2) earned.

41. Find the annual rate of interest, compounded quarterly, equivalent to an annual simple interest rate of 6%, if the term is (a) 2 years, (b) 1 month.

42. For each \$100 of maturity value, an investor might redeem savings bonds 2 years 1/2 month before maturity date for \$92. Would a person who owned bonds with a maturity value of \$1,000 have gained by redeeming them in this way in order to invest at 3 1/2%, compounded semiannually? On maturity date how much would he have gained (or lost)?

43. Given a nominal annual rate of 8%, converted on June 1 and December 1 of each year, find by 3 methods the present value on December 1, 1972 of \$100,000 due on March 15, 1980. (Take March 15 as 3 1/2 months after the preceding December 1.)

44. Under compound interest, how much would be owing at the end of (a) 1 year, (b) 3 years, on a \$5,000 debt transacted today if the following set of repayments were made: \$800 at the end of 4 months and \$1,000 at the end of 10 months? Money is worth an effective annual rate of 5%.

45. Prove or disprove:

(a) If a sum of money doubles in n years at some compound interest rate, then for every $x > 0$ it has value 2^x in nx years.

(b) If a sum A accumulates at a given effective rate to pA in m periods and to qA in n periods, and if $p > 1$, $q > 1$, then $n = m \log_p q$.

46. (a) To the nearest .001 year, how long will it take \$1 to triple itself at an effective annual rate of 7%? (Do NOT use logarithms.)

(b) What assumption did you make in (a)? Demonstrate your answer by showing that, under it, \$1 actually does triple itself in the length of time you computed in (a).

47. If one had a table of $\log(1 + i)^n$, what advantage would he have in solving for n: $S = A(1 + i)^n$ or the equivalent $A = Sv^n$?

48. (a) Show that linear interpolation and the approximation of formula (1.29) give the same result for $(1 + i)^{\overline{n}+t}$.

(b) Show that linear interpolation and the approximation of formula (1.30) give the same result for $(1 + i)^{-(\overline{n}+t)}$. Note that consequently linear interpolation and formula (1.31) do not give the same result for $(1 + i)^{-(\overline{n}+t)}$.

(c) Show that the approximations given by (1.29) and (1.30) are inconsistent with each other, by accumulating a sum for $\overline{n} + t$ periods and discounting the result for the same term according to those formulas. Are (1.29) and (1.31) also inconsistent? Suggest an approximate accumulation formula consistent with (1.30).

49. Which of the following rates will produce the largest present value for $100,000 due at the end of 3 months: (a) simple interest of 6% per year, (b) a nominal annual rate of 6%, compounded semiannually, (c) an effective annual rate of 6%? Find the difference between the largest and smallest present values.

50. If $4,000 grows to $6,000 in a certain length of time at a certain rate of interest, to what will $4,000 discount in a transaction of the same term and rate? Does your answer depend upon whether compound or simple interest is used?

51. (a) For $0 < t < 1$ and $0 < i < 1$, obtain the series expansion of $(1 + i)^t$ and an upper bound on the error in using only the first k terms of the series to express the sum.

(b) Calculate by the binomial theorem a value of $(1.02)^{1/2}$ to check exactly the tabulated value, after first determining from (a) the maximum number of terms which must be used.

(c) Use (a) to determine a numerical bound to the error when simple interest is used to approximate $(1.02)^{1/2}$. Then find the exact error to 3 significant digits.

52. Find expressions for (a) $\dfrac{\partial^p}{\partial i^p} v^n$, (b) $\dfrac{\partial^p}{\partial n^p} v^n$, (c) $\dfrac{\partial^2}{\partial i \partial n} v^n$.

Sec. 1.12, 1.13

53. At the end of 12 years, $1,000 together with interest at (.05, 4) is due. What is the equivalent sum at the end of 4 years, assuming money is worth (.06, 2)?

54. (a) Which would be preferable to an investor: (i) $1,000 in 3 years, or (ii) $1,200 in 7 years, if money is worth 5%? Name the most convenient comparison date. Show that the differences in amount obtained by valuing on different dates are equivalent.

(b) If, instead, the $1,200 accrues 6% simple interest per year from the end of the fifth year onward, which would be preferable? In this case, are the differences due to using different valuation dates equivalent?

55. At what effective annual interest rate will $1,000 at the ends of 4 and 6 years be equivalent to payments of $900 at the ends of 3 and 5 years?

56. (a) If interest is at the nominal annual rate of 6%, m = 12, what equal monthly payments at the beginning of each month would be equivalent to $1,000 at the beginning of each quarter?

(b) The same problem, except for compound interest at an effective annual rate of 6%.

57. To complete a $15,000 purchase on which payments of $7,000 down, $1,000 at the end of 6 months and $2,000 at the end of 18 months have already been made, what single sum should be paid at the end of 4 years? Assume interest is at (.06, 4).

58. Kelly owed Davis 2 sums: $200 due at the end of 3 years without interest and $300 due at the end of 10 years with 4% effective annual interest. The first debt was not paid when due.

(a) What should Kelly pay at the end of 10 years to settle both debts, if on the first debt Davis requires interest from maturity date at (.06, 2)?

(b) If Davis had been willing to accept $775 at the end of 10 years in complete settlement of the indebtedness, what effective annual rate would have been charged on the first debt?

59. Smith has the following debts: (a) a $100 note dated July 1, 1960 and maturing on July 1, 1965 with interest at (6%, 2), (b) a $200 note payable without interest on January 1, 1966, (c) a $500 note dated January 1, 1965 and maturing on May 1, 1965 with simple interest at 6%. How much should Smith pay on April 1, 1965 to cancel the debts, if money is worth (4%, 4)?

60. The executor of Ehrlich's estate finds the following among the deceased's papers: loans made by Ehrlich, namely, (i) a $6,000 note signed 3 years ago and due in 5 years with interest at an effective annual rate of 5%, (ii) a $3,500 note due in 7 1/2 years with interest for 10 years at (.04, 2), (iii) $500 due in 5 months with simple interest at 6% for 240 days, (iv) a 180-day non-interest-bearing note for $300 due in 127 days; debts of Ehrlich, namely, (v) a $1,000 note of 1 year ago due with interest at an effective annual 4% rate two years hence and (vi) a $2,000 note payable in 3 years with interest for 5 years at (.06, 4). If money is worth (.05, 2), what will be the net value of these papers one year from now, when the estate is to be settled?

61. Robertson owes $10,000 payable at the end of one year. He offers to repay his loan by making equal payments at the end of each 6 months for the next 2 years. If money is worth 4%, $m = 2$, determine the size of the semiannual payment.

62. To the nearest .001 year, find when a $15,000 payment will repay debts of $5,000 due immediately and $10,000 due in 18 months, with (a) an effective annual 6% rate and the pure compound interest method, (b) an effective annual 6% rate and the customary approximate method(s), (c) an annual 6% simple interest rate.

63. With a line diagram describe the meaning of

$$(1.02)^{10} + (1.02)^{12} + (1.02)^{14} + \cdots + (1.02)^{120};$$

simplify and evaluate it, without using logarithms.

Sec. 1.14

64. (a) Approximate i without use of tables, if in 23.45 periods a unit principal produces a unit in interest.

(b) At the rate obtained, determine the actual compound interest earned.

65. Find to the nearest dollar the amount to which $1 will accumulate in 100 years at 7% per year (a) approximately, without interest tables, (b) exactly.

66. For a deposit of $17.18 a bank promises to pay $25.00 at the end of 7 1/2 years. (a) Its advertisements speak of "compounding your interest continuously at 5.00%" so that you "earn a guaranteed yield of 6.07%." What are these rates? (b) The bank permits early withdrawal on the 5.00% basis in (a), to date of withdrawal, but it asserts that the yield is then less than 6.07%. Discuss the assertion.

67. (a) Find the error in obtaining $(1.07)^{50}$ by linear interpolation between $(1.06)^{50}$ and $(1.08)^{50}$ and compare it with the absolute value of the maximum error given by Example 1.6. (This problem should convince the reader that under certain conditions linear interpolation for $(1 + i)^n$ may give quite unsatisfactory results.)

(b) (For students of finite differences.) Find the error in obtaining $(1.07)^{50}$ by second order interpolation, or an equivalent method, using $(1.06)^{50}$, $(1.08)^{50}$ and $(1.05)^{50}$.

Supplementary List (Problems 68-124)

68. Find the annual force of interest earned in the following cases:

(a) A principal invested for a year earns interest at 4% paid at the end of each half year, with that interest immediately reinvested at an annual rate of (4%, 2);

(b) $8 interest is paid every 18 months on a $100 loan.

69. Would a person needing $3,000 for 6 years be wisest to (a) take a loan at 6%, compounded monthly, (b) sell bonds yielding 6.30%, effective, or (c) borrow from a friend who will accept $4,200 in 6 years as repayment?

70. Given $10,000 invested for 3 1/2 years. At what nominal rate of interest, compounded monthly, would the same interest payment result as at 6% simple interest per year? Are these rates equivalent?

71. (a) Furniture priced at $5,000 is bought for $1,000 down and a note for the balance to be repaid with interest at (.06, 4) in 7 years. However, 2 years 1 1/2 months after the purchase the furniture store goes into bankruptcy, and the note is liquidated by sale to a firm discounting notes at (.066, 2). What amount thereby becomes available to the store's creditors?

(b) Same problem, if the rate on liquidation is (.06, 4).

72. A note for $5,000, bearing interest at (5%, 2), matures in 12 years. What nominal annual rate, compounded semiannually, will be earned by a purchaser who buys the note after 3 years for $5,000?

73. Should A withdraw money from a savings account earning (.03, 4) to lend B $5,000, to be repaid with $500 interest at the end of 3 years? Solve in 2 ways.

74. A \$400 sum is invested for 3 years at (.04, 2) and then reinvested at (.04, 4) for 7 years. What is the equivalent level nominal annual rate of interest compounding continuously?

75. Find the maximum difference between results of the various familiar methods for discounting \$10,000 at (.06, 2) for terms of any length between 6 and 10 years, inclusive.

76. If for the next 4 years there are investment possibilities which are deemed equally safe, list the rates below in a prudent investor's order of preference. Do not use any tables. The choices are to lend at (a) an effective annual rate of 6%, (b) a nominal annual rate of 6%, compounded semiannually, (c) a constant annual force of interest of 6%, (d) an effective annual rate of 5% for half the term and of 7% for the other half, (e) an annual force of interest of 5% for half the term and 7% thereafter, (f) a simple interest rate of 6% per year.

77. On merchandise having a list price of \$2,500, a retailer may pay cash and receive a discount of 1% off list price, or he may sign a \$2,500, 90-day note bearing 6% simple interest per year. What annual rate of simple interest does he actually pay if he does not take the cash option?

78. How much interest is earned by a unit sum in 10 periods at an effective rate i per period, such that

$$\log (1 + i) = .03440 \log e?$$

79. (a) If a bill of \$2,000 is 8 months overdue me, would I gain by accepting a non-interest-bearing note for \$2,225 payable in 14 months, if money is worth (.06, 2)? (b) At what rate (j, 2) would I come out exactly even?

80. What nominal annual rate of interest convertible every 8 months is equivalent to the rate (5.25%, 2)?

81. A 180-day, \$500 loan bearing simple interest at 5% per year was not paid when due but, instead, was extended 12 months, at a compound rate of (.06, 12). How much interest was paid for the use of the \$500?

82. If the force of interest δ_t at time t is such that $\delta_t = (1 - .01t) \ln 1.05$, find the present value of a unit due at the end of 20 years.

83. If a varying annual force of interest $\delta_t = 2(.06 + ct)$, c a constant, is equivalent over the period $0 \leq t \leq 2$ to a level annual force of interest of 10%, find c.

84. How long, in years and months, will it take \$75 to accumulate to \$100, if interest is at the nominal annual rate of 3%, compounded semiannually?

85. Equal sums were invested 5 years ago in two different funds. The first fund guaranteed an effective semiannual rate of 2%; the second guaranteed a 3 1/2% effective annual rate for the first 5 years, but stipulated an increase at the end of the 5 years, if experience warranted. If the rate of the second now becomes 5% per year and remains at that level, when will the two funds again be of equal size?

86. Three years ago $1,000 was placed in a savings account. For the first year 1% interest was added every 3 months; since then 1 1/4% has been the 3-month rate. At the end of 18 months $500 was withdrawn, and 6 months ago, $400. What amount is now left in the account?

87. (a) If money is worth a simple interest rate per time unit and if debts of maturity values $A_1, A_2, \cdots, A_k$ are payable at the ends of $n_1, n_2, \cdots, n_k = n$ time units, respectively, where $n_h < n$ $(h \neq k)$, show by valuing all the debts at time n that payment of $A = \sum_{h=1}^{k} A_h$ at time t, called the <u>equated time</u>, where $t = \sum_{h=1}^{k} n_h A_h / A$, would be equally satisfactory. Does this result depend upon the choice of n as comparison date? Note that in the result the actual interest rate is immaterial.

(b) For money worth an effective rate i per time unit, obtain an exact formula for finding the equated time, that is, the time at which a single payment of A is equivalent under the effective rate i to the given payments. Show that at least for small $(n - n_h)$, the equated time is approximately $\sum_{h=1}^{k} n_h A_h / A$ again. (It can be shown that this approximate equated time favors the debtor, i.e., is too great; for an interesting proof, see, for instance, D.W.A. Donald, <u>Compound Interest and Annuities-Certain</u> [Cambridge, 1953], pp. 38, 39.)

88. Find, approximately and exactly, the equated time (see Problem 87) for paying debts of $500 due in 2 years and $300 due in 5 years, money being worth an annual 6% effective rate.

89. (a) If the current annual rate of interest is 4%, compounded semiannually, in how many years would a $500 payment liquidate existing debts of $100 due in 4 years, together with interest at 6%, compounded quarterly, for 7 years, and of $400 due in 12 years? Assume that in the interim nothing is paid on the existing debts. (Note that the equated time principle of Problem 87 does not apply.)

(b) If the $500 were paid at the end of 6 years, at what rate per year, compounded semiannually, would the debts have been valued?

90. A construction company is willing to repay $2,500 after 10 years for every $1,000 loaned to it.

(a) If a lender agreed to accept earlier repayment at the interest rate determined by the original contract, what sum to the nearest $100 at the end of 8 years would settle a $75,000 loan?

(b) What effective annual interest rate is the construction company offering?

91. Prove or disprove:

(a) If a unit is accumulated for $2n$ interest periods at an effective rate i and is then discounted for n periods at rate $2i$, less than the unit remains. Assume $i > 0$.

(b) Investment of A will buy either (1) F receivable at the ends of both n and $3n$ interest periods, or (2) 2F receivable at the end of $2n$ interest periods. If money is worth $i > 0$ per interest period, the prudent investor chooses (2).

(c) If a force of interest is doubled, every discrete equivalent rate of interest with the same time unit is more than doubled. Assume the rates are positive.

92. Determine the effective annual interest rate i earned by each of the investments below, using simple interest for the fractional interest period. Per unit of original investment,
(a) 1.05040 can be obtained by selling after 15 months;
(b) 1.15000, after 63 months.

93. According to a certain annuity mortality table, of 965,939 men living at age 30 there will be 684,986 alive at age 65. What equal payment should each of the men aged 30 make, in order that:

(a) Each one who survives to age 65 receive 1? Assume no interest. (In life insurance mathematics, this is called the probability that a 30-year-old man will live to age 65.)

(b) Each one who survives to age 65 receive 1? Assume 3% effective annual interest. (In life insurance mathematics, this is called the present value of a pure endowment of 1 at age 65 to a man of age 30.)

(c) Each one, or his heirs, receive 1 at the date of his 65th birthday? Assume 3% effective annual interest.

94. (a) Compare where possible the relative size of the 4 factors for computing time in simple interest problems, and give a mathematical relation comparing interest amounts where numerators are invariant but denominators differ.

(b) Show for a transaction of less than 1 year, that the maximum difference in interest on A at a simple interest rate i, as determined by the 4 methods of calculating time, can be expressed by $(7/360 + d_a/26{,}280)Ai$, where d_a is the approximate number of days.

95. (a) If $\delta_t = ac^t$ is the annual force of interest operating at exact time t and if $S(0) = 1$, show that

$$S(t) = e^{a(c^t-1)/\ln c}$$

and that during the $(n + 1)$th year the effective annual rate equivalent to the forces δ_t, $n \le t \le n + 1$, is given by

$$e^{ac^n(c-1)/\ln c} - 1.$$

(b) If the annual force of interest increases continuously and uniformly from .03 now to .07 ten years from now, find to 4 significant figures the effective annual rate earned for the year commencing 2 years from now.

96. Discuss $\lim_{m \to 0} i^{(m)}$.

97. Savings accounts are insured up to $15,000. A bank pays interest at (4%, 4). If an account is opened with $4,500, at the end of how many quarters will it last contain less than $15,000 assuming

(a) no deposits or withdrawals take place;

(b) $150 is deposited at the end of every quarter year? (Hint: algebraically simplify your equation of value.)

98. Equal sums are invested at 6% per annum, one at simple interest and the other at an effective annual rate. When will the compound amount be double the simple interest amount?

99. In 1957 the U.S. Government began to issue Series E Savings Bonds, such that per \$3 investment, \$4 was to be returned in 8 years 11 months. What nominal annual rate of interest, compounded semiannually, did an investor in this type of bond earn if he held it to maturity?

100. A debt of \$800, due at the end of 6 years together with interest for 10 years at 5%, is to be replaced by a promise to pay, instead, the necessary equal amounts at the ends of 3 and 5 years. The creditor assumes money is worth 5%, compounded semiannually, for the first 4 years and 4%, compounded quarterly, thereafter. What size of payment is required?

101. If i, $i^{(4)}$ and δ are all equivalent rates, express (a) $i^{(4)}$ as a series in powers of δ, (b) δ as a series in powers of $i^{(4)}$.

102. Given a nominal annual rate of 3% compounded every 8 months.

(a) What nominal annual rate with semiannual conversions is equivalent?

(b) What simple interest rate is equivalent in a 1-year transaction, if for the 3% rate (i) the compound interest method is used? (ii) an approximate method is used?

103. Show that the excess of the interest on a unit invested for n time units at a nominal rate per time unit of (j, m) over that at an effective rate per time unit of j is approximately

$$\frac{n(m-1)}{2m} j^2 (1+j)^{n-1}.$$

What restrictions are needed?

104. Under a constant annual force of interest δ money doubles in 46.2 years. In approximately how many years will it grow 2 1/2 times under a nominal annual rate of interest numerically equal to δ but convertible only once in 2 years? Use $\ln 2 = .693$.

105. (a) At an annual force of interest the amount of \$10,000 at the end of one year is \$18 (to the nearest dollar) larger than the amount at the equal annual effective rate. Find the rate.

(b) Same problem, except for a \$27 excess at the end of 2 years.

106. A note for \$1,000 is signed on September 12 with the provision that the borrower may repay it in any amounts and at any times he desires within one year, and that each payment shall first be applied to the interest then due, with any balance reducing (and any deficiency increasing) the principal of the debt. A simple interest rate of 12% is to be used. Payments are made as follows: \$50 on March 15, \$250 on May 2 and \$400 on June 24. What final payment remains to be made at the end of the year? Does the compound interest principle have any bearing on this problem? Assume that the year contains the date February 29.

107. On an original debt of A, bearing interest at rate i per time unit, a partial payment A' is made after t_1 time units. Find expressions for the sum owing at time t_2 $(t_2 > t_1)$ assuming (a) simple interest, with A' being first applied to the interest accrued, (b) compound interest with interest compounded at times t_1 and t_2. Note that simplified results fall in the form of one or more simple or compound interest accumulations.

108. (a) A father leaves $30,000 to be so divided among his 3 children that each will receive the same amount on the first anniversary of the father's death following the child's 21st birthday. At the date of the father's death, John is 16, Mary 14 and Edward 12. If the money is earning 5%, compounded semiannually, what sum will each child receive?

(b) To what portion of the inheritance does each fall heir?

(c) How much more would Edward have received if his father had left the money in three equal shares, with payment deferred as at present?

109. Which of the following is (a) the most favorable, (b) the least favorable: Earning an effective rate (i) of i_1 for n periods, followed by i_2 for the next n periods, where $i_1 \neq i_2$; (ii) of $(i_1 + i_2)$ for n periods, and then nothing; (iii) of $(i_1 + i_2)/2$ for 2n periods. Given $i_1 > 0$, $i_2 > 0$.

110. Interpret $\int_0^c e^{\int_0^h \delta_t dt} \delta_h dh \qquad (c > 0)$.

111. (a) Show that the number of interest periods n required for A to accumulate to cA at an effective rate i per period is

$$n = \frac{\ln c}{i}\left(1 + \frac{i}{2} - \frac{i^2}{12} + \frac{i^3}{24} - \cdots\right), \quad i > 0.$$

(b) Derive a formula for the corresponding simple interest result.

112. (a) Show that

$$i = i^{(m)} + \frac{1 - \frac{1}{m}}{2!} i^{(m)2} + \frac{(1 - \frac{1}{m})(1 - \frac{2}{m})}{3!} i^{(m)3} + \cdots.$$

Is any restriction on $i^{(m)}$ needed?

(b) Use (a) to obtain $(1 + i) = e^{\delta}$, where δ replaces $i^{(m)}$ as $m \to \infty$.

113. (a) Find the balance on December 31, 1975 in a savings account which pays 1 3/4% interest each June 30 and December 31 and which has the following activity:

January 1, 1960 - $1,000 deposit	January 1, 1968 - $200 deposit
July 1, 1964, - $500 withdrawal	July 1, 1972 - $400 deposit.
January 1, 1965 - $300 withdrawal	

(b) Assuming the account is closed out on December 31,

1975, when does it contain exactly \$575? \$400? Less than \$575? Less than \$400?

114. When are \$10 and \$20 payable 35 periods afterwards equivalent, (a) at a 2% effective rate of compound interest, (b) at 2% simple interest per period?

115. (a) In terms of an effective rate i and a constant, derive a 2-term formula for the number of time units required for a unit sum to grow to e, and test its accuracy for $i = .01$ and $.08$.

(b) Repeat (a) for a nominal rate (j, m) and test the accuracy of the approximation for $j = .10$, $m = 5$.

116. Twelve years ago Johnson made a \$1,000 investment in a concern, upon which he has received a \$200 return at the end of each 2 years. However, the concern fails, just after the last payment. If the \$1,000 capital is lost but the \$200 payments have all been kept invested at (.05, 4), what effective annual interest rate did Johnson earn during the term of the investment?

117. The assets of a fund invested at the beginning and the end of a year were A and B respectively, and the total interest income was I. Assuming that the fund was invested at an average annual force δ during the year, show that

$$\delta \doteq I/[(A + B)/2]$$

and that an approximately equivalent effective rate of interest i is given by

$$i \doteq I/[(A + B - I)/2].$$

Also show that the same approximation for i results from the assumption that noninterest income earns one-half year's interest during the year.

118. (a) Tom Rowland inherited \$50,000, invested at (6%, 4). What sum is in the fund at the beginning of the 10th year, if at the end of every year Tom has withdrawn 20% of his balance?

(b) Withdrawals are made as in (a) until the fund has been reduced to just less than \$10,000. When does this situation occur, and how much is then in the fund?

119. A gift of \$40,000 is presented a college on condition that it be allowed to accumulate for 10 years and that each year thereafter 4/5 of the interest earnings on the accumulated fund be given as scholarships, the remaining 1/5 of the interest being added to the fund, until the end of the year in which the fund grows to \$100,000; that thereafter, all the interest earnings be awarded as scholarships. If it is assumed that the fund can be invested at 4% for the first 10 years and thereafter at 5%, find (a) the amount in the fund at the end of 15 years, (b) the number of \$1,000 scholarships (payable immediately) that may be awarded at the end of 16 years, according to the agreement, (c) at the end of how many years the fund will first exceed \$100,000.

120. If, at the end of every interest period, a man spends twice the interest earned at rate i on an investment, how much will he have, per dollar invested, right after his nth expenditure? How long can such spending continue?

121. A man with a sum invested at rate i spends at the end of 1, 2, 3, ··· interest periods 3/2, 3, 9/2, ··· times his interest earnings of the period, respectively. His 14th expenditure exactly wipes out his remaining investment.

(a) At what rate of interest were the funds invested?

(b) In what year does the expenditure exactly equal the balance remaining just after it has been made?

122. Solve without tables.

(a) Given $i^{(2)} = .04$, find $i^{(4)}$.

(b) Given $i/i^{(2)} = 1.0172$, find i.

(c) Given $i/i^{(4)} = 1.0241$ and $i/i^{(2)} = 1.0160$, find $(1 + i)^{1/4}$.

(d) Given $i/i^{(3)} = 1.0303$, find $i^{(3)}$.

123. Show that $\frac{\partial}{\partial m} i^{(m)} \doteq - \delta^2/(2m^2)$.

124. Show that $1 - v = iv$ and verbally explain why this equation is true.

CHAPTER 2

RATES OF INTEREST-IN-ADVANCE AND RATES OF DISCOUNT

2.1. Introduction. For most interest theory and for most applications, it is considered that interest is credited at the ends of stated intervals. However, there are instances in both theory and practice where the interest for an interval is credited at the beginning of the interval. We shall speak of such interest as interest-in-advance. The interest discussed in the preceding chapter might be labelled "interest-in-arrears" but, for convenience and to follow common usage, we shall continue to refer to it by the simpler term "interest."

For the discrete case, a theory of interest-in-advance may be developed which is analogous to, but distinct from, the theory of interest presented in the previous chapter. For the continuous case, with interest credited momently, we will find it is immaterial whether interest is considered payable in advance or arrears, and, consequently, the continuous theory remains unchanged.

When interest is credited in arrears, accumulation is a simple process while the inverse process of discounting or finding the present value is a little less obvious. For interest-in-advance, the discounting procedures are simpler than those for accumulation. In fact, it happens that the rate of interest-in-advance may be considered as a rate of discount on the sum due at the end of the period.

To begin to clarify matters regarding these basic rates, we make the following general definitions, in which the basic differences from the general definition of rate of interest in Chapter 1 appear in capital letters:

The General Definition of Rate of Interest-in-Advance: A rate of INTEREST-IN-ADVANCE, applicable over a given interest interval and expressed in terms of some time unit, is the ratio of the interest payable for the interval at the BEGINNING of the interval, to the product of the CORRESPONDING principal (invested from the start of that interval) and of the number of time units in the interval;

The General Definition of Rate of Discount: A rate of DISCOUNT, applicable over a given DISCOUNT interval and expressed in terms of some time unit, is the ratio of the DISCOUNT for the interval, payable at the BEGINNING of the interval, to the product of the ACCUMULATED AMOUNT AT THE END of that interval and of the number of time units in the interval.

More briefly, the rate of interest-in-advance during a given interval is numerically equal to the interest credited at the beginning of the interval on a unit of principal, per unit of time; whereas the rate of discount for the interval numerically equals the discount in the interval per unit of final sum at the end of the interval, per unit of time. That the mathematical relations derived from these two general definitions are usually identical will be shown as we proceed. As in Chapter 1, these definitions fit for the simple, compound, nominal and effective rates we shall soon introduce. We temporarily bypass discussion of the concept "corresponding principal" in the definition of rate of interest-in-advance, but do tackle it in Section 2.3 after other related concepts have been treated.

One observes, as the fundamental distinction between interest rates (whether in arrears or in advance) and discount rates, that the former are based on principal at beginning of the interval and the latter on final amount. It follows that any problem of value may be phrased in terms of an interest rate, a discount rate or a rate of interest-in-advance. Of these, the most common in long-term investments is the compound interest rate. While it will continue to be our most basic rate, the present chapter develops other rates which are of mathematical interest and which have some applicability.

Most authors have treated discount rates, but not (by our meaning) rates of interest-in-advance. They point to the simple discount rates commonly charged on short-term loans by banks and other lending institutions. They recognize that compound discount rates are encountered so infrequently in computation that published tables of functions based on them are rare. Of course, as a bank keeps its funds invested in short-term loans, repeatedly taking the repayment of one loan made at a simple discount rate as the source of funds for another such loan, through this series of transactions it is actually accumulating its funds by compound discount; but its computations are in respect to each individual loan and hence involve no compound discount theory.

In fact, the chief numerical application of formulas of compound discount is by accountants in one fairly uncommon method of depreciation. Thus, compound discount has somewhat limited applicability, but compound interest-in-advance has some importance in annuity theory (Chapter 3) and in life insurance mathematics. For this reason, our emphasis will be on compound interest-in-advance, and the compound discount theory will be treated rather incidentally. However, we shall stress simple discount (rather than simple interest-in-advance) because of its use in financial practice, and because its theory is less clumsy.

2.2. Effective rate of interest-in-advance. In Chapter 1 the basic rate of interest was taken to be the compound rate per interest period, denoted by i and termed effective rate. Later, nominal rates were introduced. In the present chapter, a similar development will be followed for interest-in-advance, but in view of the more restricted field of application and because many ideas of the first chapter will carry over more or less directly, the discussion will be quite brief.

For an effective rate of interest-in-advance, the interest period and the time unit must coincide. By effective rate of interest-in-advance we then mean the ratio of (a) the interest, payable for any time unit at the beginning of the time unit on the initial principal of the time unit, to (b) that same initial principal, assuming that such interest may be invested immediately on the same basis as the original principal. Such a rate will be denoted by d, the notation being determined by the fact that very often the rate is interpreted as a rate of discount. When the time unit is a year, we shall call d an effective annual rate of interest-in-advance. The precise meaning of "initial principal" will shortly become clear.

2.3. Accumulating by an effective rate of interest-in-advance. If a principal of A is invested for one interest period at the effective rate of interest-in-advance d, interest of dA will be payable at the beginning of the interest period and the principal of A repayable at the end of the interest period. According to the definition in the previous section, the interest dA is promptly invested on the same terms as A and will produce interest of d^2A immediately and repayment of principal dA at the end of the interest period. Similarly, the new interest d^2A is invested to produce d^3A in interest and d^2A in repayment of principal, at the beginning and end of the interest period, respectively, and so on. The fund at the end of the interest period is the entire principal of the period, namely,

$$A + dA + d^2A + \cdots = A(1 - d)^{-1},$$

provided that d, as always in practical applications and as assumed henceforth in this book, is less than 1. Thus an initial principal A invested at the beginning of the period under the effective rate of interest-in-advance d accumulates to $A(1 - d)^{-1}$ by the end of the period. In other words, the principal has accumulated by the factor $(1 - d)^{-1}$. However, $A(1 - d)^{-1}$ is not just the accumulated principal of the period; it is also the entire principal invested for the period. Whether the lender is actually in possession of it is immaterial. He has it, if all the payments of interest-in-advance and principal, or their equivalent, have been made. At the other extreme, if he has received no payments at all, this same fund, $A(1 - d)^{-1}$, is of course credited to him. In any case, $A(1 - d)^{-1}$ is the value of his investment at the end of the first interest period.

If the investment is continued on the same terms for n periods, then the accumulated value S at the end of the n periods will be given by the formula

$$S = A(1 - d)^{-n}. \tag{2.1}$$

This formula is comparable to formula (1.4).

The total compound interest-in-advance earned on A is

$$S - A = A\left[(1 - d)^{-n} - 1\right]. \tag{2.2}$$

One may verify this result by summing the total interest-in-advance of each of the n interest periods. The total interest-in-advance earned in the first period is

$$dA + d^2A + d^3A + \cdots = dA(1 - d)^{-1}$$

which is the same as applying the rate d to the entire principal $A(1 - d)^{-1}$ of the period. The total interest-in-advance of each period is similarly obtained, and for the whole term the total is then

$$dA(1 - d)^{-1} + dA(1 - d)^{-2} + \cdots + dA(1 - d)^{-n} \tag{2.2a}$$

which is reducible to the right member of (2.2).

One notes that the concept of accumulating a principal A under an effective rate of interest-in-advance d over an interest period is complicated by the fact that the interest is payable at the *beginning* of the period, and to be properly accounted for in the accumulated value at the *end* of the period must be considered as reinvested to earn interest-in-advance. Each new element of interest-in-advance must similarly be reinvested. Thus, in regard to any interest period, there is a distinction between the interest-in-advance payable on the initial principal of the period and the total interest-in-advance earned for the period (and based on the entire principal of the period), e.g., dA and $dA(1-d)^{-1}$ respectively for period 1. The effective rate of interest-in-advance d is obtainable from the general definition (Section 2.1) in relation to *either* the initial principal *or* the entire principal in the role of "corresponding principal" (meaning, of course, the principal on which the interest-in-advance in the numerator is based); thus

$$d = dA/A = dA(1 - d)^{-1}/[A(1 - d)^{-1}];$$

and the definition of it might have allowed for this fact. There are no such ramifications in accumulating a principal A under an effective rate of interest (in arrears) i over an interest period, as the interest iA falls due at the time the accumulated value is to be reckoned, and is the total interest for the period on the one and only principal of the period.

Thus far, we have taken the viewpoint of the investor who, in exchange for an initial principal of A, lent at an effective rate of interest-in-advance d, has the equivalent sum $S = A(1 - d)^{-n}$ n periods later. The concepts may be clarified by considering two possible arrangements with borrowers.

First, the borrower may agree to pay interest-in-advance each period as it falls due and, at the end of n periods, to repay the initial principal lent him. The borrower's contract is summarized in Figure 2.1.

Receive	A							
Pay	dA	dA	dA	dA	…	dA	dA	A
Time	0	1	2	3	…	n-2	n-1	n

Fig. 2.1

This borrower is concerned only with initial principal, and not with any entire principal. (However, the lender, in keeping continually invested all funds related to this transaction, would enter into one or more additional transactions (probably with different borrowers) on each interest payment date, so as to have an entire principal at work in the first period of $A(1 - d)^{-1}$, in the second period of $A(1 - d)^{-1}(1 + d + d^2 + \cdots) = A(1 - d)^{-2}$, etc.) Returning to our borrower, we see that the value by rate d, at time n, of his interest payments is given by (2.2a). Note that the term $dA(1 - d)^{-n}$ in that expression represents, to the borrower, the value at time n of his interest payment, dA, at time 0; while (as previously pointed out) the creditor views $dA(1 - d)^{-n}$ as his total interest-in-advance of the nth period. Note too that at time n the value at rate d of what the borrower has received and what he has paid are equal (to S); in fact, A now and the set of the borrower's payments are equivalent sets of sums at rate d.

Second, consider the borrower who wants to make a single payment at time n, consisting of all the interest of the transaction, S - A, and of repayment of the principal A. When he receives A, he immediately in effect borrows also from the lender $dA + d^2A + d^3A + \cdots$ for the interest payments then due, so that at the end of the first period he owes the entire principal $A(1 - d)^{-1}$ of the first period. Each successive period he is automatically extended further credit to cover deferred payments of interest-in-advance, and in the end must make the single payment $S = A(1 - d)^{-n}$. Likewise, his receipt of A and payment of S are equivalent sums at rate d.

Thus, it follows that $S = A(1 - d)^{-n}$ represents the value at the end of n time units, at an effective rate of interest-in-advance d, of (1) the borrower's proceeds, namely A at time 0, (2) the set of repayments by the borrower, (3) the creditor's initial loan of A, and (4) the set of amounts received by the creditor in payment of his initial loan of A. These concepts may at first be difficult to grasp, but they are logical and with persistent study will become clear.

<u>2.4. Discounting by an effective rate of interest-in-advance; effective rate of discount.</u> If the effective rate of interest-in-advance is d, then the <u>present, or discounted, value</u> of a sum S due at the end of n interest periods is the principal A which if invested now at the rate of interest-in-advance d would accumulate to S. It follows from equation (2.1) that

$$A = S(1 - d)^n. \tag{2.3}$$

This present value formula (2.3) is comparable to formula (1.6).

From equation (2.3), one sees that the total discount on S is

$$S - A = S[1 - (1 - d)^n] .$$

In particular, when $n = 1$, the discount is

$$S[1 - (1 - d)] = Sd$$

and the effective rate of discount (the ratio of the amount of discount payable in a unit of time at the start of that unit, to the amount accumulated at the end of that unit) is

$$Sd/S = d.$$

Thus, as mentioned in the introduction to the chapter, the effective rate of interest-in-advance d in respect to a principal A at the beginning of an interest period is equal to the effective rate of discount on the amount $S = A(1 - d)^{-1}$ due at the end of the period. Further, formula (2.3) indicates that, for an n-period transaction, A is the present value of S under the effective rate of discount d, the discount factor for each discount period being $(1 - d)$.* In fact, formula (2.3) is the basic formula of the theory of compound discount and would appear early in a systematic development of that topic. In such a development, it might be obtained from the difference equation

$$A_k = A_{k-1} - dA_{k-1} \quad \text{with} \quad k = 1, 2, \cdots, n,$$

where A_k is the present value after k discount periods of $A_0 = S$ and where $A_n = A$. This method is like that used in deriving $S = A(1 + i)^n$ in Chapter 1.

Although the notions of interest-in-advance and of compound discount are closely related, the important distinction mentioned in the introduction must be noted. If d is considered as a rate of interest-in-advance and is used to calculate such interest for an interest period, it is applied to the initial principal A. However, when d is thought of as a rate of discount and is used to calculate the discount over a discount period, it must be applied to the final amount S. The discount, so determined, equals the total interest-in-advance earned for the period, including interest on interest. Since this is also the

---

*As an interest period is associated with an interest rate, so a discount period is associated with a discount rate.

interest-in-advance of the period on the entire principal of the period, the definitions of effective rate of discount, and of effective rate of interest-in-advance based on entire principal, are mathematically the same although they are different concepts.

2.5. Nominal rates of interest-in-advance and of discount. As in Chapter 1, by nominal rate is meant a compound rate applicable over an interest (or discount) period which may be different from the time unit. By a nominal rate of interest-in-advance f, converted m times per time unit and denoted by (f, m), we shall mean (1) the interest period is one-mth of a time unit, (2) interest is payable at the beginning of each such period, (3) interest is reinvested immediately on the same terms as the original principal, and (4) according to the general definition,

$$f = \frac{\text{The interest payable at the beginning of an interest period}}{\text{The corresponding principal invested from the beginning of the interest period, times } 1/m}.$$

It follows that f/m is the effective rate of interest-in-advance for a time unit one-mth that of the nominal rate. For example, corresponding to the nominal annual rate of interest-in-advance $(f = 4\%, 4)$ is the effective quarterly rate of interest-in-advance $d = 1\%$. Here, as in Chapter 1, one may sometimes wish to set $m = 1$ and use $(f = d, 1)$.

A principal A at the beginning of an interest period under the rate (f, m) will earn interest of Af/m payable immediately, and by means of the method of Section 2.3, the accumulation will amount to

$$A(1 - f/m)^{-1}$$

by the end of the period. In this case, the accumulation factor per interest period is $(1 - f/m)^{-1}$, and if the investment is continued on the same basis for N time units, the accumulated value S at the end of the term is

$$S = A(1 - f/m)^{-mN}. \tag{2.4}$$

The corresponding present value formula is

$$A = S(1 - f/m)^{mN}. \tag{2.5}$$

On the basis of equation (2.5), one may interpret (f, m) as a nominal rate of discount, compounded m times each time unit.

Formulas (2.4) and (2.5) correspond to formulas (1.9) and (1.10) of the previous chapter. Again, as there, it is usually more convenient to use the corresponding effective rates, and hence proceed by the basic equations (2.1) and (2.3).

2.6. Equivalent rates i and d, and others. In Section 1.7 two rates, independent of their kinds, were defined to be equivalent over a specified term if a given principal invested for that term under each rate would accumulate to the same amount. It was there shown that two compound rates equivalent over one term are equivalent over all terms. The present extension of equivalent rates is to the case where at least one of the rates is a rate of interest-in-advance or of discount.

Now let i and d be equivalent effective rates of interest and interest-in-advance with the same interest period. Then a unit invested for one interest period under each rate accumulates to the same amount by the end of the period, as indicated on the line diagram, Figure 2.2.

$A = 1$ (at 0) —————— $S = 1 + i = 1/(1 - d)$ (at 1)

Fig. 2.2

From the relation

$$1 + i = 1/(1 - d) \qquad (2.6)$$

we obtain

$$i - d = id, \qquad (2.7)$$

$$i = d(1 + i) \qquad (2.8)$$

and

$$i = d/(1 - d). \qquad (2.9)$$

To interpret these relations, we recall that on the unit principal, interest-in-advance d is payable at the beginning of the period corresponding to interest-in-arrears i payable at the end of the period. Equation (2.7) indicates that i exceeds d by the interest of one period on d.* Equations (2.8) and (2.9) express i as the accumulated value at the end of the period of d invested at the beginning of the period at rate i (or at the equivalent rate d).

The explanations of equations (2.7)-(2.9) are simple illustrations of a very important technique of mathematics of finance

*For example, when $i = 4\%$, then by the basic equation (2.6), $d = 3.85\%$, and when $d = 4\%$, the equivalent rate $i = 4.17\%$. For computing equivalent rates, knowledge of the definition (hence, essentially of equation (2.6)) is sufficient; more direct formulas such as (2.9) or (2.11) are not too necessary, although eventually they should become second nature.

and mathematics of life insurance. This technique, called a verbal interpretation, consists of explaining the truth of an equation (or possibly a very minor modification of the equation), in words and/or by means of a line diagram. It enables a person to check his reasoning and to clarify it. When practiced in the technique, he can derive and prove formulas verbally. In general, verbal interpretations serve to heighten understanding and appreciation of our subject and ultimately to simplify it.

Again, from equation (2.6), we have

$$v = (1 + i)^{-1} = 1 - d \tag{2.10}$$

and, from equation (2.8),

$$d = iv \tag{2.11}$$

whence, by equation (2.10),

$$d = i(1 - d) \tag{2.12}$$

which also follows easily from equation (2.9). Of these relations (2.10) and (2.11) assume importance in life insurance mathematics. Equation (2.10) shows, as was previously remarked, that $1 - d$ may be used as a discount factor. From equations (2.11) and (2.12) it is seen that d is the present value of i due at the end of the interest period; that is, d at the beginning of the period is equivalent to i at the end of the period. This relation could have been used as the starting point for the theory of interest-in-advance, but we have developed the theory directly from its own definitions rather than having it depend on the theory of interest-in-arrears.

One may proceed as in Section 1.7 to discuss equivalent rates of interest-in-advance (f_1, m_1) and (f_2, m_2) with the same basic time unit. One sees from the definition of equivalent rates that

$$(1 - f_1/m_1)^{-m_1} = (1 - f_2/m_2)^{-m_2},$$

and hence,

$$(1 - f_1/m_1)^{m_1} = (1 - f_2/m_2)^{m_2}. \tag{2.13}$$

Equation (2.13) states the equality of present values of a unit under each rate for one time unit. All the conclusions of Chapter 1 in regard to compound equivalent rates follow in the same manner from (2.13).

Further, one may develop relations linking equivalent nominal rates (f, m) and (j, m), having the same time unit, just as was done for equivalent effective rates d and i. From the basic equation

$$1 + j/m = (1 - f/m)^{-1} \tag{2.14}$$

one may obtain such results as

$$j - f = jf/m. \tag{2.15}$$

Equation (2.7) is the special case of equation (2.15) with $m = 1$. Solution of equation (2.15) for j and f, respectively, yields

$$j = f(1 + j/m) = f(1 - f/m)^{-1} \tag{2.16}$$

and

$$f = j(1 - f/m) = j(1 + j/m)^{-1}. \tag{2.17}$$

It is sometimes convenient to have the notation $d^{(m)}$ signifying the nominal rate of interest-in-advance, converted m times per time unit, which is equivalent to the effective rate d per time unit. Here, $d^{(m)}$ is the special case of (f, m) which is equivalent to d, just as in Chapter 1 $i^{(m)}$ was the special case of (j, m) equivalent to i. Using the definition of equivalent rates, or from equation (2.13) with appropriate changes in notation, one obtains

$$1 - d = (1 - d^{(m)}/m)^m. \tag{2.18}$$

The relations

$$d = 1 - (1 - d^{(m)}/m)^m \tag{2.19}$$

and

$$d^{(m)} = m\left[1 - (1 - d)^{1/m}\right] \tag{2.20}$$

are then available for computing the effective rate equivalent to $d^{(m)}$ and, conversely, the nominal rate converted mthly which is equivalent to the effective rate d. If, in addition, d is equivalent to i, then, by use of formula (2.10), equation (2.20) may be expressed as

$$d^{(m)} = m(1 - v^{1/m}) = v^{1/m}\, i^{(m)}. \tag{2.21}$$

In all the foregoing relations, (2.6) to (2.21), d, (f, m) and $d^{(m)}$ could wear their other hats and stand for rates of discount. In fact, the relations are usually presented from the discount point of view. In that context, for example, equations (2.19) and (2.20) express what is apparent from the definition of discount rates, namely, that d and $d^{(m)}/m$ are the discount on a unit sum for a single discount period, here a time unit and an mth of a time unit, respectively.

It is interesting to note that $d < d^{(m)}$ for $m > 1$ and $0 < d < 1$. This fact may be shown by expanding the right member of equation (2.19) to obtain

$$d^{(m)} - \frac{m-1}{2m}(d^{(m)})^2 + \cdots .$$

Or, from equation (2.18), one may argue that in discounting a unit sum for a time unit by d, the rate is applied to the unit sum for the whole period, while in discounting by $d^{(m)}$, the rate $d^{(m)}/m$ is applied in successive mths of the time unit to the decreasing amounts $1, 1 - d^{(m)}/m, (1 - d^{(m)}/m)^2, \cdots$. Hence, $d^{(m)}$ has to be larger in order to produce the same amount of discount over the time unit as does d. One may similarly conclude, either from equation (2.21) or by verbal argument, that $d^{(m)} < i^{(m)}$, when the rates are equivalent and m is finite. Since in Chapter 1 we had $i^{(m)} < i$ for $m > 1$, it follows for $i > 0$ that

$$d < d^{(m)} < i^{(m)} < i \quad \text{for} \quad m > 1 \text{ and finite.}$$

In Appendix Table II, d and some of the rates $d^{(m)}$ equivalent to the tabulated rates i are listed. The reader may wish to note their progression in accordance with the inequalities above and may also wish to check some of the rates.

As illustration, the nominal annual rate $(f, 12)$ of interest-in-advance convertible monthly, equivalent to a nominal annual rate of interest of (4%, 2), can be found by equating accumulations over a six-month period, as follows:

$$(1 - f/12)^{-6} = 1.02.$$

Solution for f yields

$$\begin{aligned} f &= 12\left[1 - (1.02)^{-1/6}\right] \\ &= 12(.0032\,950) \quad \text{or } 2d^{(6)} \quad \text{when } i \text{ is } 2\% \\ &= 3.954\%. \end{aligned}$$

Then too, for the effective annual rate d of discount equivalent to these rates, the equating of present values of 1 due at the end of a year gives us

$$1 - d = (1.02)^{-2}, \quad d = 3.883\%.$$

To complete the picture, the effective annual rate i of interest is 4.040%. The foregoing results are observed to conform to the inequalities above.

2.7. Force of interest-in-advance. Given a time unit and time origin, by the force of interest-in-advance at time t we mean the nominal rate of interest-in-advance, convertible momently, which operates in the instant at time t. As mentioned in Section 2.1 such a force of interest-in-advance is the same as the equivalent force of interest, since, as a consequence of the infinitesimal character of the interest periods, it is immaterial whether interest is considered to be paid at the beginning or the end of the period. To verify this equality of the forces in the case of constant rates, let us suppose δ is the force of interest and that i, d and $d^{(m)}$ are rates equivalent to δ. Then, the equivalent force of interest-in-advance is equal to

$$\begin{aligned}\lim_{m\to\infty} d^{(m)} &= \lim_{m\to\infty} m\left[1 - (1 - d)^{1/m}\right] \\ &= \lim_{t\to 0} \frac{1 - (1 - d)^t}{t} \\ &= -\ln(1 - d) \\ &= \ln(1 + i), \quad \text{by (2.6)} \\ &= \delta, \quad \text{the force of interest.}\end{aligned}$$

Accordingly, it is unnecessary to introduce any new notation or theory in respect to force of interest-in-advance. For example, the accumulated value of 1 invested for a time unit under the force of interest-in-advance δ is equal to $(1 - d)^{-1}$, since d is equivalent to δ, and by the foregoing relations,

$$(1 - d)^{-1} = e^{\delta} .$$

This accumulation factor e^{δ} and the corresponding discount factor $e^{-\delta}$ are precisely what were obtained previously in the continuous theory of interest. Alternatively, the reader may discern that use of the second form of equation (2.21) quickly produces $\lim_{m\to\infty} d^{(m)} = \delta$ and that equivalent rate considerations then yield the factors e^{δ} and $e^{-\delta}$ for accumulating and discounting.

In the general case, for every t in the interval $0 \le t \le n$, let the variable force δ'_t of interest-in-advance be equivalent to the corresponding variable force δ_t of interest. Also let $S(t)$ be a differentiable function of t denoting the value of $S(0) = A$ accumulated to time t by the forces of interest.

Then by the interest-preserving property of equivalent rates and by rate definition based on entire principal,

$$\delta'_t = \begin{cases} \lim\limits_{h\to 0^+} \dfrac{S(t+h) - S(t)}{S(t+h)\,h} \\[2ex] \lim\limits_{h\to 0^-} \dfrac{S(t) - S(t+h)}{S(t)\,(-h)} \end{cases}$$

$$= \frac{1}{S(t)} \frac{d}{dt} S(t)$$

$$= \delta_t \text{ by (1.16).}$$

We have shown that equivalent forces of interest and interest-in-advance are equal, and so all the results of Section 1.8 regarding forces of interest hold also for forces of interest-in-advance.

That in the continuous case the theories of interest and interest-in-advance are the same, while in the discrete case they are not, is an illustration of a continuous theory being somewhat simpler than its discrete counterpart. It is also clear that while it may be possible to obtain a continuous result by taking a limit case of the corresponding discrete formula, it may not be possible to reverse the process and to infer the discrete formula from its continuous image.

To pass from the force δ to the equivalent rates i and d, and vice versa, the following series expressions are useful:

$$\delta = \ln(1 + i) = i - \frac{i^2}{2} + \frac{i^3}{3} - \frac{i^4}{4} + \cdots \tag{2.22}$$

$$= -\ln(1 - d) = d + \frac{d^2}{2} + \frac{d^3}{3} + \frac{d^4}{4} + \cdots \tag{2.23}$$

$$i = e^{\delta} - 1 = \delta + \frac{\delta^2}{2!} + \frac{\delta^3}{3!} + \frac{\delta^4}{4!} + \cdots \tag{2.24}$$

$$d = 1 - e^{-\delta} = \delta - \frac{\delta^2}{2!} + \frac{\delta^3}{3!} - \frac{\delta^4}{4!} + \cdots. \tag{2.25}$$

To complete the picture, there are also series linking equivalent rates i and d as follows:

$$i = (1 - d)^{-1} - 1 = d + d^2 + d^3 + d^4 + \cdots \qquad (2.26)$$

$$d = 1 - (1 + i)^{-1} = i - i^2 + i^3 - i^4 + \cdots . \qquad (2.27)$$

For the usual magnitude of rates, the series above all converge, and their successive terms diminish rapidly in numerical value, so that consequently we may calculate one equivalent rate from another to any desired degree of accuracy by the use of a relatively few terms in the appropriate series expansion.

For an interesting equivalent rates problem, the reader is referred to Example 2.2 in Section 2.12.

2.8. Force of discount.* We have seen that d, (f, m) and $d^{(m)}$ may be interpreted as rates of discount. Similarly, $\lim_{m\to\infty} d^{(m)}$ may be considered as a force of discount which is the usual term applied to it. From this point of view, one might have started with the limiting case of the general definition of rate of discount in Section 2.1 to obtain the variable force of discount δ''_t, namely,

$$\delta''_t = \begin{cases} \lim_{h\to 0^+} \dfrac{A(t) - A(t+h)}{A(t)\ h} \\[2ex] \lim_{h\to 0^-} \dfrac{A(t+h) - A(t)}{A(t+h)\,(-h)} \end{cases}$$

so that

$$\delta''_t = -\frac{1}{A(t)}\frac{dA(t)}{dt} = -\frac{d \ln A(t)}{dt}, \qquad (2.28)$$

where $A(t)$ represents the discounted value, under variable forces of discount, of $A(0) = S$ due at the end of t time units.

Equation (1.16) may be compared with this result. Differences hinge on differing time origins and orientations as well as notation. In the notation and time sense of δ''_t, the equivalent force of interest δ_t by definition is

$$\delta_t = \begin{cases} \lim_{h\to 0^+} \dfrac{A(t) - A(t+h)}{A(t+h)\ \ h} \\[2ex] \lim_{h\to 0^-} \dfrac{A(t+h) - A(t)}{A(t)\ (-h)} \end{cases}$$

which results again in the right members of (2.28). Therefore,

*This section can be omitted in a first reading.

$\delta''_t = \delta_t = \delta'_t$; that is, if the forces of discount, interest and interest-in-advance are equivalent, those forces are equal.

From equation (2.28) there now follows the differential equation

$$-dA(t) = A(t)\,\delta_t dt$$

which might have been taken as the starting point. The left member is actually positive since, with A(t) decreasing as t increases, dA(t) < 0; and the momentary discount, to first order of differentials, is equal to $A(t)\,\delta_t dt$. From the second form of equation (2.28), we have

$$d \ln A(t) = -\delta_t dt$$

which, upon integration over the range t = 0 to t = N, with A(N) = A, yields

$$A = S\,e^{-\int_0^N \delta_t dt}\,.$$

This relation is equation (1.18) for discounting under variable forces of interest operating in reverse order to the forces above but producing the same result. For constant forces of discount $\delta_t = \delta$ and for N = 1 and S = 1, we get

$$A = e^{-\delta}$$

which, of course, is the discount factor previously obtained.

2.9. Simple discount. Let us consider a transaction involving an initial principal A and a final amount S at the end of a term of t time units, where, since we shall be concerned with simple rates, the term is presumably short. The difference S - A may be considered as simple interest on the principal A at the interest rate i per time unit, such that

$$S - A = Ait$$

and

$$S = A(1 + it).$$

Equally well, S - A may be regarded as simple discount on the amount S (for by simple discount we mean that all the discount is calculated directly on the final amount) at the discount rate d per time unit. By the general definition of rate of discount one has

$$d = (S - A)/(St)$$

or

$$S - A = Sdt. \tag{2.29}$$

From this relation, there follows the formula

$$A = S(1 - dt) \tag{2.30}$$

for finding the present or discounted value of S due in t time units under a simple discount rate of d per time unit. For a fixed $S > 0$, to keep A positive in equation (2.30), one must have

$$t < 1/d;$$

this places a restriction on the number of time units which was not encountered in our study of any other kind of rate. For example, at a simple discount rate of 5% a year, a transaction is limited to less than 20 years; in practice, such a limit is not very important because simple rates are confined to transactions of much shorter duration. Finally, by solving equation (2.30) for S, one obtains

$$S = A/(1 - dt) \tag{2.31}$$

as the formula for the accumulated value of a principal A invested for t time units at a simple discount rate d.

It was remarked in the introduction to this chapter, that a rate of simple discount is used by bankers and others in making short-term loans. Such a rate is frequently termed a "rate of interest-in-advance" but the discount terminology seems preferable. For instance, suppose a bank grants a \$1,000 six-month loan at an annual simple discount rate of 6%. The borrower is given immediate use of 1,000(1 - .06/2) = \$970; that is, a discount of \$30 has been charged against the \$1,000 due at the end of the six months. On the other hand, one could imagine that the bank actually transfers \$1,000 to the borrower, and the borrower immediately pays the bank \$30 interest-in-advance on the loan so that he ends up having the use of \$970. In this case, one considers that the borrower makes two payments to the bank: namely, the \$30 of interest-in-advance and the repayment of the \$1,000 principal at the end of the six months. These two payments are separated in time and cannot be combined to give an accumulated value without some assumption as to the reinvestment or compounding of the interest. Since the simple interest-in-advance interpretation is complex and unrealistic in regard to the practical transaction and is intractable in respect to theory, it is better to employ simple discount terminology, and we shall do so.

A simple discount rate may be equivalent to another rate or rates. For instance, when a simple interest rate i and a simple discount rate d each accumulate an initial principal A to the same amount S in t time units, they are said to be equivalent over a term of t time units. As the factor A may be cancelled from the relation

$$A(1 + it) = A/(1 - dt),$$

it follows that the equivalence does not depend on the size of the principal A. By further simplification, one obtains

$$i - d = idt, \tag{2.32}$$

$$i = d/(1 - dt) \tag{2.33}$$

and

$$d = i/(1 + it) \tag{2.34}$$

which, for $t = 1$, are the same as equations (2.7), (2.9) and (2.11) for effective rates of compound interest and compound discount. The presence of t in equations (2.33) and (2.34) shows that the equivalence of the simple rates i and d depends on the term of the transaction. Thus, an annual simple discount rate of 6% is equivalent to an annual simple interest rate of 6.03% over a one-month term and to an annual simple interest rate of 6.38% over a one-year term. This example illustrates a principle; for from equation (2.33) or (2.34), or verbally, one sees that a positive rate of simple discount is always smaller than an equivalent rate of simple interest, and that the difference grows as the term increases.

For the equivalent simple rates i and d, we have $S - A = Ait = Sdt$ so that

$$Ai = Sd. \tag{2.35}$$

If A and S have been determined, equation (2.35) is a convenient relationship between i and d. From it one might imagine that the equivalence of i and d does not depend on t, but implicitly it does since, on substituting $A(1 + it)$ for S in equation (2.35) one gets

$$i = (1 + it)d,$$

or formula (2.34) again. Incidentally, formula (2.35) brings home the fact that interest is computed on principal and discount on final amount.

Illustrative Example 2.1 at the end of the chapter may be provocative.

2.10. Other remarks. For rates of interest-in-advance and rates of discount, one may develop in detail the topics of transactions with nonintegral terms, comparison of values under equal compound and simple rates, equivalent values and equations of value, as was done in Chapter 1 for interest rates. However, as the procedures are parallel to those of Chapter 1 and the rates of less importance, the discussion here is brief. In fact, change of rate-form in the previous treatment of equivalent values and equations of value does not alter the conclusions reached. Thus, only the first two topics deserve special mention.

Because accumulating and discounting under a force of discount are valid for all time periods, integral or not, it follows that these processes are likewise valid with a compound rate of discount for all time periods. In the case of a term $n = \overline{n} + t$, $0 < t < 1$, as defined in Section 1.10, it is sometimes convenient to replace the compound rate by an equal simple rate of discount for the nonintegral t time units. For example,

$$A = S(1 - d)^{\overline{n}+t} \tag{2.36}$$

may be approximated by

$$A \doteq S(1 - d)^{\overline{n}}(1 - dt). \tag{2.37}$$

An inquiring reader will wonder which one of the equations (2.36) or (2.37) yields the greater result. This question leads to the comparison of (1) the value V_t of a sum V_0, available at time 0 and discounted or accumulated to time t under the compound rate $d > 0$ according to the formula

$$V_t = V_0(1 - d)^{-t}, \quad \text{all real } t, \tag{2.38}$$

with (2) the value V_t^s of V_0, discounted or accumulated to time t by the equal simple rate d, according to the formulas

$$V_t^s = V_0[1 - d(-t)], \; -1/d < t \leq 0 \tag{2.39}$$

$$V_t^s = V_0/(1 - dt) \quad , \; 0 \leq t < 1/d. \tag{2.40}$$

Analysis (Problem 42) brings out the following conclusions:

$$V_t = V_t^s \;, \quad t = 0 \text{ or } \pm 1$$

$$V_t > V_t^s \;, \quad -1/d < t < -1 \text{ or } 0 < t < 1$$

$$V_t < V_t^s \;, \quad -1 < t < 0 \text{ or } 1 < t < 1/d.$$

Thus, use of simple discount for fractional periods less than one discount period in duration favors the debtor, since, compared with compound discount, in discounting (the case $-1 < t < 0$ above) it produces greater proceeds, and inversely, in accumulating (the case $0 < t < 1$) it produces a smaller accumulated value. In the previous chapter we found that the use of simple interest for terms less than one interest period favors the creditor, instead. Returning now to the comparison of equations (2.36) and (2.37), we conclude that the debtor would prefer the method of (2.37).

2.11. Summary. The rates introduced in this chapter are dual in character. On the one hand, they may be regarded as rates of interest-in-advance, and for the calculation of such interest are applied to an appropriate principal (usually the initial principal). On the other hand, they serve as rates of discount, and for the calculation of discount are applied to the amount payable at the end of the discount interval. In the case of compound rates, it is immaterial which interpretation is used for finding accumulated and discounted values, as the resulting formulas are the same. Our emphasis has been on compound interest-in-advance rather than compound discount as the former has wider application. For simple rates, the discount interpretation was preferred.*

There is now at hand a considerable variety of rates and some relation summaries may be useful. To begin with, for equivalent compound rates i, $i^{(m)}$, δ, d, $d^{(m)}$ having the same time unit, we have found that

$$(1 - d)^{-1} = (1 - d^{(m)}/m)^{-m} = e^{\delta} = (1 + i^{(m)}/m)^{m} = 1 + i \quad (2.41)$$

and it follows that for $i > 0$,

$$d < d^{(m)} < \delta < i^{(m)} < i, \quad m > 1 \text{ and finite.} \quad (2.42)$$

For convenience of reference, a more complete summary of the relationships among these equivalent compound rates is given in the

*As the rates of Chapter 2 have both an interest and a discount interpretation, one may inquire whether there is a dual meaning for the rates of Chapter 1 also. The answer is affirmative, but brings in a concept of discount-in-arrears which seems devoid of practical content. The interested reader might give thought to the net discount on the sum S due at the end of one discount period, discount being at the effective rate i. This net discount is equal to

$$Si - Si^2 + Si^3 - \cdots = S - S/(1 + i).$$

accompanying table. The formula appearing in a given row and given column expresses the rate at the left of the row in terms of the rate at the top of the column.

TABLE 2.1

Relationships Among Equivalent Rates

Rate	i	$i^{(m)}$	δ
i	i	$(1 + i^{(m)}/m)^m - 1$	$e^\delta - 1$
$i^{(m)}$	$m[(1 + i)^{1/m} - 1]$	$i^{(m)}$	$m(e^{\delta/m} - 1)$
δ	$\ln(1 + i)$	$m \ln(1 + i^{(m)}/m)$	δ
$d^{(m)}$	$m[1 - (1 + i)^{-1/m}]$	$i^{(m)}/(1 + i^{(m)}/m)$	$m(1 - e^{-\delta/m})$
d	$i/(1 + i)$	$1 - (1 + i^{(m)}/m)^{-m}$	$1 - e^{-\delta}$

Rate	δ	$d^{(m)}$	d
i	$e^\delta - 1$	$(1 - d^{(m)}/m)^{-m} - 1$	$d/(1 - d)$
$i^{(m)}$	$m(e^{\delta/m} - 1)$	$d^{(m)}/(1 - d^{(m)}/m)$	$m[(1 - d)^{-1/m} - 1]$
δ	δ	$-m \ln(1 - d^{(m)}/m)$	$-\ln(1 - d)$
$d^{(m)}$	$m(1 - e^{-\delta/m})$	$d^{(m)}$	$m[1 - (1 - d)^{1/m}]$
d	$1 - e^{-\delta}$	$1 - (1 - d^{(m)}/m)^m$	d

Any of these formulas can easily be established by going back to the basic notion of equivalent rates, that a unit of principal invested for a given term under each rate will accumulate to the same amount. The given term may be taken as $1/m$ or 1 time unit, as convenience suggests.

Again we repeat that, because interest or discount theory and applications can be handled readily by means of a few basic principles such as equivalence of rates and equations of value, there is no need to follow formulas slavishly. It is not particularly necessary, for example, to know the formulas in the table, as the relationship required in any instance can be obtained quickly by use of the principle of equivalence.

2.12. Illustrative problems for this chapter. As many ideas and methods of this chapter closely parallel those of Chapter 1, only three additional examples are given. No prior reference has been made to Example 2.3, a problem about depreciation of an asset by compound discount techniques.

Example 2.1

(a) Turner receives \$100 and agrees to repay it in 6 months with simple interest at 10% per annum. What equivalent annual rate of simple discount might he have been charged? If, after 6 months, Turner fails to repay the loan but instead asks and receives a 6-month extension, what would be the equivalent annual simple discount rate during the extension? for the year?

Solution: For the original loan the equivalent simple discount rate d, according to definition, would be

$$d = \frac{5}{105(1/2)} = 9.52\%.$$

When Turner receives the extension, the presumption is that the lender turns the original \$5 interest into principal and considers himself to be lending \$105 at 10% for the next 6 months. The new equivalent simple discount rate d' for the extension is given by

$$d' = \frac{105(.1)(1/2)}{105[1 + .1(1/2)](1/2)} = \frac{.1}{1.05} = d$$

as might have been immediately evident. However, for the year period, the equivalent rate d'' becomes

$$d'' = \frac{5 + 105(.1)(1/2)}{105[1 + .1(1/2)]} = \frac{10.25}{110.25} = 9.30\%.$$

Upon reflection one sees that the rate d'' is the annual simple discount rate equivalent in a one-year transaction to a nominal annual interest rate of (.10, 2), while $d = d'$ is the corresponding rate equivalent in a half-year transaction to (.10, 2).

(b) Solve the problem assuming all rates are nominal annual rates compounded semiannually.

Solution: For the original loan, we have the equal accumulations at (f, 2) and (.10, 2) of

$$100(1 - f/2)^{-1} = 100(1.05),$$

which, upon simplification, yields $f = d = 9.52\%$ again. Similarly, during the period of the extension, there result the accumulations

$$105(1 - f'/2)^{-1} = 105(1.05),$$

or $f' = f = d$. Finally, for the entire year

$$100(1 - f''/2)^{-2} = 100(1.05)^2$$

and still $f'' = f = d$.

The extension injects an automatic compounding. Where compound rates are involved, no change in equivalent rates takes place, in contrast to the simple-rate situation over half-year and year terms.

Example 2.2

Let i, $i^{(m)}$, $d^{(m)}$ and d be equivalent rates with the same time unit. If

$$\sum_{m=1}^{\infty} (-1)^m \left(\frac{1}{i^{(m)}} - \frac{1}{d^{(m)}} \right) = 0.048790,$$

find d.

Solution: From equation (2.15)*

$$i^{(m)} - d^{(m)} = i^{(m)} d^{(m)}/m.$$

Therefore,

$$\sum_{m=1}^{\infty} (-i)^m \left(\frac{1}{i^{(m)}} - \frac{1}{d^{(m)}} \right) = - \sum_{m=1}^{\infty} (-i)^m/m$$

$$= i - i^2/2 + i^3/3 - \cdots$$

$$= \ln(1 + i) = \delta = .048790.$$

From Table II we see that the rate d equivalent to this δ is $d = 4.7619\%$. Alternatively, d can be found to the same accuracy from the first 3 terms of the infinite series in equation (2.25).

Example 2.3

A car costing \$3,500 will have a trade-in value of \$1,500 at the end of 5 years. By use of the constant-percentage (or reducing-balance) method of depreciation,

(a) find the annual rate of depreciation, and

(b) construct the depreciation schedule.

Solution: Depreciation is the decline in value of a physical asset which cannot be remedied by current repairs. There are several methods by which accountants calculate it, in order to

*While the reader could not be expected to remember this relation, in his attempt to simplify the left member he would derive it from the basic idea of equivalent rates $i^{(m)}$, $d^{(m)}$:

$$1 + i^{(m)}/m = (1 - d^{(m)}/m)^{-1} .$$

determine at any time the book value of the asset, which we shall define as its original cost less all depreciation to date. Usually such depreciation is obtained with no accounting for interest, but nevertheless some of our theory may apply. For instance, this problem introduces the depreciation method mentioned in Section 2.1 as an application of compound discount techniques. As the name "constant-percentage method" implies, the depreciation charge of any set period is a fixed percentage of the book value of the asset at the beginning of the period.

(a) By every depreciation method, the book value of the asset must be reduced from the original cost to the assumed salvage value at the end of the estimated useful lifetime of the asset. In this problem this purpose is accomplished by solving

$$3{,}500(1 - d)^5 = 1{,}500$$

for d, the annual rate of depreciation. We obtain

$$d = 1 - (1{,}500/3{,}500)^{1/5} = 1 - .84412 = .15588,$$

so that the annual reduction in book value is at the rate 15.588%.

(b) At the end of year k, the book value B_k is seen to be

$$B_k = 3{,}500(1 - .15588)^k, \quad k = 0, 1, 2, \cdots, 5$$

or

$$\begin{aligned} \log B_k &= \log 3{,}500 + k \log(.84412) \\ &= 3.544068 - .073595\, k, \end{aligned}$$

in which $\log(.84412) = \log[(1{,}500/3{,}500)^{1/5}]$ was obtained in the solution of (a). The depreciation schedule, Table 2.2, is self-explanatory, except perhaps for the portion which introduces for comparison the very popular straight-line method. By that method the depreciation charge is a constant amount per period, namely, in this case $(3{,}500 - 1{,}500)/5 = \$400$ per year, and consequently

$$B_k = 3{,}500 - 400\, k, \quad k = 0, 1, 2, \cdots, 5.$$

Note that the book values by the constant-percentage method at the ends of years 1-4 are less than the corresponding book values by the straight-line method. This is not mere happenstance, as the reader's solution of Problem 66 (c) will bring out.

TABLE 2.2

Depreciation Schedule

	Constant-Percentage Method			Straight-Line Method	
(1) End of Year k	(2) $\log B_k$ $= 3.544068$ $-.073595\ k$	(3) Book Value B_k	(4) Depreciation Charge $(4)=(3)_{-1}-(3)$	(5) Book Value $B_k = 3{,}500$ $-400\ k$	(6) Depreciation Charge
0	3.544068	$3,500.00	$	$3,500.00	$
1	3.470473	2,954.40	545.60	3,100.00	400.00
2	3.396878	2,493.90	460.50	2,700.00	400.00
3	3.323283	2,105.20	388.70	2,300.00	400.00
4	3.249688	1,777.00	328.20	1,900.00	400.00
5	3.176093	1,500.00	277.00	1,500.00	400.00

The amounts in columns (3) and (4) are given to the nearest 10¢, since the logarithms in column (2) limit accuracy in column (3) to at best 5 significant figures.

For an automobile or similar asset, which actually does depreciate most rapidly in the early years, the constant-percentage method may be expected to give reasonably true results. In selecting between these two methods when depreciating such an asset, one would weigh against this advantage of greater accuracy the much easier computation by the straight-line method.

PROBLEM LIST 2

Basic List (Problems 1-42)

Sec. 2.1-2.4

1. A sum of $512 is accumulated for 6 years, the first 3 years at $i = 8\%$ and the final 3 years at $d = 4\%$. What is the final sum?

2. (a) In approximately how many years will money double at an effective annual rate d of interest-in-advance, given $\ln 2 = .693$?

(b) In how many complete years will 1 invested at the annual effective rate $d = 7.544\%$ of interest-in-advance accumulate to approximately twice the amount of 1 invested at the effective annual rate $i = 4\%$ of interest?

3. In a transaction of n time units, let A, S and d have their usual meanings. In this notation express what a borrower of A should pay n time units later, if he pays

(a) dA at the beginning of each period;
(b) dA at the end of each period;
(c) $dA(1 - d)^{-1}$ at the beginning of each period;
(d) $dA(1 - d)^{-1}$ at the end of each period.

4. In n years, \$100 grows to \$900 at an effective annual rate of discount which is to be assumed for the following.

(a) To what will \$100 grow (i) in $n/2$ years, (ii) in $2n$ years?

(b) What is the discounted value of \$100 (i) for n years, (ii) for $n/2$ years, (iii) for $2n$ years?

5. An investor puts \$1,000 into a firm which over the next 10 years grows in value at 10% per year and another \$1,000 into a firm which in the same period decreases by 10% per year. Does the investor make a net gain or loss? How much?

6. A savings account of \$10,000 is growing by interest at (4%, 4) per year and is being depleted at the end of every year by withdrawals of 10% of the balance. When will the account first fall below \$1,000, and to the nearest dollar what will be its balance then?

Sec. 2.5

7. Find the present value of \$1,000 due at the end of 18 months if the nominal annual rate of interest-in-advance is 4%, compounded quarterly.

8. On the assumption there is equal security, which is the better investment: a bond which pays a nominal annual rate of interest of 4 1/4% converted semiannually or a note which pays a nominal annual rate of discount of 4% converted quarterly?

9. Decide by verbal reasoning whether $(1 - f/m)^{-m}$ is larger than $(1 - f)^{-1}$ when $m > 1$ and $0 < f < 1$.

10. Sketch the graph of the accumulated value of \$1,000 invested for 10 years at an annual rate $f = 10\%$ of interest-in-advance with frequency of conversion m varying from 1/10 to $+\infty$.

Sec. 2.6

11. At how great an effective annual rate of (1) interest, (2) discount could a person afford to borrow in order to pay cash for goods on which the terms are 2% discount for cash or full price in 90 days?

12. A man has real estate property worth \$10,000 increasing in value at a net rate of 3% per annum. After 10 years he needs \$10,000 which he can borrow at an effective annual rate of interest-in-advance $d = 4.8\%$, using his property as security for the loan. If he makes no payments at all on the loan, when should the lender take over the property? Justify a nonintegral result.

13. A has just received \$192 from B and has promised to repay it at $d = .04$ in 1 year. Besides, he owes B \$1,000 due in 2 years. If B agrees instead to accept \$1,500 in full payment of the debts 6 years from now, (a) at what effective annual rate of interest are the debts being accumulated? (b) at what effective annual rate of interest-in-advance?

14. A lender of A immediately receives interest-in-advance of dA, which he reinvests immediately on the same terms. However, he reinvests the second payment of interest-in-advance

at an equivalent rate of interest i. What total sum will he have accumulated at the end of one period?

15. If i and d are equivalent effective rates, derive the simplest expression for X in the notation of the chapter, in order to make the 2 sets of payments in the line diagram equivalent at the given rates.

	0	1	2	...	n-2	n-1	n
Y receives:	2A						
Y pays:	$dA+\frac{d^2A}{i}$	$dA+\frac{d^2A}{i}$	$dA+\frac{d^2A}{i}$	...	$dA+\frac{d^2A}{i}$	$dA+\frac{d^2A}{i}$	X

16. (a) Find the interest rate equivalent to a discount rate of k^{-1} and the discount rate equivalent to an interest rate of k^{-1}, with the same time unit and with $0 < k^{-1} < 1$.

(b) Show that when i and d are equivalent compound rates

$$\text{(i)}\quad i = d + d^2 + \frac{d^3}{1 - d} \doteq d(1 + d)$$

$$\text{(ii)}\quad d = i - i^2 + i^3v \doteq i(1 - i).$$

17. Assume that all unspecified rates below are equivalent, with a common time unit.

(a) Simplify to a function of i:

$$\frac{i^2}{1 + i} + v^{1/2}(1 - d)^{3/2}\left(1 + \frac{i^{(12)}}{12}\right)^{18}\left(1 - \frac{d^{(4)}}{4}\right)^{-10} - \frac{d^2}{1 - d}\,.$$

(b) Find

$$\left(1 + \frac{i^{(6)}}{6}\right)^{20} \quad \text{if} \quad (1 - d)^{10}\left(1 - \frac{d^{(3)}}{3}\right)^{-20} e^{-10\delta} = (1.1)^{-12}.$$

18. Given $(f = .06, 4)$, find the equivalent rates
(a) d (b) $(f, 12)$ (c) $(j, 4)$ (d) $(j, 12)$ (e) i (f) δ.

19. Given $(.06, 4)$, find the equivalent rates
(a) d (b) $(f, 12)$ (c) $(f, 4)$ (d) $(j, 12)$ (e) i (f) δ.

20. If j and f, and $i^{(m)}$ and $d^{(m)}$, are equivalent rates of interest and discount, verbally interpret

(a) $\frac{j}{m}\left(1 - \frac{f}{m}\right) = \frac{f}{m}$ (b) $\frac{j}{m} = \frac{f}{m}\left(1 - \frac{f}{m}\right)^{-1}$ (c) $\frac{j}{m} - \frac{f}{m} = \frac{j}{m}\cdot\frac{f}{m}$

(d) $i = (1 + i^{(m)}/m)^m - 1$ (e) $i^{(m)}/m = (1 + i)^{1/m} - 1$

(f) $d^{(m)}/m = 1 - v^{1/m}$ (g) $d^{(m)}/m = v^{1/m}\, i^{(m)}/m$.

21. (a) Find the effective rate of interest-in-advance which is 90% of the equivalent effective rate of interest.

(b) Express in terms of x: the effective rate of discount which is x times the corresponding effective rate of interest, $0 < x < 1$.

22. (a) Given $d^{(4)} = 4\%$, find the equivalent rate $i^{(2)}$.

(b) Find the nominal annual rate of discount, convertible monthly, which is equivalent to a nominal annual rate of interest of 4%, compounded quarterly.

23. In each part let the rates involved be equivalent. Solve without using interest tables.

(a) Given $i^{(4)} = 5.39\%$, calculate $d^{(2)}$.

(b) Given $i/d^{(2)} = 1.0596$, approximate i.

(c) Given $d/d^{(2)} = 0.99$, find $v^{1/2}$ and d.

(d) If $d^{(2)}/d^{(4)} = 0.995$, find d.

(e) If $i^{(m)} = 0.09179$ and $d^{(m)} = 0.08973$, find $d^{(2)}$.

24. (a) Show that $v^{1/m} + \frac{d^{(m)}}{m} = 1$, where v is at rate i equivalent to $d^{(m)}$.

(b) Show that $d^{(m)} = d^{(2m)}\ (1 - d^{(2m)}/4m)$.

(c) Express $i^{(m)}$ as a function of $i^{(2m)}$.

Sec. 2.7, 2.8

25. Let all the rates below have the same time unit. Find the force of discount correct to six significant figures

(a) If the effective rate of interest is 10%;

(b) If the nominal rate of interest is 10%, $m = 2$;

(c) If the effective rate of discount is 10%;

(d) If the nominal rate of interest-in-advance is 20%, $m = 2$.

26. (a) Calculate the rates d, $d^{(4)}$, $i^{(4)}$ and i equivalent to a force of 4% per time unit.

(b) Find the effective annual rate of discount equivalent over one year to a variable annual force of interest $\delta_t = .03t$, $0 \leq t \leq 1$.

27. Let all rates used be equivalent.

(a) Prove $\delta - d = \frac{1}{2} i^2 - \frac{2}{3} i^3 + \frac{3}{4} i^4 - \cdots$.

(b) Show that

(i) $\delta = \frac{i + d}{2} - \frac{i^2 - d^2}{4} + \frac{i^3 + d^3}{6} - \cdots$

(ii) $\delta \doteq i\left(1 + \frac{i}{2}\right)^{-1}$, $\delta \doteq d\left(1 - \frac{d}{2}\right)^{-1}$

(iii) $\sinh \delta = \frac{i + d}{2} \doteq \delta$.

(c) Express δ in terms of $i^{(m)}$ and $d^{(m)}$ corresponding to the formulas in (b).

28. (a) Develop a rule similar to $n \doteq \frac{.693}{i} + .35$ (see Example 1.3 (d)) for the number of time units required for money to double itself at a force of discount. Is your rule exact or approximate? Explain.

(b) In how many years will money double at an annual force of discount of 6%? (Cf. Example 1.3 (a).)

29. (a) Simplify $\frac{1}{d^{(m)}} - \frac{1}{i^{(m)}}$.

(b) Given that $i^{(4)} = .05$, calculate the equivalent $d^{(4)}$.

(c) Simplify $\left(\frac{1}{d^{(2)}} - \frac{1}{i^{(2)}}\right)^2 \Big/ \left(\frac{1}{d^{(12)}} - \frac{1}{i^{(12)}}\right)$ assuming the rates are equivalent.

(d) Simplify and discuss $\frac{1}{d^{(\infty)}} - \frac{1}{i^{(\infty)}}$.

30. Place each of the following sums on a line diagram in such a way that they are equivalent payments: $(1 + i)^n$, $(1 - d)^n$, v^2, $e^{2n\delta}$ $(1 - d)^{-3}$. Assume that i, d, δ are equivalent rates with the same time unit.

Sec. 2.9

31. (a) To earn 1% simple interest per month on 60-day notes, at what annual simple discount rate should a bank discount notes?
(b) If a business can earn 1% effective a month on funds, what maximum rate (f, 12) of interest-in-advance could it offer to encourage immediate payment of accounts receivable in 2 months?

32. Eight months ago, A invested \$885 at 6% simple interest per year. He now withdraws his accumulation and lends it at an annual simple discount rate of 6% for the next 7 months. At what single nominal annual rate of interest-in-advance compounded quarterly might he equally profitably have invested his \$885 for the 15-month period?

33. On receipt of \$100 from B, repayable in 20 days, A pays B \$1. At what rate is A paying (a) simple discount? (b) simple interest? (c) compound discount at the rate (f, 12) per year? (d) compound interest at the rate (j, 4) per year? Are these rates equivalent?

34. On July 6, A lent C \$1,200 due in 180 days with simple interest at 6%. He plans to discount it at Bank B, which charges 6% simple discount, as soon as he can get \$1,200 for it. On what date will that be?

35. Smith signed a note on December 12, 19-- reading as follows: "Ninety days after date, for value received, I promise to pay to the order of A. Jones \$200." Jones was actually charging an 8% simple discount rate. After 30 days he discounted the note at The National Bank, at a 6% simple discount rate, and it immediately rediscounted the note at a Federal Reserve Bank at a 4% simple discount rate. (a) What is The National Bank's net profit from the transaction? (b) What simple interest rate did Jones earn during the time he held the note?

36. A signs a 1-year note for \$1,000 and receives \$940 from the bank. At the end of 9 months he pays \$197. To what in effect does this reduce the face of the note?

37. What annual rate $(j, 2)$ is equivalent to a simple discount rate of 8% per year in a transaction of length (a) 3 months? (b) 6 months? (c) 12 months?

38. In the following, assume a transaction of N time units.
(a) Express the simple discount rate equivalent to (i) (j, m); (ii) (f, m); (iii) δ.
(b) Let the effective rates i and d be equivalent to the simple rates r and d'. Show that r and d' are of form $i^{(p)}$ and $d^{(p)}$, respectively.

Sec. 2.10

39. In a 6-month transaction in which $S = \$1,000$, what is the difference between the simple discount and the compound discount, at an annual discount rate of $d = 7.84\%$?

40. (a) Use $S = A(1 - d)^{-\overline{n}-t}$ to obtain the approximations

(i) $S \doteq A(1 - d)^{-\overline{n}-1}[1 - d(1 - t)]$

(ii) $S \doteq A(1 - d)^{-\overline{n}}/(1 - dt)$

(iii) $S \doteq A(1 - d)^{-\overline{n}}(1 + dt)$.

(b) Which of the four expressions for S should a debtor like most? least?

41. Describe the rationale used in discounting 1 under each of the following, and list the values in increasing order of magnitude, where $\overline{n}$ = a positive integer and $0 < t < 1$:

(a) $(1 + r)^{-\overline{n}-t}$ (b) $(1 - r)^{\overline{n}+t}$

(c) $(1 + r)^{-\overline{n}-1}[1 + r(1 - t)]$ (d) $(1 - r)^{\overline{n}}(1 - rt)$

(e) $(1 + r)^{-\overline{n}}/(1 + rt)$ (f) $(1 - r)^{\overline{n}+1}/[1 - r(1 - t)]$.

42. Work out the conclusions drawn from equations (2.38)-(2.40). On a single axis system, sketch the graphs of V_t, V_t^s and $V_t - V_t^s$.

Supplementary List (Problems 43-68)

43. Find an approximate value of $\delta_1 - \delta_2$, where δ_1 is the force of interest equivalent to an effective rate of interest-in-advance of 5% and δ_2 is the force of interest equivalent to an effective rate of interest of 5%.

44. (a) Instead of payments of \$400 and \$100 2 and 6 years from now, respectively, A wishes to make equal payments X at the ends of 2, 4 and 6 years. Find X, using a simple discount rate of 5%, by valuing (i) at the end of 2 years, (ii) at the end of 6 years.
(b) Note that different values of X result; i.e., the valuation date affects the result. Demonstrate with equations of value whether this would also be true at simple interest, compound discount, compound interest.

45. In a circular seeking capital, organizers of a loan company state that they anticipate that every dollar of capital will double in 10 years. Assume that at any time 90% of company funds would be invested. What nominal rate of interest-in-advance (f, 2) on invested funds would the organizers then have presumed?

46. (a) If money doubles at an effective annual discount rate d in n years, in how many years will it be (i) 8 times its original size? (ii) 6 times?
(b) Same problem, at a simple discount rate d per year.
(c) Same problem, at an effective annual interest rate i.
(d) Same problem, at a simple interest rate i per year.

47. For how many time units must a sum be discounted to be reduced 25%, at (a) a simple discount rate d? (b) a simple interest rate i? (c) an effective rate of interest-in-advance d? (d) an effective rate of interest i? (e) a force of discount δ?

48. Give a pair of series expansions linking equivalent rates (a) $d^{(m)}$, d; (b) $i^{(m)}$, i; (c) $d^{(m)}$, $i^{(m)}$; (d) $d^{(m)}$, δ; (e) $i^{(m)}$, δ.

49. (a) Find (i) $\frac{d}{di}\delta$ (ii) $\frac{d}{dv}\delta$ (iii) $\frac{d}{dd}\delta$.
(b) Find an expression for $\frac{d}{d\delta}d^{(m)}$.

50. (a) A \$105, 3-month loan from which \$5 interest was deducted immediately, was renewed 10 times for 3-month periods by payment of \$5 interest at renewal date. What effective annual rate of interest was paid?
(b) Suppose that the \$5 payments were not made on renewal dates. What amount should be paid to discharge the debt at the end of the 10th renewal period?

51. Prove or disprove:
(a) It is preferable to borrow at (f = .06, 2) than at (.06, 4).
(b) As a lender, I would prefer a level discount rate d per period for 5 periods to successive discount rates $d + 2k$, $d + k$, d, $d - k$, $d - 2k$. Assume $0 < |k| < v/2$, where v is at rate i equivalent to d.
(c) If i and d are equivalent rates, and also i' and $2d$, then $i' > 2i$. Given: $i > 0$, $i' > 0$.
(d) If $i^{(m)}$ and $d^{(p)}$ are equivalent rates of interest and interest-in-advance between 0 and 1, and if m and p are positive integers, then $i^{(m)} > d^{(p)}$.
(e) If $0 < d < 1$, then $d < d^{(1/2)}$.

52. For i and d equivalent rates, show that

(a) $$\sum_{k=0}^{n-1} v^k = \frac{1 - v^n}{d} = \frac{1 - v^{n-1}}{i} + 1$$

(b) $$\sum_{k=1}^{n} (1 + i)^k = \frac{(1 + i)^n - 1}{d} = \frac{(1 + i)^{n+1} - 1}{i} - 1.$$

53. Brown receives $1,000 from White in return for his promise to repay $100 at the end of every month for 11 months. White immediately sells the contract to a bank.

(a) Find the amount which White receives if the bank charges a 6% simple discount rate.

(b) How much less would White receive if the bank charged (f = .06, 12)?

(c) Find the annual rate of simple discount which Brown pays.

(d) Explain the method you would use to obtain the annual rate (f, 12) which Brown pays.

54. Let f be the nominal semiannual rate of interest-in-advance convertible monthly equivalent to an effective annual rate of interest i, and let δ be the biennial force of interest equivalent to a nominal annual rate of interest (f, 1/2). Express δ in terms of i.

55. The accumulation of a sum for 2N interest periods at (f = j, m) for any N of the periods and at (j, m) for the remaining N periods is equal to the accumulation of the same sum at (2j', m) for N periods. Express j' in terms of j, m and/or N, and describe your answer in equivalent-rates terminology.

56. I invest two equal sums, one at an effective annual rate of interest-in-advance d and the other at (f = d, 2). At the end of 20 years, my accumulations to the nearest dollar are $1,220 and $1,000, respectively. Find d to the nearest integral percent.

57. Consider the expressions (a) $(i - \delta)/\delta^2$ and (b) $(\delta - d)/\delta^2$, where i, d, δ are equivalent rates with $0 < \delta < 1$. Show that one of them slightly exceeds 1/2 and the other is slightly less than 1/2. Which one is nearer to 1/2?

58. If d, $d^{(m)}$ and $i^{(m)}$ are equivalent rates with m > 1 and $0 < i^{(m)} < m$, and if money doubles in n periods at discount rate d per period, show that each of the following is an approximation to n and determine which is the best one:
(a) $(\ln 2)/d^{(m)}$; (b) $(\ln 2)/i^{(m)}$; (c) $(\ln 4)/(i^{(m)} + d^{(m)})$.

59. Two sums, one invested at 10% simple interest and the other at 9% simple discount, are now equal. At what times, past and future, are they also equal? Sketch the graphs of both on the same axis system.

60. A savings bank lends A for a period in return for a promise of S at the end of the period. At the time of the loan it receives a deposit of A; it pays deposit interest at rate i per period (less than its discount rate d on loans). Express (a) its net percentage gain during the period on A; (b) the increment in its discount rate, if when its deposit interest rate is increased k% it is to maintain its same net percentage gain on A.

61. (a) Prove, algebraically and verbally, that for equivalent rates i and d, $i(1 - d)^{1/2} = d(1 + i)^{1/2}$.

(b) Prove further that the expressions in (a) equal $(id)^{1/2}$ and approximately $(i + d)/2$.

(c) Prove that $2(i - d)/(i + d)$ is an approximation for the equivalent force δ, and also the expressions in (a) and (b).

(d) Compare to 5 significant figures the values given by each of these approximations for δ with the true value when $i = 8\%$.

62. (a) A building which cost \$100,000 is assumed to have a useful lifetime of 100 years and a salvage value of \$10,000 then and to depreciate continuously at a constant rate. Find the annual force of depreciation.

(b) Same as (a), except it is assumed there is no salvage value.

(c) Same as (b), except it is also assumed that it will cost \$10,000 to tear down the old building (i.e., "salvage value" = - \$10,000).

(d) For the building in (a), find to the nearest dollar the total depreciation charged in the tenth year and the book value at the end of 10 years.

63. At a force of interest δ, a unit doubles in 23.1 years. In how many years will it quadruple at a nominal rate of interest-in-advance numerically equal to δ and convertible 3 times in every 2 years? Given ln 2 = .693. Answer to the nearest tenth of a year.

64. (a) In respect to a unit sum at the end of n interest periods, show that when the effective rate of discount d is doubled, the amount of discount earned during the n periods is increased by

$$(1 - d)^n \left[1 - (1 - i)^n\right] ,$$

where i is the effective rate of interest equivalent to d.

(b) When a unit is discounted at a rate of discount $d > 0$, show that the increase in discount, when the time is doubled from n to $2n$ discount periods, may be expressed as $v^n(1 - v^n)$, where v is at the equivalent rate i. Also find for what n such doubling of the term halves the present value, and obtain these present values.

(c) Which produces a greater increase in discount: (i) doubling the time, or (ii) doubling the discount rate?

65. Find x if

$$\lim_{p\to\infty} .0609^{(p)} - \lim_{h\to 0} \left\{ \left[(1.03)^h - 1\right] /h \right\} = \lim_{k\to\infty} \left\{k\left[1 - (1 - x)^{1/k}\right]\right\} .$$

66. Let the original cost of an asset be C, its salvage value at the end of n years be S and its annual rate of depreciation be d (expressed as a decimal).

(a) Show that the depreciation charge D_k for year k $(1 \le k \le n)$ by the constant-percentage method is $Cd(1 - d)^{k-1}$. (Note that this result, being precisely the product of the depreciation rate d and the book value at the beginning of year k, validates the name of the method.)

(b) The depreciation fund at the end of year k equals $\sum_{h=1}^{k} D_h$. Show that it also equals the original cost less the book value at the end of year k.

(c) Show that the book value of an asset by the straight-line method of depreciation exceeds that by the constant-percentage method by the greatest amount when

$$k = n \frac{\log(1 - S/C) - \log\left[-\ln(S/C)\right]}{\log(S/C)} .$$

Assume book values B_k are continuous functions of k, $0 \le k \le n$.

67. Graph on one axis system the curves representing the accumulation and present value of 1 at equal effective rates of interest and interest-in-advance.

68. (a) Explain the assertion that a banker making short-term loans at a simple discount rate d, in the long run is essentially investing at compound interest-in-advance.

(b) Show that

(i) the banker should prefer a single loan of term t to one for term $t_1 < t$ followed immediately by one for term $t - t_1$; i.e., he should prefer longer-term loans.

(ii) the banker should prefer in a set of k loans, wherein the proceeds of any loan after the first arises immediately from the repayment of its predecessor, with the last loan being repaid at a fixed time n, that all k loans have different terms. (Hint: consider the cases $k = 2$, $k > 2$.)

(c) Demonstrate whether these same statements would be true for a lender at a simple interest rate i.

CHAPTER 3

ANNUITIES-CERTAIN

3.1. Terminology. In the previous chapters, we considered various expressions for the accumulated value and the present value of a single payment. The next main step in the theory is to treat accumulation and discounting formulas for series of periodic payments, or annuities. The word annuity may originally have implied a series of annual payments but is now used to indicate any set of periodic payments, for example, monthly payments on a mortgage loan, a monthly income to a retired employee, or weekly benefits under accident insurance.

A number of terms have been used to classify and describe various types of annuities. Unfortunately these expressions have varied usage, some of which is confusing. One is tempted to discard most terminology and to describe each annuity explicitly as it appears. However, it is convenient to have brief phrases to signify standard forms of annuities, and we shall introduce some terms for that purpose.

The annuities we shall deal with are called annuities-certain. A number of authors explain the use of "certain" as implying that the annuity has a fixed number of payments, and not an uncertain number such as would be the case for a life annuity payable while a given individual survives. There is also the implication that the payments are assumed certain to be made on their given due dates, and are not contingent upon some event which cannot be entirely foretold, say, on the survival of the annuitant as in the case of a life annuity.

While these implications are closely related, the second is more general, as the case of the perpetual annuity (called a perpetuity) brings out. Perpetuity payments are not contingent but are considered certain to be made as stipulated, even though they continue forever and thus are unlimited in number. Essentially, a perpetuity is a limiting case of an annuity-certain with a fixed number of payments, and is always considered to belong in the category of annuities-certain. Since all the annuities we shall discuss are annuities-certain, the word certain will be dropped and the term annuity in each case shall mean annuity-certain.

In general, we shall work with discrete annuities with equal intervals between successive payment dates. This constant interval will be called the payment period; in some cases it may be a year or a number of years, while in others, a quarter, a month, or a week. The limiting case is that in which the payment period is infinitesimal and the annuity is payable continuously. In such a case the annuity is called continuous. Since to specify an annuity the payment period must be stated, it will be immediately clear from the context whether a discrete or continuous annuity is being considered, and it will usually be unnecessary to be explicit about the matter in referring to the annuity. Frequently the payment period and the interest period of a discrete annuity are identical, with payments and interest conversions on the same dates; we shall call such an annuity a simple annuity.

In the case of discrete annuities a distinction must be made between annuities with payments at the beginnings of the payment periods and those with payments at the ends of the payment periods. That for continuous annuities this distinction disappears, is another example of the greater simplicity of continuous theory in comparison with the corresponding discrete theory. We shall use the phrase ordinary annuity to imply an annuity having its payments at the ends of payment periods, as the standard annuity functions have been developed and tabulated for this case.*

An annuity with payments at the beginnings of the payment periods will be called an annuity-due. Thus, the phrase ordinary annuity will indicate that each payment is considered to belong to the payment period preceding its date, while for an annuity-due each payment is considered to refer to the payment period following its date. A common example of payments under an ordinary annuity is wages, while rent payments (which are traditionally made in advance) form an annuity-due.

A concept which will be used frequently is that of annuity term. By this is meant the total interval extending from the

*Such annuities have frequently been called "immediate annuities." The term "immediate," however, is also used to indicate that the first payment period begins at the present. As the modifier "immediate" is both confusing and ambiguous, we have preferred to use the term "ordinary." Where it is clear from the context what type of annuity is meant, no modifier will be used.

beginning of the first payment period to the end of the last payment period. For an annuity with payments at the ends of the periods, the annuity term begins one payment period before the first payment date and extends to the time of the last payment. For an annuity-due, the annuity term begins at the time of the first payment and extends one payment period beyond the date of the last payment.

It may happen that the annuity term does not begin at the present, but instead starts at some future date. In such cases the annuity is called a *deferred annuity*. Any such annuity may be thought of either as a deferred ordinary annuity or as a deferred annuity-due, but usually one of these terms is more appropriate or more convenient. The interval from the present to the beginning of the annuity term is called the *period of deferment*. In the following, unless it is specifically indicated that an annuity is deferred, it will be assumed that the annuity term commences with the present.

The *value of an annuity* on any date whatsoever is the total of the values on that date of all the annuity payments, i.e., the single payment on that date equivalent to the entire set of annuity payments. Two important special cases are more or less self-defined but should be mentioned. *The present value of an annuity* denotes the total of the present values of the payments of the annuity, and while usually taken at the beginning of the annuity term, may also be calculated in respect to any date prior thereto. The *accumulated value of an annuity* means the total of the accumulated values of the payments of the annuity, and is almost always taken as of the end of the annuity term rather than later. Unless the contrary is stated, evaluation by compound interest is understood.

3.2. Basic annuity functions. Let us consider the following standard ordinary annuity which, as indicated on the line diagram, consists of payments of 1 at the end of each interest period for n periods. It should be noted that (a) the payment

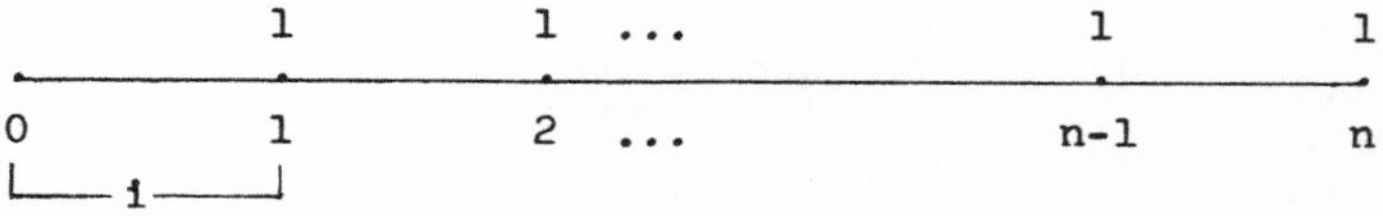

Fig. 3.1

period equals the interest period, (b) payments are at the ends of the periods, and (c) the annuity term begins immediately. The two main annuity functions are defined as the present value (at the beginning of the term) and the accumulated value (at the end of the term) of this standard annuity. At an interest rate i per conversion period, the present value of this annuity is denoted by $a_{\overline{n|}\,i}$ (read a angle n at i). Its accumulated value is denoted by $s_{\overline{n|}\,i}$. To recapitulate:

> $a_{\overline{n|}\,i}$ = the present value, at the beginning of its term, of an annuity of 1 per interest period, payable at the end of each interest period for n periods, n being a positive integer and interest being at the effective rate i per period.
>
> $s_{\overline{n|}\,i}$ = the accumulated value, at the end of its term, of an annuity of 1 per interest period, payable at the end of each interest period for n periods, n being a positive integer and interest being at the effective rate i per period.*

Thus, the complete annuity symbol prescribes (1) the present value, a, or accumulated value, s; (2) the number of interest periods, n, which in this case also equals the number of payments; and (3) the rate of interest i per interest period. Where the interest rate, however, is understood to be known, or need not be specifically known, the symbols are sometimes abbreviated to just $a_{\overline{n|}}$ and $s_{\overline{n|}}$. Again, we emphasize that $a_{\overline{n|}}$ is the value of the standard ordinary annuity one payment period before the first payment, and $s_{\overline{n|}}$ is the value of this annuity at the time of the last payment.

If, in determining the present value of the annuity, we discount the last payment first, then the next to last payment, and so on, we obtain the equation of value

$$a_{\overline{n|}\,i} = v^n + v^{n-1} + v^{n-2} + \cdots + v^2 + v. \tag{3.1}$$

The terms of the right member form a geometric progression with common ratio $v^{-1} = 1 + i$, and it follows that

$$a_{\overline{n|}\,i} = \frac{1 - v^n}{i}\,. \tag{3.2}$$

---

*These definitions are more general than those given in the International Actuarial Notation. For instance, in the International Notation, $a_{\overline{n|}\,i}$ = the value of an annuity-certain of 1 per annum for n years, the payments being made at the ends of each year (and interest being at the effective rate i per year).

Similarly, for the accumulated value we have the expressions

$$s_{\overline{n}|i} = 1 + (1 + i) + (1 + i)^2 + \cdots + (1 + i)^{n-2} + (1 + i)^{n-1} \qquad (3.3)$$

and

$$s_{\overline{n}|i} = \frac{(1 + i)^n - 1}{i} . \qquad (3.4)$$

(In the trivial case $i = 0$, formulas (3.2) and (3.4) are invalid, but formulas (3.1) and (3.3) give $a_{\overline{n}|} = s_{\overline{n}|} = n$.)

These formulas express the annuity functions $a_{\overline{n}|i}$ and $s_{\overline{n}|i}$ in terms of the discount and accumulation functions v^n and $(1 + i)^n$. Thus, it would always be possible, although tedious, to calculate any desired value of $a_{\overline{n}|i}$ or $s_{\overline{n}|i}$ from tables of v^n and $(1 + i)^n$; but the frequency with which such values are required makes tables of the standard annuity functions extremely useful. (See Table I in the Appendix.) For example, the present value of monthly salary payments of \$1,000 for a year at the nominal annual rate (.03, 12) is $1{,}000\, a_{\overline{12}|.0025} = \$11{,}807.25$, and the accumulated value is $1{,}000\, s_{\overline{12}|.0025} = \$12{,}166.38$.

Formulas (3.1) and (3.3) indicate that tables of $a_{\overline{n}|i}$ and $s_{\overline{n}|i}$ may be obtained by cumulative summation of powers of v and of $(1 + i)$. For the computation of single values, or check values, formulas (3.2) and (3.4) are particularly useful.

3.3. Identities for the annuity functions. A number of significant and useful identities involving $a_{\overline{n}|i}$ and $s_{\overline{n}|i}$ can be obtained. To begin with, we have the relations

$$a_{\overline{n}|i} = v^n\, s_{\overline{n}|i} \qquad (3.5)$$

and

$$s_{\overline{n}|i} = (1 + i)^n\, a_{\overline{n}|i} \qquad (3.6)$$

which are readily verified by simple algebra. These relations may also be established by the principle of equivalence. We know that the sum $a_{\overline{n}|i}$ at time 0 is equivalent to the annuity payments, and so is the sum $s_{\overline{n}|i}$, at time n. Now $v^n\, s_{\overline{n}|i}$ at time 0 is equivalent to $s_{\overline{n}|i}$ at time n and, hence, is equivalent to the annuity payments. Since $a_{\overline{n}|i}$ and $v^n\, s_{\overline{n}|i}$ at time 0 are each equivalent to the annuity payments, they must be equivalent to each other, and having the same date, are equal. Similarly, $s_{\overline{n}|i}$ and $(1 + i)^n\, a_{\overline{n}|i}$ at time n are each equivalent to the annuity payments, and, in consequence, are equal.

If, in this argument, we replace $a_{\overline{n|}i}$ by "present value of the annuity at the beginning of the term," and $s_{\overline{n|}i}$ by "accumulated value of the annuity at the end of the term," we see that the reasoning is not limited to the standard annuity but applies to any annuity. Thus, for such present and accumulated values the present value of any annuity is equal to v^n times its accumulated value and the accumulated value equals $(1 + i)^n$ times the present value of the annuity, where n is the number of interest periods in the annuity term. Once we have found either the present value or the accumulated value of an annuity, it is easy to find the other, although it is often easier to obtain them independently.

The following addition formulas are useful for various purposes including the situation where tables do not extend far enough to give $a_{\overline{n|}i}$ or $s_{\overline{n|}i}$ directly:

$$a_{\overline{h+k|}i} = a_{\overline{h|}i} + v^h a_{\overline{k|}i} \; ; \tag{3.7}$$

$$s_{\overline{h+k|}i} = s_{\overline{h|}i}(1 + i)^k + s_{\overline{k|}i} \; . \tag{3.8}$$

These may be established by grouping terms in equations (3.1) and (3.3) for the case $n = h + k$, as follows:

$$\begin{aligned} a_{\overline{h+k|}i} &= v + v^2 + \cdots + v^h + v^h(v + v^2 + \cdots + v^k) \\ &= a_{\overline{h|}i} + v^h a_{\overline{k|}i} \; ; \end{aligned}$$

$$\begin{aligned} s_{\overline{h+k|}i} &= 1 + (1+i) + \cdots + (1+i)^{k-1} + (1+i)^k \left[1 + (1+i) + \cdots + (1+i)^{h-1}\right] \\ &= s_{\overline{k|}i} + (1 + i)^k s_{\overline{h|}i} \; . \end{aligned}$$

Essentially the same argument may be expressed by means of a line diagram (see Figure 3.2). Verbally, the value at time h of

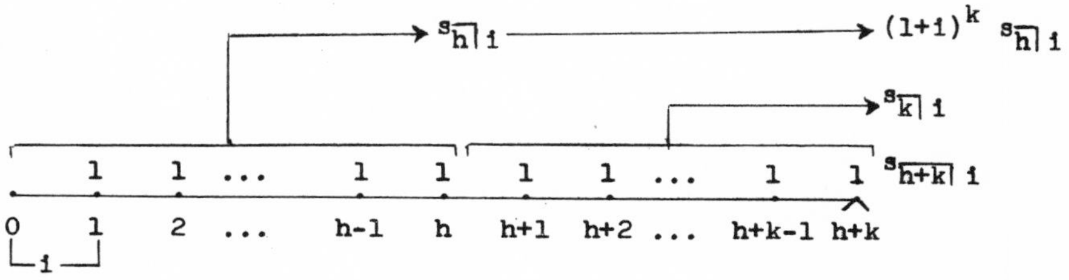

Fig. 3.2

the first h payments is $s_{\overline{h}|i}$ and this accumulated to time $h + k$ amounts to $(1 + i)^k s_{\overline{h}|i}$. In addition, the last k payments must be valued at time $h + k$. If we consider h as the time origin, the last k payments form a standard annuity and their value at the end of the term is $s_{\overline{k}|i}$. Added together, these values represent the accumulated value of the unit simple ordinary annuity of $h + k$ payments.

It will be left to the reader, as an instructive exercise, to use the line-diagram method to establish formula (3.7). If the line-diagram method is understood it is unnecessary to "know" formulas (3.7) and (3.8), as their application in a particular case will be obvious from a suitable diagram.

As a final remark on formulas (3.7) and (3.8) it should be noted that permutation of h and k will not change the left members of equations (3.7) and (3.8) but will give alternative expressions for the right members; for example,

$$a_{\overline{h+k}|i} = a_{\overline{k}|i} + v^k a_{\overline{h}|i} .$$

To calculate $a_{\overline{150}|.08}$ or $s_{\overline{150}|.08}$ from our tables, we may take (h, k) or (k, h) as (50, 100), (60, 90) or (70, 80). For instance,

$$\begin{aligned} a_{\overline{150}|.08} &= a_{\overline{100}|.08} + v^{100} a_{\overline{50}|.08} \\ &= 12.494318 + (.0004546)(12.233485) \\ &= 12.49988, \end{aligned}$$

$$\begin{aligned} s_{\overline{150}|.08} &= s_{\overline{50}|.08}(1.08)^{100} + s_{\overline{100}|.08} \\ &= (573.770156)(2199.761256) + 27484.515704 \\ &= 1,289,641.90, \end{aligned}$$

answers which seem astounding.

For the purpose of computing tables of $a_{\overline{n}|i}$ and $s_{\overline{n}|i}$ and, as we shall see later, for dealing with annuities-due, the simple linear recurrence relations (or difference equations) satisfied by these functions are important. In the case of $a_{\overline{n}|i}$, the relation can be obtained by setting up an equation of value for comparison date 1 between the present value $a_{\overline{n}|i}$ and

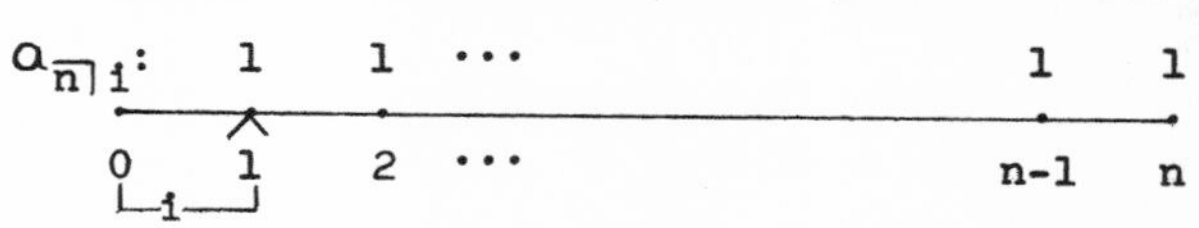

Fig. 3.3

the annuity payments. We obtain

$$a_{\overline{n}|i}\,(1 + i) = 1 + a_{\overline{n-1}|i} \tag{3.9}$$

since, as of time 1, the first payment has value 1 and the remaining payments may be considered as forming a standard annuity with time origin at 1 and with a term of n - 1 periods. This relation, connecting the consecutive values $a_{\overline{n-1}|i}$ and $a_{\overline{n}|i}$, may be arranged in various ways to suit the problem on hand.

To obtain an analogous relation for $s_{\overline{n}|i}$, we consider a standard annuity with n + 1 payments and set up an equation of

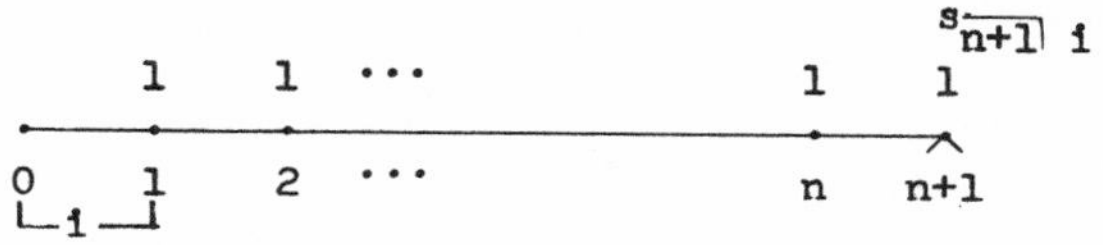

Fig. 3.4

value at time n + 1 between $s_{\overline{n+1}|i}$ and the payments in the form

$$s_{\overline{n}|i}\,(1 + i) + 1 = s_{\overline{n+1}|i}. \tag{3.10}$$

The left member values the payments by taking in one group the first n payments, and handling the final payment by itself. In fact, formula (3.10) can be obtained from equation (3.8) by setting h = n, k = 1.

Other meaningful identities are obtainable by rearranging equations (3.2) and (3.4) to give

$$1 = i\,a_{\overline{n}|i} + v^n \tag{3.11}$$

and

$$(1 + i)^n = i\,s_{\overline{n}|i} + 1. \tag{3.12}$$

As Figure 3.5 indicates, each of formulas (3.11) and (3.12) can

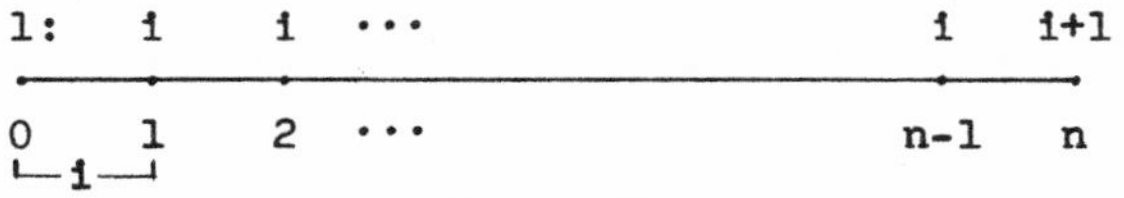

Fig. 3.5

be regarded as an equation of value between 1 (invested at time 0 for n periods to earn interest at rate i per period) and the annuity of interest payments, plus the repayment at the end of the investment term of the unit principal. For equation (3.11) the comparison date is at 0 and for equation (3.12) it is at time n.

Division of equation (3.11) by $a_{\overline{n}|i}$ leads to

$$\frac{1}{a_{\overline{n}|i}} = i + \frac{v^n}{a_{\overline{n}|i}}$$

$$= i + \frac{1}{(1+i)^n a_{\overline{n}|i}}$$

or

$$\frac{1}{a_{\overline{n}|i}} = i + \frac{1}{s_{\overline{n}|i}} . \tag{3.13}$$

Now $1/a_{\overline{n}|i}$ (or $a^{-1}_{\overline{n}|i}$) is the periodic payment of a simple annuity with level payments at the end of each interest period for n periods and with present value of 1. Similarly, $1/s_{\overline{n}|i}$ (or $s^{-1}_{\overline{n}|i}$) is the periodic payment of such an annuity with an accumulated value at the end of its term of 1. Equation (3.13) is verbally interpreted in Example 3.3. Need for values of $1/a_{\overline{n}|i}$ and $1/s_{\overline{n}|i}$ arises so often as to suggest their tabulation rather than calculation each time as reciprocals of $a_{\overline{n}|i}$ and $s_{\overline{n}|i}$, respectively. Referring back to the identity (3.13), however, we see that the value of $1/a_{\overline{n}|i}$ exceeds the value of $1/s_{\overline{n}|i}$ by the fixed value i. The practical consequence is that it is unnecessary to have tables of both $1/a_{\overline{n}|i}$ and $1/s_{\overline{n}|i}$, as the values for one function are easily obtained from those of the other. In this book, $1/s_{\overline{n}|i}$ is tabulated, and by merely adding i to it one gets $1/a_{\overline{n}|i}$. For example, in order to find what level payment W at the end of every month for a year is equivalent to \$1,000 at the end of the year, at an annual rate (.03, 12), we solve $W\, s_{\overline{12}|.0025} = 1{,}000$ as

$$W = 1{,}000(1/s_{\overline{12}|.0025}) = \$82.19$$

directly rather than by division. Likewise, if the \$1,000 were available at the beginning of the year, we would have

$$W = 1{,}000(1/a_{\overline{12}|.0025}) = 1{,}000(.0025 + 1/s_{\overline{12}|.0025}) = \$84.69.$$

It is sometimes useful to know that, as a function of i, $1/a_{\overline{n}|}$ is more nearly linear than $1/s_{\overline{n}|}$, $a_{\overline{n}|}$ or $s_{\overline{n}|}$.

Innumerable other identities can be obtained for the functions $a_{\overline{n}|i}$ and $s_{\overline{n}|i}$ but the foregoing relations are the ones with most significance for theory and for application.

<u>3.4. Ordinary annuities with constant payments.</u> In this section, we shall consider both simple annuities in which interest periods and payment periods exactly coincide and more general annuities in which they do not. In either case, there is the implication that the total number of payments of the annuity is a positive integer. While the number of interest periods may also be an integer, it need not be in the more general case. For instance, if interest is compounded annually and payments are monthly, a half-year, or ten-and-one-half-year, annuity term would be quite possible. Regardless of the character of the number of interest periods, say n, in the term of the annuity, in the mathematical development to follow the expressions $(1 - v^n)/i$ and $[(1 + i)^n - 1]/i$ will occur. When n is either zero, or positive but not an integer, we now define for $i > 0$

$$a_{\overline{n}|i} = (1 - v^n)/i, \qquad s_{\overline{n}|i} = [(1 + i)^n - 1]/i,$$

so that formulas (3.2) and (3.4) hold for all nonnegative numbers n and positive i, in the present instance by definition, and in the previous as a consequence of the verbal definitions of $a_{\overline{n}|i}$ and $s_{\overline{n}|i}$. For completeness, we also define $a_{\overline{n}|0} = s_{\overline{n}|0} = n$ for n either zero, or positive and nonintegral; thus $a_{\overline{n}|0} = s_{\overline{n}|0} = n$ for all nonnegative n. For n nonintegral, all the numbered formulas of Section 3.3 hold including formula (3.13) (provided every annuity term is nonnegative), even though the verbal definitions do not apply. In fact, no very simple verbal meaning exists here; the reader may wish to explore the thought further in Problem 125.

We shall now seek to find the present value and accumulated value of the general annuity indicated below in Figure 3.6. The work will be detailed and rather lengthy, befitting its importance. The section concludes with a numerical example.

Payments		W	W	...	W	W
Interest Periods	0	q	2q	...	n-q	n
Payment Periods	0	1	2	...	$\frac{n}{q} - 1 = np-1$	$\frac{n}{q} = np$

Fig. 3.6

To fix ideas, we list the notation to be used:

p = number of payment periods in an interest period. The number p is positive but not necessarily integral. However, generally when it is introduced, p is an integer.

q = number of interest periods in a payment period; q is positive but need not be an integer. Note that p and q are reciprocals.

n = number of interest periods in the term of the annuity; n is positive but need not be an integer.

$np = n/q$ = total number of payments, assumed to be integral and positive.

W = the amount of the periodic payment. For ordinary annuities, W is payable at the end of the payment period.

$R = pW$ = the total of the annuity payments in an interest period, that is, the (annuity) rent per interest period.

i = effective rate of interest per interest period.

A = present value of the annuity, as of the beginning of the term.

S = accumulated value of the annuity, as of the end of the term.

By discounting the individual payments to the present (i.e., one payment period before the first payment), beginning with the last payment, we obtain

$$A = W[v^n + v^{n-q} + v^{n-2q} + \cdots + v^q] . \qquad (3.14)$$

The expression in brackets is the sum of n/q terms of a geometric progression with common ratio $(1 + i)^q$. It follows that

$$A = W \frac{1 - v^n}{(1 + i)^q - 1} . \qquad (3.15)$$

Formula (3.15) may be regarded as the basic formula for the present value of an ordinary annuity with constant payments. If n is not an integer, formula (3.15) is a good means for finding A. If $q = 1$, the formula simplifies to

$$A = W \frac{1 - v^n}{i} = W a_{\overline{n}|i} . \qquad (3.16)$$

This is the simple case, where interest and payment periods coincide. For other cases, the formula can be rearranged in several ways, so that one is essentially dealing with an equivalent simple annuity. The methods are as follows:

(a) The equivalent-interest-rate method. The idea simply is to make interest and payment periods coincide by working with the equivalent interest rate per payment period. By this device, the annuity is transformed into a simple annuity. Specifically, the interest rate per payment period, i', equivalent to rate i per interest period is determined by the relations $1 + i' = (1 + i)^q = (1 + i)^{1/p}$. In terms of i', formula (3.15) may be written as

$$A = W \frac{1 - (1 + i')^{-np}}{i'} = W a_{\overline{np}|i'} \; . \qquad (3.17)$$

To get the meaning of this result, one notes that by changing from the rate i to the equivalent rate i' per payment period, that is, by taking a new interest period which coincides with the payment period, the annuity is reduced to a simple annuity of W per period for $n/q = np$ periods. The simplification, however, is more apparent than real since $i' = (1 + i)^q - 1$ will usually be an irregular rate for which function values are not tabulated.

The basic distinction between the equivalent-interest-rate method and the two equivalent-payment methods which follow is that in the former, as we have observed, the basic time unit is the payment period, whereas in the latter it is the interest period. That is to say, to simplify the problem, method (a) uses an adjusted interest rate but unchanged payments, while methods (b) and (c), as their names suggest, use instead suitably adjusted payments and an unchanged interest rate. This alternative device avoids the objection to method (a), so that (b) and (c) have become the recognized methods for computing annuity values.

The idea behind them is to form a simple annuity by working with a set of fictitious annuity payments -- at the ends of the interest periods -- equivalent to the set of actual payments. That two methods alike in idea are treated is because method (b) is advantageous when q is integral, whereas method (c) may be when p is integral.

(b) The first equivalent-payment method. If n is integral, and whether q is integral or not, but especially if it is, convenience of computation may be obtained by rearranging formula (3.15) as

$$A = W \frac{i}{(1 + i)^q - 1} \; \frac{1 - v^n}{i}$$

or

$$A = \frac{W}{s_{\overline{q}|i}}\, a_{\overline{n}|i} \,.$$ (3.18)

The right member of formula (3.18) may be interpreted as the
present value of an annuity of $W/s_{\overline{q}|i}$ at the end of each interest
period for n periods. In other words, the original annuity of
W at the end of each q interest periods may be replaced by an
equivalent simple annuity of $W/s_{\overline{q}|i}$.

This interpretation brings out "the idea," by means of which
one can immediately write down equation (3.18) without recourse
to formula (3.15). To see this fact more clearly, consider the
case of q an integer. The line diagram depicting a typical
payment period (Figure 3.7) helps us to determine the desired
payment X at the end of each interest period, equivalent to W
at the end of the payment period.

| Equivalent Payments | X | X $\cdots$ | X | X |
| Actual Payments | | | | W |

Payment Periods h   h+1

Interest Periods 0   1   2 $\cdots$ q-1   q
                  $\lfloor$___ 1 ___$\rfloor$

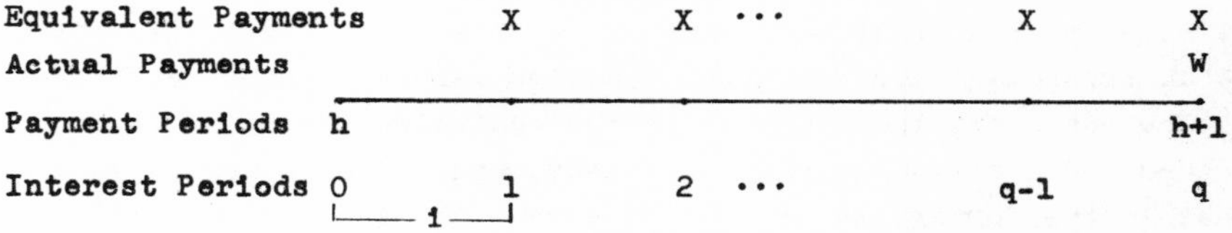

Fig. 3.7

There results the equality $X\, s_{\overline{q}|i} = W$, or $X = W/s_{\overline{q}|i}$, the equiv-
alent payment. The whole actual annuity is thus equivalent to
the annuity shown in Figure 3.8, with time unit the interest
period.

$\dfrac{W}{s_{\overline{q}|i}}\quad \dfrac{W}{s_{\overline{q}|i}}\quad \cdots\quad \dfrac{W}{s_{\overline{q}|i}}\quad \dfrac{W}{s_{\overline{q}|i}}\quad \cdots\qquad \dfrac{W}{s_{\overline{q}|i}}\quad \dfrac{W}{s_{\overline{q}|i}}\quad \cdots\quad \dfrac{W}{s_{\overline{q}|i}}$

0   1   2 $\cdots$ q   q+1 $\cdots$ n-q n-q+1 $\cdots$ n
$\lfloor$_1_$\rfloor$

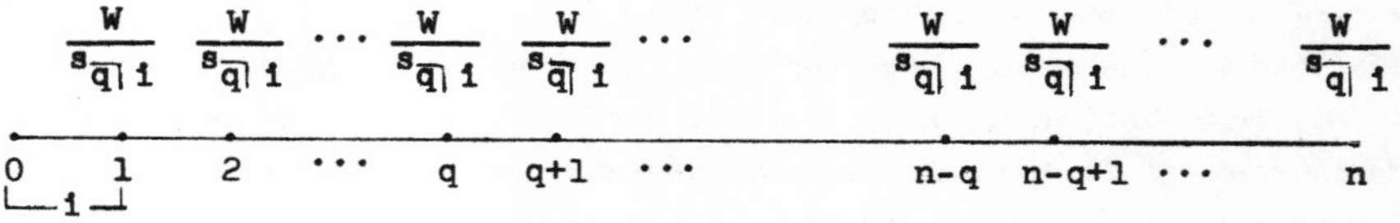

Fig. 3.8

Its present value, therefore, is

$$A = \frac{W}{s_{\overline{q}|i}}\, a_{\overline{n}|i}$$

as given by formula (3.18). In fact, in any problem of this
type, the easiest method of solution is to think what the equivalent payment at the end of each interest period is and to use it
as the payment of a simple annuity.

When q is not an integer, the interpretation still applies, but the formula is not as evident from the "idea." To use this method numerically for q not an integer, special tables of $s_{\overline{q|}}$ and/or its reciprocal are required. These appear in Table I for the useful values of $q = 1/2, 1/3, 1/4, 1/6, 1/12$ corresponding to the customary integral values of p.

(c) <u>The second equivalent-payment method.</u> If n is an integer, and if $p = 1/q$ is also an integer, one may choose to rearrange formula (3.15) to the form

$$A = p\, W \frac{i}{p\left[(1+i)^{1/p} - 1\right]} \frac{1 - v^n}{i}$$

or

$$A = R \frac{i}{i^{(p)}} a_{\overline{n|}i}. \qquad (3.19)$$

The notation $a^{(p)}_{\overline{n|}i}$ is often used to denote the present value, at the beginning of the term, of an annuity with rent of 1 per interest period, payable in installments of $1/p$ at the end of each pth of an interest period for a term of n interest periods, interest being at the effective rate i per period. Similarly, $s^{(p)}_{\overline{n|}i}$ is used to denote the accumulated value of such an annuity at the end of its term. In the important special case of $n = 1$, we see by accumulating the separate payments and summing the resulting geometric progression that

$$s^{(p)}_{\overline{1|}i} = \frac{1}{p}\left[1 + (1+i)^{1/p} + (1+i)^{2/p} + \cdots + (1+i)^{(p-1)/p}\right] = \frac{i}{i^{(p)}}.$$

Hence, formula (3.19) can be rewritten in the form

$$A = R a^{(p)}_{\overline{n|}i} = R s^{(p)}_{\overline{1|}i}\, a_{\overline{n|}i}. \qquad (3.19a)$$

To interpret formulas (3.19) we consider the line diagram for the present case (Figure 3.9). We see that the given annuity is

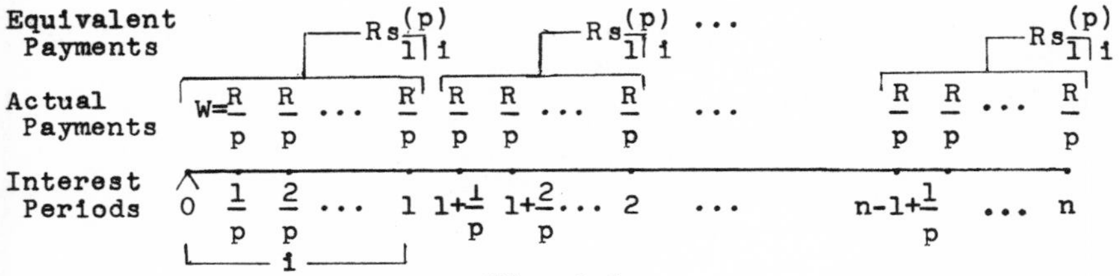

Fig. 3.9

equivalent to an annuity of R $s^{(p)}_{\overline{1}|i} = R\ i/i^{(p)}$ at the end of each interest period within the term, hence has present value R $s^{(p)}_{\overline{1}|i}\ a_{\overline{n}|i} = R\ \frac{i}{i^{(p)}}\ a_{\overline{n}|i}$. Once again one is enabled to write down the formula without reference to formulas (3.19) by means of "the idea" of obtaining equivalent payments at the ends of interest periods, namely p W $s^{(p)}_{\overline{1}|i}$, and valuing them as the simple annuity that they form. For this purpose, some useful values of $s^{(p)}_{\overline{1}|i} = i/i^{(p)}$ are tabulated (Table II).

Actually, all the formulas (3.17)-(3.19) theoretically apply for all positive real values of n, p and q, but tabulated values are, of course, limited. Unlike most published tables, Appendix tables make formulas (3.18) and (3.19) equally desirable for computation when p = 2, 3, 4, 6, 12. Certainly, tabulated values of both $s^{(p)}_{\overline{1}|}$ and $s^{-1}_{\overline{1/p}|}$ are unnecessary since $s^{-1}_{\overline{1/p}|} = p\ s^{(p)}_{\overline{1}|}$. They are both given here so that the reader can develop his own preference after experience with both forms; and also so that he can adapt easily to varied practice in the literature and tables. For computation observe that greater exactness is obtained from our tabulated $s^{-1}_{\overline{1/p}|}$ than our $s^{(p)}_{\overline{1}|}$. Also observe that the formulas (3.18) and (3.19) differ only in their labels for the equivalent payment at the end of each interest period, namely, W $s^{-1}_{\overline{1/p}|}$ and R $s^{(p)}_{\overline{1}|}$ respectively. Historically the $s^{(p)}_{\overline{1}|}$ form has had the emphasis and it will have the stress in this book as well.

The reader should note that for annuities, even for nonintegral periods, compound interest -- not simple interest approximations thereto -- is assumed.

Formulas for the accumulated value S on the date of the last payment, corresponding to formulas (3.14)-(3.19), are readily obtained by multiplying by $(1 + i)^n$ or independently. The starting formula is

$$S = W[1 + (1 + i)^q + (1 + i)^{2q} + \cdots + (1 + i)^{n-q}] \quad (3.20)$$

which, summed, yields

$$S = W\ \frac{(1 + i)^n - 1}{(1 + i)^q - 1}\ . \quad (3.21)$$

The accumulated value of the simple annuity

$$S = W\, s_{\overline{n}|\, i} \qquad (q = 1 = p) \tag{3.22}$$

is a special case of formula (3.21). In the general case, the equivalent-interest-rate method produces

$$S = W\, s_{\overline{np}|\, i'} \qquad \left[1 + i' = (1 + i)^q\right], \tag{3.23}$$

while the equivalent-payment methods in turn give

$$S = \frac{W}{s_{\overline{q}|\, i}}\, s_{\overline{n}|\, i} \tag{3.24}$$

and

$$S = R\, s^{(p)}_{\overline{n}|\, i} = R\, s^{(p)}_{\overline{1}|\, i}\, s_{\overline{n}|\, i} = R\, \frac{i}{i^{(p)}}\, s_{\overline{n}|\, i}. \tag{3.25}$$

Note that when $R = n = 1$ in formula (3.25), there results $s^{(p)}_{\overline{1}|\, i} = i/i^{(p)}$, which is familiar.

In the solution of problems, we urge the use of line diagrams and careful reasoning, based upon sound basic understanding of notations and "the ideas" underlying the formulas. The following example serves to illustrate: Payments at the rate of $1,000 per year are to be made for 10 years in equal installments at the end of every (a) quarter, (b) half-year, (c) year, (d) 8 months. Find both the present value and the accumulated value of each annuity if interest is at the annual rate (.04, 2).

<u>Solution:</u> (a) Figure 3.10 aids us in determining the equivalent payment at the end of each semiannual interest period and in completing the solution. Immediately,

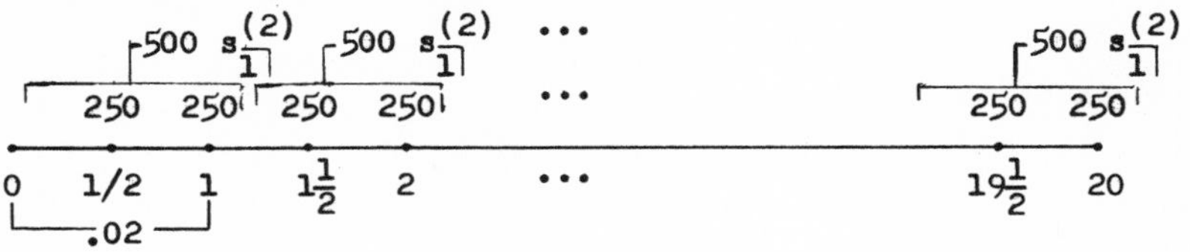

Fig. 3.10

$$A = 500\, s^{(2)}_{\overline{1}|\,.02}\, a_{\overline{20}|\,.02} = 250\, s^{-1}_{\overline{1/2}|\,.02}\, a_{\overline{20}|\,.02} = \$8,216.39;$$

$$S = 500\, s^{(2)}_{\overline{1}|\,.02}\, s_{\overline{20}|\,.02} = 250\, s^{-1}_{\overline{1/2}|\,.02}\, s_{\overline{20}|\,.02} = \$12,209.13.$$

As a crude check for reasonableness, we note that

$$A < nR = 10,000 < S.$$

(b) In the simple case, we have directly

$$A = 500\, a_{\overline{20|}\,.02} = \$8,175.72;$$

$$S = 500\, s_{\overline{20|}\,.02} = \$12,148.68.$$

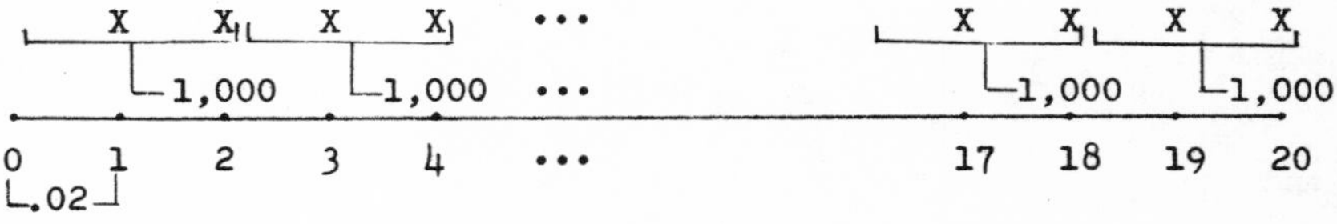

Fig. 3.11

(c) Figure 3.11 indicates that the equivalent payment can be found from the equation

$$X\, s_{\overline{2|}\,.02} = 1,000.$$

Then

$$A = X\, a_{\overline{20|}\,.02} = \frac{1,000}{s_{\overline{2|}\,.02}}\, a_{\overline{20|}\,.02} = \$8,094.77;$$

$$S = X\, s_{\overline{20|}\,.02} = \frac{1,000}{s_{\overline{2|}\,.02}}\, s_{\overline{20|}\,.02} = \$12,028.40.$$

(d) In this instance, tabulated values are not available for either equivalent-payment method, since $q = 4/3$ and neither p

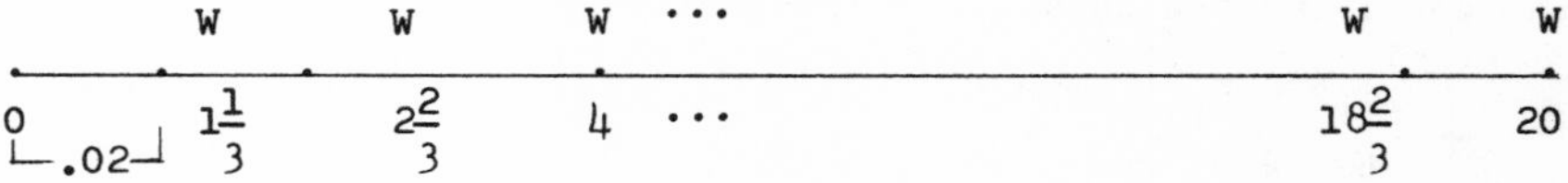

Fig. 3.12

nor q is an integer. From the basic formula (3.15) with $W = 2/3\ (1,000)$, we have

$$A = \frac{2,000}{3}\, \frac{1 - (1.02)^{-20}}{(1.02)^{4/3} - 1} = 8,148.674 \doteq \$8,148.67;$$

$$S = 8,148.674\, (1.02)^{20} = \$12,108.50.$$

Such a problem as (d) rarely occurs, but is included for completeness.

A oomparison of the results is worthwhile in itself and as a check on the reasonableness of the answers. As is to be expected, the greater the frequency of payment, the greater are the present values and the accumulated values.

Examples 3.2 and 3.5 further illustrate ordinary annuities.

3.5. Annuities-due. An annuity-due may be considered as an ordinary annuity which has its term beginning and ending one payment period earlier than is actually the case. Hence, the present value or the accumulated value for an annuity-due may be obtained by determining A or S for the corresponding ordinary annuity and multiplying such value by the accumulation factor for one payment period. For example, the standard annuity-due of 1 payable at the beginning of each interest period for n periods

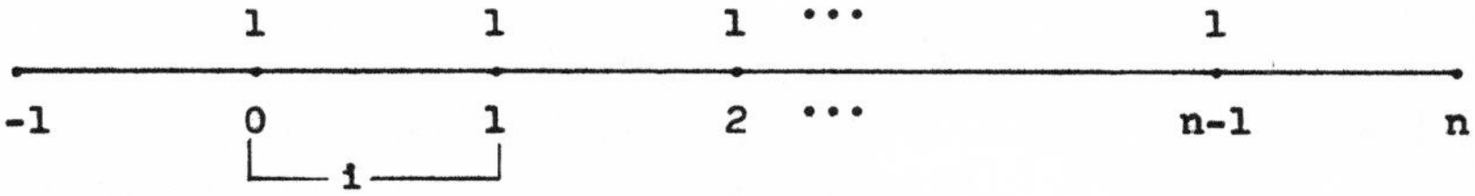

Fig. 3.13

may be considered as an ordinary annuity with term from -1 to $n - 1$. Its present value, as of time 0 when the first payment is made, is denoted by $\ddot{a}_{\overline{n}|i}$. It is given by the formula

$$\ddot{a}_{\overline{n}|i} = a_{\overline{n}|i}(1 + i) \tag{3.26}$$

where $a_{\overline{n}|i}$ represents the value at -1, and $1 + i$ accumulates this value to time 0. The accumulated value, denoted by $\ddot{s}_{\overline{n}|i}$ and found one payment period after the final payment, is similarly determined by the formula

$$\ddot{s}_{\overline{n}|i} = s_{\overline{n}|i}(1 + i) \tag{3.27}$$

where $s_{\overline{n}|i}$ represents the value at time $n - 1$.

Alternatively, one may argue that a payment of 1 at the beginning of an interest period is equivalent to a payment of $1 + i$ at the end, so that an annuity-due of 1 is equivalent to an ordinary annuity of $1 + i$, having the present and accumulated values above.

Denoting by d the equivalent effective rate of interest-in-advance per interest period, that is, $d = i/(1 + i)$, we may write these formulas in the forms

$$\ddot{a}_{\overline{n}|i} = \frac{1 - v^n}{d} \tag{3.28}$$

and

$$\ddot{s}_{\overline{n}|i} = \frac{(1 + i)^n - 1}{d} . \tag{3.29}$$

These lead to the identities

$$1 = d\,\ddot{a}_{\overline{n}|i} + v^n \tag{3.30}$$

and

$$(1 + i)^n = d\,\ddot{s}_{\overline{n}|i} + 1 \tag{3.31}$$

which are analogous to formulas (3.11) and (3.12) but are based on the concept of interest being paid in advance, that is, as an annuity-due, during the investment term.

By use of formula (3.9), equation (3.26) may be changed to the form

$$\ddot{a}_{\overline{n}|i} = 1 + a_{\overline{n-1}|i}, \tag{3.32}$$

which one may also obtain directly from the line diagram by considering the annuity as an initial payment of 1 plus an ordinary annuity with term n - 1. Similarly, from equation (3.10), formula (3.27) may be written as

$$\ddot{s}_{\overline{n}|i} = s_{\overline{n+1}|i} - 1. \tag{3.33}$$

To obtain this from the line diagram, one adds and subtracts a payment of 1 at time n. The n + 1 positive payments have value $s_{\overline{n+1}|i}$ at time n and, when account is taken of the negative payment, the formula results.

If tabulated values of $a_{\overline{n}|i}$ and $s_{\overline{n}|i}$ are available, formulas (3.32) and (3.33) provide such an efficient way of obtaining values of $\ddot{a}_{\overline{n}|i}$ and $\ddot{s}_{\overline{n}|i}$ that these latter quantities need not be tabulated even if they are often encountered.

Let us consider now a more general annuity-due of W at the beginning of each payment period, where there are q interest periods in a payment period, p payment periods in an interest period and n interest periods in the annuity term, with the total number of payments, np = n/q, an integer; in other words, the basic notation is the same as in the preceding section but payments are now on a due basis. There are added the new notations $\ddot{a}^{(p)}_{\overline{n}|i}$ and $\ddot{s}^{(p)}_{\overline{n}|i}$ denoting, as expected, the present value at the beginning of the term and the accumulated value at the end of the term, respectively, of an annuity-due of 1 per interest period, payable in installments of 1/p at the beginning of each pth of an interest period for a term of n interest periods, interest being at the effective rate i per period.

Formulas for the present value A, at the time of the first payment, may be obtained by multiplying formulas (3.14)-(3.19) by the accumulation factor $(1 + i)^q = (1 + i)^{1/p}$ and, of course, by other more direct means as well. Thus

$$A = W[v^{n-q} + v^{n-2q} + \cdots + v^q + 1] . \qquad (3.34)$$

There follows

$$A = W \frac{1 - v^n}{1 - v^q} \qquad (3.35)$$

and, for the special case of the simple annuity-due,

$$A = W \frac{1 - v^n}{d} = W\ddot{a}_{\overline{n}|\,i} = Wa_{\overline{n}|\,i}\,(1 + i) = W(1 + a_{\overline{n-1}|\,i}) \qquad (3.36)$$

which, naturally, is merely W times the standard annuity-due present-value forms.

The equivalent-interest-rate method, with $1 + i' = (1 + i)^q = (1 + i)^{1/p}$ as before, yields

$$A = W\,\ddot{a}_{\overline{np}|\,i'} . \qquad (3.37)$$

To it, the previous objection of i' ordinarily being an untabulated rate still applies.

If n is an integer, a more general annuity-due is usually evaluated by one of the equivalent-payment methods. The first of these provides the present value

$$A = \frac{W}{s_{\overline{q}|\,i}}\,a_{\overline{n}|\,i}\,(1 + i)^q = \frac{W}{a_{\overline{q}|\,i}}\,a_{\overline{n}|\,i} = W(i + \frac{1}{s_{\overline{q}|\,i}})\,a_{\overline{n}|\,i} \qquad (3.38)$$

where, preferably, q is an integer. In this case, the set of payments $W/a_{\overline{q}|\,i}$ at the <u>end</u> of every interest period within the annuity term is equivalent to the actual set of payments W at the beginning of every payment period, since each such payment W is equivalent to a simple ordinary annuity of $W/a_{\overline{q}|\,i}$ for q periods. At first it may seem peculiar that an annuity-due is replaced by an equivalent ordinary annuity, but annuity tables dictate this course. To obtain the present value by the formula $A = \frac{W}{\ddot{a}_{\overline{q}|\,i}}\,\ddot{a}_{\overline{n}|\,i}$, the equivalent payments being at the <u>beginning</u> of the interest periods, would not be convenient from the usual tables.

When n and p are both integers, it is convenient to use the second equivalent-payment method which yields

$$\left.\begin{aligned} A &= R\,\ddot{a}^{(p)}_{\overline{n}|i} = R\,a^{(p)}_{\overline{n}|i}\,(1+i)^{1/p} = R\,\frac{i}{i^{(p)}}\,(1+i)^{1/p}\,a_{\overline{n}|i} \\ &= R\,\frac{i}{d^{(p)}}\,a_{\overline{n}|i} = R\,\ddot{s}^{(p)}_{\overline{1}|i}\,a_{\overline{n}|i} \end{aligned}\right\} \quad (3.39)$$

where $R = pW$ and, from Table 2.1 or otherwise,

$$d^{(p)} = i^{(p)}/(1 + i^{(p)}/p) = i^{(p)}/(1 + i)^{1/p} .$$

Therefore, since it follows that

$$\ddot{s}^{(p)}_{\overline{1}|i} = \frac{i}{d^{(p)}} = \frac{i}{i^{(p)}} + \frac{i}{p} ,$$

$\ddot{s}^{(p)}_{\overline{1}|}$ need not be tabulated when tables of $s^{(p)}_{\overline{1}|}$ are available, for $\ddot{s}^{(p)}_{\overline{1}|}$ is readily obtained by adding i/p to $s^{(p)}_{\overline{1}|}$. This form is usually computationally preferable to the equally correct

$$\ddot{s}^{(p)}_{\overline{1}|} = s^{(p)}_{\overline{1}|}\,(1 + i)^{1/p} .$$

Of course,

$$\ddot{s}^{(p)}_{\overline{1}|} = \frac{1}{p}\,\frac{i}{1 - v^{1/p}} = a^{-1}_{\overline{1/p}|}/p$$

also. This form affirms the equivalence of expressions (3.38) and (3.39), and Appendix tables permit calculation by either formula when $p = 2, 3, 4, 6, 12$. That is to say, the equivalent payment at the end of each interest period is

$$R\,\ddot{s}^{(p)}_{\overline{1}|} = W\,a^{-1}_{\overline{1/p}|} .$$

Corresponding to the formulas for the present value of the annuity-due, are those for its accumulated value. These formulas for S, the value one payment period following the final payment, are obtained by multiplying the present-value formulas by $(1 + i)^n$, or otherwise, and some of these are

$$S = W\left[(1 + i)^q + (1 + i)^{2q} + \cdots + (1 + i)^n\right] \quad (3.40)$$

$$S = W\,\frac{(1 + i)^n - 1}{1 - v^q} \quad (3.41)$$

$$S = W\,\frac{(1 + i)^n - 1}{d} = W\,\ddot{s}_{\overline{n}|i} \quad (q = 1) \quad (3.42)$$

$$S = \frac{W}{s_{\overline{q}|i}}\,s_{\overline{n}|i}\,(1 + i)^q = \frac{W}{a_{\overline{q}|i}}\,s_{\overline{n}|i} \quad (3.43)$$

$$\left.\begin{aligned} S &= R\, \ddot{s}^{(p)}_{\overline{n}|i} = R\, s^{(p)}_{\overline{n}|i} (1+i)^{1/p} = R\, \frac{i}{i^{(p)}} (1+i)^{1/p}\, s_{\overline{n}|i} \\ &= R\, \frac{i}{d^{(p)}}\, s_{\overline{n}|i} = R\, \ddot{s}^{(p)}_{\overline{1}|i}\, s_{\overline{n}|i} \,. \end{aligned}\right\} \quad (3.44)$$

The reader should strive to understand rather than "know" the formulas of this section. In every case a line diagram can serve to suggest a method one may use. For example, a merchant may wish to know the size of the monthly installment, first payment due immediately, to charge on a $500 refrigerator if payments are to continue for 3 years and interest is at the effective annual rate of 8%. As the first step in the solution, we would draw a line diagram, having the equivalent payments at times 1, 2, 3:

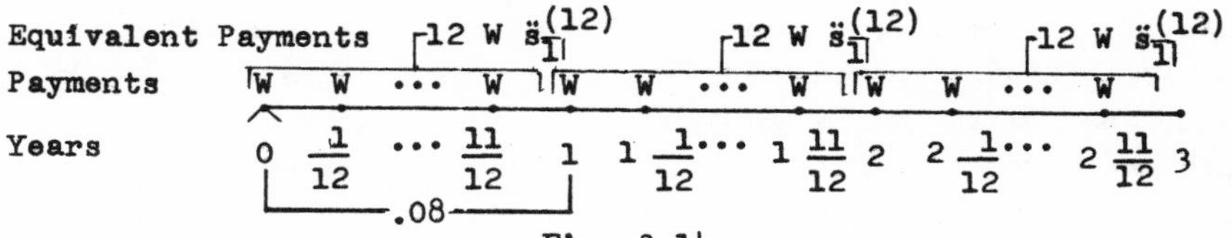

Fig. 3.14

Showing the equivalent payments suggests the equation

$$500 = 12\, W\, \ddot{s}^{(12)}_{\overline{1}|.08}\; a_{\overline{3}|.08}$$

from which

$$W = 500\, (s^{-1}_{\overline{3}|.08} + .08)/(12\, s^{(12)}_{\overline{1}|.08} + .08) = \$15.50.$$

Alternatively by use of the equivalent payment of (3.38) or by further reduction of the computational form above,

$$W = 500\, a_{\overline{1/12}|.08} / a_{\overline{3}|.08} \,.$$

On the other hand, if a regular payment were also to be made at the end of 3 years, it would be best to value the first payment separately, and the others in groups of 12, so that

$$500 = W(1 + 12\, s^{(12)}_{\overline{1}|.08}\; a_{\overline{3}|.08}) \,.$$

<u>3.6. Deferred annuities.</u> To determine present and accumulated values for deferred annuities involves no essentially new formulas and no new tabulated functions. However, for the present value, one must be careful in determining the period of deferment, that is, the period from the present to the beginning of

the annuity term. If the annuity is considered as an ordinary annuity, the period of deferment extends from the present to one payment period before the first payment. If the annuity is considered as an annuity-due, the period of deferment is from the present to the time of the first payment. The following methods are then available to find the present value of a deferred annuity.

(a) The value of the annuity at the beginning of the annuity term may be found and this value discounted for the period of deferment.

(b) The deferred annuity may be considered as an annuity with term extending from the present to the end of the annuity term less an annuity with term extending over the period of deferment. The present value of the deferred annuity is easily obtained as the difference in the present value of these two annuities.

For example, if interest is at the effective rate of 3% per year the present value on January 1, 1965 of an annuity of \$100 per month for 15 years, with first payment on January 1, 1975, is seen from Figure 3.15 to be equal to

$$1{,}200\left(i/d^{(12)}\right)a_{\overline{15|}}v^{10} = \$10{,}831.97$$

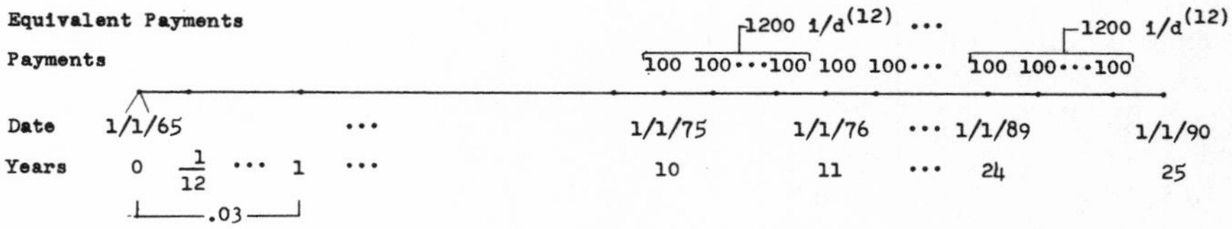

Fig. 3.15

or from Figure 3.16, with use of the fictitious payments in

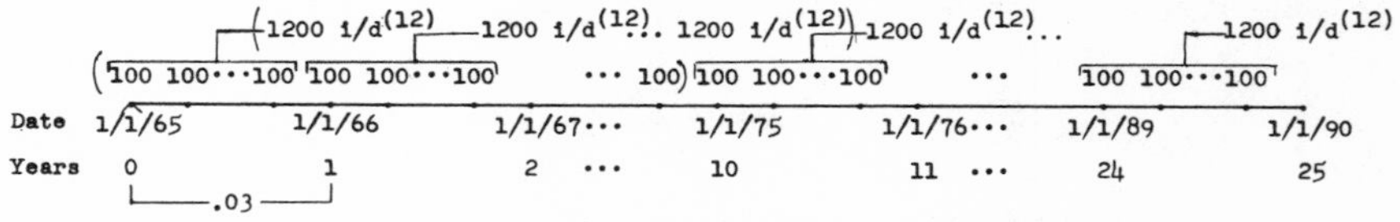

Fig. 3.16

parentheses, to

$$1,200\left(1/d^{(12)}\right)\left[a_{\overline{25|}} - a_{\overline{10|}}\right] = \$10,831.97$$

again, where all values are calculated at the rate of 3%. That these methods should give the same numerical result is clear from equation (3.7). It should be added that the second method may be inconvenient if the deferment period does not contain a whole number of interest periods, and that it is inapplicable if the interest rate of the deferment period differs from that of the term of the annuity.

It often happens that a deferred annuity-due may be regarded conveniently as a deferred ordinary annuity, with term beginning one payment period before the first payment. In the example here, it would not be convenient to do so, as it would lead to a deferment period of 9 11/12 years. Brief consideration at the start of any problem should bring out the most efficient method of solution.

A rough estimate to check the reasonableness of an answer is always useful. Treating the annuity of our example as approximately equivalent to a lump sum payment of 1,200 (15) = \$18,000 at the midpoint of its term, we have as rough estimates of the present value

$$18,000\, v^{17\frac{1}{2}} \doteq 18,000\, v^{17} \doteq \$11,000.$$

To denote the present value of a deferred annuity with a deferment period of m interest periods, one merely prefixes $m|$ to the regular annuity notation, e.g., $_{m|}a^{(p)}_{\overline{n|}i}$ and $_{m|}\ddot{a}^{(p)}_{\overline{n|}i}$. In the example, we have evaluated 1,200 $_{10|}\ddot{a}^{(12)}_{\overline{15|}.03}$ in preference to 1,200 $_{9\frac{11}{12}|}a^{(12)}_{\overline{15|}.03}$.

To find the accumulated value of a deferred annuity, one accumulates the various payments to the end of the annuity term. But this is precisely what was done in obtaining our previous formulas for S so that these are still applicable, as is also the previous annuity notation for accumulated values. Thus, for the preceding illustration, if the end of the annuity term is taken to be January 1, 1990, the accumulated value is 1,200 $\ddot{s}^{(12)}_{\overline{15|}}$ $= 1,200 \dfrac{1}{d^{(12)}} s_{\overline{15|}}$ at 3%.

Finding the value of an annuity on any date is an easy step forward, for the methods brought out in valuing annuities due and deferred are appropriate here also. These methods consist of

(1) valuing the annuity at the beginning or end of its term, and then accumulating or discounting this value to the required date, and (2) breaking up the annuity for valuation into two or more convenient component parts, possibly by the insertion of fictitious payments. For example, the value of the annuity of our example is

$$1{,}200\,\left(i/d^{(12)}\right) a_{\overline{15}|}\, v^5 \qquad \text{on January 1, 1970}$$

and, on January 1, 1980, is

$$1{,}200\left(i/d^{(12)}\right) a_{\overline{15}|}(1+i)^5 \quad \text{or} \quad 1{,}200\,\left(i/d^{(12)}\right) s_{\overline{15}|}\, v^{10}$$

$$\text{or } 1{,}200\,\left(i/d^{(12)}\right)\left[s_{\overline{5}|} + a_{\overline{10}|}\right],$$

where all values are at 3% interest. See also Example 3.1.

3.7. Varying annuities. Sometimes annuities are encountered in which the payments are not level. For example, it is often assumed that population increases geometrically from year to year, so if a community maintained a constant tax rate, its tax revenues might form an annuity with payments in increasing geometric progression. Then too, annual interest payments on a debt on which a constant amount of principal is retired each year would constitute a decreasing annuity with its payments in arithmetic progression.

Various methods are in use for valuing varying annuities. If such an annuity has only a few payments, or if the payments are of irregular size or frequency, direct evaluation by summing the values of the individual payments may be the best, or even the only practical, method.

A method which is suitable when the payments are in arithmetic progression is to break the annuity up into an equivalent set of level annuities. Let us consider the annuity of Figure 3.17

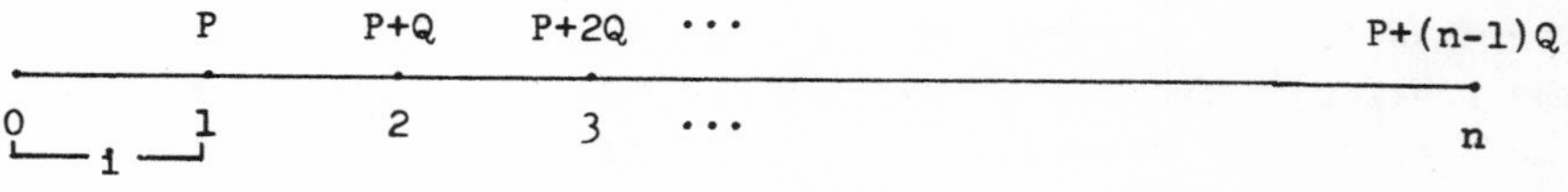

Fig. 3.17

which has first payment P and common difference Q. Its accumulated value may be determined if we level out the payments as in Figure 3.18.

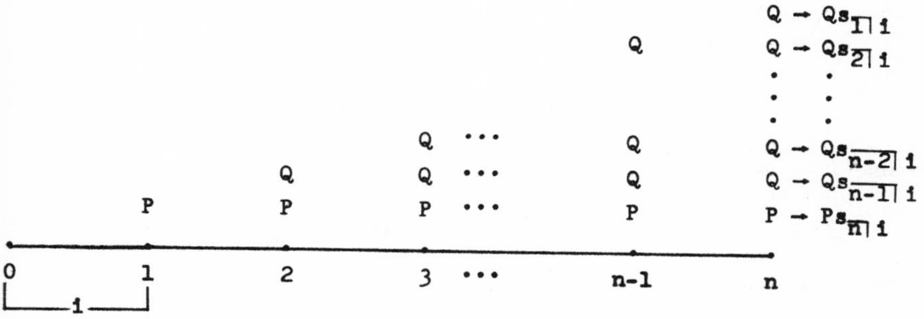

Fig. 3.18

Thus, at rate i

$$S = P\,s_{\overline{n}|} + Q \sum_{t=1}^{n-1} s_{\overline{t}|} = P\,s_{\overline{n}|} + \frac{Q}{i}\left[\sum_{t=1}^{n-1} (1+i)^t - (n-1)\right]$$

$$= P\,s_{\overline{n}|} + \frac{Q}{i}\left[\sum_{t=0}^{n-1} (1+i)^t - n\right]$$

$$= P\,s_{\overline{n}|} + Q\,\frac{s_{\overline{n}|} - n}{i}\,. \qquad (3.45)$$

For the present value A, we have

$$A = S\,v^n = P\,a_{\overline{n}|} + Q\,\frac{a_{\overline{n}|} - nv^n}{i}\,. \qquad (3.46)$$

Other applications of the handy "levelling method" occur in Example 3.4.

A more general method is one which uses finite differences.* Let us consider the annuity shown in Figure 3.19 where interest is at the effective rate i per interest period. The present

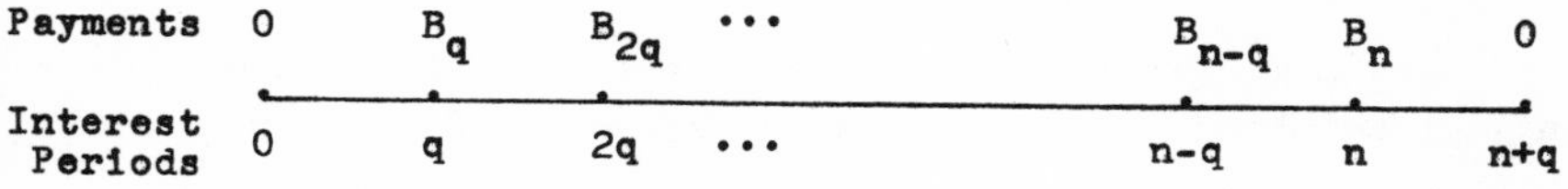

Fig. 3.19

value may be written as

$$A = \sum v^h B_h \qquad (h = q, 2q, \cdots, n)$$

$$= \sum v^h B_h \qquad (h = 0, q, \cdots, n) \qquad (\alpha)$$

*At this point the reader may wish to detour to the Appendix to study the brief introduction to the calculus of finite differences which is given there for the purposes of this book.

since $B_0 = 0$. Then

$$(1 + i)^q A = \sum v^{h-q} B_h \qquad (h = q, 2q, \cdots, n)$$

$$= \sum v^h B_{h+q} \qquad (h = 0, q, \cdots, n) \qquad (\beta)$$

since $B_{n+q} = 0$. Subtraction of (α) from (β) yields

$$[(1 + i)^q - 1] A = \sum v^h \underset{q}{\Delta} B_h \qquad (h = 0, q, \cdots, n)$$

where $\underset{q}{\Delta} B_h = B_{h+q} - B_h$. This leads to

$$A = \frac{1}{(1 + i)^q - 1} \sum v^h \underset{q}{\Delta} B_h \qquad (h = 0, q, \cdots, n). \qquad (3.47)$$

When q = 1, the notation q below Δ is suppressed, and the formula simplifies to

$$A = \frac{1}{i} \sum_{h=0}^{n} v^h \Delta B_h. \qquad (3.48)$$

Formulas (3.47) and (3.48) are useful in cases where the payments B_h are in arithmetic progression. In some cases, one may wish to apply the procedure a second time and thereby obtain

$$A = \frac{1}{[(1 + i)^q - 1]^2} \sum v^h \underset{q}{\Delta^2} B_h \qquad (h = -q, 0, q, \cdots, n) \quad (3.49)$$

where $\underset{q}{\Delta^2} B_h = \underset{q}{\Delta} B_{h+q} - \underset{q}{\Delta} B_h$. For q = 1,

$$A = \frac{1}{i^2} \sum_{h=-1}^{n} v^h \Delta^2 B_h. \qquad (3.50)$$

In every case the summation runs over all possible nonzero differences.

To obtain accumulated values for these annuities, we may first find A and then use the general relation $S = A(1 + i)^n$.

For a level annuity of W, all the differences $\underset{q}{\Delta} B_h$ are zero except $\underset{q}{\Delta} B_0 = W$ and $\underset{q}{\Delta} B_n = -W$. Putting these in formula (3.47), we obtain our previous formula (3.15). Similarly, formula (3.48) will yield our previous formula (3.16).

As further illustrations of the application of these formulas, we consider a number of annuities including some of standard form. Throughout, interest is assumed to be at the effective rate i per interest period.

(a) Annuity with payments in arithmetic progression. We return to the annuity previously discussed, with its n payments $P, P + Q, P + 2Q, \cdots, P + (n - 1)Q$ forming a simple annuity. From formula (3.48), we obtain

$$A = \frac{1}{i}\left(P + \sum_{h=1}^{n-1} v^h Q - v^n \left[P + (n - 1)Q\right]\right)$$

which may be simplified to formula (3.46).

(b) Standard increasing annuity. This annuity consists of payments of $1, 2, 3, \cdots, n$ at the ends of the first, second, third, $\cdots$, nth periods, respectively. The symbol $(Ia)_{\overline{n|}}$ is used to denote the present value, and $(Is)_{\overline{n|}}$ its accumulated value. By formula (3.48)

$$(Ia)_{\overline{n|}} = \frac{1}{i}\left[\sum_{h=0}^{n-1} v^h - nv^n\right]$$

or

$$(Ia)_{\overline{n|}} = \frac{\ddot{a}_{\overline{n|}} - nv^n}{i} \quad . \tag{3.51}$$

Then

$$(Is)_{\overline{n|}} = (1 + i)^n (Ia)_{\overline{n|}} = \frac{\ddot{s}_{\overline{n|}} - n}{i} \quad . \tag{3.52}$$

These, of course, can also be obtained by setting $P = Q = 1$ in formulas (3.46) and (3.45) and simplifying or else, very easily, directly by the levelling technique.

(c) Standard decreasing annuity. Here the payments are n, $n - 1, n - 2, \cdots, 2, 1$ at the ends of the first, second, third, $\cdots$, $(n-1)$th, nth periods, respectively. The present value is denoted by $(Da)_{\overline{n|}}$ and the accumulated value by $(Ds)_{\overline{n|}}$. Then, from formula (3.48),

$$(Da)_{\overline{n|}} = \frac{1}{i}\left[n + \sum_{h=1}^{n} v^h(-1)\right]$$

which reduces to

$$(Da)_{\overline{n|}} = \frac{n - a_{\overline{n|}}}{i} \quad . \tag{3.53}$$

Alternatively, formula (3.53) results from simplifying the expression given by formula (3.46) with $P = n$ and $Q = -1$. For $(Ds)_{\overline{n|}}$, we have the formulas

$$(Ds)_{\overline{n|}} = (Da)_{\overline{n|}} (1 + i)^n = \frac{n(1 + i)^n - s_{\overline{n|}}}{i}. \tag{3.54}$$

It is interesting to note that the combination of the standard increasing annuity and the standard decreasing annuity forms a level ordinary annuity with payment n + 1. Thus for instance,

$$(Ia)_{\overline{n}|} + (Da)_{\overline{n}|} = (n+1)\,a_{\overline{n}|}\,.$$

One also notes, by appropriate splitting into level annuities, that

$$(Is)_{\overline{n}|} = \sum_{h=1}^{n} s_{\overline{h}|} \tag{3.55}$$

and

$$(Da)_{\overline{n}|\,i} = \sum_{h=1}^{n} a_{\overline{h}|\,i}\,. \tag{3.56}$$

One consequence is that formulas (3.55) and (3.56) may be used to provide summation checks in the calculation of tables of $s_{\overline{n}|\,i}$ and $a_{\overline{n}|\,i}$, respectively. They also offer a speedy yet basic means of deducing formulas (3.52) and (3.53).

(d) <u>Example 3.6.</u> This is a more complicated example solved by the finite difference technique.

If the annuity payments form a geometric progression, their present value may be found by direct use of geometric progression formulas. Equations (3.47) and (3.48) will be of no assistance as the differences of geometric payments are geometric, nor can one readily break the annuity up into a set of level annuities. If payments are as indicated in the line diagram, with

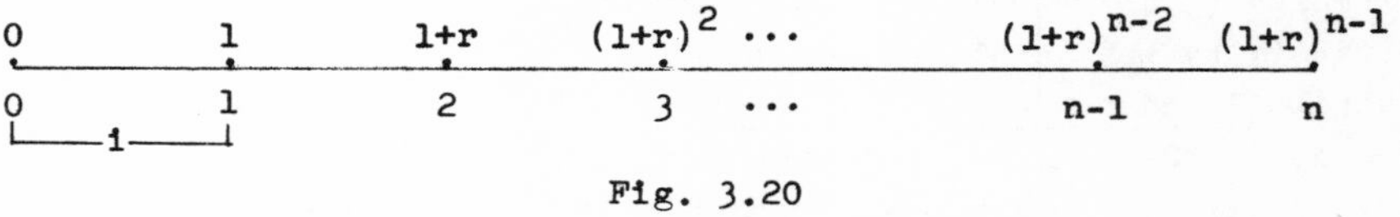

Fig. 3.20

r > -1, then

$$A = \sum_{h=1}^{n} v^h(1+r)^{h-1} = \frac{v\left[1-\left(\frac{1+r}{1+i}\right)^n\right]}{1-\frac{1+r}{1+i}},$$

that is,

$$A = \frac{1-\left(\frac{1+r}{1+i}\right)^n}{i-r} \tag{3.57}$$

which may be valued by logarithms, or by setting

$$\frac{1+r}{1+i} = 1+i_1 \text{ if } r > i, \text{ and } \frac{1+r}{1+i} = \frac{1}{1+i_2} = v_2 \text{ if } r < i.$$

If $r = i$, formula (3.57) is indeterminate but one sees by going back to the original expression for A, that $A = nv$. Finally,

$$S = A(1 + i)^n = \begin{cases} \dfrac{(1 + i)^n - (1 + r)^n}{i - r}, & r \neq i \\ n(1 + i)^{n-1}, & r = i. \end{cases} \tag{3.58}$$

<u>3.8. Continuous annuities.</u> Heretofore, we have dealt with discrete annuities with finite intervals between payment dates. We now consider annuities for which the payment period is infinitesimal, that is, payments are made continuously. For discrete annuities we developed formulas for the present and accumulated values by geometric and other sums. In the case of continuous annuities integrals will replace sums. Also, as previously mentioned, the distinction between ordinary annuities and annuities-due disappears.

It is convenient here to start with a general case and to specialize afterwards to particular cases. We consider an annuity payable continuously for n time units, where n may be any positive real number. For this annuity, the rate of payment (per time unit) at time t is $r(t)$, where $r(t)$ is a well-behaved, differentiable function. Let $A(t)$ represent the present value at time t of the payments remaining to be made during the interval from t to n. Then $A(0) = A$, the present value of the whole annuity, and $A(n) = 0$ since payments terminate at n. For the fixed time unit, let δ be the force of interest and i the equivalent effective rate of interest, so that $v = e^{-\delta}$. By thinking of $A(t)$ as the fund at time t which, together with interest, will provide the subsequent annuity payments, and considering the rate of decrease of $A(t)$ at time t, we arrive at the differential equation

$$\frac{-d\,A(t)}{dt} = r(t) - \delta\,A(t) \; ; \tag{3.59}$$

that is, $A(t)$ decreases at a rate equal to the excess of the rate of outgo, the payment rate $r(t)$, from the fund at time t, over the rate of income, namely the rate $\delta A(t)$ of interest accrual at that time.

If we rearrange equation (3.59) in the form

$$-d\,A(t) + \delta\,A(t)\,dt = r(t)\,dt$$

and multiply through by the integrating factor $e^{-\delta t} = v^t$, we obtain

$$-d[v^t A(t)] = v^t r(t)dt.$$

Integrating from 0 to n, and taking into account that A(0) = A and A(n) = 0, we get as present value formula

$$A = \int_0^n v^t r(t)dt. \tag{3.60}$$

We have obtained formula (3.60) by starting with the differential equation (3.59), and the procedure is illustrative of such an approach to basic formulas in actuarial mathematics. Alternatively, we might have arrived at the integral in formula (3.60) by setting up a sum approximately equal to the present value of the annuity, and considering the limit case. Interpreted, formula (3.60) seems very logical and enables one to think readily in terms of integrals when valuing continuous annuities. For r(t)dt is (approximately) the annuity payment in an instant at time t having (approximately) the present value $v^t r(t)dt$; and when the present values of all the momentary annuity payments are summed, by means of integration, the present value of the whole annuity naturally emerges.

For the accumulated value S at a constant force δ, we have the expressions

$$S = A\, e^{\delta n} = A(1 + i)^n = \int_0^n (1 + i)^{n-t}\, r(t)dt\ . \tag{3.61}$$

By using integration by parts in the right member of (3.60), we obtain a formula analogous to formulas (3.47) and (3.48). The initial step is to write $v^t\ dt$ $(= e^{-\delta t}dt)$ as $d(\frac{v^t}{-\delta})$. Then

$$A = \int_0^n r(t)\ d\left(\frac{v^t}{-\delta}\right)$$

$$= \left[r(t)\left(\frac{v^t}{-\delta}\right)\right]_0^n + \frac{1}{\delta}\int_0^n v^t\ d[r(t)]\ ,$$

so that

$$A = \frac{r(0) - r(n)v^n}{\delta} + \frac{1}{\delta}\int_0^n v^t\ d[r(t)]\ . \tag{3.62}$$

One notes that formula (3.62) appears less simple than, say, formula (3.48) of the discrete case, as there are terms in addition to the integral.

As illustrations of the application of formulas (3.60)-(3.62), we take:

(a) $r(t) = 1$. Then A is denoted by $\bar{a}_{\overline{n}|\,i}$, S by $\bar{s}_{\overline{n}|\,i}$, the bar over the a and s being used to denote that the annuity is payable continuously. One obtains

$$\bar{a}_{\overline{n}|\,i} = \int_0^n v^t\,dt = \frac{1 - v^n}{\delta} \tag{3.63}$$

and

$$\bar{s}_{\overline{n}|\,i} = \int_0^n (1 + i)^{n-t}\,dt = \frac{(1+i)^n - 1}{\delta}. \tag{3.64}$$

We see that

$$\bar{a}_{\overline{n}|\,i} = \frac{i}{\delta}\, a_{\overline{n}|\,i} \doteq \left(1 + \frac{i}{2}\right) a_{\overline{n}|\,i} \tag{3.65}$$

and

$$\bar{s}_{\overline{n}|\,i} = \frac{i}{\delta}\, s_{\overline{n}|\,i} \doteq \left(1 + \frac{i}{2}\right) s_{\overline{n}|\,i}\ , \tag{3.66}$$

so that a continuous level annuity of 1 is roughly equivalent to a discrete ordinary annuity with payment $1 + \frac{i}{2}$, or interpreted otherwise, to a discrete annuity of 1 paid in the middle of each interest period. Since values of i/δ are available in Table II, the middle members of formulas (3.65) and (3.66) are convenient ones for calculation.

(b) $r(t) = t$. Here A is denoted by $(\bar{I}\bar{a})_{\overline{n}|\,i}$ and S by $(\bar{I}\,\bar{s})_{\overline{n}|\,i}$, the notation $\bar{I}$ indicating that payments are increasing continuously in accordance with $r(t) = t$. Then

$$(\bar{I}\,\bar{a})_{\overline{n}|\,i} = \int_0^n v^t\, t\,dt = -\frac{nv^n}{\delta} + \frac{1}{\delta}\int_0^n v^t\,dt = \frac{\bar{a}_{\overline{n}|\,i} - nv^n}{\delta} \tag{3.67}$$

and

$$(\bar{I}\,\bar{s})_{\overline{n}|\,i} = \int_0^n (1 + i)^{n-t}\, t\,dt = \frac{\bar{s}_{\overline{n}|\,i} - n}{\delta}. \tag{3.68}$$

(c) $r(t) = n - t$. In this case A is denoted by $(\bar{D}\,\bar{a})_{\overline{n}|\,i}$, S by $(\bar{D}\,\bar{s})_{\overline{n}|\,i}$, where

$$(\bar{D}\,\bar{a})_{\overline{n}|\,i} = \int_0^n v^t(n - t)dt = \frac{n}{\delta} + \frac{1}{\delta}\int_0^n v^t(-dt) = \frac{n - \bar{a}_{\overline{n}|\,i}}{\delta} \tag{3.69}$$

and

$$(\bar{D}\,\bar{s})_{\overline{n}|\,i} = \int_0^n (1 + i)^{n-t}(n - t)dt = \frac{n(1 + i)^n - \bar{s}_{\overline{n}|\,i}}{\delta}. \tag{3.70}$$

We observe (1) that the values of these increasing or decreasing continuous annuities are not merely i/δ times the values of counterpart discrete annuities, and (2) that the combination of the two continuous annuities in (b) and (c) yields a continuous level annuity of n per time unit.

We encounter continuous annuities again in Examples 3.7 and 3.8.

3.9. Perpetuities. As was pointed out in Section 3.1, a perpetuity is an annuity which is assumed to continue for an unlimited term, i.e., forever. The notion is not without practical significance. For example, the dividends of a preferred stock, the coupons of a nonredeemable bond, the harvests of a forest and the replacements of a permanent improvement such as a telephone line or highway, may all be regarded in terms of perpetuities. It is clear that the accumulated value of a perpetuity is undefined, but in most instances in practice the present value is determinate. The present values $B_h v^h$ of the payments B_h $(h = 0, q, 2q, \cdots)$ of a perpetuity form the term sequence of an infinite series and this infinite series, of course, may or may not converge. Standard tests can be applied to determine whether the series does in fact converge.

Formulas for the present value of an ordinary perpetuity with level payments W every q interest periods can be obtained by having $n \to \infty$ in formulas such as (3.15), (3.17), (3.18) or (3.19). Since when $n \to \infty$, $v^n \to 0$ and $a_{\overline{n}|i} \to \frac{1}{i}$, we obtain the present value formulas

$$A = \frac{W}{(1 + i)^q - 1} \tag{3.71}$$

$$A = \frac{W}{i'} \tag{3.72}$$

$$A = \frac{W}{s_{\overline{q}|i}} \frac{1}{i} \tag{3.73}$$

$$A = \frac{R}{i^{(p)}} \quad . \tag{3.74}$$

Of these formulas, (3.71) is most basic and, perhaps, the most useful. It can be obtained, from first principles, by means of an equation of value with comparison date at the end of q

interest periods.

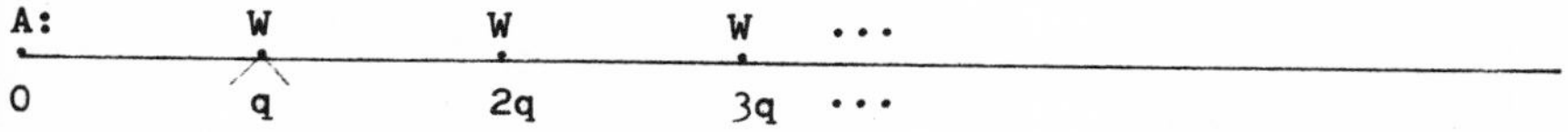

Fig. 3.21

Thus

$$A(1 + i)^q = W + A$$

since, as of the comparison date, the second and following payments form a perpetuity with present value equal to A again. Rearrangement of the equation gives

$$A\left[(1 + i)^q - 1\right] = W.$$

As the left member represents the interest for q periods on the principal A, one sees that the perpetuity payments may be regarded as periodic interest payments on A. This is especially clear when q = 1 and the equation becomes simply

$$Ai = W.$$

In other words, level perpetuity payments must precisely equal the interest on the principal and thereby preserve the principal intact; for larger payments would deplete the principal, eventually exhausting it and thus preventing indefinite continuation of the annuity, while smaller payments would cause the principal to be augmented and in time to increase without bound.

The notation $a_{\overline{\infty}|i}$ is an abbreviation for $\lim\limits_{n\to\infty} a_{\overline{n}|i}$. In this notation, the special case $n \to \infty$ of equation (3.11) yields

$$1 = i\, a_{\overline{\infty}|i} \, ,$$

implying that equivalent to a loan of 1 is a perpetual annuity of interest payments i, with no repayment at all of principal. It is interesting to note that $a_{\overline{n}|i}$ can be expressed as the difference of two perpetuities, one deferred, namely

$$a_{\overline{n}|i} = a_{\overline{\infty}|i} - v^n a_{\overline{\infty}|i} = a_{\overline{\infty}|i} - {}_{n|}a_{\overline{\infty}|i}$$

and thus that $a_{\overline{n}|} \doteq a_{\overline{\infty}|}$ provided n is large. For example, at 8%, $a_{\overline{50}|} = 12.23^+$, $a_{\overline{100}|} = 12.49^+$, and $a_{\overline{\infty}|} = 12.50$ precisely.

If the perpetuity payments are on a due basis, formulas for the present value can be obtained by multiplying the preceding numbered equations by $(1 + i)^q = (1 + i)^{1/p}$ or by letting $n \to \infty$ in equations (3.35), (3.37), (3.38) and (3.39); thus

$$A = \frac{W}{1 - v^q} \tag{3.75}$$

$$A = W\,\frac{1 + i'}{i'} = \frac{W}{d'} \tag{3.76}$$

$$A = \frac{W}{a_{\overline{q|}\,i}}\,\frac{1}{i} \tag{3.77}$$

$$A = \frac{R}{d^{(p)}}\,. \tag{3.78}$$

In particular, $\ddot{a}_{\overline{\infty|}\,i} = 1/d$.

Similarly, since $\lim_{n\to\infty} nv^n = 0$, the perpetuity analogues of formulas (3.46) and (3.51) are

$$A = \frac{P}{i} + \frac{Q}{i^2} \tag{3.79}$$

and

$$(Ia)_{\overline{\infty|}} = \frac{1}{id}\ , \tag{3.80}$$

and both of these have interesting verbal interpretations. For the geometric varying perpetuity, formula (3.57) yields

$$A = \frac{1}{i - r} \qquad (r < i). \tag{3.81}$$

Present values of the geometric increasing perpetuity when $r \geq i$ and of the standard decreasing annuity (with $n \to \infty$) do not exist.

For continuous perpetuities, one has from formula (3.60) the relation

$$A = \int_0^\infty v^t\, r(t)dt\ . \tag{3.82}$$

In particular, if $r(t) = 1$, then

$$A = \bar{a}_{\overline{\infty|}\,i} = \frac{1}{\delta} \tag{3.83}$$

and if $r(t) = t$

$$A = (\bar{I}\,\bar{a})_{\overline{\infty|}\,i} = \frac{1}{\delta^2}\ . \tag{3.84}$$

3.10. Summary and illustrative examples. In this chapter we have extended our theory to cover series of regularly spaced payments. The remaining chapters will discuss important practical applications of annuities, but in a sense all the basic theory is now developed.

The reader who looks on this chapter as a list of 84 formulas must by now be discerning the inadequacy of his approach. It is far better to concentrate on fundamental ideas by means of which any problem can be attacked with confidence regardless of whether it follows any exact pattern which has been presented. In this summary, only fundamental ideas will be mentioned.

In any particular instance, one wishes to deal with the value of an annuity on some date. While such a value is simply the sum of the values on that date of the individual payments, typically this sum can be simplified, at the very least by the introduction of tabulated annuity and related functions. Thus it is very important that the reader grasp precisely the definitions and notations. Then by means of line diagrams, equations of value, and basic formulas, problems can be attacked and solved.

The ordinary simple annuity of constant payments W has present value one payment period before the first payment, of

$$A = W a_{\overline{n|}\,i} = W \frac{1 - v^n}{i}$$

and accumulated value at the time of the final payment, of

$$S = W\, s_{\overline{n|}\,i} = W \cdot \frac{(1 + i)^n - 1}{i} = A(1 + i)^n \ .$$

Valuing a simple annuity on any other date can be accomplished by accumulating or discounting A or S to that date, or by more elegant means such as separation of payments into two or more groups for valuation or supplying fictitious payments at convenient dates. For instance, annuities-due and deferred annuities are handled in this fashion. A perpetuity may be treated as a limiting case.

More generally, one has for the ordinary annuity of constant payments W

$$A = W(v^n + v^{n-q} + \cdots + v^q) = W \frac{1 - v^n}{(1 + i)^q - 1} = \frac{W}{s_{\overline{q|}\,i}} a_{\overline{n|}\,i} = R \frac{i}{i^{(p)}} a_{\overline{n|}\,i},$$

and $S = A(1 + i)^n$ as usual. The sum form for A is suggested by a line diagram and, being the sum of a geometric progression, it produces the second form from which the others follow, although in practice one writes the others directly with the purpose of (1) replacing the actual payments W with equivalent payments $W/s_{\overline{q}|\,i} = R\ i/i^{(p)}$ at the end of each interest period and (2) valuing the resulting simple annuity. Extension to other level payment annuities follows by the methods of the preceding paragraph.

Special techniques for handling discrete varying annuities include (1) direct evaluation, (2) the formation of level annuities and (3) finite difference and algebraic methods.

For continuous annuities one thinks in terms of integrals, e.g.,

$$A = \int_0^n v^t\ r(t)dt.$$

Frequently, several solutions of a problem are possible. The reader is advised to cultivate (1) the ability to set up these alternative solutions and (2) the skill to recognize and write initially the most useful form. Verbal reasoning, developed through practice, produces deeper insights into the subject.

We conclude this chapter with some illustrative examples employing and extending the theory which has been developed thus far. Reference has already been made to each of these examples.

Example 3.1

Reconsider Example 1.1.

Solution:

(a) After inserting fictitious payments of R at the ends of 9 and 10 half-years in the line diagram of the original solution, we may write

$$R(s_{\overline{7}|.03} - s_{\overline{2}|.03}) = 1{,}050(1.03)^9 + 10{,}000(1.03)^6 + 20{,}000(1.06)^8,$$

which again yields R = \$8,022.69.

(b) The construction and significance of the table should be reviewed.

(c) The simplest solution has already been given but the result is immediate from the annuity equation (based on valuation at the present)

$$R'\,a_{\overline{5}|} = R\,a_{\overline{5}|}\,v^3\ .$$

Example 3.2

Ten years ago A borrowed \$10,000 from B at (.06, 12) per year and agreed to repay the loan in equal semiannual installments over a 15-year period. In addition to the payment now due, A would like to pay off the rest of the debt. What sum should B ask if money is presently worth an effective annual rate of 5%?

Solution: B should demand the commuted (present) value of the remaining payments, valued at 5%. The size of the level payment W is determined from

$$10{,}000 = \frac{W}{s_{\overline{6}|.005}} \, a_{\overline{180}|.005}$$

$$= \frac{W \, a_{\overline{90}|.005}}{s_{\overline{6}|.005}} [1 + (1.005)^{-90}]$$

to be W = \$512.69. Then in addition to the regular payment at the end of 10 years, A could pay

$$2(512.69) \, s^{(2)}_{\overline{1}|.05} \, a_{\overline{5}|.05} = \$4{,}494.17$$

in complete settlement of the debt. Alternatively,

$$512.69 \, s^{-1}_{\overline{1/2}|.05} \, a_{\overline{5}|.05} = \$4{,}494.17.$$

Note that the drop in interest rate causes A's cash payment to increase, from

$$\frac{512.69}{s_{\overline{6}|.005}} \, a_{\overline{60}|.005} = \$4{,}364.94$$

if there had been no change, to \$4,494.17.

Example 3.3

For n a positive integer, verbally interpret

$$\frac{1}{a_{\overline{n}|i}} = i + \frac{1}{s_{\overline{n}|i}} \quad . \tag{3.13}$$

Solution: We know that 1 buys a simple ordinary annuity of $1/a_{\overline{n}|i}$ for n periods and also that a simple ordinary annuity of $1/s_{\overline{n}|i}$ accumulates in n periods to 1. Let us study the periodic payments which the investment of a unit at rate i over an n-period term can provide. First of all, there is $1/a_{\overline{n}|i}$. Secondly, the interest i might be paid each period and in lieu of accepting the unit back after n periods the investor might receive the annuity payments $1/s_{\overline{n}|i}$ each period. Thus at rate i, a unit provides n payments of $1/a_{\overline{n}|i}$ or n payments of i and n payments of $1/s_{\overline{n}|i}$, all at the end of every interest period. Consequently, the periodic payment $1/a_{\overline{n}|i}$ equals the sum of the separate periodic payments i and $1/s_{\overline{n}|i}$. The argument is summarized in the line diagram below.

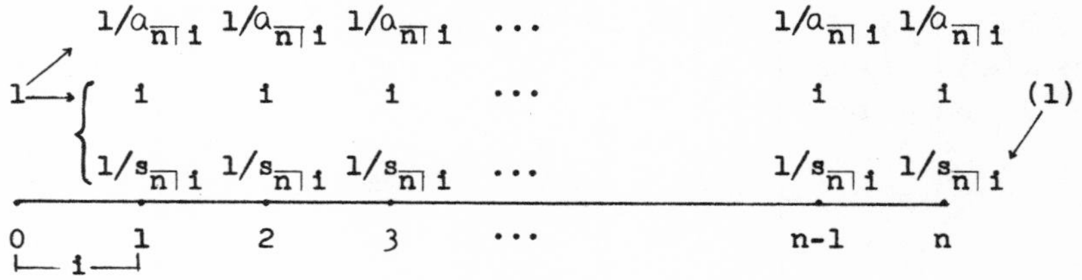

Fig. 3.22

Example 3.4

An annuity of $50 at the end of every month for a year is to be followed by a monthly annuity of $100 for 8 months and is then to be reduced to $10 a month for the next 10 months. At an annual rate of (.06, 12) find both the present value and the accumulated value of all the payments.

Solution: Figure 3.23 summarizes the facts of the problem.

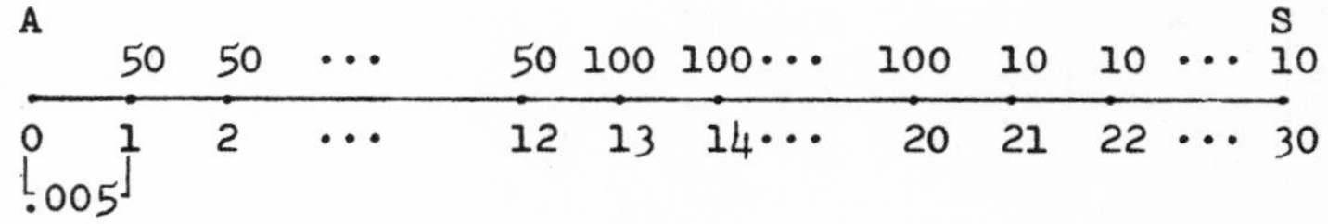

Fig. 3.23

The direct solutions

$$A = 50\, a_{\overline{12}|} + 100\, a_{\overline{8}|}\, v^{12} + 10\, a_{\overline{10}|}\, v^{20}$$

$$S = A(1 + i)^{30} = 50\, s_{\overline{12}|}\, (1 + i)^{18} + 100\, s_{\overline{8}|}\, (1 + i)^{10} + 10\, s_{\overline{10}|}\ ,$$

where all functions are at rate $i = 0.5\%$, are possible but not the most efficient. For obtaining A, the alternative technique for treating the $100 and $10 deferred annuities, and the varying annuity levelling and finite difference methods, all produce the same simple form; and similar methods give S. To illustrate by the level annuity method, we have for finding A the annuities in Figure 3.24, all with term beginning at the present. The sum

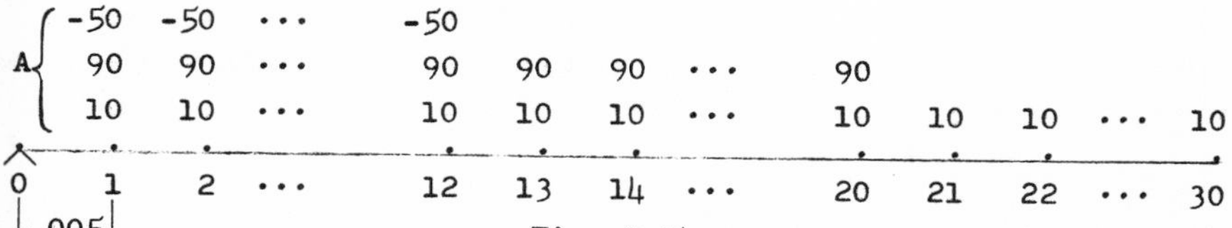

Fig. 3.24

of the payments at any time is the actual payment then made. We obtain at 0.5%

$$A = 10\ a_{\overline{30}|} + 90\ a_{\overline{20}|} - 50\ a_{\overline{12}|} = \$1{,}405.86.$$

For S the line diagram is constructed so that the terms of the level annuities all expire at the end of 30 months.

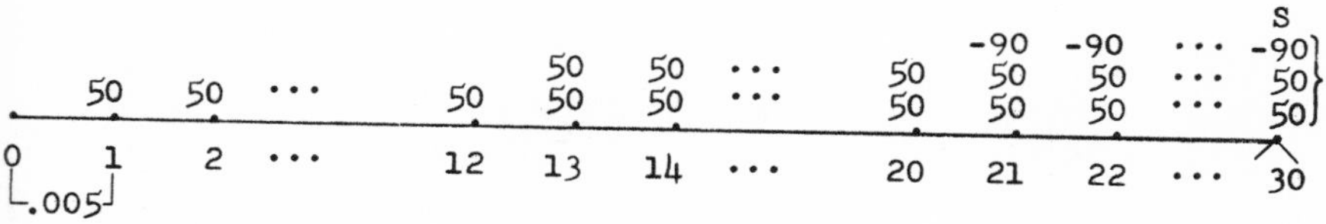

Fig. 3.25

$$S = 50\ s_{\overline{30}|} + 50\ s_{\overline{18}|} - 90\ s_{\overline{10}|} = \$1{,}632.77.$$

Example 3.5

At an effective annual rate of 6%, how many quarterly $50 payments can be made from an $1,100 fund? What final withdrawal can be made 3 months later?

Solution: Where n is the number of years in the annuity term, we seek as a first step the bracketing integral values n which most nearly satisfy the equation

$$200\ s^{(4)}_{\overline{1}|.06}\ a_{\overline{n}|.06} = 1{,}100$$

or $1/a_{\overline{n}|.06} = .18586$, whence $1/s_{\overline{n}|.06} = .12586$ and $6 < n < 7$. Thus payments continue for 6 and a fraction years, i.e., for some integral number $4n$ of quarters with $24 < 4n \le 28$. By use of linear interpolation we can determine an estimated number of quarters, as follows:

4n	n	$1/s_{\overline{n}\|.06}$		
24	6	.14336	.01750	.02422
		.12586		
28	7	.11914		

$$4n \doteq 24 + \left(\frac{1750}{2422}\right)4 = 26.89\ .$$

It now appears that 26 withdrawals of \$50 can be made followed by a smaller one at the end of the 27th quarter, but this result must be verified and the final payment X found. Proceeding on

1,100:	50	50	50	50	50	...	50	50	50	X } 50-50}
Yr.	0			1		...	6			7
	└── .06 ──┘									

Fig. 3.26

this estimate, we have from the line diagram

$$200\ s^{(4)}_{\overline{6\ 3/4}|.06} - 50 + X = 1{,}100(1.06)^{6\ 3/4}$$

from which we may obtain X according to either the relation

$$X = 1{,}100(1.06)^{6\ 3/4} - 50\left[\frac{(1.06)^{6\ 3/4} - 1}{(1.06)^{1/4} - 1} - 1\right]$$

or the relation

$$X = \left(1{,}100(1.06)^{6} - 200\ s^{(4)}_{\overline{1}|.06}\ s_{\overline{6}|.06}\right)(1.06)^{3/4}$$

$$- 50\ \left[(1.06)^{1/2} + (1.06)^{1/4}\right] .$$

Finally, X = \$38.09. Since $0 < X < 50$, we now conclude definitely that 26 withdrawals of \$50 and one of \$38.09 at the end of the 27th quarter exhaust the \$1,100 fund.

Example 3.6

The annual payment of a varying annuity at time h years from the present is $(h + 1)^2$, where $h = 0, 1, 2, \cdots , 10$. Find the present and accumulated values of this annuity at the annual rate (.05, 2).

Solution: The line diagram can be constructed in terms of interest periods with payments at the ends of $t = 2h$ $(h = 0, 1, 2, \cdots , 10)$ half-years. We have here a varying annuity-due in which the payments have constant second differences, and the differences (with difference interval 2) may be

$\underset{2}{\Delta^2} B_t$	1	2	2	2	2	2	2	2	2	2	2	-142	121	0
$\underset{2}{\Delta} B_t$	0	1	3	5	7	9	11	13	15	17	19	21	-121	0
$B_t = B_k$	0	0	1	4	9	16	25	36	49	64	81	100	121	0
t	-4	-2	0	2	4	6	8	10	12	14	16	18	20	22
k	-2	0	2	4	6	8	10	12	14	16	18	20	22	24

Fig. 3.27

shown on the line diagram along with the payments B_t. By adapting formula (3.49) we can find the present value A' of an ordinary annuity at time $t = -2$. Thus, with the summation over even integers and $k = t + 2$

$$A' = \frac{1}{[(1.025)^2 - 1]^2} \sum v^k \underset{2}{\Delta^2} B_k \qquad (k = -2, 0, 2, \cdots, 22)$$

$$= \frac{1}{[(1.025)^2 - 1]^2}\left[(1.025)^2(1) + \sum v^k(2) + v^{20}(-142) + v^{22}(121)\right]$$

$$(k = 0, 2, 4, \cdots, 18).$$

The summation over $k = 0, 2, \cdots, 18$ reduces to $2a_{\overline{20|}\,.025}/a_{\overline{2|}\,.025}$. Therefore, the required values, A at time $t = 0$ and S at time $t = 22$, are

$$A = A'(1.025)^2$$

$$= \frac{1}{(1.025)^2 - 2 + v^2}\left[(1.025)^2 + \frac{2\,a_{\overline{20|}}}{a_{\overline{2|}}} - 142v^{20} + 121v^{22}\right] = \$349.65;$$

$$S = 349.65\ (1.025)^{22} = \$601.95 \doteq \$602.$$

This solution illustrates the theory. A person equipped with a calculating machine might, of course, prefer to obtain A directly from

$$A = 1 + 4v^2 + 9v^4 + \quad \cdots \quad + (h + 1)^2\, v^{2h} + \quad \cdots \quad + 121v^{20}.$$

Example 3.7

Obtain the 2nd formula of Problem 117 in List 1, by assuming that noninterest income accrues uniformly throughout the year.

Solution: Total net income during the year is $B - A$, of which I is net interest income. The assumption that noninterest net income, $B - A - I$, accrues uniformly within a year implies that it is earned continuously in equal amounts within equal intervals and, therefore, that the interest accumulation on it at the end of the year is

$$(B - A - I)(\bar{s}_{\overline{1|}\,i} - 1).$$

The total net interest income of the year is this sum plus interest for a full year on the initial assets A. Accordingly,

$$I = Ai + (B - A - I)(\bar{s}_{\overline{1|}\,i} - 1).$$

By use of the relation

$$\bar{s}_{\overline{1|}\,i} = \frac{i}{\delta} \doteq 1 + \frac{i}{2}$$

one finds that the effective annual net interest rate earned is

$$i \doteq \frac{2\,I}{A + B - I} \quad .$$

This result has been widely used by insurance companies.

Example 3.8

Show that

(a)
$$\frac{\partial}{\partial n}\,\bar{a}_{\overline{n|}} = v^n$$

(b)
$$\int_0^n v^h\;\bar{a}'_{\overline{n-h|}}\,dh = \int_0^n v'^h\;\bar{a}_{\overline{n-h|}}\,dh\;,$$

where primed symbols indicate values based on a force of interest δ' and unprimed symbols, values based on a force δ .

Solution: This example is included to illustrate two useful results from calculus, namely, Leibnitz' rule for differentiation of an integral* and the rule for change of order of integration in a double integral.

(a) We are required to differentiate in regard to the upper limit of the integral; that is,

$$\frac{\partial}{\partial n}\,\bar{a}_{\overline{n|}} = \frac{\partial}{\partial n}\int_0^n v^t\,dt$$

$$= v^n$$

by Leibnitz' rule. The student may check that the result is not quite so immediate by the method $\frac{\partial}{\partial n}\left(\frac{1-v^n}{\delta}\right)$.

(b) What a surprising formula we are to prove! From the left member, we have

---

*Leibnitz' rule for differentiation of an integral. Let

$$F(x) = \int_{h=g_1(x)}^{h=g_2(x)} f(h,x)\,dh\;,$$

where g_1 and g_2 are differentiable functions in the closed interval $x_1 \le x \le x_2$, and where $f(h,x)$ is continuous, and $f_x(h,x)$ exists, in the region $x_1 \le x \le x_2$, $g_1(x) \le h \le g_2(x)$. Then

$$\frac{dF(x)}{dx} = \int_{h=g_1(x)}^{h=g_2(x)} \frac{\partial f(h,x)}{\partial x}\,dh + f(g_2,x)\,\frac{dg_2}{dx} - f(g_1,x)\,\frac{dg_1}{dx}\;.$$

$$\int_0^n v^h \bar{a}'_{\overline{n-h}|}\, dh = \int_0^n v^h \left(\int_0^{n-h} v'^{\,t}\, dt \right) dh = \int_0^n \int_0^{n-h} v^h\, v'^{\,t}\, dt\, dh.$$

Here, we are asked to integrate first in regard to t and then in regard to h, whereas we would prefer the opposite order.

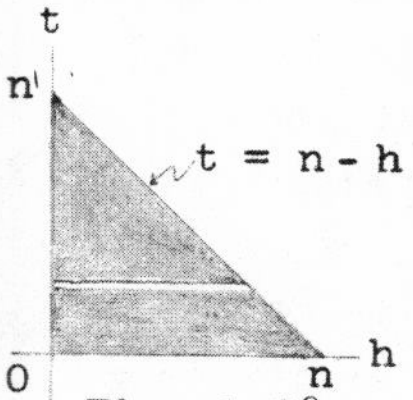

Fig. 3.28

Figure 3.28, in which the region of integration is shaded, helps one to set the appropriate limits when making the change of order. Note that when h is the first variable of integration, it varies from 0 to the diagonal line, namely to $h = n - t$, and that t ranges from a minimum of 0 to a maximum of n. Therefore

$$\int_0^n v^h \bar{a}'_{\overline{n-h}|}\, dh = \int_0^n \int_0^{n-t} v'^{\,t}\, v^h\, dh\, dt = \int_0^n v'^{\,t} \left(\int_0^{n-t} v^h\, dh \right) dt$$

$$= \int_0^n v'^{\,t}\, \bar{a}_{\overline{n-t}|}\, dt$$

$$= \int_0^n v'^{\,h}\, \bar{a}_{\overline{n-h}|}\, dh$$

by change of the variable of integration from t to h.

The reader will appreciate this method the more when he discovers how unfruitful is the approach

$$\int_0^n v^h\, \bar{a}'_{\overline{n-h}|}\, dh = \int_0^n v^h\, \frac{1 - v'^{\,n-h}}{\delta'}\, dh.$$

A more convenient alternative uses the result from part (a),

$$v^h\, dh = d\, \bar{a}_{\overline{h}|}$$

with the interest rate constant, and integration by parts. Thus

$$\int_0^n v^h\, \bar{a}'_{\overline{n-h}|}\, dh = \int_0^n \bar{a}'_{\overline{n-h}|}\, d\, \bar{a}_{\overline{h}|}$$

$$= \left[\bar{a}'_{\overline{n-h}|}\, \bar{a}_{\overline{h}|} + \int \bar{a}_{\overline{h}|}\, v'^{\,n-h}\, dh \right]_0^n$$

$$= \int_0^n \bar{a}_{\overline{h}|}\, v'^{\,n-h}\, dh$$

$$= \int_0^n \bar{a}_{\overline{n-t}|}\, v'^{\,t}\, dt \qquad (t = n - h)$$

$$= \int_0^n v'^h \, \bar{a}_{\overline{n-h}|} \, dh.$$

3.11. Further remarks. The reader will by now have become aware that undergirding the mathematics of compound interest is a well-developed and consistent system of notation. Initially confusing, it later becomes extremely useful to the student of the subject. We now make the following additions to the pattern of notation:

$I_{\overline{h}|}$ (as in $(I_{\overline{h}|}s)_{\overline{n}|}$) implies h unit increases to h, with the annuity remaining level at h for the balance of its term; the payments are 1, 2, ⋯ , h, h, ⋯ (to end of term).

$(Is)^{(p)}_{\overline{n}|}$ = the accumulated value of an increasing ordinary annuity of payments t/p at the ends of each pth part of the tth interest period ($t = 1, 2, \cdots, n$); that is, there are p payments of $1/p$ each, then p payments of $2/p$, etc.

$(I\bar{s})_{\overline{n}|}$ = the accumulated value of a continuous annuity with level rate of payment h throughout the hth interest period ($h = 1, 2, \cdots, n$).

$(I^{(p)}s)^{(p)}_{\overline{n}|}$ is left to the reader. See Problem 68. Now that the pattern of symbols is set, the student should have little trouble deducing consistent forms for present values, decreasing annuities, annuities-due, etc.

The Problem List which follows is long. There are a great many annuity problems which are interesting and instructive. We suggest a sample in the following paragraph and propose the reader proceed to further sampling. To help the reader obtain his sample, we have subdivided the List into the following four categories: Basic List and Supplementary Lists A: More Practice, B: More Insights and C: More Applications. Each of Lists A, B and C is roughly graded, advancing from easier problems to the more difficult. We suggest that the reader's sample contain problems in all four categories and of varying degrees of difficulty.

Among the practical problems in the List, we call the reader's attention especially to two particular types which have not been explicitly mentioned in our exposition: (1) reinvestment (see Problem 83 in particular, and also Problems 151, 169, 170); and (2) various financial problems such as budgeting, comparison of costs of competing equipment, or reasonable expenditures to prolong life of equipment (see Problems 80, 81, 147-149, 168). In the theoretical area are problems about characteristics of compound interest functions, not only the multiplicity of interrelationships, identities and inequalities; but also the analytic properties, such as continuity, differentiability and monotonicity as in Problems 60, 139, 141, and 142. From the theoretical considerations, practical implications can be drawn; and the practical problems give clearer insights into the theory and its limitations; and from experience in both the practical and the theoretical aspects come heightened understanding, skill and enjoyment.

PROBLEM LIST 3

Basic List (Problems 1-83)

Sec. 3.1-3.3

1. (a) By cumulative summation of powers of v, obtain the tabulated values of $a_{\overline{n}|.01}$, n = 1, 2, 3, 4. Use (3.2) to check $a_{\overline{4}|.01}$.

(b) Note that $a_{\overline{4}|.01} = 3.90$. Check arithmetically that this result implies that a loan of 3.90 can be fully repaid in 1 year by payments of 1 at the end of each quarter, with payments providing interest at 1% on the loan balance outstanding during the period as well as reducing the outstanding loan balance.

(c) In terms of the loan in (b) and alternatives to it, explain senses to the lender and to the borrower in which $s_{\overline{4}|.01} = 4.06$ is the accumulated value of $a_{\overline{4}|.01}$.

2. By use of (3.1) and (3.3) only, show that

$$a_{\overline{54}|} = a_{\overline{50}|} + \sum_{t=51}^{54} v^t = a_{\overline{50}|} + v^{50} a_{\overline{4}|} = a_{\overline{50}|} + v^{54} s_{\overline{4}|}$$

$$= a_{\overline{4}|} + \sum_{t=5}^{54} v^t = a_{\overline{4}|} + v^4 a_{\overline{50}|} = (s_{\overline{4}|} + a_{\overline{50}|})v^4$$

$$= a_{\overline{60}|} - \sum_{t=55}^{60} v^t = a_{\overline{60}|} - v^{54} a_{\overline{6}|} = (s_{\overline{60}|} - s_{\overline{6}|})v^{60}.$$

Consider the usefulness of each of the forms above for computation at a tabulated interest rate using Appendix tables and a desk calculator.

3. Simplify and interpret your result:

$$s_{\overline{5}|i}[1 + (1 + i)^5 + (1 + i)^{10} + (1 + i)^{15} + (1 + i)^{20}] .$$

4. Set up and complete a 2-way table in which each one of the functions $(1 + i)^n$, v^n, $s_{\overline{n}|}$ and $a_{\overline{n}|}$ is expressed in turn in terms of each one of the other functions (and no more) and possibly i. For example, the entry in the 1st line, 2nd column is $1/v^n$, expressing the 1st-row $(1 + i)^n$ in terms of the 2nd-column v^n.

5. Having available only $(1.03)^{31} = 2.500$, $(1.03)^{-31} = 0.4000$, $s_{\overline{31}|.03} = 50.00$, $a_{\overline{31}|.03} = 20.00$, compute

(a) $s_{\overline{62}|.03}$ (c) $s_{\overline{32}|.03}$

(b) $a_{\overline{93}|.03}$ (d) $a_{\overline{32}|.03}$

independently of the others and then do some checks (e.g., calculate (b) using (a)).

6. Given that money quadruples at the effective annual rate i in n years, and that $s_{\overline{2n}|i} = 300$, find $a_{\overline{\infty}|i}$.

7. Simplify:

(a) $$\frac{a_{\overline{40}|i}}{a_{\overline{20}|i}\,(2 - i\,a_{\overline{20}|i})}$$

(b) $$\frac{s_{\overline{n+20}|} - s_{\overline{n+10}|}}{s_{\overline{n+10}|} - s_{\overline{n}|}} - \frac{a_{\overline{n+10}|} - a_{\overline{n}|}}{a_{\overline{n+20}|} - a_{\overline{n+10}|}}\,.$$

8. Solve (a) and (b) by different methods, to find in each case an integral n:

(a) $a_{\overline{n}|.085} = 10.900$, (b) $s_{\overline{n}|.06} \doteq 9{,}000$.

9. Solve without the use of tables:

(a) Find i if $s_{\overline{3}|i} = 3.31$.

(b) If $a_{\overline{n}|i} = 10$ and $s_{\overline{n}|i} = 25$, find i.

(c) If $s_{\overline{n}|i} = 50$ and $s_{\overline{2n}|i} = 150$, find the values of $(1 + i)^n$, $s_{\overline{3n}|i}$, i, and also $a_{\overline{n}|i}$ (both with and without using the value of i).

(d) Given $(1 + i)^n = 1.2$, evaluate $$\frac{s_{\overline{2n+1}|i} - s_{\overline{2n}|i}}{a_{\overline{n}|i} - a_{\overline{n-1}|i}}\,.$$

(e) Given $a^{-1}_{\overline{n}|i} = .05$, evaluate $$\frac{a_{\overline{2n}|i}}{(a_{\overline{n}|i})^2} + i.$$

(f) Given $(1 + i)^{20} = 2.25$, evaluate $$\frac{s_{\overline{20}|i} + a_{\overline{5}|i}}{s_{\overline{10}|i} + a_{\overline{15}|i}}\,.$$

10. Prove:

(a) $$\sum_{k=0}^{n} (s_{\overline{k}|} + a_{\overline{n-k}|}) = a_{\overline{n}|}\, s_{\overline{n+1}|}\,.$$

(b) $$\sum_{k=1}^{n} \frac{s_{\overline{k}|}\, v^{n+k}}{(a_{\overline{n}|})^2} = \frac{n\, a^{-1}_{\overline{n}|} - 1}{(1 + i)^n - 1}\,.$$

11. Without interest tables, solve for i and n, the equations

$$s_{\overline{n}|i} = 45.7620, \quad s_{\overline{n+1}|i} = 50.4229,$$

and find the value of $s_{\overline{2n}|i}$.

12. Note that the definitions of $a_{\overline{n}|i}$ and $s_{\overline{n}|i}$ in Sec. 3.2 do not apply for n = 0. Nevertheless, consider the formulas of Sec. 3.3 for indication of how $a_{\overline{0}|i}$ and $s_{\overline{0}|i}$ might be defined. In fact, how are they defined? (Section 3.4.)

Sec. 3.4

13. Find the accumulated value at the end of 10 years of an annuity of \$100 per month during the 10 years if interest is at (a) 4% effective per year, (b) 4% per year compounded quarterly, (c) 4% per year compounded monthly, given $s_{\overline{120}|1/3\%} = 147.249805$. Are your answers consistent?

14. Calculate the present value of an annuity of \$1,000 at the end of each year for 20 years if interest is at an annual rate of (a) (.04, 1), (b) (.04, 2), (c) (.04, 4). Are your answers consistent?

15. A savings account is begun with a deposit of \$1,000. At the end of each 2 years thereafter \$400 is deposited, except at the end of the 16th year when \$900 is withdrawn and nothing is deposited. Give an expression for the amount on deposit at the end of 20 years if interest is at 3% per annum compounded semi-annually.

16. What is represented by

(a) $50 \dfrac{1 - e^{-n\delta}}{e^{\delta/2} - 1}$ (b) $s^{-1}_{\overline{1/4}|.03}\, a_{\overline{20}|.03} /4$?

17. (a) What payment at the end of each quarter is equivalent at (.04, 4) per year to
(i) \$100 at the end of each year,
(ii) \$100 at the end of each month,
(iii) \$200 at the end of each year and \$50 at the end of each month?
(b) Same problem, if interest is at (.04, 2) per year.

18. Show how you would find the present value of an annuity of \$100 at the end of each month for 39 months if interest is at 6%, m = 2.

19. Calculate the value (to the nearest integer) of $\sum_{t=1}^{40} a_{\overline{t/4}|.04}$.

20. Payments of \$500 are to be deposited into a fund at the end of each quarter for 15 years. If during the first 10 years the fund earns interest at the annual rate of 6%, compounded monthly, and during the last 5 years at the effective annual rate of 6%, find the accumulated amount in the fund at the end of 15 years.

21. If a car, on which the balance due after down payment is \$2,000, is financed by monthly payments of \$174.90 for a year, at what effective annual rate of interest is the lender operating?

22. Simplify:

(a) $(1 - i^{(p)} a^{(p)}_{\overline{n|}\,i})(1 + i^{(p)} s^{(p)}_{\overline{n|}\,i})$

(b) $\dfrac{1}{a^{(p)}_{\overline{n|}\,i}} - \dfrac{1}{s^{(p)}_{\overline{n|}\,i}}$.

Sec. 3.5

23. If the annuity in Problem 13 were changed to an annuity-due, what would the accumulated values become? Solve independently of Problem 13 and then check using Problem 13.

24. If the annuity in Problem 14 were changed to an annuity-due, what would the present values become? Solve independently of Problem 14 and then check using Problem 14.

25. At an effective annual rate of 6%, the present value of an ordinary annuity of R per year payable quarterly for 20 years is \$10,000. At the same rate of interest, what is the present value of an annuity-due of R per year payable monthly for 20 years?

26. (a) At 6% per year compounded monthly, what payment at the end of each month for a year is equivalent to a payment of \$1,000 (i) at the end of the year, (ii) at the beginning of the year? How is the answer to (ii) related to the answer to (i)?

(b) Same as (a), except find the equivalent payment at the beginning of each month for a year.

(c) In selecting the form of equivalent payments in a general annuity situation, why would one tend to favor the ordinary basis, as in (a), over the due basis, as in (b)?

27. (a) At 6% effective per year, what payment at the end of the year is equivalent to payments of \$100

(i) at the end of each month in the year?

(ii) at the beginning of each month in the year?

(b) Same as (a), except find the equivalent payment at the beginning of the year.

28. Express as a single symbol:

(a) $v + a_{\overline{1|}}\, a_{\overline{n-1|}}$ (d) $d\, \ddot{s}_{\overline{n|}} / d^{(m)}$

(b) $(\ddot{s}_{\overline{n|}} - s_{\overline{n|}})/d$ (e) $(s^{-1}_{\overline{n-1|}} - s^{-1}_{\overline{n|}})\, s_{\overline{n-1|}}$

(c) $s_{\overline{n|}} + \ddot{s}_{\overline{2n|}}\, \ddot{s}^{-1}_{\overline{n|}} - \ddot{s}_{\overline{n|}}$ (f) $v^n s_{\overline{n|}}\, s^{-1}_{\overline{1/m|}} / (mv^{1/m})$

(g) $(s^{(m)}_{\overline{1|}} + \frac{1}{m})(1 + i)^{n+1}\, a_{\overline{n|}}\, i^{(m)} v^{1/m}/i$.

29. Prove, both algebraically and verbally: $\dfrac{1}{\ddot{a}^{(p)}_{\overline{n|}}} = d^{(p)} + \dfrac{1}{\ddot{s}^{(p)}_{\overline{n|}}}$.

Note the special case $\ddot{a}^{-1}_{\overline{n|}} = d + \ddot{s}^{-1}_{\overline{n|}}$.

30. Consider the validity of the formulas of Sec. 3.3 with all the annuities changed to annuities-due. Make whatever changes are necessary to produce corresponding identities.

31. Verbally interpret $\ddot{s}^{(p)}_{\overline{1}|i} = s^{(p)}_{\overline{1}|i} + \frac{i}{p}$.

32. Jones is obligated to make mortgage payments of $100 at the end of each month for 15 years. In place of the monthly payments, he arranges to make quarterly payments at the beginning of each quarter for 15 years. If money is worth a nominal annual rate of 6%, compounded quarterly, what should be the size of the quarterly payment?

33. To accumulate a sum of $10,000 at (.05,2) per year by means of $400 payments at the end of each year, (a) how many regular $400 payments are needed; and (b) what payment 1 year after the last regular payment will complete the fund?

34. (a) An annuity of $1,000 a year for 25 years, payments at the end of each year, is to be altered so as to become payable (i) semiannually in arrears; (ii) semiannually in advance; (iii) semiannually, first payment in three months. Find the equivalent payments in each case with interest at the effective annual rate of 4%.

(b) Under each alternative (i) to (iii) in (a), annuity payments in a year total less than $1,000. At the beginning of the 25-year period, what cash payment should the annuitant make so as to receive $1,000 every year under each option in (a)?

Sec. 3.6

35. Find an expression for the present value of an annuity of $1,000 per year for 8 years, first payment at the end of 2 1/2 years, if interest is at the annual rate (4%, 4).

36. In terms of $a_{\overline{n}|.01}$ and no other tabulated functions, express the present value at the nominal annual rate (4%, 4) of 10 payments of $100, the first to be made at the end of 5 years and the remaining payments thereafter at 2-year intervals.

37. If interest on a savings fund is at the nominal annual rate of 4%, compounded monthly, give an expression for the monthly withdrawal at the beginning of each month for 120 months, first withdrawal at the end of 5 years, which can be provided by making annual deposits of $1,000 into the fund at the beginning of each year for 5 years.

38. At a nominal annual rate of 6% compounded semiannually, what payment made at the end of every month for 5 years will provide during the next 5-year period

(a) $100 at the end of every month (give a numerical answer),

(b) $1,000 at the end of every year (give an expression only).

39. What annual payment for 5 years, first payment at the end of 6 years, is equivalent to $500 at the beginning of each year for 15 years? Interest is at an annual (.05, 4).

40. Express the value today at 1/2% effective per month of 15 semiannual payments of \$500, the first due in 4 months.

41. Abrams buys an article costing \$1,300 by making a cash payment of \$300 and promising to make level monthly payments for 10 years, with the first payment 30 months after the sale. Find the monthly payment, at an annual rate (4%, 2).

42. Simplify solely by use of a line diagram:

(a) $a_{\overline{35}|}(1 + v^{35}) + a_{\overline{18}|}\, v^{70}$

(b) $\ddot{a}^{(2)}_{\overline{100}|} - (\ddot{a}^{(2)}_{\overline{20}|} - \ddot{a}^{(2)}_{\overline{8}|})\, v^{80}$.

Sec. 3.7

43. Find the present value under the effective rate i per period of an annuity for n periods under which the payment at the end of the kth period is $1 + (n - k + 1)i$. Interpret your result.

44. (a) If interest is at the effective rate of 5% per year, obtain the accumulated amount at the end of 20 years of an annuity-due with payments of \$100 per month in the first 10 years, and of \$200 per month in the second 10 years.

(b) Same problem, except reverse the order of the payments.

45. Find a simplified expression for the present value, at the effective annual rate i, of an annuity with payments:

10, 11, ··· , 19 at the ends of years 1-10,
21, 23, ··· , 39 at the ends of years 11-20,
42, 45, ··· , 69 at the ends of years 21-30.

46. Simplify the sums:

(a) $\sum_{h=1}^{n} a_{\overline{h}|i}$, (b) $\sum_{h=1}^{n} s_{\overline{h}|i}$, (c) $\sum_{h=1}^{n} a_{\overline{2h}|i}$.

47. Payments of t are made at the end of every month in the tth year ($t = 1, 2, \cdots, 10$). Show that the accumulated value of this annuity at the end of 10 years, at the monthly rate i, is

$$\frac{1}{i}\left(\frac{s_{\overline{120}|}}{a_{\overline{12}|}} - 10\right).$$

48. Give a simplified expression in terms of tabulated functions for the accumulated value of an annuity of monthly payments of 32 for the first year, 34 for the second year, 36 for the third year, ··· , 90 for the final year. Interest is at an effective annual rate i.

49. Verbally interpret

(a) $\ddot{s}_{\overline{n}|i} = i(Is)_{\overline{n}|i} + n$ (c) $n = i(Da)_{\overline{n}|i} + a_{\overline{n}|i}$

(b) $\ddot{a}_{\overline{n}|i} = i(Ia)_{\overline{n}|i} + nv^n$ (d) $n(1+i)^n = i(Ds)_{\overline{n}|i} + s_{\overline{n}|i}$.

50. An annuity is to provide \$1,000 at the beginning of each quarter for 3 years and then \$4,000 at the beginning of each quarter for another 4 years. Obtain expressions in good

computational form for substitution from Appendix tables for the accumulated value of this annuity if interest is at (a) 6% per year compounded quarterly, (b) 6% per year compounded monthly.

51. Prove that $\ddot{a}_{\overline{10|}}\ s_{\overline{9|}} = (Is)_{\overline{9|}} + (Da)_{\overline{9|}}$.

52. If interest is at the effective annual rate of 5%, find the present value of an annuity-due with annual payments increasing geometrically in ratio 1.03 and with annuity term of (a) 20 years, (b) infinity. Assume the first payment is 1.

53. Simplify to a single symbol:

(a) $\frac{1}{i}[\ddot{s}_{\overline{n+1|}} - (n+1)] - (n+1)$ (d) $(Is)^{(p)}_{\overline{n|}}/(Is)_{\overline{n|}}$

(b) $\frac{1}{n}[(Ia)_{\overline{n|}} + (D\ddot{a})_{\overline{n|}}]$ (e) $\sum_{t=0}^{n-1}\ {}_{t|}a_{\overline{n-t|}}$

(c) $(I\ddot{s})_{\overline{h+k|}} - (I_{\overline{h|}}\ddot{s})_{\overline{h+k|}}$ (f) $(Da)_{\overline{5|}} + {}_{5|}(Da)_{\overline{5|}} + 5a_{\overline{5|}}$.

54. For the annuity having payment t^2 at the end of t interest periods ($t = 1, 2, \cdots, 11$) and interest rate i, state which of the following express its present value:

(a) $[\ddot{a}_{\overline{11|}} + 2(Ia)_{\overline{10|}} - 121\ v^{11}]/i$

(b) $(\ddot{s}_{\overline{1|}} + 2\ \ddot{a}_{\overline{10|}} - 142\ v^{10} + 121\ v^{11})/i^2$

(c) $(\ddot{s}_{\overline{2|}} - 144\ v^9 + 263\ v^{10} - 121\ v^{11})/i^3$

(d) $(1 + i)\dfrac{\partial}{\partial i}\ a_{\overline{11|}} + (1 + i)^2\ \dfrac{\partial^2}{\partial i^2}\ a_{\overline{11|}}$.

55. Which of the following are equal to $\sum_{t=10}^{25} s_{\overline{t|}i}$?

(a) $(\ddot{s}_{\overline{25|}i} - \ddot{s}_{\overline{9|}i} - 16)/i$ (d) $(Is)_{\overline{25|}i} - (Is)_{\overline{9|}i}(1 + i)^{16}$

(b) $(s_{\overline{25|}i} - s_{\overline{9|}i} - 16v)/d$ (e) $(Is)_{\overline{16|}i}(1 + i)^9 + 16s_{\overline{9|}i}$

(c) $(s_{\overline{26|}i} - s_{\overline{10|}i} - 16)/i$ (f) $(Is)_{\overline{25|}i} - (Is)_{\overline{9|}i}$

(g) $(I_{\overline{16|}}s)_{\overline{25|}i}$.

56. In construction of financial tables at a fixed rate of interest, say for $t = 1, 2, \cdots, n$, one often can (and often does) find the initial value, calculate each other value from its immediate predecessor and employ summation checks. For example, for the function $(1 + i)^t$, these are $(1 + i)^1 = 1 + i$, $(1 + i)^t = (1 + i)^{t-1}(1 + i)$ and

$$\sum_{t=1}^{n}(1 + i)^t = \ddot{s}_{\overline{n|}} = \begin{cases} s_{\overline{n+1|}} - 1 \text{ or } s_{\overline{n|}}(1 + i), \text{ if those annuity values have been independently calculated} \\ [(1 + i)^n - 1](1 + i)/i, \text{ otherwise.} \end{cases}$$

As a check on the summation value, note that when $n = 1$ all members produce $(1 + i)$ and when $n = 2$, $(1 + i) + (1 + i)^2$. Proceed in this same fashion to describe table construction for (1) v^t, (2) $s_{\overline{t}|}$, (3) $a_{\overline{t}|}$, (4) $(Da)_{\overline{t}|}$, (5) $(Is)_{\overline{t}|}$, (6) $(Ds)_{\overline{t}|}$, (7) $(Ia)_{\overline{t}|}$.

Sec. 3.8

57. Find the present value of momently payments at the rate of \$100 per year for 15 years if interest is at 4% per year compounded semiannually.

58. Find the present value of an annuity with momently payments under which the annual rate of payment is t for $0 \le t \le n$ and is $2n - t$ for $n \le t \le 2n$. Assume interest is at the effective annual rate i, and simplify your formula.

59. Show that $(\bar{I}\,\bar{s})_{\overline{n}|} = \int_0^n \bar{s}_{\overline{h}|}\,dh$ and

$$(\bar{D}\,\bar{a})_{\overline{n}|} = \int_0^n \bar{a}_{\overline{t}|}\,dt.$$

60. Differentiate in regard to (a) i, (b) n:

(1) $\bar{a}_{\overline{n}|i}$ (3) $(\bar{I}\,\bar{s})_{\overline{n}|i}$

(2) $\bar{s}_{\overline{n}|i}$ (4) $(\bar{D}\,\bar{a})_{\overline{n}|i}$.

61. A man has \$40,000 in a fund paying interest at the rate of 4% per annum, compounded continuously. If he withdraws money continuously at the rate of \$2,400 per year, how long will the fund last? (Given: $\ln 3 = 1.09861$.)

62. True or false? Explain. The annuities are valued at an effective rate i equivalent to a force δ.

(a) $\bar{a}_{\overline{n}|}^{-1} = \delta + \bar{s}_{\overline{n}|}^{-1}$

(b) $(1 + i)^n\, \bar{s}_{\overline{n}|}^{-1} - (1 + i)^{2n}\, \bar{s}_{\overline{2n}|}^{-1} = \bar{s}_{\overline{n}|}^{-1} - \bar{s}_{\overline{2n}|}^{-1}$

(c) $\bar{a}_{\overline{p+q}|} = \bar{a}_{\overline{p}|} + v^p\, \bar{a}_{\overline{q}|}$

(d) $\bar{a}_{\overline{n}|}\, e^{\delta} = 1 + \bar{a}_{\overline{n-1}|}$

(e) $\bar{a}_{\overline{n}|} = a_{\overline{n}|}\, e^{\delta/2}$.

63. How does $(\bar{I}\,\bar{a})_{\overline{n}|}$ compare in size with $(\bar{a}_{\overline{n}|})^2$?

64. If $A(t)$ denotes the present value of payments to be made from time t to time n under a continuous annuity with rate of payment $r(t)$ at time t, $0 \le t \le n$, (a) write an integral for $A(t)$ and (b) find $\frac{d}{dt} A(t)$ using (a).

65. Find the present and accumulated values of the continuous annuity having for $0 \le t \le n$, (a) $r(t) = (1 + r)^t$; (b) $r(t) = t^2$.

66. If $\delta_t = 1/(t + 2)$ per time unit for $0 \le t \le 2$, find the present value of an annuity
(a) of 1 at times t = 1 and 2;
(b) payable continuously at the rate of 1 per time unit for the interval $0 \le t \le 2$;
(c) payable continuously at the rate of t at time t, $0 \le t \le 2$.

67. Express
(a) i/δ (1) as an annuity, (2) in terms of $s_{\overline{1}|}^{(p)}$;
(b) $\bar{s}_{\overline{n}|}$ in terms of (1) $s_{\overline{n}|}^{(p)}$, (2) $\ddot{s}_{\overline{n}|}^{(p)}$, and check that $\bar{s}_{\overline{n}|} = \frac{i}{\delta} s_{\overline{n}|}$ follows in each case;
(c) $(I\bar{s})_{\overline{n}|}$ in terms of (1) $(Is)_{\overline{n}|}$, (2) $(Is)_{\overline{n}|}^{(p)}$.

68. (a) Define $(I^{(p)}a)_{\overline{n}|}^{(p)}$ consistent with other notation and such that $(\bar{I}\bar{a})_{\overline{n}|} = \lim_{p\to\infty} (I^{(p)}a)_{\overline{n}|}^{(p)}$.
(b) Show that $(I^{(p)}a)_{\overline{n}|}^{(p)} = (\ddot{a}_{\overline{n}|}^{(p)} - nv^n)/i^{(p)}$.

Sec. 3.9

69. Find the present value of \$60 at the end of each quarter in perpetuity, at the annual rate (a) (.12, 12), (b) (.12, 4), (c) (.12, 2).

70. A fund of \$10,000 is invested at an effective annual rate of 5% for the purpose of providing as soon as possible a \$2,000 annual scholarship forever. How many years must pass until the first \$2,000 payment? What smaller payment could be made 1 year earlier and still permit scholarships of \$2,000 each year thereafter?

71. Assuming an effective annual rate of interest of 2%, compute the present value of a perpetuity with first payment of \$20 at the end of 1 year, \$19 at the end of 2 years, \$18 at the end of 3 years, etc., until a payment of \$10 is reached, after which payments remain level at \$10.

72. A perpetuity with momently payments has annual rate of payment r(t) as follows:

For $0 \le t < 25$, $r(t) = 100t$
For $25 \le t$, $r(t) = 2{,}500$.

Find a simplified expression for its present value.

73. A perpetuity is payable continuously at the rate $1 + t^2$. If $\delta = .05$, find the present value of this perpetuity.

74. In terms of perpetuities interpret

(a) $\ddot{a}_{\overline{n}|} = \frac{1}{d} - \frac{v^n}{d}$ (c) $\frac{1}{d^{(p)}} = \frac{1}{i^{(p)}} + \frac{1}{p}$

(b) $\ddot{s}_{\overline{n}|} = \frac{(1+i)^n}{d} - \frac{1}{d}$ (d) $(\ddot{a}_{\overline{\infty}|})^2 - (a_{\overline{\infty}|})^2 = \ddot{a}_{\overline{\infty}|} + a_{\overline{\infty}|}$.

75. Verbally interpret $$(Ia)_{\overline{n}|} = \frac{\ddot{a}_{\overline{n}|}}{i} - \frac{nv^n}{i} = \frac{a_{\overline{n}|}}{d} - \frac{nv^n}{i}.$$

76. (a) From prior problems or otherwise, obtain formulas in terms of rates only for (1) $(I\ddot{a})_{\overline{\infty}|}$, (2) $(Ia)^{(p)}_{\overline{\infty}|}$, (3) $(I\ddot{a})^{(p)}_{\overline{\infty}|}$, (4) $(I^{(p)}a)^{(p)}_{\overline{\infty}|}$, (5) $(I^{(p)}\ddot{a})^{(p)}_{\overline{\infty}|}$.

(b) Calculate as easily as possible with $i = .01$ and $p = 12$:

(i) (1) $a_{\overline{\infty}|}$, (2) $\ddot{a}_{\overline{\infty}|}$, (3) $\bar{a}_{\overline{\infty}|}$, (4) $a^{(p)}_{\overline{\infty}|}$, (5) $\ddot{a}^{(p)}_{\overline{\infty}|}$, (6) $(Ia)_{\overline{\infty}|}$, (7) $(I\bar{a})_{\overline{\infty}|}$, (8) $(\bar{I}\bar{a})_{\overline{\infty}|}$, and

(ii) the values in (a).

77. A perpetuity of $100 a month is to be divided equally between A and B, but A is to receive the full annuity until it is B's turn to receive the remaining perpetuity. At an annual rate (.08, 4), how many full payments does A get? How should the next payment be split between A and B?

Sec. 3.10

78. Find to the nearest cent:

(a) The present value of an ordinary annuity of $1.00 per year for 62 years at 3% per annum, compounded annually.

(b) The accumulated value of an ordinary annuity of $1.00 per year for 20 years at 3% per annum convertible semiannually.

(c) The present value of an ordinary annuity of $1.00 per year payable semiannually for 20 years at 3% per year effective.

(d) The accumulated value of a continuous annuity of $1.00 per year for 20 years at an effective rate of 3% per year.

(e) The present value of a perpetuity of $1.00 at the end of each quarter, first payment 10 years from now, at 4% per year, compounded quarterly.

(f) The accumulated value of an annuity-due of $1.00 per year payable semiannually for 18 years at 2.01% per annum, compounded annually.

79. If interest is at 4% per annum compounded semiannually, express each of the following in good computational form for substitution from Appendix tables:

(a) The value today of an annuity of 10 semiannual payments of $100, first payment 2 years from now (give 2 answers);

(b) The present value of an annuity-due of 10 annual payments of $100;

(c) The present value of an annuity-due of 9 quarterly payments of $100;

(d) The accumulated value of an ordinary annuity of 120 monthly payments of $100;

(e) The accumulated value of an ordinary annuity of 120 semiannual payments of $100;

(f) The value 5 years after the first payment of a continuous annuity having level annual rate of payment of $100 and payable for 15 years;

(g) Same as (f) except payments continue forever;

(h) The present value of an ordinary simple annuity having 16 $100 semiannual payments followed by 14 $70 semiannual payments and concluding with 10 \$90 semiannual payments (have $a_{\overline{n}|}$ the only interest function in your answer).

80. (a) Given the following payments anticipated to be made by a business over a long period of time:

\$50,000 at the end of each half year
\$10,000 spread uniformly over each month
\$80,000 at the end of every 3 years
\$40,000 at the beginning of every 5 years.

At an effective annual rate of interest i, what is the equivalent annual cost in mid-year?

(b) Which is more economical: to buy an article costing \$100 and having a 5-year lifetime or to buy a competing article costing \$150 and having an 8-year lifetime? Money is worth (.05, 2) per year. (Hint: compare equivalent semiannual costs.)

81. (a) Per \$1,000 worth of lumber, how much could a company afford to spend at purchase date in treating the lumber, if its service lifetime would thereby be increased from 10 to 15 years? Assume that money is worth 3 1/2% effective per year and that in each case the scrap value will be \$50.

(b) The company in (a) elects not to treat the lumber at purchase date; how much could it afford to pay, instead, at the end of 10 years to extend the lifetime by 5 years?

82. (a) At an annual rate of (.03, 4), how many semiannual payments of \$50 must be made before a fund of \$1,000 is obtained? To complete the \$1,000 fund 6 months after the last regular \$50 payment, how large a payment should be made at that time?

(b) Same problem, except that a fund of \$970 is required.

83. Reinvestment rates. In practice it often happens that interest income cannot earn the same rate as the invested sums which produce that income. In such a case, we say that the reinvestment rate i differs from the investment rate i'. Usually $i < i'$. Let us consider

(a) The generalized accumulated value of a single principal; the generalized present value of a single sum. Let A be invested for n periods and interest income at rate i' be paid each period and reinvested at rate i for the balance of the n-period term. What sum S results in n periods; and given S, what is its present value?

(b) The generalized accumulated value of an annuity. Assume that each annuity payment B_t $(t = 1, 2, \cdots, n)$ produces interest income at rate i' per period and that those interest income amounts are reinvested at rate i. What is the whole accumulated value S after n periods? To what does this simplify if $B_t = R$ $(t = 1, 2, \cdots, n)$? Solve the level case in a second way also.

(c) The generalized present value of an annuity. This concept might be defined as the sum of the present values obtained by applying the present value form in (a) n times, with S in turn $B_1, B_2, \cdots, B_n$ and terms of $1, 2, \cdots, n$ periods, respectively. The result would be unwieldy. Therefore, we define the present value of an annuity having an n-period term, as the principal such that (1) the annuity payments produce interest income each period at rate i' on that principal, and (2) the remaining portions of the annuity payments are accumulated at rate i to replace that principal. Show that

$$A = \sum_{t=1}^{n} B_t v^t / [1 + (i' - i) a_{\overline{n}| i}]$$

in the general case, and

$$A = R a_{\overline{n}| i} / [1 + (i' - i) a_{\overline{n}| i}] = R\, s_{\overline{n}| i} / (1 + i' s_{\overline{n}| i})$$

in case $B_t = R$ for all t; cf. (a). Note that these present values are unrelated to the generalized accumulated values in (b).

(d) What these results become if (1) $i = i'$, (2) $i = 0$.

(e) The following problems which illustrate reinvestment theory.

(i) Find the accumulated amount at the end of 10 years of $1,000 invested to yield 10% payable annually if the interest income can be reinvested (1) at an effective annual rate of 4%, (2) at a nominal annual rate of 4% convertible semiannually.

(ii) Find the present value of $1,000 due at the end of 5 years to an investor who considers that the original principal should earn 6% payable annually but that reinvestment of income will be at the nominal annual rate (4%, 2).

(iii) A man invests $10,000 to earn 7% payable annually and reinvests the interest at 3% compounded annually. At the end of 5 years, the accumulated interest will be invested to earn 6% payable annually with reinvestment of its interest income at 3% compounded annually. Find the total accumulation at the end of 10 years.

(iv) Given an annuity of $1,000 payable at the end of each year for 10 years. Assume that each annuity payment will earn 6% per year payable semiannually and that such interest income can be reinvested at 4% per year compounded semiannually. Show that the accumulated amount at the end of 10 years can be simplified to

$$1{,}500\, s_{\overline{20}| .02}\, s^{-1}_{\overline{2}| .02} - 5{,}000.$$

(v) Find the present value of an annuity of $1,000 at the end of each year for 15 years to an investor who seeks a return of 8% payable annually on his original principal and will accumulate the balance of the annuity payments at the rate of 4% compounded annually to replace his capital at the end of 15 years.

(vi) The same as (v) but with the replacement fund earning 4% per year compounded semiannually.

Supplementary List A: More Practice (Problems 84-105)

84. Given: at .02, $v^{35} = 1/2$. Without tables obtain numerical values of

(a) $1/a_{\overline{35}|}$, $1/s_{\overline{35}|}$, $a_{\overline{35}|}$, $s_{\overline{35}|}$;

(b) $a_{\overline{70}|}$, $s_{\overline{70}|}$, $a_{\overline{17.5}|}$, $s_{\overline{17.5}|}$;

(c) $(Ia)_{\overline{35}|}$, $(Is)_{\overline{35}|}$, $(Da)_{\overline{35}|}$, $(Ds)_{\overline{35}|}$;

(d) $a_{\overline{\infty}|}$, $(Ia)_{\overline{\infty}|}$;

(e) $_{35|}a_{\overline{35|}}$, $_{36|}\ddot{a}_{\overline{35|}}$, $_{35|}a_{\overline{70|}}$, $_{70|}a_{\overline{35|}}$,

$_{35|}(Ia)_{\overline{35|}}$, $(I_{\overline{35|}}a)_{\overline{70|}}$, $_{35|}a_{\overline{\infty|}}$, $_{35|}(I_{\overline{35|}}a)_{\overline{\infty|}}$.

85. (a) If interest is at the annual rate of 4%, compounded semiannually, to how much will deposits of \$100 at the end of each month for 20 years accumulate by the end of 20 years?

(b) If the deposits were at the beginning of each month, what would be the accumulated amount at the end of 20 years?

86. Give a simplified formula for the present value of an annuity of \$100 at the beginning of each month for 10 years, if interest is at the force of 4% per year.

87. Given that the annual force of interest is .05, find the present value of a perpetuity payable momently under which the annual rate of payment at time t is $e^{.01t}$.

88. An ordinary annuity has semiannual payments of \$800, \$750, \$700, ... , \$350. Show that at an effective semiannual rate of 2%, its present value simplifies to

$$25{,}000 - 2{,}200\, a_{\overline{10|}}.$$

89. To the nearest dollar, find the present value of an annuity of \$200 per year payable in semiannual installments for 15 years, if interest is at 6% compounded quarterly and the first payment is at the end of 2 years.

90. Find the accumulated value of an ordinary annuity of 1 at the end of each period for 20 periods, at a force of interest 3δ per period, where δ is the force equivalent to an effective rate of 4%.

91. Express as a single symbol:

(a) $a_{\overline{100|}.04}(1 + v^{100} + v^{200})$

(b) $s_{\overline{50|}.01} + (1.01)^{50}$

(c) $v(1 + a_{\overline{40|}.02})$

(d) $(a_{\overline{39|}.03} + s_{\overline{36|}.03})(1.03)^{40}$

(e) $(a_{\overline{4|}.05} + s_{\overline{6|}.05})v^{60}$.

What usefulness do the expressions above have?

92. Given $s_{\overline{n|}} = 10$ and $\ddot{s}_{\overline{n|}} = 11$, find i, $\ddot{a}_{\overline{\infty|}}$, $a_{\overline{n|}}^{-1}$, $_{3n|}a_{\overline{2n|}}$, and to the nearest integer, n.

93. If $\ddot{a}_{\overline{10|}} - \ddot{a}_{\overline{9|}} = .5$, find without tables:

(a) $\ddot{a}_{\overline{9|}} - a_{\overline{9|}}$

(b) $\ddot{a}_{\overline{19|}} - \ddot{a}_{\overline{18|}}$

(c) $a_{\overline{27|}} - a_{\overline{26|}}$

(d) $s_{\overline{19|}} - s_{\overline{18|}}$

(e) $s_{\overline{36|}}/a_{\overline{9|}}$

(f) $\ddot{s}_{\overline{9|}} - \ddot{s}_{\overline{8|}}$.

94. A loan is repaid in 10 years by annual payments of k ($k = 1, 2, \cdots, 10$). If interest is at the annual effective rate of 4%, determine the total amount of interest paid.

95. Describe an annuity having payments of a round sum and

(a) $A = 100\left[v^7 + s_{\overline{12}|}^{-1}\left(a_{\overline{115}|} - a_{\overline{7}|}\right)\right]$

(b) $S = 100\left[(1 + i)^7 + s_{\overline{12}|}^{-1}\left(s_{\overline{115}|} - s_{\overline{7}|}\right)\right]$

(c) $S = 100\left[(1 + i)^7 + a_{\overline{12}|}^{-1}\left(s_{\overline{115}|} - s_{\overline{7}|}\right)\right]$.

96. An ordinary perpetuity consists of 5 annual payments of 1 followed by 5 annual payments of 2, repeating in that sequence of payments of 1 and 2 forever. At an annual effective rate i, express the present value of the perpetuity in terms of values of $s_{\overline{n}|}$ and i.

97. Find x in terms of just i and annuities having terms shorter than 5 interest periods, if

$$x \cdot {}_{17|}a_{\overline{15}|} = \ddot{a}_{\overline{35}|}^{(p)} - \ddot{a}_{\overline{20}|}^{(p)} .$$

98. Estimate, and then obtain exactly, the accumulated value at the end of 21 years of an increasing ordinary annuity with monthly payments of \$100 in the first year, \$110 in the second year, \$120 in the third year, up to \$200 in the 11th year, after which payments remain at \$200 for the final 10 years. Assume annual rates of (a) (4%, 1) and (b) (4%, 12). Given: at 1/3%, $s_{\overline{12}|} = 12.2224629$, $s_{\overline{132}|} = 165.4714518$, $s_{\overline{252}|} = 393.9400531$, $(1 + i)^{120} = 1.4908327$.

99. (a) Find an expression for the present value, at an effective annual rate i, of an infinite series of annual payments commencing at \$5,000 with each succeeding payment 90% of the previous payment, the first payment being due 6 months hence.
(b) Same as (a), except that the payments are semiannual.

100. Express in terms of annuity symbols of the form $R\, a_{\overline{n}|i}^{(p)}$ or $R\, \ddot{a}_{\overline{n}|i}^{(p)}$ or $R\, {}_{h|}a_{\overline{n}|i}^{(p)}$:

(a) $\dfrac{1 - (1.015)^{-12}}{12\left[(1.015)^{1/3} - 1\right]}$ (c) $100\, a_{\overline{2}|.03}^{-1}\, a_{\overline{40}|.03}$

(b) $\dfrac{1 - (1.02)^{-20}}{1 - (1.02)^{-1/4}}$ (d) $100\, \dfrac{i}{i^{(2)}}\, a_{\overline{10}|i}\, v^6$

(e) $50\left(\dfrac{.04}{.04^{(4)}} + .01\right)\left(a_{\overline{25}|.04} - a_{\overline{5}|.04}\right)$.

101. Find the accumulated amount at 3.95% interest of a special 15-year annuity-certain in which each annual payment after the first is 1% less than the preceding payment, the final payment being \$100. From this amount deduce a formula for the present value of the annuity at date of issue, check

this formula independently, and calculate it. Given $(.99)^{15} = 0.86005835$.

102. (a) If $(Da)_{\overline{31}|i} = 367$ to the nearest integer, find i.
(b) If $(Da)_{\overline{n}|.02} = 526$ to the nearest integer, find n.

103. At a fixed rate $i > 0$, indicate the largest of the following:

(a) $(a_{\overline{19}|} - a_{\overline{7}|})/s_{\overline{2}|}$ (d) $\ddot{a}^{(2)}_{\overline{15}|} - \ddot{a}^{(2)}_{\overline{9}|}$

(b) $(a_{\overline{21}|} - a_{\overline{9}|})/a_{\overline{2}|}$ (e) $\ddot{a}_{\overline{15}|} - \ddot{a}_{\overline{9}|}$

(c) $v^5(a^{(3)}_{\overline{10}|} - a^{(3)}_{\overline{4}|})$ (f) $(1 + i)^6(\ddot{a}_{\overline{22}|} - \ddot{a}_{\overline{16}|})$.

104. Describe an annuity having present value of

(a) $10\, a_{\overline{20}|} - \dfrac{s_{\overline{10}|} - 10}{i} v^{20}$

(b) $\dfrac{1}{i}(h - a_{\overline{hk}|}/ s_{\overline{k}|})$

(c) $10[(1 + 20\, i)a_{\overline{10}|} - 10]/[(1 + i)^{1/12} - 1]$

(d) $\sum_{t=1}^{10} t\, a_{\overline{t}|}$, and find a simple expression for its present value.

105. Describe perpetuities (the payments of which are not interest functions) that have the following present values:

(a) $1/(i\delta)$ (c) $(\ddot{s}_{\overline{n}|} - n)/\left(i[(1 + i)^n - 1]\right)$

(b) $(n - {}_{n|}a_{\overline{t}|})/d$ (d) $\ddot{a}_{\overline{n}|}/i$.

Supplementary List B: More Insights (Problems 106-142)

106. Money triples in n years, n an integer, at an annual interest rate i assumed to be the earnings rate forever. A fund is developed by a unit deposit at the end of each year for n years. By verbal reasoning alone, describe a simple ordinary annuity, term commencing at the end of the n years, which the fund can provide, if the annuity is to continue (1) for n years, (2) for 2n years, (3) forever.

107. For $i > 0$ and all positive integral n, state (without reference to tables) which of the following are <u>false</u>:

(a) $s_{\overline{n}|}/\ddot{s}_{\overline{n}|} = v$

(b) $s_{\overline{n}|} = s_{\overline{n-1}|} + (1 + i)^n$

(c) $s_{\overline{n}|} = \ddot{s}_{\overline{n-1}|} + 1$

(d) $v^m s_{\overline{n}|} = \begin{cases} a_{\overline{m}|} - a_{\overline{m-n}|} & \text{if } m>n \\ a_{\overline{m}|} + s_{\overline{n-m}|} & \text{if } m<n \end{cases}$

(e) $s_{\overline{n}|} > 1$

(f) $a_{\overline{n}|} < \bar{a}_{\overline{n}|} < \ddot{a}_{\overline{n}|} < n$

(g) $a_{\overline{2n}|} > a_{\overline{n}|}$

(h) $a_{\overline{n}|i'} > a_{\overline{n}|i}$, where $i' > i$

(i) $s^{-1}_{\overline{n}|} \le \dfrac{1}{n} \le a^{-1}_{\overline{n}|}$

(j) $a^{-1}_{\overline{n}|} = (1 + i)^n s^{-1}_{\overline{n}|}$

(k) $s^{(p)}_{\overline{1}|} > 1$.

108. Which of the following formulas are <u>false</u>?

(a) $s_{\overline{100}|} = s_{\overline{40}|} + s_{\overline{60}|}(1+i)^{40}$ (e) $\bar{s}_{\overline{n}|}^{-1} = \delta\, s_{\overline{n}|}^{-1}/i$

(b) $a_{\overline{150}|} = a_{\overline{100}|} + v^{50}\, a_{\overline{50}|}$ (f) $(I\ddot{a})_{\overline{\infty}|} = (a_{\overline{\infty}|} + 1)^2$

(c) $\ddot{a}_{\overline{n}|} = a_{\overline{n+1}|} - 1$ (g) $(Ia)_{\overline{\infty}|} = a_{\overline{\infty}|} + (a_{\overline{\infty}|})^2$

(d) $(Ia)_{\overline{n}|} = a_{\overline{n}|} + \frac{1}{i}(a_{\overline{n}|} - nv^n)$ (h) ${}_{h|}a_{\overline{n}|}/a_{\overline{3}|} = {}_{h-2|}\ddot{a}_{\overline{n}|}/s_{\overline{3}|}$.

109. True or false? If false, correct the right member.

(a) $\ddot{a}_{\overline{n}|}(1+i)^{n-1} = \ddot{s}_{\overline{n}|}$

(b) ${}_{m|}\ddot{a}_{\overline{n}|} = {}_{m+1|}a_{\overline{n}|}$

(c) $\ddot{a}^{(p)}_{\overline{\infty}|\,i} = 1/p + a_{\overline{\infty}|\,i'}$, if i' is properly chosen

(d) $\ddot{s}_{\overline{n}|}/s_{\overline{n}|} = \ddot{a}_{\overline{n}|}/a_{\overline{n}|}$

(e) $i(Is)_{\overline{n}|} = \delta(\bar{I}\,\bar{s})_{\overline{n}|}$

(f) $a_{\overline{x+y}|} = a_{\overline{x}|} + {}_{x|}a_{\overline{y}|}$.

110. Which of the following are equal to ${}_{h|}\ddot{a}_{\overline{k}|}$?

(a) $\ddot{a}_{\overline{h+k}|} - \ddot{a}_{\overline{h}|}$ (c) $a_{\overline{h+k-1}|} - a_{\overline{h-1}|}$

(b) $a_{\overline{h+k}|} - a_{\overline{h}|}$ (d) ${}_{h-1|}a_{\overline{k}|}$.

111. Give 2 expressions in terms of tabulated functions, for each of ${}_{m|}\bar{a}_{\overline{n}|\,i}$, ${}_{m|}\ddot{a}_{\overline{\infty}|\,i}$, ${}_{m|}(Ia)_{\overline{n}|\,i}$, ${}_{m|}(Ia)_{\overline{\infty}|\,i}$.

112. If $3a^{(2)}_{\overline{n}|\,i} = 2\,a^{(2)}_{\overline{2n}|\,i} = 45\, s^{(2)}_{\overline{1}|\,i}$, find i.

113. Both verbally and algebraically, prove that

(a) $a_{\overline{n}|}[1 + (1+i)^n + (1+i)^{2n} + \cdots + (1+i)^{9n}]$

$$= v^n s_{\overline{10n}|} = a_{\overline{n}|} + s_{\overline{9n}|}$$

(b) $s_{\overline{n}|} = a_{\overline{n}|} + i\, a_{\overline{n}|}\, s_{\overline{n}|}$.

114. Prove that

$$i\,a_{\overline{n}|}\,s_{\overline{n+1}|} = i\,\ddot{a}_{\overline{n+1}|}\,s_{\overline{n}|} = d\,a_{\overline{n}|}\,\ddot{s}_{\overline{n+1}|} = \ddot{s}_{\overline{n}|} - a_{\overline{n}|} = s_{\overline{n+1}|} - \ddot{a}_{\overline{n+1}|}.$$

115. Verbally interpret (a) $i^{(p)}\, s^{(p)}_{\overline{1}|\,i} = i$ and

(b) $i^{(p)}\, s^{(p)}_{\overline{n}|\,i} + 1 = (1+i)^n$.

116. Simplify $s^{(1/p)}_{\overline{np}|}\, s_{\overline{p}|}/p$ and justify your result by verbal reasoning.

117. (a) A man is investing 1 per year in p equal installments each year. Find a formula for the amount he has accumulated immediately after his (np)th payment, if interest is credited at effective annual rate i at the end of each year, except that for new investment during any year simple interest at rate i is credited for that year. Assume p and n are positive integers.

(b) Does the usual formula for the accumulation of an annuity payable p times each year produce a higher value? lower value? or the same value as in (a)?

(c) Same as (a), except that new investment during any year earns interest for that year at an effective annual rate $i' < i$.

118. (a) Show that for p a positive integer

$$a_{\overline{n}|}^{(p)} \doteq a_{\overline{n}|}\left(1 + \frac{p-1}{2p}\, i\right)$$

and determine the direction of the error.

(b) Compare the values of $a_{\overline{25}|.06}^{(2)}$ and $a_{\overline{25}|.06}^{(12)}$ by this, and the true, formula.

(c) Does the approximation in (a) apply when $q = 1/p$ is a positive integer?

(d) What approximations for $\ddot{a}_{\overline{n}|}^{(p)}$ and $\bar{a}_{\overline{n}|}$ are consistent with the approximation above for $a_{\overline{n}|}^{(p)}$?

119. Prove or disprove: the limiting forms of $a_{\overline{n}|i}^{(p)}$ and $\ddot{a}_{\overline{n}|i}^{(p)}$ are equal, when (1) $n \to \infty$, (2) $p \to \infty$, (3) $i \to \infty$.

120. Show that

$$\frac{a_{\overline{n}|}}{a_{\overline{m}|}} = \frac{\ddot{a}_{\overline{n}|}}{\ddot{a}_{\overline{m}|}} = \frac{{}_{h|}a_{\overline{n}|}}{{}_{h|}a_{\overline{m}|}} = \frac{a_{\overline{n}|}^{(p)}}{a_{\overline{m}|}^{(p)}} = \frac{(I_{\overline{n}|}a)_{\overline{\infty}|}}{(I_{\overline{m}|}a)_{\overline{\infty}|}} = v^{n-m}\frac{s_{\overline{n}|}}{s_{\overline{m}|}} = 1 - \frac{s_{\overline{m-n}|}}{s_{\overline{m}|}},$$

the last expression holding if $m \not< n$; and extend the list.

121. Express each of the following as a single symbol:

(a) $\ddot{a}_{\overline{1}|}^{(m)}\,\ddot{a}_{\overline{n}|}$ (c) $\ddot{a}_{\overline{n+1/m}|}^{(m)} - 1/m$

(b) $\ddot{s}_{\overline{1}|}^{(m)}\,a_{\overline{n}|}$ (d) $s_{\overline{1}|}^{(m)}\,a_{\overline{n}|} + \frac{1}{m}(1 - v^n)$

(e) $\left(1 + \frac{i^{(m)}}{m}\right) a_{\overline{n}|}^{(m)}$.

122. Which of the following are equal?

(a) $\dfrac{\ddot{a}_{\overline{n}|} - a_{\overline{n}|}}{\ddot{s}_{\overline{n}|} - s_{\overline{n}|}}$ (b) $\dfrac{\ddot{a}_{\overline{n}|}^{(p)} - a_{\overline{n}|}^{(p)}}{\ddot{s}_{\overline{n}|}^{(p)} - s_{\overline{n}|}^{(p)}}$ (c) $m\dfrac{\ddot{a}_{\overline{n}|}^{(m)} - a_{\overline{n}|}^{(m)}}{\ddot{s}_{\overline{n}|} - s_{\overline{n}|}}$.

123. Match each expression in the first column with its equivalent in the second column:

(a) $i\,a_{\overline{n}|}\,s_{\overline{n}|}$ (1) $(1 + i)^n - v^n$

(b) $i\,a_{\overline{n}|}\,(Is)_{\overline{n}|}$ (2) $s_{\overline{n}|} - a_{\overline{n}|}$

(c) $i\,a_{\overline{n}|}\,(is_{\overline{n}|} + 2)$ (3) $\ddot{s}_{\overline{n}|} - a_{\overline{n}|}$

(d) $i\,[(Da)_{\overline{n}|} + (Is)_{\overline{n}|}]$ (4) $(Is)_{\overline{n}|} - (Ia)_{\overline{n}|}$.

124. Show that $(I\ddot{s})_{\overline{n}|} + (D\ddot{a})_{\overline{n-1}|} = \ddot{s}_{\overline{n}|}\,\ddot{a}_{\overline{n}|}$.

125. (a) What is the amount of the final payment of the annuity which has its present value denoted by $a_{\overline{n}|}$, where $n = \bar{n} + t$, $0 < t < 1$, if the time of the final payment is taken as (1) $\bar{n} + t$, (2) $\bar{n}$, (3) $\bar{n} + 1$? In case (1) the final payment is sometimes approximated by t. Comment.

(b) The last payment under the annuity represented by $a^{(4)}_{\overline{n+1/12}|}$ (n a positive integer) is taken as 1/12 at the end of the annuity term. Give an expression for the error in the final payment, and indicate its direction.

126. Verbally interpret: (1) $(Ia)_{\overline{\infty}|} = \ddot{a}_{\overline{\infty}|}\,a_{\overline{\infty}|}$ and (2) $d(Ia)_{\overline{\infty}|} = a_{\overline{\infty}|}$.

127. For n an even positive integer, which of the following are exact?

(1) $a^{(1/2)}_{\overline{n}|} = a_{\overline{n}|}/(1 + \frac{i}{2})$ (2) $a^{(1/2)}_{\overline{n}|}/a^{(1/4)}_{\overline{n}|} = 1 + i + \frac{i^2}{2}$

(3) $\ddot{a}^{(1/2)}_{\overline{n}|} = 2\,a_{\overline{n}|}/a_{\overline{2}|}$.

128. Arrange in increasing order of magnitude:

(a) $s_{\overline{n}|}$, $\ddot{s}_{\overline{n}|}$, $\bar{s}_{\overline{n}|}$ (b) $(I\ddot{s})_{\overline{n}|}$, $(I\bar{s})_{\overline{n}|}$, $(\bar{I}\,\bar{s})_{\overline{n}|}$

(c) $(Ds)_{\overline{n}|}$, $(Is)_{\overline{n}|}$, $(n + 1)s_{\overline{n}|}/2$, $(n + n^2)/2$.

129. True or false?

(a) If d is a simple discount rate equivalent to an effective rate i in an n-period transaction, $d = \frac{i}{n}a_{\overline{n}|i}$.

(b) If $i^{(m)}$ and $d^{(m)}$ are equivalent rates, and if also $i'^{(p)}$ and $d'^{(p)}$ are equivalent, then

$$\frac{m}{d^{(m)}} - \frac{p}{d'^{(p)}} = \frac{m}{i^{(m)}} - \frac{p}{i'^{(p)}}.$$

(c) $d\sum_{t=1}^{n}\ddot{a}_{\overline{t}|}\,\ddot{s}_{\overline{t}|} = (I\ddot{s})_{\overline{n}|} - (D\ddot{a})_{\overline{n}|}$.

(d) The accumulated value of an ordinary annuity paying $s_{\overline{t}|}$ at time t $(t = 1, 2, \cdots, n)$ is $(Ds)_{\overline{n}|}$.

130. Express $a^{(p)}_{\overline{1}|i}$, $\ddot{a}^{(p)}_{\overline{1}|i}$ and $\ddot{a}^{(p)}_{\overline{1}|i} - a^{(p)}_{\overline{1}|i}$ in terms of one or more of i, d, $i^{(p)}$, $d^{(p)}$, p and no other symbols.

131. If tables of $\ddot{a}_{\overline{n}|}$, $\ddot{s}_{\overline{n}|}$ and $\ddot{a}^{(p)}_{\overline{1}|}$ were given rather than tables of $a_{\overline{n}|}$, $s_{\overline{n}|}$ and $s^{(p)}_{\overline{1}|}$, what equivalent-payment formulas for present and accumulated values of ordinary annuities and annuities-due would you use? Begin by defining $\ddot{a}_{\overline{n}|}$ and $\ddot{s}_{\overline{n}|}$ for n nonnegative and not a positive integer.

132. Simplify, preferably using verbal reasoning:

(a) $s_{\overline{n}|}\, s^{-1}_{\overline{2n}|} + s_{\overline{2n}|}\, s^{-1}_{\overline{n}|} - s_{\overline{3n}|}\, s^{-1}_{\overline{2n}|}$

(b) $s_{\overline{3n}|}\, s^{-1}_{\overline{n}|} - i(s_{\overline{n}|} + s_{\overline{2n}|})$

(c) $[(1 + i)^n + 1]\, s^{-1}_{\overline{2n}|}$.

133. Prove or disprove:

(a) $(s^{-1}_{\overline{n}|} - s^{-1}_{\overline{n+m}|})\, a_{\overline{n+m}|} = s^{-1}_{\overline{n}|}\, a_{\overline{m}|}$

(b) For every nonnegative i and m, and for every positive n,

$$0 < {}_{m|}a_{\overline{2n}|}/s_{\overline{n}|} < 2 .$$

134. Prove, both verbally and algebraically:

(a) $(D\ddot{s})_{\overline{n}|} = [n(1 + i)^n - s_{\overline{n}|}]\, \ddot{a}_{\overline{\infty}|}$

(b) $(D\ddot{s})_{\overline{n}|} = (Ds)_{\overline{n+1}|} - s_{\overline{n+1}|}$

(c) $(D\ddot{s})_{\overline{n}|} = (D\ddot{s})_{\overline{t}|}(1 + i)^{n-t} + (n - t)(\ddot{s}_{\overline{n}|} - \ddot{s}_{\overline{n-t}|}) + (D\ddot{s})_{\overline{n-t}|}$.

135. (a) Prove that, for every nonnegative h and k (and also $h - k$, in (ii) and (iv))

(i) $a_{\overline{h+k}|} = a_{\overline{h}|} + v^h a_{\overline{k}|}$

(ii) $a_{\overline{h-k}|} = a_{\overline{h}|} - v^h s_{\overline{k}|}$

(iii) $s_{\overline{h+k}|} = s_{\overline{h}|} + (1 + i)^h s_{\overline{k}|}$

(iv) $s_{\overline{h-k}|} = s_{\overline{h}|} - (1 + i)^h a_{\overline{k}|}$.

(b) With the Appendix tables, how might a result in (a) have been used in Example 3.5 to determine precisely the number of \$50 payments?

136. (a) Show that a perpetuity of 1 at the end of every interest period, with interest at 1% effective for 10 periods and thereafter 3%, is equivalent to a varying perpetuity at 1%.

(b) In (a) for 1%, 3%, 1% read 3%, 1%, 3%.

(c) Extend (a) to the case of 3 rates: 1% for 10 periods, then 3% for 15 periods and thereafter 2%.

137. Which is larger: the present value at rate i of

(a) a level ordinary annuity of n payments of n each, made at the end of every 2 interest periods, or

(b) a simple ordinary annuity of n payments of $a_{\overline{n}|i}$?

138. Define $(I^{(p)}a)^{(2p)}_{\overline{n}|}$ and obtain a formula for it, similar to the result $(I^{(p)}a)^{(p)}_{\overline{n}|} = (\ddot{a}^{(p)}_{\overline{n}|} - nv^n)/i^{(p)}$ in Problem 68.

139. In solution of equations of value for i or n, an important question is whether there is a unique (exact) result. For the basic interest functions, verify each of the following statements:

(a) For fixed $i > 0$

(1) and for all real n, $(1 + i)^n$ continuously increases with n (and v^n decreases), so there is a unique n for every value of $(1 + i)^n > 0$.

(2) $s_{\overline{n}|}$ continuously increases with n $(n \geq 0)$; so there is a unique n for every value of $s_{\overline{n}|} \geq 0$.

(3) $a_{\overline{n}|}$ continuously increases with $n (n \geq 0)$; so there is a unique n for every value of $a_{\overline{n}|}$, where $0 \leq a_{\overline{n}|} < 1/i$.

(b) For fixed $n > 0$

(1) $(1 + i)^n$ continuously increases and v^n continuously decreases as i increases $(i \geq 0)$; so there is a unique i for every value of $(1 + i)^n$, where $(1 + i)^n \geq 1$, and for every value of v^n, where $0 < v^n \leq 1$.

(2) As i increases $(i \geq 0)$,

(i) for $0 < n < 1$: $s_{\overline{n}|}$ continuously decreases, $n \geq s_{\overline{n}|} > 0$,

(ii) for $n = 1$: $s_{\overline{n}|} = 1$ (constant),

(iii) for $n > 1$: $s_{\overline{n}|}$ continuously increases, $s_{\overline{n}|} \geq n$; so in cases (i) and (iii) there is a unique i for every value of $s_{\overline{n}|}$ within the range of $s_{\overline{n}|}$ in the case; but in case (ii) there is no unique i.

(3) $a_{\overline{n}|}$ continuously decreases as i increases $(i \geq 0)$; so there is a unique i for every value of $a_{\overline{n}|}$, where $n \geq a_{\overline{n}|} > 0$.

Thus, if f denotes one of the basic interest functions (those above or $s^{-1}_{\overline{n}|}$ or $a^{-1}_{\overline{n}|}$), the result of, say, inverse interpolation for i or n, based on f = a constant, is an approximation to the <u>unique</u> exact result, except in the cases $s_{\overline{1}|i} = 1$ and $s^{-1}_{\overline{1}|i} = 1$ (which are satisfied by all $i \geq 0$).

140. Prove

(a) $s_{\overline{1/2}|i}\,(1 + i)^{1/2} = 1 - s_{\overline{1/2}|i}$

(b) $s_{\overline{n+1/2}|i} - s_{\overline{n}|i} = (1 - s_{\overline{1/2}|i})(1 + i)^{n-1/2}$, $n \geq 0$.

141. The graphs of $s_{\overline{n}|}$ as a function of i $(0 \leq i < \infty)$ are to be sketched, for various values of n, on a single axis system.

(a) Sketch the graphs of $s_{\overline{1}|i}$ and $s_{\overline{2}|i}$.

(b) Using only the results of (a), Problems 139 and 140, and point-plotting not requiring tables, sketch the graphs of $s_{\overline{n}|}$ for $n = 1/2, 3/2, 5/2$.

142. Consider in turn the variability of $i^{(m)}$, $d^{(m)}$, $s^{(m)}_{\overline{1}|}$ and $\ddot{s}^{(m)}_{\overline{1}|}$, where all rates used are equivalent, by proving that

(a) As a function of m with m positive, and $m > \delta$ in the cases of $d^{(m)}$ and $\ddot{s}_{\overline{1}|}^{(m)}$, and with i positive and fixed, $i^{(m)}$ and $\ddot{s}_{\overline{1}|}^{(m)}$ decrease, $d^{(m)}$ and $s_{\overline{1}|}^{(m)}$ increase; and

(b) As a function of i with $i > 0$ and with m positive and fixed, all four functions increase, except that $s_{\overline{1}|}^{(m)}$ is constant if $m = 1$ and decreases if $m < 1$.

Supplementary List C: More Applications (Problems 143-170)

143. (a) A man aged 35 undertakes to accumulate $50,000 by the end of 20 years. If he can invest funds to earn an annual rate of 6%, $m = 4$, what amount invested at the end of each 6 months during the 20 years will enable him to reach his goal?
(b) If the semiannual payments were invested at the beginning rather than at the end of each half year, how large should they be?

144. Life insurance proceeds of $25,000 were left to a boy aged 16 on condition that they were to be held by the company at interest until he reached age 21 and at that time applied to purchase an annuity-certain of 19 annual payments, the first due at age 21. The payments for ages 21 to 24 are to be one third as large, and for ages 25 to 29 to be two thirds as large, as for ages 30 to 39. The company operates on a 3% basis, but allowed an extra 1% interest (a total of 4%) while the proceeds were at interest. The boy is now age 21. Express his first annuity payment in simplified form.

145. An account, just opened without deposit, will grow by $500 deposits at the end of each year for 20 years and by interest thereon. How many withdrawals of $1,000 can the fund sustain, if such withdrawals, once begun, are to continue annually for the balance of the 20-year period? The fund earns 4% effective a year.

146. A fund grows at an effective quarterly rate of 1%, with $1,000 deposits each July 1 and withdrawals of $510 on October 1 in each year of a deposit. Give a simple expression for the amount in the fund just after the 9th withdrawal.

147. Machinery costing $100,000 would do the work of 4 people each earning $4,000 a year, but would cost about $1,100 to maintain; and interest at 7.5% on the $100,000 would have to be paid each year. Assume that annual net savings can be invested at an effective annual rate of 4%, and that all annual costs are at the end of the year. In approximately how many years would the machine pay for itself?

148. An industrial plant has 18 employees, each at $5,000 a year, to do a certain job. Four employees at the same salary and a machine could do the job. Assuming that the life of the machine is 12 years and that maintenance costs $5,000 per year, give an expression for the price which could be paid for it if a saving of $25,000 per year is desired. The capital invested must earn (.125, 1) per annum. Level annual payments during the life of the machine are to be made into a fund earning (.05, 1)

per annum so as to replace the capital. Assume for convenience that all costs are payable at the end of the year.

149. Find the equivalent annual cost (at the end of the year) of a building which (1) costs $500,000 to build, (2) has salvage value of $50,000 after 50 years when it must be replaced, (3) has annual upkeep, spaced uniformly throughout the year, of $10,000, and (4) has quinquennial maintenance, except in its final year, of $20,000. Interest is at 4% per year.

150. To accumulate $5,000 at the end of 10 years, what equal sums should be invested at the beginning of each quarter at 2% per quarter, if the interest on these sums is paid each quarter and is reinvestable at only 1% per quarter?

151. At the end of each year for 15 years, a lender of $10,000 receives from the borrower repayments of $1,000, which he immediately reinvests at an effective annual rate of 5%. What is the growth in his capital in the 15-year period? To the nearest 1/4%, what effective annual rate of interest (1) has he earned; (2) has the borrower paid?

152. A man borrows $5,000 at an effective annual rate of 5% in order to invest it at a nominal annual rate of (.07, 2). He is to repay his loan by equal payments at the end of each year for 12 years. At the end of the 12 years, what is his accumulated profit?

153. A note for a debt of $2,000, being repaid at 6% effective per year by 20 level quarterly payments, is sold just before the 12th payment. (1) Give an expression for the amount received, if money is then worth (.06, 12) per year. (2) Does the seller make a net gain by this transaction? Explain.

154. During his 4 academic years a college student receives a scholarship of $100 a month except during June, July and August. Show that the value of the scholarship at the date of the first payment, at an effective rate i per month, is

$$100\ \ddot{a}_{\overline{48|}}(1 - s_{\overline{3|}}\ s^{-1}_{\overline{12|}})\ .$$

155. A loan of $20,000 made on January 1, year N, is repayable in 25 years by level semiannual payments on the basis of an annual rate of (.05, 2). On January 1 and July 1 of year (N + 5) payments of $2,000 each were made in addition to the regular payments. Regular payments were made in year (N + 6). Calculate the payment, to begin January 1, year (N + 7), which will keep the term of the loan unaltered.

156. A fund of $10,000 is invested at a force of interest of 4% per annum. Out of the fund an annuity is to be paid continuously at the annual rate of $100(1 + e^{.08t})$ t years from now ($t \geq 0$). Find (a) the number of years until the fund is exhausted and (b) the maximum size of the fund.

157. (a) From fund A, which initially contains exactly the sum needed to make continuous level payments at annual rate 1 for n years, those payments are withdrawn and put into fund B. If both funds earn effective annual rate i, after how many years t are they equal?

(b) Fund C grows for n years by continuous level payments at annual rate 1, but thereafter continuous level withdrawals at annual rate 1 are made. At effective annual rate i, at what time t (where $n + t \geq n$) is the fund (1) a maximum, (2) zero?

158. A man has just retired after working exactly 36 years for one employer. He started at a $3,600 annual salary and each year had an increase of 3.5% of his salary of the previous year.

(a) At what annual salary did he retire?

(b) What were his total career earnings?

(c) He is to receive each year a pension of 50% of his average salary of the last 5 years. What is the amount of this annual pension, and what percentage is it of his career average salary?

159. A deposits $10,000 in a savings fund to accumulate for 20 years with compound interest at the rate of i per year. B invests $10,000 in property which yields a net annual rental at the end of each year of j times the value of the property at the beginning of the year, and deposits the rent received each year in a savings fund to accumulate with compound interest at the rate of i per year. The value of the property in which B invests increases annually over the 20-year period at the rate of 5% over each 4-year period. B sells the property at the end of 20 years for its value at that time. What value of j will produce equal accumulations for A and B over the 20-year period?

160. The potential purchaser of an ordinary perpetuity of $100 per annum will have expenses of 22 1/2 % of the first payment, 21 1/4% of the second, 20% of the third, etc., until a uniform rate of 7 1/2% is reached. To realize 5% after expenses on the transaction, what price should he offer for the perpetuity?

161. An article costing $275 is bought for a down payment of $50 plus 6 semiannual payments of $50. What effective annual rate (to the nearest 0.1%) is money worth to the merchant?

162. (a) A property producing a level annual income forever is left in equal shares to institutions A, B, C and D, with each of A, B and C in succession to have the whole income for a time before final reversion to D. Determine to the nearest year the length of time A, B and C should have the income. Interest is at 4% effective per year.

(b) Show how you would determine partial payments to each institution to keep the shares strictly equal.

163. A began 6 years ago when his son B was 8 years old to make equal deposits at the end of each month to provide $2,500 at the beginning of each year for 4 years, starting when B enters college at age 18. Deposits are to be continued until the beginning of B's 4th college year and accumulated at a nominal annual rate of 5% compounded semiannually. A has been unable to make any deposits during the last 2 years, but he now plans to resume the original monthly deposits at the end of each month and to make additional level deposits at the end of each year sufficient to make up the deficiency in past deposits. Develop an expression for determining the amount of the additional annual payments.

164. An advance of $10,000 is being repaid by an ordinary annuity for 30 years, on the basis of an annual rate of 5%

effective. Immediately after the 10th payment, the creditor and debtor agree to reduce the effective interest rate thereafter to 3 1/2%, provided each future annuity payment is increased an equal amount over its immediate predecessor so as to liquidate the loan in 10 years. Under the new arrangement, what is the decrease in the total amount of interest paid?

165. A has just reached his 21st birthday and wishes to make the first of 20 equal quarterly withdrawals from a savings account which was intended to provide him with $150 a quarter for the next 5 years. The savings account was opened on his 11th birthday with the first of what were to be 40 equal quarterly deposits on the assumption that the bank would continue its then interest rate of 1% per quarter. On his 16th birthday the bank changed its interest rate to 1 1/4% per quarter, and subsequent deposits were changed to provide $150 a quarter on the assumption that the new interest rate would continue. The bank has just changed to "continuous interest" at $\delta = 1\ 1/4\%$ per quarter, and it is assumed that this rate will continue. Find the amounts of the deposits and the withdrawals. Given $e^{-1/4} = .778801$.

166. (a) A fund at 5% per year is established by payments of $1,000, $900, $800, ··· , $100 at the beginnings of successive years 1, 2, 3, ···, 10. There are withdrawals of $300 at the ends of years 1, 2, 3, ··· as long as possible. At the end of how many years will the final regular withdrawal occur, and (to the nearest dollar) what final payment 1 year later will exhaust the fund?

(b) Same as (a), except that the withdrawals are $100, $200, $300, ··· .

167. Successive annual payments of 20, 19, 18, ··· are made each May 1, starting May 1, 1975 into a trust fund earning (.03, 1) per year. No payment is made in 1995. Beginning in 1996, annual withdrawals are made each May 1 of 1, 2, 3,···. When the year arrives in which it is impossible to withdraw the scheduled amount, the trust terminates on May 1 with the withdrawal of the balance. Find the termination date and, to the nearest dollar, the amount of the last withdrawal.

168. An old machine costs $350 per year to operate and the cost of repairs is $75 per year. It has a probable life of 10 years and a scrap value then of $400. It turns out 300 units of production a year.

A new machine which would replace it produces 400 units per year, costs $3,000 new and has a probable life of 20 years and no scrap value. It requires annual expenditures of $350 for operation and $50 for repairs.

Assuming interest at 5% effective per year, find the value of the old machine assuming the same unit cost of production for both machines. Assume the work done by each machine, operating costs and costs of repair occur continuously.

169. At the end of each period for kn periods (k and n positive integers), a unit is deposited in a savings account at rate i per period. After every n periods, the investor's entire accumulation to date is reinvested in bills paying rate r per period, and the returns from the bills are invested each period in the savings account, until the next bill purchase date. Show that the final fund might also be obtained at the single rate $j = (1 + r\, s_{\overline{n}|i})^{1/n} - 1$, by accumulating equal sums, j/r, paid

at the end of every one of the kn periods, with no reinvestments.

170. A life insurance company issues a policy with a level annual premium of \$100. The company guarantees 3% interest, compounded annually, on the fund built up from 87.5% of the premiums received. The company, however, credits an additional .36% above the guaranteed rate, with all accretions from this source kept separate and accumulated at 3 1/2% compounded annually. Prove that at the end of n years the total fund will exceed the guaranteed fund by $65.205\, s_{\overline{n}|.035} - 64.890\, s_{\overline{n}|.03}$.

CHAPTER 4

AMORTIZATION AND SINKING FUNDS

4.1. Introduction. In the preceding chapter we concentrated on two problems, namely, obtaining (1) the present value and (2) the accumulated value of any annuity. The first -- how to determine the present value of any annuity -- is the problem of finding the amount which if invested at present would, under the given rate of interest, be exactly sufficient to provide the annuity payments as they fall due. Having determined the present value of an annuity, one could verify that it would, if invested, be sufficient to produce the given payments. In fact, one can exhibit each annuity payment as consisting of two portions, one of which is interest on the remaining invested capital and the other a reduction in the invested capital. This verification is interesting but not particularly necessary if the sole purpose is the determination of the present value of the annuity.

In many cases in practice one starts with a given present value and determines an annuity equivalent to it. An important example is that of a mortgage loan repayable by equal monthly payments over a term of years, the payments to include both interest and repayment of principal. A first problem is the determination of the monthly payment. A second concern of both the lender and the borrower is the division of each payment into interest and principal portions. The lender requires this information, as the interest received is income to him and is taxable as such. For the borrower, the interest paid may be considered as a deductible allowance from his taxable income. Furthermore, knowledge of the amount of outstanding principal at every payment date is useful if (as is often the case) the borrower has the right at every payment date to hasten repayment of the loan either by paying the full outstanding principal or the difference between it and any future scheduled outstanding principal. In all these cases a complete analysis of the annuity is required which will show the outstanding principal at every stage, and the interest and principal components of each payment.

Such repayment of a loan by means of an annuity is called

amortization of the loan. More explicitly, by amortization of a loan we shall mean: (a) the loan is repaid by an annuity, generally by equal payments, except possibly the final one; and (b) each annuity payment is first applied to pay interest on the outstanding principal, and the balance of the payment is applied to reduce the outstanding principal. This requirement (b) provides a process for tracing the progress of the loan -- from initial principal, through all succeeding amounts of outstanding principal, to final extinction.

The second main problem of Chapter 3 was how to determine the accumulated value of any given annuity, that is, to find the amount to which the annuity payments would accumulate by the end of their term, under a given interest rate. Analysis of the growth of the fund was not our object. However, if one has need for a specific amount in the future -- for example, to purchase some costly item, to provide for replacement of equipment, or to repay the principal of a loan on which interest alone is paid the creditor currently -- the purchaser or borrower may wish (or be required) to accumulate this sum by regular deposits, usually level in amount and usually made at equal intervals. A fund so developed is called a sinking fund. After the periodic deposits to the sinking fund are determined, it may be useful to show by a schedule the growth of the fund period by period, due to interest earnings as well as the regular deposits. The study of sinking funds, in particular for debt repayment, is the second main topic of this chapter. Finally, the amortization and sinking-fund methods of repaying loans will be compared.

In dealing with the theory we shall make the important simplifying assumption that the interest period coincides with the payment period. If initially this were not the case, one could always find the effective rate of interest per payment period that would be equivalent to the given rate of interest and then proceed to work with this effective rate. Since now there will be no need to distinguish between interest and payment periods, we shall simply write "period," without modifier.

The notation we shall use for the discrete amortization case will be as follows:

i = the effective rate of interest per period

n = the number of periods in the annuity term

R_h = the annuity payment made at the end of period h

A_h = the outstanding principal at the end of period h,

after the payment R_h has been made. In other words, A_h is the interest-bearing principal for the period $(h + 1)$. Then A_0 represents the original principal A, and it is assumed that A_n is zero.

The sinking-fund case, together with its notation, will be presented in Section 4.7.

4.2. Amortization by an ordinary level annuity. Since amortization of this type is by far the most important case in practice, it will be treated first and separately, even though its theory could be obtained by specializing the general amortization theory. To fix ideas, we give the line diagram which indicates that a loan of A is to be repaid by payments of R at the end of each period for n periods.

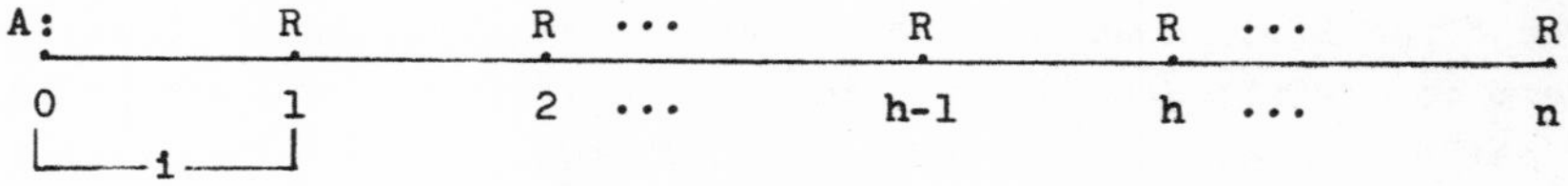

Fig. 4.1

Since the principal outstanding at the beginning of period h is A_{h-1}, the interest component of the payment R made at the end of the period is iA_{h-1} and the balance of the payment reduces the principal from A_{h-1} to A_h. Hence, as basic equation, we have

$$R = iA_{h-1} + A_{h-1} - A_h, \quad h = 1, 2, \cdots, n. \tag{4.1}$$

This may be rearranged as

$$-A_h + (1 + i)A_{h-1} = R$$

which, on multiplication by v^h, becomes

$$-(v^h A_h - v^{h-1} A_{h-1}) = -\Delta(v^{h-1} A_{h-1}) = Rv^h. \tag{4.2}$$

If we sum both sides of this equation over the range $h = 1$ to $h = n$, and take into account that $A_0 = A$ and $A_n = 0$, we obtain

$$A = R\, a_{\overline{n}|i} \tag{4.3}$$

or

$$R = A/a_{\overline{n}|i} \tag{4.4}$$

which determines the annuity payment.

One might have obtained formula (4.3) directly by arguing that, since the only payments made on the loan are those of the annuity, the annuity must be equivalent to the original principal, and hence, by use of the present as comparison date, the present value of the annuity must equal A. However, our starting formula (4.1) has the advantage of expressing explicitly condition (b) of the definition of amortization, and it has confirmed formula (4.3). Then too, it leads quickly, as we shall now see, to formulas for the outstanding principal A_h.

If in formula (4.2) we change h to g, and sum over the range g = 1 to g = h, we obtain

$$-v^h A_h + A = R\, a_{\overline{h}|\, i}$$

or

$$A_h = A(1 + i)^h - R\, s_{\overline{h}|\, i}. \tag{4.5}$$

Similarly, by summing over the range g = h + 1 to g = n, we have

$$v^h A_h = R \sum_{g=h+1}^{n} v^g = R\, v^h\, a_{\overline{n-h}|\, i}$$

or

$$A_h = R\, a_{\overline{n-h}|\, i}. \tag{4.6}$$

Formula (4.5) is called the <u>retrospective formula</u> for A_h. It indicates that the outstanding principal at the end of period h is the difference in the values at that time of the original principal and the annuity of past payments. On the other hand, formula (4.6) expresses the outstanding principal at the end of period h as the present value of the remaining payments and, as such, is called the <u>prospective formula</u> for A_h.

That A_h is the same whether obtained retrospectively or prospectively may be mathematically clear, but there is merit in the following verbal demonstration of equality, in which all values are understood to be determined according to the original interest assumption or set of assumptions and the time unit is chosen equal to the interest period:

Original principal = Present value of payments

{Value at time h of the original principal} = {Value at time h of all the payments}

= {Value at time h of past payments} plus {Value at time h of future payments}.

Therefore,

{Value at time h of the original principal} less {Value at time h of past payments} = {Value at time h of future payments},

that is,

Retrospective formula for A_h = Prospective formula for A_h.

The demonstration is general and applies in every amortization situation, not merely in the special case treated in this section.

It is important to understand that the equivalence of retrospective and prospective expressions for outstanding principal presupposes a single interest rate assumption or predetermined set of rates, such as 4% for the first 10 years and 3% thereafter. To make a subsequent change of assumption destroys the equivalence, as the reader may see by carefully retracing the preceding arguments and comparing the results. By reference to Example 3.2, the point can be made numerically. There, B is to receive the value of the future payments at the new rate of (.05, 1) instead of the originally assumed rate, (.06, 12). That value is $4,494.17 according to the 5% prospective valuation given in the solution. The corresponding 5% value obtained retrospectively is

$$10{,}000(1.05)^{10} - 2(512.69)\ s^{(2)}_{\overline{1}|.05}\ s_{\overline{10}|.05} = \$3{,}232.58,$$

which is quite a different amount and hardly a value for which B should settle. However, the illustrative prospective value at (.06, 12), namely, $4,364.94 in the solution, could, to the nearest dollar (but not as easily), be obtained retrospectively from

$$10{,}000(1.005)^{120} - \frac{512.69}{s_{\overline{6}|.005}}\ s_{\overline{120}|.005}.$$

Let us now analyze the hth payment under amortization by an ordinary level annuity. The interest component in the hth payment is $i\ A_{h-1}$ and, from formulas (4.6) and (3.2), we have

$$i\ A_{h-1} = i\ R\, a_{\overline{n-h+1}|} = R(1 - v^{n-h+1}). \tag{4.7}$$

Then, the principal component of the hth payment is $R - i\ A_{h-1}$ $= R - R(1 - v^{n-h+1})$ or

$$R\ v^{n-h+1}. \tag{4.8}$$

This expression (4.8) could also be obtained by taking the principal component as $A_{h-1} - A_h$ and applying formulas (4.6) and (3.1).

On the basis of these results we can readily exhibit an amortization schedule showing how repayment of the loan progresses and giving the interest and principal components of each payment. See Table 4.1.

TABLE 4.1

Amortization Schedule

For a loan of an initial principal $A = R\, a_{\overline{n}|}$ to be amortized by payments of R at the end of each period for n periods. Interest at the effective rate i per period.

(1) Period	(2) Interest for period h	(3) Payment on principal at end of period h	(4) Outstanding principal after the payment at end of period h
h	$i\, A_{h-1}$	R - (2)	$A_h = A_{h-1}$ - (3)
0			$R\, a_{\overline{n}|}$
1	$R(1 - v^n)$	$R\, v^n$	$R\, a_{\overline{n-1}|}$
2	$R(1 - v^{n-1})$	$R\, v^{n-1}$	$R\, a_{\overline{n-2}|}$
⋮	⋮	⋮	⋮
h	$R(1 - v^{n-h+1})$	$R\, v^{n-h+1}$	$R\, a_{\overline{n-h}|}$
⋮	⋮	⋮	⋮
n - 1	$R(1 - v^2)$	$R\, v^2$	$R\, a_{\overline{1}|}$
n	$R(1 - v)$	$R\, v$	0
Totals	$nR - R\, a_{\overline{n}|}$ $= nR - A$	$R\, a_{\overline{n}|} = A$	$R(n - a_{\overline{n}|})/i$ $= (nR - A)/i$

From the preceding formulas and Table 4.1, some additional observations have become apparent:

(a) The repayments of principal are in geometric progression with common ratio $1 + i$. At each stage, the principal component increases by interest on the principal portion of the previous payment.

(b) The total interest paid is $nR - A$, that is, the total of the payments less the original principal.

(c) The total of the payments on principal is equal, of course, to the original principal A.

(d) The total interest paid is i times the sum of the outstanding principal column. This follows because at each step the interest is calculated on outstanding principal.

(e) In any numerical problem, checks on accuracy are available through column totals and also through the final schedule value, A_n, which should be 0.

(f) Any line or set of lines of the schedule can be calculated independently of the rest of the schedule.

For illustration, suppose that a loan of \$1,000.00 is to be amortized over 5 years by equal annual payments including interest at the effective annual rate of 6%. The annual payment R is given by $1,000/a_{\overline{5}|.06}$ = \$237.40. See Table 4.2. Rounding

TABLE 4.2

Amortization Schedule

For a loan of \$1,000 to be amortized by payments of \$237.40 at the end of each year for 5 years. Interest at 6% compounded annually.

(1) Year h	(2) Interest for year h $i\,A_{h-1}$	(3) Payment on principal at end of year h 237.40 - (2)	(4) Outstanding principal after the payment at end of year h $A_h = A_{h-1} - (3)$
0	\$	\$	\$1,000.00
1	60.00	177.40	822.60
2	49.36	188.04	634.56
3	38.07	199.33	435.23
4	26.11	211.29	223.94
5	13.44	223.96	- 0.02
Totals	\$186.98	\$1,000.02	\$3,116.31

errors have accumulated to \$.02 in the fifth line because the calculations have been carried to only two decimals. In practice, the final payment would be adjusted to \$237.38. In longer schedules, adjustments might be made at intervals. The totals are useful in checking the accuracy of the table. The reader should check that the numerical totals approximate their theoretical counterparts in Table 4.1.

In a practical situation an amortization schedule may involve considerable computation. For example, if the loan is to be amortized by monthly payments over 25 years, the schedule will contain 301 lines. The computation can be organized in several ways. One might proceed line by line in succession, using the relations indicated in the column headings of the general schedule. If this is done, it would be advisable to calculate in advance check values at periodic intervals (e.g., every 5 or 10 lines) by means of the expressions in the columns of the general schedule (Table 4.1). Alternatively, any one of the columns (2), (3) or (4) could be calculated by itself and the remaining columns obtained by their relations to it. A good discussion of the possibilities is given by D.W.A. Donald in Sec. 5.8-5.11 of his book Compound Interest and Annuities-Certain (Cambridge University Press, 1953, reprinted in 1956 and 1963). Of course, the calculation of amortization schedules can be carried through readily by high-speed electronic computers.

Amortization by a perpetuity is a contradiction in terms, but it is a limiting case. The reader can satisfy himself that in this case $A_h = A$ for $h = 0, 1, 2, \cdots$ and $R = Ai$ = the interest component of each payment, so that the principal component of each payment is zero. That is to say, interest alone is paid and the outstanding principal after every payment is exactly the original principal.

4.3. Amortization by an ordinary varying annuity. We consider here a loan of A to be repaid by an annuity with varying payments $R_1, R_2, \cdots, R_n$, as indicated in the line diagram below.

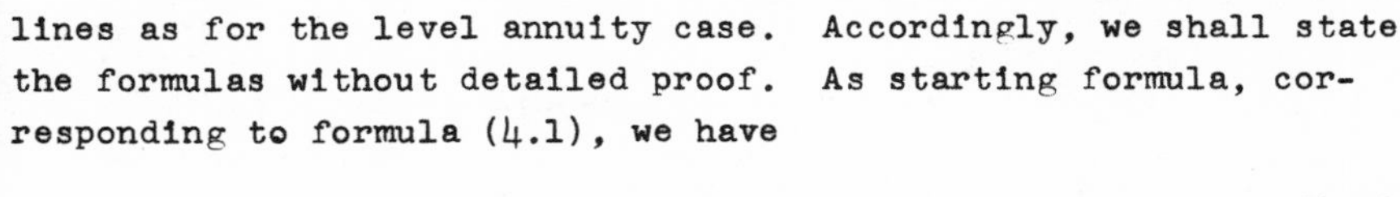

Fig. 4.2

Formulas for this case can be developed on exactly the same lines as for the level annuity case. Accordingly, we shall state the formulas without detailed proof. As starting formula, corresponding to formula (4.1), we have

$$R_h = i\,A_{h-1} + A_{h-1} - A_h, \qquad h = 1, 2, \cdots, n. \tag{4.9}$$

This leads to

$$-\Delta(v^{h-1} A_{h-1}) = R_h\, v^h \tag{4.10}$$

and

$$A = \sum_{h=1}^{n} R_h\, v^h \tag{4.11}$$

$$A_h = A(1 + i)^h - \sum_{g=1}^{h} R_g(1 + i)^{h-g} \tag{4.12}$$

$$A_h = \sum_{g=h+1}^{n} R_g\, v^{g-h}\,. \tag{4.13}$$

Formula (4.11) shows that the payments are equivalent to A, and formulas (4.12) and (4.13) are retrospective and prospective formulas for the outstanding principal.

An interesting feature here is that the outstanding principal will increase over any period for which the annuity payment is smaller than the interest on the outstanding principal at the beginning of the period. This may be seen by rearranging equation (4.9) to the form

$$A_h = A_{h-1} + (i\,A_{h-1} - R_h)$$

which indicates that if R_h is less than $i\,A_{h-1}$, the deficiency is added to the outstanding principal, in other words, is capitalized. This situation may arise, for instance, in the early periods if the loan is repaid by an annuity of increasing payments. It cannot happen if payments are level since, in that case, the outstanding principal decreases at the end of period h by the positive amount given by formula (4.8).

Let us consider the case of a cash offer for two annual $100 payments followed by three annual $1,100 payments. An investor desiring 5% on his money could spend

$$A = 1{,}100\ a_{\overline{5}|.05} - 1{,}000\ a_{\overline{2}|.05} = \$2{,}903.01$$

for the promise of the annuity payments. Of course, his principal outstanding would increase during the first two years, for the $100 payments are inadequate to meet his interest requirements. The amortization schedule in Table 4.3 tells the full story.

TABLE 4.3

Amortization Schedule

For a loan of $2,903.01 to be repaid by successive payments of $100, $100, $1,100, $1,100, $1,100 at the ends of each of 5 consecutive years. Interest at 5% compounded annually.

(1) Year h	(2) Interest for year h	(3) Payment on principal at end of year h	(4) Outstanding principal after the payment at end of year h
0	$	$	$2,903.01
1	145.15	-45.15	2,948.16
2	147.41	-47.41	2,995.57
3	149.78	950.22	2,045.35
4	102.27	997.73	1,047.62
5	52.38	1,047.62	0.00
Totals	$596.99	$2,903.01	$11,939.71

Example 4.2 illustrates a useful form of amortization by a varying annuity.

4.4. Amortization by level payments and a final smaller payment.

It may happen that the loan of A is to be repaid by fixed level payments of R, made at the end of each period for as long as necessary, and a final smaller payment fR, $0 < f < 1$, made one period after the last full payment. As this is a special case of repayment by a varying annuity, the formulas of the preceding section can be adapted for it. The number of full payments R is evidently the largest integer $\bar{n}$ satisfying the relation

$$A > R\, a_{\overline{\bar{n}}|i} \,. \tag{4.14}$$

The line diagram for the transaction is then

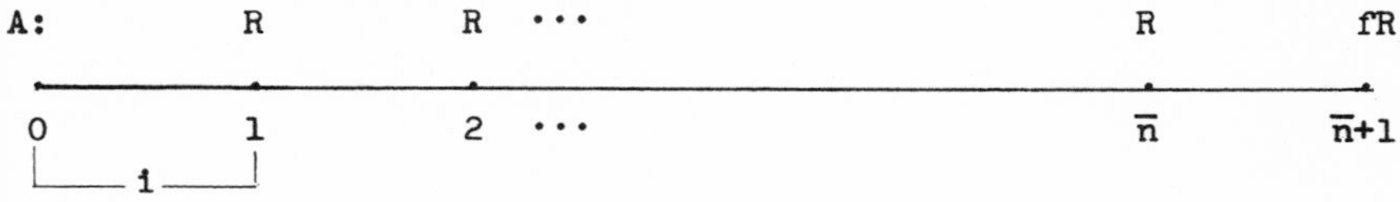

Fig. 4.3

To determine the final fractional payment fR, we may first calculate the outstanding principal $A_{\bar{n}}$ by use of the retrospective formula (4.12), which gives in this case

$$A_{\bar{n}} = A(1 + i)^{\bar{n}} - R\, s_{\overline{\bar{n}}|i} \,. \tag{4.15}$$

Since the final payment must repay $A_{\bar{n}}$ with interest, we have

$$fR = A_{\bar{n}}(1 + i) = A(1 + i)^{\bar{n}+1} - R\, \ddot{s}_{\overline{\bar{n}}|i} \,. \tag{4.16}$$

The right member of equation (4.16) might also be obtained by setting the retrospective formula for $A_{\bar{n}+1}$ equal to zero, and then solving for fR.

An interesting alternative procedure for determining fR is obtained by applying equation (4.11). This yields

$$A = R\, a_{\overline{\bar{n}}|i} + fR\, v^{\bar{n}+1}$$

$$= R\left[a_{\overline{\bar{n}}|i} + f(a_{\overline{\bar{n}+1}|i} - a_{\overline{\bar{n}}|i})\right]$$

or

$$f = \frac{(A/R) - a_{\overline{\bar{n}}|i}}{a_{\overline{\bar{n}+1}|i} - a_{\overline{\bar{n}}|i}} \,. \tag{4.17}$$

This is precisely the relation one would obtain for f if one linearly interpolated between the points $(\bar{n}, a_{\overline{\bar{n}}|})$ and $(\bar{n} + 1, a_{\overline{\bar{n}+1}|})$ to find the value of $\bar{n} + f$ that would make $a_{\overline{\bar{n}+f}|}$ equal to A/R. The value of f so obtained is not an exact solution for the equation $a_{\overline{\bar{n}+f}|} = A/R$* but it is an exact solution for our problem of determining the final payment fR. Accordingly, the calculation may be carried out to the full degree of accuracy of the tabulated values of $a_{\overline{n}|i}$.

For instance, if a loan of \$1,000 is to be amortized at 6% by annual payments of \$250 for as long as necessary and a final smaller payment one year later, then we find from

$$1{,}000 > 250 \quad a_{\overline{n}|.06}$$

that $\bar{n} = 4$ regular payments of \$250 are necessary. The direct method for obtaining the final payment fR produces

$$fR = 1{,}000(1.06)^5 - 250(s_{\overline{5}|.06} - 1) = \$178.95.$$

Alternatively, by the interpolation method

$$f = \frac{4 - a_{\overline{4}|.06}}{a_{\overline{5}|.06} - a_{\overline{4}|.06}} = 0.715809$$

and $fR = \$178.95$ again. The reader may wish to supply the amortization schedule.

4.5. Amortization by a continuous annuity. In essence, the case of a loan being amortized by a continuous annuity has been treated already when we considered the present value of such an annuity (Section 3.8). All that is necessary is to change the point of view and reinterpret some of the notation. Let us suppose then that a loan of A is to be amortized by an annuity payable continuously for n time units. As before, the rate of payment per time unit at time t is denoted by $r(t)$, and the force of interest and the equivalent effective rate for the time unit by δ and i, respectively. However, now $A(t)$ will be used to represent the outstanding principal at time t. It follows that $A(0) = A$ and $A(n) = 0$.

At time t, the rate of payment of interest is $\delta A(t)$ and the total rate of payment is $r(t)$. The excess, $r(t) - \delta A(t)$, represents the rate of decrease of the outstanding principal, hence

*Because $a_{\overline{t}|}$ is not a linear function of t.

$$-\frac{d\,A(t)}{dt} = r(t) - \delta\,A(t). \qquad (4.18)$$

This is precisely the same as formula (3.59). It is therefore clear that the present value at time t of future annuity payments, the $A(t)$ of (3.59), is identical with the outstanding principal at time t. It should be noted how formula (4.18) expresses the amortization principle, namely, that payments are first applied toward interest and the balance toward repayment of principal.

Following the method of the present value discussion in Section 3.8 we obtain the various amortization equations, namely

$$-d\,A(t) + \delta\,A(t)dt = r(t)\,dt$$

$$-d\left[v^t\,A(t)\right] = v^t\,r(t)\,dt \qquad (4.19)$$

$$A = \int_0^n v^t\,r(t)\,dt \qquad (4.20)$$

$$A(t) = A(1+i)^t - \int_0^t (1+i)^{t-s}\,r(s)\,ds \qquad (4.21)$$

$$A(t) = \int_t^n v^{s-t}\,r(s)\,ds, \qquad (4.22)$$

formulas (4.20)-(4.22) being obtained by integrating equation (4.19) over the ranges indicated. The reader will recognize that formulas (4.21) and (4.22) are the retrospective and prospective expressions, respectively, for the outstanding principal at time t. As in the case of discrete varying annuities, the outstanding principal may increase for a time, namely, whenever $r(t) - \delta A(t) < 0$.

In the particular case where a loan A is to be amortized over n time units by payments at the constant rate r per time unit, we have the relations

$$A = r\,\bar{a}_{\overline{n}|\,i} \qquad (4.23)$$

$$A(t) = A(1+i)^t - r\,\bar{s}_{\overline{t}|\,i} \qquad (4.24)$$

$$A(t) = r\,\bar{a}_{\overline{n-t}|\,i}. \qquad (4.25)$$

<u>4.6. Amortization at a rate of interest i' in excess of the lender's rate i.</u> There are instances where, in addition to the regular interest payments, extra charges are made on outstanding principal for some special purpose such as insurance on the life

of the debtor, insurance against default of payments, or the payment of commission to agents. If the loan is amortized at the lender's yield rate, and the extra charges are a fixed percent of the amounts of outstanding principal according to such amortization, no additional amortization relations are involved. A well-known example is Federal Housing Administration mortgage loans which might be amortized on the basis of a nominal annual rate of 5%, compounded monthly, with an additional 1/2% charge against outstanding principal for loan insurance. The extra charges decrease from year to year and so also does the total monthly payment by the same amount.

However, if the loan is amortized at a rate i' in excess of the lender's yield rate i, so that excess interest payments of $(i' - i)$ times the amounts of outstanding principal are available for the special purpose in question, the borrower's total periodic payment remains fixed. Further, as we shall see, some interesting relations can be developed for this case. Before discussing these, we present in Table 4.4 a simple numerical illustration of a \$1,000 loan amortized over 5 years by annual payments including interest at the effective annual rate of 5%, of which 1% is used for, say, loan insurance, and the remainder represents the lender's yield rate.

TABLE 4.4

Amortization Schedule

For a loan of \$1,000 to be amortized by payments of $R = 1{,}000/a_{\overline{5}|.05}$ = \$230.9748 at the end of each year for 5 years. Lender's yield rate 4%. Excess interest at rate of 1% used for loan insurance.

(1) Year	(2) Interest for year h	(3) Excess interest for year h	(4) Net payment to lender for year h	(5) Interest portion of net payment to lender (2) - (3)	(6) Payment on principal at end of year h	(7) Outstanding principal at end of year h
h	$.05\ A_{h-1}$	$.01\ A_{h-1}$	R - (3)	$= .04\ A_{h-1}$	R-(2)=(4)-(5)	$A_h = A_{h-1}$-(6)
0	\$	\$	\$	\$	\$	\$1,000.0000
1	50.0000	10.0000	220.9748	40.0000	180.9748	819.0252
2	40.9513	8.1903	222.7845	32.7610	190.0235	629.0017
3	31.4501	6.2900	224.6848	25.1601	199.5247	429.4770
4	21.4738	4.2948	226.6800	17.1790	209.5010	219.9760
5	10.9988	2.1998	228.7750	8.7990	219.9760	0.0000
Totals	\$154.8740	\$30.9749	\$1,123.8991	\$123.8991	\$1,000.0000	\$3,097.4799

Columns (2), (6) and (7) form a regular 5% amortization schedule for the loan, while columns (3) and (4) show the distribution of the yearly payments into excess interest and net payment to the lender. Columns (5) and (6) distribute the net payments to the lender into interest and principal portions. The borrower makes a fixed annual payment of $230.9748; the lender receives increasing net payments, as shown in column (4).

Returning to the general case, we attach primes to functions based on the amortization interest rate i' and assume that unprimed functions are based on the lender's interest rate i. For a loan of A amortized over n periods, the total periodic payment will be

$$R = A/ a'_{\overline{n|}}.$$

The principal outstanding at the end of h periods is

$$A'_h = R\, a'_{\overline{n-h|}}$$

and the excess interest in the payment $(h + 1)$ is

$$(i' - i)A'_h = (i' - i)R\, a'_{\overline{n-h|}}. \tag{4.26}$$

Then the net payment to the lender at the end of the period $(h + 1)$ is

$$R - (i' - i)R\, a'_{\overline{n-h|}} = Rv'^{\,n-h} + i\, A'_h , \tag{4.27}$$

where the first term in the right member represents the payment on principal and the second term is the lender's interest. From the left member it is clear that these net payments form an increasing series.

There are some interesting expressions for determining, as of the end of the hth period, the present value at rate i of the remaining excess interest payments. Denoting this quantity by E_h we have

$$E_h = R(i' - i)\left[a'_{\overline{n-h|}}\, v + a'_{\overline{n-h-1|}}\, v^2 + \cdots + a'_{\overline{1|}}\, v^{n-h}\right]$$

$$= R(i'-i)\left[(v'+ v'^2+\cdots+v'^{\,n-h})v+(v'+v'^2+\cdots+v'^{\,n-h-1})v^2+\cdots+ v'v^{n-h}\right]$$

which, by collecting terms with v', v'^2, etc., we may rearrange to

$$E_h = R(i' - i)\left[a_{\overline{n-h|}}\, v' + a_{\overline{n-h-1|}}\, v'^2 + \cdots + a_{\overline{1|}}\, v'^{\,n-h}\right].$$

This last expression is of the same form as the first but with the primes interchanged within the brackets [cf. Example 3.8(b)]. To simplify it, we perform the multiplication by $i' - i$, and when we multiply by i' we use the first expression for E_h but when we multiply by i, we use the last. The result is

$$E_h = R\,[(1 - v'^{\,n-h})v + (1 - v'^{\,n-h-1})v^2 + \cdots + (1 - v')v^{n-h}$$
$$- (1 - v^{n-h})v' - (1 - v^{n-h-1})v'^2 - \cdots - (1 - v)v'^{\,n-h}]$$

which simplifies to

$$E_h = R\,[a_{\overline{n-h}|} - a'_{\overline{n-h}|}] = R\,a_{\overline{n-h}|} - A'_h\,. \qquad (4.28)$$

Thus, the present value at rate i of the remaining excess interest payments is the excess of (a) the value at rate i of the remaining periodic payments over (b) the outstanding principal, a result that might have been foreseen.

As of the end of the period h, the present value at rate i of the remaining net payments to the lender should equal the outstanding principal A'_h. To show this, we use the left member of equation (4.27), and find that the present value in question equals

$$R\,a_{\overline{n-h}|} - E_h$$

which by formula (4.28) reduces immediately to A'_h, as previously stated.

4.7. Sinking-fund method of discharging a loan. There are many ways that a loan can be repaid with interest. The amortization (or installment) method we have been discussing has the advantage that, as it is usually applied, the periodic payments are equal. For some lenders it would have the disadvantage that a varying portion of principal is repaid with each payment and would require reinvestment. The lender might prefer to receive his principal in a lump sum at the end of the loan term, and to obtain periodic interest on his whole principal throughout the term. The borrower would then have to make uniform interest payments at the end of each period within the term and to repay the principal at the end of the term. To meet this latter obligation he might decide, or be required by the terms of the loan, to make periodic deposits into a sinking or savings fund which would accumulate by the end of the term to the original principal.

We consider the case of a loan of A which is to be repaid in a single sum at the end of n periods and is to have interest on the whole principal paid at the end of each period at the rate i per period. In addition, deposits are to be made into a sinking fund with interest at the rate j per period, the deposit at the end of period h being denoted by F_h. Then, at the end of the period h, the borrower is required to provide a total payment of

$$Ai + F_h. \tag{4.29}$$

Also, since the sinking fund must accumulate to A at the end of the term, it follows that

$$\sum_{h=1}^{n} F_h(1 + j)^{n-h} = A. \tag{4.30}$$

The accumulated value of the sinking fund at the end of period h just after the sinking-fund deposit is

$$\sum_{g=1}^{h} F_g\ (1 + j)^{h-g}. \tag{4.31}$$

The borrower who, at the end of the hth period, has the amount (4.31) to offset his loan liability A may regard the difference

$$A - \sum_{g=1}^{h} F_g\ (1 + j)^{h-g} \tag{4.32}$$

as the <u>book value</u> of his debt at that time.

These expressions simplify in the case that the sinking-fund deposits are of uniform amount F. In this circumstance, it follows from equation (4.30) that

$$F = A/s_{\overline{n|}\,j} \tag{4.33}$$

and, from expression (4.29), the total payment per period is now the uniform amount

$$Ai + A/s_{\overline{n|}\,j}. \tag{4.34}$$

The accumulated value of the sinking fund at the end of period h is given by

$$Fs_{\overline{h|}\,j} = As_{\overline{h|}\,j}/s_{\overline{n|}\,j} \tag{4.35}$$

and the book value at that time by

$$A(1 - s_{\overline{h|}\,j}/s_{\overline{n|}\,j}). \tag{4.36}$$

A schedule can be constructed to show the progress of the growth in the sinking fund, as indicated in Table 4.5, page 176.

Of course, just as various amortization practices exist (Sections 4.2-4.6), there are variations in the way in which a sinking fund can be developed. To mention a few, the sinking-fund payments can form a varying annuity, an annuity-due or a continuous annuity, or they may be of fixed size with their term and final payment unknown. However, discussing such possibilities in detail is unnecessary, since the results are familiar from the previous chapter.

TABLE 4.5

Sinking-Fund Schedule

For a fund to contain $A = Fs_{\overline{n}|j}$ at the end of n periods. Payments thereto of F at the end of each period. Interest at the effective rate j per period.

(1) Period	(2) Interest for period h	(3) Increase in sinking fund in period h	(4) Amount in sinking fund at end of period h	(5) Book value of debt at end of period h
h	$j \cdot (4)_{-1}$	$F + (2)$	$(4)_{-1} + (3)$	$A - (4)$
0			0	A
1	0	F	$F = Fs_{\overline{1}|}$	$A - Fs_{\overline{1}|}$
2	$F[(1 + j) - 1]$	$F(1 + j)$	$Fs_{\overline{2}|}$	$A - Fs_{\overline{2}|}$
3	$F[(1 + j)^2 - 1]$	$F(1 + j)^2$	$Fs_{\overline{3}|}$	$A - Fs_{\overline{3}|}$
⋮	⋮	⋮	⋮	⋮
h	$F[(1 + j)^{h-1} - 1]$	$F(1 + j)^{h-1}$	$Fs_{\overline{h}|}$	$A - Fs_{\overline{h}|}$
⋮	⋮	⋮	⋮	⋮
n	$F[(1 + j)^{n-1} - 1]$	$F(1 + j)^{n-1}$	$Fs_{\overline{n}|}$	$A - Fs_{\overline{n}|} = 0$
Totals	$F[s_{\overline{n}|} - n]$ $= A - nF$	$Fs_{\overline{n}|} = A$	$F(\ddot{s}_{\overline{n}|} - n)/j$ $= [(1 + j)A - nF]/j$	$(n+1)A - F(\ddot{s}_{\overline{n}|} - n)/j$ $= nA - (A - nF)/j$

We have now seen two ways of discharging a debt by uniform periodic payments, namely, the sinking-fund method with payments as in formula (4.34), and the amortization method previously discussed. Under the simplest case of the latter method, the periodic payment to contain interest at rate i per period would be

$$A/a_{\overline{n}|\,i} = Ai + A/s_{\overline{n}|\,i} \tag{4.37}$$

[see formula (3.13)]. If, as is usually the case, the lender's interest rate i exceeds the rate which the borrower earns in his sinking fund, comparison of formulas (4.34) and (4.37) indicates that the periodic payment for the amortization method would be less than the total periodic payment for the sinking-fund method. In fact, as shown numerically in Example 4.1, it would be possible for the borrower to pay a somewhat higher rate than i under the amortization method and still have a periodic payment not in excess of that of the sinking-fund method. The reason is that payments on principal in the amortization method save the borrower interest at the loan rate, while deposits in the sinking fund earn interest at rate j which was assumed less than the loan rate.

Thus the borrower usually finds the amortization method the more economical. In addition, he may prefer the convenience of making a single periodic payment and the facility for diminishing his debt, rather than shouldering the responsibility of accumulating a sinking fund.

In the mathematical sense, if $i = j$, the sinking-fund and amortization methods are closely parallel and more or less identical. The following statements can be made for the case of level payments:

(a) The periodic payments are the same, namely

$$Ai + A/s_{\overline{n}|\,i} = A/a_{\overline{n}|\,i} .$$

(b) The increase in the sinking fund over period h is

$$\frac{A}{s_{\overline{n}|}}\left[s_{\overline{h}|} - s_{\overline{h-1}|}\right] = \frac{A}{s_{\overline{n}|}}(1+i)^{h-1} = \frac{A}{a_{\overline{n}|}}v^{n-h+1}$$

which, by formula (4.8), represents the principal repaid by the amortization payment at the end of that same period.

(c) The accumulated sinking fund by the end of period h is

$$\frac{A}{s_{\overline{n}|}}s_{\overline{h}|} = \frac{A}{a_{\overline{n}|}}\left[v^n + v^{n-1} + \cdots + v^{n-h+1}\right] = \frac{A}{a_{\overline{n}|}}\left[a_{\overline{n}|} - a_{\overline{n-h}|}\right] = A - A_h,$$

that is, equals the total principal repaid under the amortization method by the end of that same period.

(d) The book value of the debt at the end of period h is

$$A - \frac{A}{s_{\overline{n}|}} s_{\overline{h}|} = \frac{A}{s_{\overline{n}|}} [s_{\overline{n}|} - s_{\overline{h}|}]$$

$$= \frac{A}{a_{\overline{n}|}} [a_{\overline{n}|} - v^{n-h} a_{\overline{h}|}] = \frac{A}{a_{\overline{n}|}} a_{\overline{n-h}|} = A_h ,$$

the principal outstanding at the same time under amortization. The result is immediate from (c).

(e) Under the amortization method, the interest in the first payment is iA and in the (h+1)th payment is $iA_h = i(A - \frac{A}{s_{\overline{n}|}} s_{\overline{h}|})$ by (d). Thus, the interest saved in the (h+1)th payment is $i \frac{A}{s_{\overline{n}|}} s_{\overline{h}|}$ which equals the interest earned in the (h+1)th period by the sinking fund.

4.8. Illustrative problems. In this chapter the theory of two well-known methods of debt repayment has been presented, and several numerical illustrations as well. The examples which follow further illustrate amortization and sinking-fund theory, and some of them, besides, are intended to enlarge the reader's understanding of amortization procedures, uses of sinking funds and methods of debt repayment. Reference to Examples 4.1 and 4.2 has been made earlier. Examples 4.3-4.5, not previously mentioned, deal with some practical complications.

Example 4.1

To repay a loan of \$2,000 in 5 years, a debtor promises to make semiannual interest payments at (.055, 2) per year and to accumulate a sinking fund by semiannual deposits invested at (.04, 2). What is the equivalent amortization rate?

Solution: The debtor can afford the same semiannual expense under amortization as under the sinking-fund method, namely,

$$2{,}000(.0275) + 2{,}000\, s^{-1}_{\overline{10}|.02} = 55.00 + 182.65 = \$237.65 .$$

Therefore,

$$2{,}000 = 237.65\, a_{\overline{10}|i}$$

or

$$a^{-1}_{\overline{10}|i} = .118825 .$$

By linear interpolation, we find 2i, the equivalent nominal annual rate of amortization, converted semiannually, to be 6.53%. This rate is and should be larger than both rates named in the problem.

Example 4.2

A loan of $1,000 is to be repaid by 5 annual $200 payments (which, of course, repay the principal), plus interest at 6% each year on the outstanding principal.

(a) Find the present value at 6% of (i) the principal repayments, (ii) the interest payments, (iii) the total payments.

(b) Compare the progress of repayment of the debt with that of the 6% amortization example in Section 4.2.

Solution: This example has been included to illustrate a different contract for debt repayment. Of course, it is actually a form of amortization by a varying annuity. The line diagram gives the pertinent data.

Payments of Interest		60	48	36	24	12
Payments of Principal		200	200	200	200	200
Years	0	1	2	3	4	5

(interval 0–1: .06)

Fig. 4.4

(a) The present value at 6% of (i) the principal repayments is $200\, a_{\overline{5}|.06} = \$842.47$ and of (ii) the interest payments is $12(Da)_{\overline{5}|.06} = 12(5 - a_{\overline{5}|.06})/.06 = \$157.53$, so that (iii) the present value of the total payments is $842.47 + 157.53 = \$1{,}000$, as is proper since the valuation rate and the investment rate are the same.

(b) Table 4.6 giving the comparison of amounts of debt outstanding indicates that within the repayment interval the outstanding principal in the present instance is less than that in the other amortization case. This result could have been anticipated since total payments here in each of the first two years exceed the $237.40 under amortization. The amortization schedule

TABLE 4.6

Debt Outstanding (in $)

End of Year	0	1	2	3	4	5
Present Example	1,000.00	800.00	600.00	400.00	200.00	0.00
Sec. 4.2 Example	1,000.00	822.60	634.56	435.23	223.94	0.00

(Table 4.2) shows principal payments increasing from \$177 to \$224, such payments exceeding the \$200 principal payment of this example only in the last 2 years.

Example 4.3

(a) A large investor is considering the purchase of bonds which will pay \$2,500 at the end of every 6 months until their redemption at the end of 10 years, at which time \$101,000 will be paid, in addition to the regular \$2,500. The investor anticipates an initial expense of \$1,000. He can earn 3% effective each year on a sinking fund to be built by level semiannual deposits in advance to replace loss of capital when the \$101,000 is paid. If he desires to earn 2% semiannually on his entire initial outlay, what price should he offer?

(b) Suppose that, instead of making semiannual sinking-fund deposits, he plans to invest immediately at 3% effective per year the single sum necessary to replace loss of capital when the \$101,000 is paid. If the other conditions remain unchanged, what price should he offer?

Solution: (a) An investor who pays \$101,000 would earn approximately 2.5% semiannually. Then the investor desiring only 2% would be willing to pay more than \$101,000. An orderly way for such an investor to ensure that at redemption he has his full initial capital is to build a sinking fund to contain the excess over the \$101,000 redemption value. Thus the problem "makes sense."

Assume that the investor offers a price A and that by semiannual deposits F, invested at an effective annual rate of 3%, he builds a sinking fund to contain S at the end of 10 years. His initial outgo, the interest-bearing capital, is $A+1{,}000+F$. At the end of every 6 months in the first 9 1/2 years, his \$2,500 income must pay F and also the interest on this capital. Thus,

$$2{,}500 = F + .02(A + 1{,}000 + F).$$

At the end of 10 years the proceeds, $101{,}000 + S + 2{,}500$, must provide interest on the capital and refund the capital; that is,

$$101{,}000 + S + 2{,}500 = 1.02(A + 1{,}000 + F) = 1.02(2{,}500 - F)/.02$$

from the first relation. Therefore,

$$S = 24{,}000 - 51\ F = 2\ F\ \ddot{s}^{(2)}_{\overline{10|}.03}\ .$$

Consequently,

$$F = \frac{24{,}000}{2(i/d^{(2)})\, s_{\overline{10}|} + 51} \text{ at } .03 = \$322.40$$

and by the first equation

$$A = \frac{2{,}500 - 1.02\ F}{.02} - 1{,}000 = 124{,}000 - 51\ F = \$107{,}557.60.$$

It is interesting to note from the relations for S and A that

$$S = A - 100{,}000 = \$7{,}557.60.$$

(b) The fund S at the end of 10 years is produced by a single deposit of $S(1.03)^{-10}$ earning 3% per year. From the lines of the previous solution, initial outgo is $A + 1{,}000 + S(1.03)^{-10}$, and semiannually for 9 1/2 years

$$2{,}500 = .02\left[A + 1{,}000 + S(1.03)^{-10}\right],$$

while at the end of 10 years

$$101{,}000 + S + 2{,}500 = 1.02\left[A + 1{,}000 + S(1.03)^{-10}\right]$$
$$= \frac{1.02}{.02}(2{,}500).$$

Thus S = \$24,000. Accordingly, from the first relation

$$A = 124{,}000 - 24{,}000(1.03)^{-10} = \$106{,}141.75.$$

In both (a) and (b) it has been possible (and simpler) to avoid involved equations of value at (.04, 2) by accounting for each exchange of money separately.

Example 4.4

How much should a prospective purchaser of two annual \$100 payments and three subsequent annual \$1,100 payments be willing to pay, if he wants to earn 5% on his investment and can replace his capital (from the balance of his income over his interest requirements) by sinking-fund deposits earning 4%?

Solution: For an investment of A, it appears that two sinking-fund deposits of 100 - .05 A, followed by three of 1,100 - .05 A = (100 - .05 A) + 1,000, must accumulate at 4% to A; or,

$$A = (100 - .05\ A)s_{\overline{5}|.04} + 1{,}000\ s_{\overline{3}|.04}$$
$$= \frac{100\ s_{\overline{5}|.04} + 1{,}000\ s_{\overline{3}|.04}}{1 + .05\ s_{\overline{5}|.04}} = \$2{,}882.58.$$

Unfortunately, the sinking-fund deposits of the first two years are negative; that is, the amounts of the interest deficiencies are borrowed from the then nonexistent sinking fund and later repaid the fund at its rate of 4%. Such a procedure seems unrealistic.

The purchaser, anticipating that the early payments might be inadequate to meet the interest, could have stipulated that he would capitalize any interest deficiencies at his regular 5% earnings rate. The calculation above would confirm his suspicions. He could see that his investment, say A', would grow at 5% (through the capitalizing) to a sum A_2 at the end of 2 years and would thereafter remain at A_2, until a payment of that amount from the sinking fund would complete the transaction. Thus,

$$A'(1.05)^2 - 100\, s_{\overline{2}|.05} = A_2$$

or

$$A' = A_2(1.05)^{-2} + 100\, a_{\overline{2}|.05}$$

and

$$A_2 = (1{,}100 - .05\, A_2)\, s_{\overline{3}|.04} = \frac{1{,}100}{s^{-1}_{\overline{3}|.04} + .05} = \$2{,}970.18,$$

so that $A' = \$2{,}879.98$. The schedule in Table 4.7 below casts further enlightenment.

TABLE 4.7

Schedule of Debt and Sinking Fund

For a loan of $2,879.98 to receive annual interest at 5%, except that when payments are insufficient to pay interest in full, the balance of the interest is capitalized at 5%. The balance (if any) of each payment to be invested in a sinking fund at 4% compounded annually. Successive payments of $100, $100, $1,100, $1,100, $1,100 at the ends of each of 5 consecutive years.

(1) Year h	(2) Interest for year h $.05\,A_{h-1}$	(3) Payment to sinking fund at end of year h*	(4) Interest at 4% on sinking fund for year h $.04\,(5)_{-1}$	(5) Amount in sinking fund at end of year h $(5)_{-1} + (3)^* + (4)$	(6) Debt outstanding at end of year h A_h
0	$	$	$	$ 0.00	$ 2,879.98
1	144.00	-44.00	0.00	0.00	2,923.98
2	146.20	-46.20	0.00	0.00	2,970.18
3	148.51	951.49	0.00	951.49	2,970.18
4	148.51	951.49	38.06	1,941.04	2,970.18
5	148.51	951.49	77.64	2,970.17	2,970.18
Totals	$735.73	$2,764.27	$115.70	$5,862.70	$17,684.68

*Except, if the sinking fund payment is negative, the debt outstanding is increased by the absolute value of such payment.

It is worthwhile to note that A, although too high, is a very good approximation to A'. The approximation A will be excessive as it is here in every instance where, according to the assumptions for it, interest deficiencies are accumulated at a lower rate than the purchaser's rate; that is, a purchaser would be willing to pay more for the set of payments if less interest is to be charged on interest deficiencies. In this problem it was soon evident that income was less than required interest for the first two years, and the approximation merely served to confirm this and to check on reasonableness. In cases, however, in which the period of interest deficiency is uncertain, knowledge that A is usually a reasonable estimate of A' -- and is too high -- may shorten the computation of A' by trial-and-error methods.

A comparison of this problem with the illustrative example of Section 4.3 is suggested.

Example 4.5

(a) A debt of A is to be repaid in n periods by level payments R which discharge interest and principal, with interest charged as follows on the debt outstanding:

Debt outstanding	Rate of interest charged on debt outstanding
$> K$ (K constant)	i' on first K and i (where $i < i'$) on balance
$\leq K$	i'

Describe how to find R.

(b) If in (a), $A = \$500$, $n = 6$, $K = \$200$, $i' = 2.5\%$ and $i = 1\%$, find R.

Solution: (a) This is a familiar variation of the ordinary amortization problem. There are two unknowns: R and also k, the least duration for which $A_h \leq K$. There will thus be two basic equations for R corresponding to equation (4.1).

The first of these, for the case $h \leq k$, is

$$R = [i'K + i(A_{h-1} - K)] + [A_{h-1} - A_h],$$

with the interest and principal components of R given in the separate brackets. It follows that

$$-A_h + (1 + i)A_{h-1} = R - (i' - i)K$$

and

$$-\Delta(v^{h-1}A_{h-1}) = [R - (i' - i)K]v^h .$$

Summation over the range h = 1 to h = k yields

$$A - v^k A_k = [R - (i' - i)K] a_{\overline{k}|i}$$

or

$$A_k = A(1 + i)^k - [R - (i' - i)K] s_{\overline{k}|i} .$$

Note that, for the first k periods, we can consider that the initial debt of A is being amortized at rate i by net payments of $R - (i' - i)K$, down to A_k outstanding after k periods.

When $h > k$, we have simply

$$R = i' A_{h-1} + A_{h-1} - A_h$$

so that, with primes denoting use of the rate i',

$$- \Delta(v'^{h-1} A_{h-1}) = R\ v'^{h} .$$

Summation from $h = k + 1$ to $h = n$ and simplification produce

$$A_k = R\ a_{\overline{n-k}|i'} .$$

We see that, in the final n-k periods, the reduced debt of A_k is amortized at rate i' by the payments of R.

We have now obtained retrospective and prospective expressions for A_k. Upon equating these and simplifying we find that

$$A = [R - (i' - i)K] a_{\overline{k}|i} + R\ v^k\ a_{\overline{n-k}|i'}$$

and

$$R = \frac{A(1 + i)^k + (i' - i)K\ s_{\overline{k}|i}}{s_{\overline{k}|i} + a_{\overline{n-k}|i'}} .$$

However, since k as well as R is unknown, the task is unfinished. But as the true single rate of interest lies between i and i', we know that

$$A\ a^{-1}_{\overline{n}|i} < R < A\ a^{-1}_{\overline{n}|i'} .$$

An estimate of R, say R^*, within this interval can be used to estimate $n - k$ (and thus k), for k is the least integer such that

$$A_k = R\ a_{\overline{n-k}|i'} \le K.$$

With this estimate of k, which will usually be correct, R can be calculated; because of the estimates, the accuracy of this R must be checked by use of the preceding inequality or otherwise.

(If the check fails, k must be estimated again and the solution repeated.)

(b) From

$$500\ a^{-1}_{\overline{6}|.01} = 86.27 < R < 500\ a^{-1}_{\overline{6}|.025} = 90.77,$$

take $R^* = \$90$. Now for estimation purposes, 6-k is the greatest integer with

$$a^{-1}_{\overline{6-k}|.025} \geq \frac{90}{200} = 0.45.$$

Thus 6-k = 2 and k is estimated to be 4, so that as trial value of R we obtain

$$R = \frac{500(1.01)^4 + 3\ s_{\overline{4}|.01}}{s_{\overline{4}|.01} + a_{\overline{2}|.025}} = \$88.93.$$

The check confirms the value of R, for

$$88.93\ a_{\overline{2}|.025} = 171.41 < 200$$

while

$$88.93\ a_{\overline{3}|.025} = 253.99 > 200.$$

An amortization schedule could readily be constructed.

4.9. Remarks about Problem List 4. We particularly cite the development of theory in certain of the problems, namely,

(1) The Makeham formula (to be met again in a different context in Chapter 5); see Problems 46 and 48;

(2) The practical problem of determination of the rate of interest in installment contracts (Problem 49);

(3) The sinking-fund method of depreciation of Problem 74. Other problems to be brought to the reader's attention include 8, 12, 16, 23 and problems about an investor's yield rate such as 62, 64, 73 (b) and 77.

PROBLEM LIST 4

Basic List (Problems 1-50)

Sec. 4.1, 4.2

1. A loan of A is being amortized by 2n equal installments. Given that $v^n = 2/3$, find (as a function of the interest rate if necessary but not of interest functions)

(a) The principal outstanding after n payments;

(b) The amount of principal repaid in the first n installments;

(c) The amount of principal repaid in the (n + 1)th payment;

(d) The amount due at the end of the term of the loan if the final n payments are defaulted.

2. (a) A loan is being amortized over 15 years by monthly installments of \$100 at the end of each month. If the interest in the 121st installment is \$36.13, determine the nominal annual rate, convertible monthly.

(b) A loan of \$1,000 is to be amortized by equal payments at the end of each 6 months for 20 years. If the total interest that will be paid is \$730.48, what effective annual rate of interest does the lender earn (if he can reinvest on the same terms)?

3. (a) If $v^{10} = .620$, find the ratio of the principal repaid in the 11th annual installment under 20-year amortization to the principal repaid in the 21st annual installment under 40-year amortization.

(b) A mortgage is being amortized by level monthly payments over 15 years including interest at 6% per year compounded monthly. Immediately after the 60th payment, a new level payment is determined at the same rate of interest to shorten the payment period so as to cause it to end 10 years from the date when the loan was made. Find the ratio of the new monthly payment to the original payment.

(c) A loan A is to be amortized by equal annual installments. Show that the total interest under amortization over $2n$ years exceeds the total interest under amortization over n years by $Ain/(1 + v^n)$.

(d) Without interest tables, find to the nearest dollar the additional interest paid if a \$10,000 loan is amortized by monthly payments at the end of each month for 30 years instead of by monthly payments for 15 years. Interest is at the annual rate (.06, 12) and you are given that $(1.005)^{-180} = .4075$.

4. Obtain a very brief solution to each of the following.

(a) A loan is being repaid by level monthly payments consisting of interest at 1/2% on the balance outstanding and of principal. The principal repaid in the current payment is \$50. Find the total of the principal repayments in the next 10 payments.

(b) To the nearest dollar, what was the initial amount of a mortgage on which semiannual payments of \$1,000 (including interest and principal repayment) have been made for 5.5 years, if interest is at (.05, 2) and the principal outstanding at the end of 5.5 years (after the \$1,000 payment) is \$5,000?

(c) A loan is being amortized at rate i over 50 periods by level payments R. At the time of the 10th regular payment, the borrower makes an additional payment, equal to the sum of the principal amounts that, according to his amortization schedule, would have been paid in his 11th through 15th regular payments. He then resumes regular payments until the loan is discharged. Give an expression for the reduction in his total interest payments due to the prepayment.

(d) A 15-year mortgage is being amortized at (.08, 4) by monthly payments of \$100. Find the amount of principal repaid in the 100th monthly payment.

(e) In amortization at rate i by level payments of R over $2n$ periods, (1) how much more interest is paid in the first n payments than the last n? (2) how much more principal is repaid in the even-numbered payments than the odd-numbered?

5. (a) A loan is to be amortized by 50 equal periodic payments with interest at 2% per period. In which payment will the interest and principal portions be approximately equal? When will the principal of the loan be approximately half repaid?

(b) A loan of $10,000 is to be amortized by equal payments at the end of each half year for (i) 20 years, (ii) 30 years. Interest is at the annual rate (.05, 2). For each case, determine in which payment the principal portion will first exceed the interest portion.

6. A debt of $10,000 is being amortized at (.12, 12) by level payments at the end of each month for 5 years. Construct just that part of the amortization schedule which analyzes payments 40 through 42; devise and use summation checks.

7. A debt of $10,000 is being amortized over 15 years by level payments at the end of each quarter year. Interest is at an annual rate of (.07, 4). Six years after the date of the loan, the borrower wishes to make a single extra payment, in addition to his regular payment, so as to shorten the amortization period by 2 years. What is the amount of the extra payment, and what is the debt outstanding 1 year later?

8. Complete the following statement: If a loan of A is amortized at rate i over n interest periods by level payments at the ends of every $1/p$ interest periods, then

(1) Each payment is of size __________,

(2) The interest in the hth payment is __________,

(3) The principal repaid in the hth payment is __________,

(4) The principal outstanding immediately after the hth payment is __________,

(5) The total interest paid in the kth interest period is __________,

(6) The total principal repaid in the kth interest period is __________.

9. (a) A loan of $1,000 is to be amortized by equal installments at the end of each month for 5 years. If the interest rate per year is (.06, 12), compute

(1) The interest portion of the 15th installment,

(2) The amount of principal repaid in the last 10 installments,

(3) The total of the interest in the 16th to 25th installments.

(b) If in (a) interest were at the effective annual rate of 6%, give expressions for the quantities required, but do not compute.

10. A loan of A is to be amortized in 16 semiannual installments R at effective annual rate i. The principal repaid in the first and last installments is $49.61 and $77.29, respectively. Find A, i and R.

11. A debt A is being amortized by n payments of R at rate i.

(a) Express the present value of (1) all repayments of principal and of (2) all the interest payments, each first at rate i and then at rate $j \neq i$.

(b) If the interest payments in (a) are subject to an income tax deduction at rate t, prove algebraically that the present values of the reduced interest payments and the capital repayments, both values at the reduced rate of interest which reflects the income tax, are together equal to the original loan.

12. A loan of A is to be amortized by level payments at the end of each period, over an n-period term. Without computation, compare the relative size of amortization-schedule entries at rate i with those at rate $i' > i$.

Sec. 4.3

13. A loan of $10,000 is being amortized at an effective annual rate i by payments $R, 2R, \cdots, 10R$ at the ends of years $1, 2, \cdots, 10$. Give expressions in terms of tabulated interest functions for R, A_h prospectively and retrospectively, and the interest in the $(h + 1)$th payment.

14. A loan is being amortized at rate i by successive payments $1, 2, 3, \cdots, 20$.

(a) Find an expression for

(1) The principal repaid in the tenth payment;

(2) The increase in the principal repaid in the tenth payment over that in the first.

(b) For approximately what range of interest rates is the initial principal greater than the principal outstanding after every payment?

15. On a debt of A being repaid by $(n + m)$ payments, of amounts $n, n - 1, n - 2, \cdots, 2, 1, 1, \cdots, 1$, set up expressions for the debt outstanding after t integral interest periods, where

(a) $0 \leq t \leq n$ (b) $n \leq t \leq n + m$.

16. A loan of $10,000 is being repaid over 10 years by semiannual payments of R for the first 5 years, then of $R + 100$ for the next 2.5 years and of $R + 150$ for the final 2.5 years. If interest is at (.08, 2), how much principal is included in the 12th payment? the 17th? What is the average principal outstanding?

17. On a loan of $2,000 being amortized at (.07, 2) per year over a 15-year period by level semiannual payments, installments $8, 9, \cdots, 12$ were missed. When payments resumed (at the end of 6 1/2 years from the date of the original loan), they were at such a level as to complete the amortization at the end of the original 15-year period. Find expressions for

(a) The total interest paid;

(b) The principal which would have been repaid by the payments which were missed.

18. A $10,000 mortgage with interest at (6%, 1) per year is being repaid by equal annual payments at the end of each year for 20 years. At the end of 10 years, the mortgage agreement is renegotiated, as follows:

(1) At the ends of years $11, 12, \cdots, 15$ only one-half the former mortgage payment will be made;

(2) Beginning at the end of year 15 interest will be at (8%, 2) per year;

(3) The debt outstanding at the end of 15 years will be repaid by 10 level semiannual payments of principal, plus simultaneous additional payments of interest on the outstanding principal.

To the nearest dollar,

(a) How much more does the debtor pay under the new arrangement than he would have under the old one?

(b) How much larger is the debt outstanding after 15 years than under the original agreement?

Sec. 4.4

19. (a) A loan of $1,000 is to be amortized by payments of $100 at the end of each quarter for as long as necessary with a final payment one quarter after the last full payment. If the interest rate per year is (.04, 4), find

(1) The principal outstanding after 8 payments,

(2) The final payment.

(b) If in (a) the interest rate per year were (.04, 2), find the final payment.

20. Level semiannual payments of $100 are to be made as long as necessary to amortize a debt of $1,000. If interest is at (.06, 12),

(a) Find when the final payment less than $100, six months after the last regular payment, should be made and its amount;

(b) Give retrospective and prospective expressions for the debt outstanding just before the 5th payment is made.

21. Same as Problem 7, except that the $10,000 debt is being amortized by quarterly payments of $250 for as long as necessary and a final smaller payment. (Keep the final payment fixed.)

22. (a) A loan of $5,000 is to be amortized by monthly payments of $50 with interest at 6% per year compounded monthly. In what payment will the principal portion be more than twice the interest portion for the first time?

(b) Criticize the following condensed proposed solution to (a): Since 139 payments are needed to amortize the loan, we require the least h such that at .5%

$$50\ v^{140-h} \geq 100(1 - v^{140-h}),$$

which turns out to be $h = 59$.

23. Show that when a loan of A is amortized by n level payments R (possibly followed by other payments which are not necessarily of size R), the principal repaid in the hth installment ($h \leq n$) is $(R - iA)(1 + i)^{h-1}$ and the total principal repaid in the first h installments is $(R - iA)s_{\overline{h|}}$. Note that

(1) It is efficient to use the first result in the solution of Problem 22;

(2) Principal repayments during the level-payment period are in geometric progression with ratio $(1 + i)$, a result useful in practice.

24. For each part, consider whether Note (2) of Problem 23 pertains, directly or indirectly, and solve.

(a) On a loan of $10,000 being amortized at 5%, the principal repaid in the tenth payment is $1,000. What is the regular level amortization payment?

(b) A loan is being amortized by monthly payments of $100 with interest at 9% per year, compounded monthly. At the end of 5 years from the initial date, the outstanding principal is $10,000. What will be the total interest paid over the second set of 5 years?

(c) Payments of \$500 are made at the end of each 4 months to discharge a loan bearing interest at (.09, 12).

(1) If the interest in the second installment is \$400, find the interest in the eighth installment.

(2) Find the total principal repaid in the first 8 payments.

25. For the case of amortization of a loan A at effective rate i, by level payments R and a final fractional payment fR, set up a general amortization schedule (including column totals) based on outstanding principals obtained (a) retrospectively, (b) prospectively. Discuss the relative merits of each table.

Sec. 4.5

26. (a) Show that

$$(1+i)^t - \bar{s}_{\overline{t}|i} / \bar{a}_{\overline{n}|i} = \bar{a}_{\overline{n-t}|i} / \bar{a}_{\overline{n}|i} ,$$

and give a verbal interpretation suited to this chapter.

(b) Give the amortization-schedule entries for the line for period h, for amortizing a debt A at effective rate i per period (time unit) by continuous level payments for n periods at the payment rate of r per period.

27. A loan of \$10,000 is to be amortized by a continuous-payment, continuously decreasing annuity over 20 years. If interest is at effective annual rate i, give expressions for

(a) The outstanding principal at the end of 5 years;

(b) The amount of interest paid in the 6th year.

Sec. 4.6

28. A debt of \$10,000 is being amortized by semiannual payments (in dollars) of 100, 100, 200, 200, 300, 300, ··· as long as necessary. The lender's rate is (.05, 2), but each stipulated payment includes an expense charge of 1/2% of the outstanding principal. Produce the 7-column amortization schedule for just the 5th year. After solving, note that during the initial years of this loan the outstanding principal increases. Without working numerically, consider the nature of the schedule entries for those years. Similarly consider the theoretical possibility of initial payments less than the requisite expense charges.

29. A company sells a property for \$10,000 which is to be paid for in equal annual payments over 10 years at 6% interest. The agent for the seller is entitled to commissions which are a part of the interest payments equivalent to a 1% interest rate. After 5 payments have been made on the mortgage, the agent requests that his remaining commissions be paid him in one sum. How much can the company pay him if the net interest earned by the company is to remain the same?

30. In the case of amortization (of a debt A in n periods by a payment R at the end of each period) at a rate of interest i' in excess of the lender's rate i, obtain a simplified expression for each of the following:

(a) The total excess interest in periods $(h + 1)$ to $(h + k)$ inclusive, where $h + k \leq n$;

(b) As of the end of the hth period, the present value at rate i of the excess interest in those same periods.

Sec. 4.7

31. (a) A loan of $10,000 is to be repaid by equal annual installments over 20 years. If the lender wishes to earn 6% annually on his whole invested capital and will replace his capital by a sinking fund accumulating at 4% effective annual interest, what should the size of the annual installment be?

(b) Just after the 12th installment is paid, the loan contract of (a) is sold to an investor who wishes to amortize his investment at 5% effective annual interest. How much should this investor pay for the contract? Does the original lender recover all his capital?

32. (a) A loan of $10,000 is being amortized by annual installments over 15 years with interest at the effective annual rate of 5%. Immediately after the 8th installment is paid, the loan contract is sold to an investor who wishes to earn 6% annually on his whole investment and to replace his principal by a sinking fund earning 4% effective annual interest. What should this investor pay for the contract?

(b) What is the largest sum (a multiple of $500) that an investor should offer for a building which he estimates will produce an annual net income of $3,000 at the end of each year for 15 years and will be worth $20,000 at the end of that time? He wishes to earn at least 6% per year on his investment and will set up a sinking fund earning 4% per year to replace his capital in excess of the $20,000 final worth of the building.

Note the similarity in the solutions of (a) and (b).

33. (a) A loan of $1,000 is to be repaid by 30 equal monthly installments out of which the lender is to receive interest on the whole principal at 1% per month for the first 20 months and 3/4% per month for the last 10 months. The balances of the installments are to be deposited into a sinking fund earning interest at 1/2% per month. Determine the monthly installment.

(b) An investor will loan $10,000 on condition that he receive a monthly income of 1/2% of the $10,000 for the next 10 years and that in addition he receive a monthly payment which will be deposited into a fund earning 4% effective per year to provide for repayment of the loan principal at the end of 10 years. Find the total monthly payment the borrower makes under these conditions.

34. (a) What should an investor pay for each of the following series of annual payments if he wishes to receive annually interest at 8% on his whole principal and will make annual deposits into a sinking fund earning 5% to recover his principal at the end of 10 years?

(1) $1,000 at the end of each year for 10 years,

(2) $10,000; $9,000; $8,000; ··· ; $1,000, with payments at the ends of years.

What difficulty would arise if the payments in (2) were in reverse order?

(b) Give an expression for the price that an investor, desiring an income at 7% effective per year, should pay for the following annual payments made at the ends of years:

$10,000 for 8 years; $8,000 for the next 7 years;
$ 5,000 for the next 5 years.

He will replace his capital by a sinking fund at 5% for the first 10 years and 4% thereafter.

35. (a) On borrowing $1,000 from B, A agrees to pay

interest to B at 6% per year at the end of each year for 10 years and to make deposits into a sinking fund earning 4% per year to repay the principal at the end of 10 years. If the interest earned on the sinking fund is considered as an offset to the interest that A pays to B, what is the net total of interest paid by A during the 10 years?

(b) To the nearest dollar, how much total interest has been earned on a sinking fund which has accumulated at 5% per year and contains $10,000 at the end of 10 years from deposits of $500, 500 + R, 500 + 2R, ⋯ , 500 + 9R at the ends of years 1, 2, 3, ⋯ , 10?

(c) Same as (b), except that the deposits were R, 1.05R, $(1.05)^2$ R, ⋯ , $(1.05)^9$ R.

36. (a) If the lender's rate under amortization is i and by the sinking-fund method is i' and if the sinking-fund rate is i'', less than i, show that, when by each method the debtor makes the same total periodic payment for the same term, then $i > i'$.

(b) If A lends B $10,000 to be amortized by 15 level annual payments consisting of principal and interest at 6%, and if A deposits a level sum at the end of each year into a sinking fund earning 5% (in order to recover his principal in 15 years), what annual rate of interest does he earn on his whole principal? Explain whether your answer is reasonable.

(c) What effective annual rate does an investor earn each year on his capital if in return for a loan of $10,000 he receives $1,500 at the end of every year for 10 years and if he sets up a sinking fund to secure his capital at the end of the period? The fund is at 5% for the first 5 years and 4% thereafter. Explain whether your answer is reasonable.

37. (a) In the light of amortization and sinking-fund theory, verbally interpret

$$\frac{1}{a^{(p)}_{\overline{n|}i}} - \frac{1}{s^{(p)}_{\overline{n|}i}} = i^{(p)} .$$

(b) If the amortization and sinking-fund effective rates are both i and in the sinking-fund method the creditor asks an effective rate i' on his capital ($i' > i$), determine a convenient expression for the borrower's extra periodic payment on a unit debt by the sinking-fund method over that under amortization, when the term is n interest periods and there are p payments per interest period. Analyze your result.

38. A purchaser wants to earn 5% on his investment and can replace his capital (from the excess of income over interest requirements) by sinking-fund deposits earning 4%. He plans to capitalize any interest deficiencies at 5%. Give an expression for the sum he should offer for each of the following incomes:

(a) Five annual $700 payments;

(b) Two annual $25 payments and three subsequent $1,150 annual payments;

(c) Two annual $1,000 payments and three subsequent $500 annual payments.

39. (a) On a $1,000 loan the debtor makes annual payments of $150 at the end of each year, consisting of (i) interest at 5% on the loan and (ii) the residue, which the creditor deposits in a principal-redemption fund which earns (.04, 1) per year.

(1) What is the book value of the debt at the end of 5 years?

(2) What final irregular payment, less than $150, should be made one year after the last $150 payment?

(b) On a loan of $1,000 at 8% effective, interest is payable at the end of each year. The creditor will accept larger payments and, after deducting his interest, will accumulate the balance at 6% effective. If the debtor pays $180, including the annual interest, on each interest date until the date when a smaller payment will discharge the loan, what will the amount of his final payment be?

(c) (1) The final smaller payment needed to complete a sinking fund one period after the last full payment may turn out to be negative. Explain.

(2) Is a negative final smaller payment possible in amortization? Explain.

40. A loan of A is being amortized at rate i by payments R_h $(h = 1, 2, \cdots, n)$ at the end of each of n periods. Show that the same total payment R_h in each of the n periods would provide a return of i to the investor on his full capital and a deposit into a sinking fund which, at rate i, would return the capital after n periods.

41. A loan is to be discharged by the sinking-fund method by means of continuous payments, both of interest and of deposits into the sinking fund. Parallel Section 4.7, giving formulas corresponding to those of the section, a sinking-fund schedule, and a comparison with amortization by continuous payments. Whenever in Section 4.7 a payment at the end of a period is given, express instead the total of the corresponding continuous payments for the period. Use δ and δ' to denote forces of interest equivalent to the effective rates i and j.

Sec. 4.8

42. How much should a prospective purchaser of a savings fund of $1,000 (which is earning 4%) and of two $100 payments and three subsequent $1,100 payments (to be made at the end of each of the next two years and of each of the following three years, respectively) be willing to pay, if he wants to earn 5% on his investment and can replace his capital at the end of the 5 years from the savings fund? He augments the savings fund by depositing each year the balance of his income over his interest requirements. Cf. Example 4.4, and construct a similar schedule of debt and sinking fund for this problem.

43. Contrast the following problem with Example 4.5:

(a) A debt of A is to be repaid in n periods by level payments R which discharge interest and principal, with interest on the debt outstanding at rate i when that debt exceeds K and at rate i' otherwise, where $i' > i$. Describe how to find R.

(b) Solve (a) for R using the data of Example 4.5 (b), and construct amortization schedules for this problem and Example 4.5 (b).

44. A debt of $1,000 is to be amortized by quarterly payments of $100 and a final fractional payment. Interest is to be charged at 2% per quarter on the first $300 of outstanding principal and at 1% per quarter on the balance, if any, of outstanding principal. If the final fractional payment is to be made one quarter

after the date of the last full payment of \$100, find when it is paid and its size. Also find the amount of principal outstanding after 5 quarters and after 10 quarters, and then draw up the amortization schedule.

45. A loan of A is being amortized in n periods by level payments R, with interest at rate i' on the first K of debt outstanding and at rate i on any excess over K, with $i' > i$. A second loan of A is being amortized at the single rate i by $\bar{n}$ level payments R, followed one period later by a final smaller payment. Obtain a simple expression for the excess of the interest in the $(h + 1)$th payment of the first loan over that in the second, assuming $h \le \bar{n}$, if

(a) $h \le k$ (where k is the least duration for which the debt outstanding in the first loan does not exceed K);

(b) $h > k$.

46. (a) A loan of C is repaid in n periods by n level principal payments plus, each period, interest at rate g on the outstanding principal of the period. Prove that the present value of this loan at rate i is

$$A = K + \frac{g}{i}(C - K), \qquad \text{(\underline{Makeham's formula})}$$

where K is the present value at rate i of the repayments of principal.

(b) Apply (a), to find the value at (.08, 4) of a mortgage of \$40,000 being repaid by quarterly payments of \$1,000 on account of principal plus interest at (.06, 4) on the outstanding principal.

(c) Same as (b), except find a generalized Makeham-type expression for the value at (1) (.08, 2), (2) (.08, 8).

47. This problem is posed so that the reader may become familiar with the Makeham formula (Problem 46), first in an evident case and then -- directly or with adaptation -- in cases in which use of the formula is very efficient.

A loan of \$5,000 is being repaid in 25 years by means of payments of \$100 at the end of every 6 months, plus semiannual interest at 2 1/4% for the period on the outstanding principal of the period.

(a) What annual amortization rate (j, 2) is actually paid?

(b) Just after the tenth payment, how much should a purchaser offer for the contract, if he can replace his capital at (.04, 2) by means of a sinking fund and wishes to realize (1) 2%, (2) 2 1/2% each payment period on his full capital?

(c) Same as (b) (2), except that he wishes to realize 2 1/2% and to build his sinking fund by level deposits.

48. (a) A loan of C is to be repaid in n periods by n level principal payments plus, each period, interest at rate g on the outstanding principal of the period. Show that the initial value A of this loan to an investor, who wants to receive interest each period during the term of the loan at rate j on his full capital and to recover his capital at the end of the term from a sinking fund earning rate i per period, is given by

$$A\left[1 + (j - i)\,a_{\overline{n}|i}\right] = K + \frac{g}{i}(C - K),$$

where K is the present value at rate i of the repayments of principal.

(b) Note that the right member of the equation in (a) is a price, call it A', given by Makeham's formula (Problem 46).

(1) Justify the result: $A = A'$ when $j = i$.

(2) Analyze loans of A and A' according to the sinking-fund method, and so derive the formula of (a).

49. Rate of interest in installment contracts. A loan of A is to be repaid by payments of R at the end of each period for n periods, and the associated (yield) rate of interest i per period is to be found. The solution depends upon definition. Some traditional definitions follow.

(a) The rate i may be defined to be such that A is the present value, at an effective rate i per period, of the installments R. Then i is the solution of $a_{\overline{n}|i} = A/R$ or of $a^{-1}_{\overline{n}|i} = R/A$ for i, say by an interpolation process.

(b) Determination of i by the United States Rule. By this method, each periodic installment is first used to pay interest that has accrued and the balance is used to reduce principal. Show that

(1) The total principal P earning interest for one period is

$$P = A\, s_{\overline{n}|i} - R(s_{\overline{n}|i} - n)/i,$$

and so $i = I/P$, where $I = nR - A$ is the total interest;

(2) The rate i by the United States Rule is the same as the rate in (a).

(c) Determination of i by the Merchant's Rule. This method requires that, at simple interest rate i per period, the accumulated value (at the end of the term) of the original debt equal the accumulated value of the installments. Then

$$A\,(1 + i\,n) = R\, \sum_{t=0}^{n-1} (1 + i\,t),$$

which can be compared with

$$A(1 + i)^n = R\, s_{\overline{n}|i} \qquad \big(\text{from (a)}\big)$$

and which the reader should solve for i.

(d) Determination of i by the Residuary Method. In this method, it is considered that for as long as necessary the whole installment is used to reduce principal and the interest payments consist of the balance of the installments after the principal has been fully repaid. Show that if $(n - 1)R \leq A$, then

(1) The total principal P earning interest for one period is

$$P = nA - n(n - 1)R/2$$

and $i = I/P$;

(2) The same rate i results as by the Merchant's Rule.

Also show that if $(n - k)R \leq A < (n - k + 1)R$, k an integer > 1, then the Residuary Method gives a rate i smaller than that by the Merchant's Rule.

(e) Determination of i by the Constant-Ratio Method. Here, the principal repaid by each installment is required to be A/n. Show that

(1) The principal portion and the interest portion of each installment are in the constant ratio A/I;

(2) The total principal P earning interest for one period is

$$P = (n + 1)A/2$$

and again $i = I/P$.

(f) The rate i may be defined as the rate payable on the whole principal at the end of each period, with the balance $(R - Ai)$ of each installment deposited in a sinking fund earning effective rate j per period and providing for the repayment of the principal at the end of the term. Show that

$$i = (R - A\ s^{-1}_{\overline{n}|j})/A.$$

(g) The rate i may be defined as the effective interest rate per period under which it may be assumed that the whole principal accumulates for the whole term, with such accumulation provided by likewise accumulating the installments in a fund earning effective rate j per period. Then

$$A(1 + i)^n = R\ s_{\overline{n}|j}\ .$$

Show that

(1) $i = (R\ s_{\overline{n}|j} - A)/(A\ s_{\overline{n}|i})$,

which should be compared with the result in (f);

(2) If $j < i$, the rates i in (f) and in (g) are less than the rate i in (a), but if $j = i$ the rates i in (f), (g) and (a) are identical.

As a numerical illustration, consider a $100 loan to be redeemed over a year by a payment of $9 at the end of each month. The following monthly rates i result, with $j = .0025$ in (f) and (g).

Method	(a), (b)	(c), (d)	(e)	(f)	(g)
i (%)	1.20	1.32	1.23	0.78	0.76

The rate of interest in installment contracts is a major topic of Chapter 6, especially as determined by the Truth-in-Lending legislation in the United States (effective date July 1, 1969). For a working rule for the present, let us assume the rate method of (a) is intended, unless in context it is clear that another method is to be used.

50. (a) A borrows $10,000 at 5% from B and promises to pay, at the end of each year for 10 years, to the noteholder (initially B) a level sum including both capital and interest. Just after A's fourth payment, B sells the contract to C at a price to yield C 6%

(1) On his capital outstanding each year;

(2) On his full investment each year, though C can reproduce his capital at only 4%.

In each case, give an expression in terms of just one tabulated interest function for C's price.

(b) Same as (a), except that A promises to repay the principal of the loan in 10 equal annual installments, together with interest at 5% on the outstanding principal.

<u>Supplementary List</u> (Problems 51-78)

51. The principal of a $50,000 debt is to be repaid by 10 annual $5,000 payments, beginning with one at the end of 5 years. Separate annual payments of interest at 5% on the outstanding principal are to be made, beginning with one at the end of 1 year. At a yield rate of 10%, give expressions for the present value of

(a) The principal repayments;
(b) The interest payments;
(c) All the payments.

52. (a) In the purchase of a home by amortization of a loan of A over n interest periods by level payments, show that the "home-owner's" equity in the home (i.e., total principal repaid) after k payments is $A\ s_{\overline{k|}}/\ s_{\overline{n|}}$.

(b) Assuming amortization by a continuous level annuity over 40 years at an effective annual rate of 8%, what portion of the original cost would the home buyer have purchased by the end of 20 years?

53. For a debt being amortized over 30 interest periods, twice the interest in the 11th payment is 3 times the principal repaid in the 21st period. Without using tables, find a good approximation to the effective interest rate per period.

54. The following exemplify methods of this chapter in non-loan situations.

(a) In considering which of 2 competitive machines to buy, a manufacturer assumes that each would have to be replaced at its original cost at the end of 35 years. The first costs \$45,000 new and would have a scrap value (after 35 years) of \$1,000. The other costs \$48,000, with an \$11,000 scrap value. At what effective annual rate of interest would the machines be equally economical?

(b) An apartment house will cost the owner \$500,000 to build and \$50,000 a year to maintain. Every 5 years renovations will cost him \$25,000. Assuming that the life of the building will be 80 years, and that all items of income and outgo take place at the ends of years, what should the annual rent be to return the owner 8% on his investment and replace his capital by a sinking fund at 5%?

55. For a loan being amortized by an ordinary varying annuity, decide which of the following express the increase in principal repaid in the $(h + 1)$th payment over that in the hth:

(a) $R_{h+1} - R_h + i(A_{h-1} - A_h)$

(b) $R_{h+1} - v\ R_h - id\ A_h$

(c) $R_{h+1} - R_h + i(R_h - i\ A_{h-1})$.

56. The outstanding principal today on a loan made 10 months ago at (.12, 12) is \$1,000.

(a) If \$100 has been received in repayment at the end of each of the 10 months, what was the original principal?

(b) If the \$100 payments are to continue, what will the outstanding principal be 10 months hence, just after the payment?

(c) Show, algebraically and verbally, that the outstanding principal in (b) is $1{,}000 - 90\ s_{\overline{10|}.01}$.

57. (a) A loan of \$1,000 is to be amortized by equal payments at the end of each month for 5 years. How much more total interest does the borrower pay if the interest rate is 6% per year rather than 3% per year, in each case compounded monthly?

(b) How would you solve (a) if the interest rates were 6% and 3% effective per year?

58. (a) On a loan of 1 being amortized by 25 level payments at effective rate i, payments 11, 12, ···, 15 were missed. Subsequent payments are to be of sufficient size to complete the amortization in the original term. Give an expression for the principal repaid in the 16th <u>actual</u> payment.

(b) Suppose that, instead of the loan in (a), 1 is being accumulated in a sinking fund, and that payments to the fund are missed and subsequent payments adjusted as in (a). Give an expression for the increase in the sinking fund in the interest period ending with the 16th <u>actual</u> payment into the fund.

59. A loan of A is being amortized by level payments R as long as necessary ($\bar{n}$ periods) and a final smaller payment one period later. Just after the hth payment, an extra payment of $(A_h - A_{h+k})$ is made, to hasten the repayment of the loan by k periods. Show that the extra payment equals both

$$R(1 - fd)\ _{\bar{n}-h-k|}a_{\overline{k|}} \text{ and } (R - Ai)(s_{\overline{h+k|}} - s_{\overline{h|}}) ,$$

and express the total saving in interest due to the extra payment.

60. (a) What should an investor give for n payments of R, to be made at the ends of $(h - 1/2)$ interest periods $(h = 1, 2, \cdots, n)$, if he wants to receive interest on his investment (at effective rate i per period) on each payment date and if he can build a sinking fund at rate j to refund his capital at the date of the last payment?

(b) To repay a loan in 20 years, a payment of $1,500 is made at the end of each year. Half of the loan will be repaid at the end of the 20 years from a sinking fund growing by deposits made at the end of each of the first 12 years and earning an effective annual rate of 5%. The balance of the $1,500 annual payment, after provision for the sinking fund, is paid to the lender and includes interest at 7% on the principal outstanding. Give an expression for the amount of the loan.

61. In amortization of a debt of A by n level payments R, show that

$$A_t = R(a_{\overline{n|}} - v^n s_{\overline{t|}})$$

and give a verbal interpretation.

62. Fifteen years ago A lent B $10,000 in return for B's promise to make the noteholder annual interest payments at 6% and to accumulate a separate sinking fund at 3% by level annuity payments to contain $10,000 at the end of 20 years from the date of the loan.

(a) What should C pay A now for this contract in order to earn 7%?

(b) At that price what would A's actual earnings rate be? Answer to the nearest 0.1%.

(c) Suppose B has missed the last 5 sinking-fund payments.

(1) Before C assumes the contract from A, what single sum might C insist B pay to the trustee of the sinking fund to bring that fund up to its contractual level?

(2) What increase in the level sinking-fund payment for the final 5 years could C require of B in lieu of the arrangement in (1)?

(3) Suppose C believes B is a bad risk as to the defaulted and future sinking-fund payments. What offer by C to A would assure C a 7% earnings rate?

63. A loan of A, effected on June 1, is to be discharged by an ordinary annuity of 240 monthly payments P at an effective annual rate i, first payment on July 1. Obtain a simple expression for the total interest in the first full <u>calendar</u> year of repayments.

64. (a) A lent $10,000 to B, who agreed to repay the loan by 20 level installments consisting of principal and interest at 5%. Immediately after receiving B's 12th payment, A sells B's note for the remaining payments to C, at a price to yield C 4%. Give an expression from which A's yield rate could be determined.

(b) Same as (a), except that A sells to C at a price which yields A 6% during the 12 periods he held the note, and we want an expression for finding C's yield rate (assuming he holds the note until the loan is fully paid).

65. (a) A lender of A must reinvest the amortization payments $A\,a^{-1}_{\overline{n}|i}$ at only i' ($i' < i$). By what sum is he short of earning compound interest at rate i on A for the whole n periods?

(b) Same, except that the lender in (a) must reinvest his periodic interest payments $i'A\,a^{-1}_{\overline{n}|i}$ at only rate i'' ($i'' < i' < i$).

(c) The lender of A requires periodic interest at rate i and return of his full capital at the end of n periods. By what sum is he short of earning compound interest at rate i on A for the whole n periods, if he can reinvest the periodic interest payments at only i' ($i' < i$)?

66. A loan at 6% is being repaid by annual payments such that (1) the hth regular payment is h times the first payment, (2) the first payment just covers the interest, and (3) the final payment (less than the regular payment at its date) is exactly sufficient to discharge the loan. In what year is repayment completed? Per $100 of original loan, what is the final payment?

67. Same as 34(a)(2), except reverse the order of the payments.

68. An amortization schedule for a 14-month loan with level monthly payments has principal outstanding at the beginning of month 5 of 500.0000. It also has interest paid in month 5 of 10.0000 and in month 6, 9.0867. Find (to the nearest .01)

(a) The principal repaid in the third and twelfth months;
(b) The original principal in two ways;
(c) The total interest paid.

69. A loan of A is to be amortized over the next n periods by periodic payments R designed to yield rate $i > 0$ per period. Show that the mean outstanding loan* is $1/(ni)$ times the total interest paid. Sometimes $A/2$ is used as an approximation to the mean outstanding loan. Show that this approximation is less than the true value.

70. Prove that the total interest paid when a loan is repaid by a level annuity is greater than when it is repaid by equal payments of principal, interest being paid on the balance outstanding during each period, but cannot be more than twice as great. Assume that payment dates are the same in both cases and exceed one in number.

---

*That is, the mean of the amounts of outstanding principal at the beginnings of the n interest periods.

71. A 5% mortgage for $12,500 was made 5 years ago on the basis of repayment over 20 years by equal annual installments covering both principal and interest. The 5th installment is now due, and the borrower wishes to pay off the mortgage in full. The mortgage company must pay its agent as a commission 10% of the portion of each scheduled installment which represents interest. It agrees to allow the borrower to discharge the mortgage upon payment of the installment due, the total amount of future commissions, and a lump sum equal to the discounted value at 4% of the future installments less commissions. To the nearest dollar, what is the full amount now payable?

72. (a) A $1,000 loan is amortized at 5% by 20 level annual payments. Show that at 3% effective, the present value of the repayments of principal is $500(5 - 3\, a_{\overline{20}|.03}\, a^{-1}_{\overline{20}|.05})$.

(b) Suppose that the principal repayments of (a) are made annually, but interest is paid monthly at 5/12% on the outstanding principal. Give a simple expression for the present value of the interest payments, at 3% effective per year.

73. On a 25-year, 6% mortgage for $40,000, the borrower has promised to pay the lender level annual payments at the end of each year and to accumulate monthly payments at 1/2% per month in a savings account to meet each of his annual payments.

(a) Give an expression for the total <u>net</u> amount of interest to be paid by the borrower, making allowance for savings-account interest.

(b) After 10 years the borrower wants to make a lump-sum payment of $5,000 in addition to his regular payment to the lender, and to discharge the mortgage in 10 more years. Give an expression for the new level payment at the end of each future year which is necessary if the lender's terms are

(1) A 7% yield for the next 10 years and a 6% yield for the past 10 years;

(2) A 7% yield over the whole 20-year term.

74. <u>Sinking-fund method of depreciation.</u> The reader has previously encountered terminology involving depreciation of a physical asset and also the straight-line and constant-percentage methods of depreciation (Example 2.3 and List 2, Problems 62 and 66). Accountants also use the sinking-fund method of depreciation in which the depreciation fund is a (mythical) sinking fund of such size that, at an assumed effective annual rate j, (mythical) level deposits F into the fund at the end of each year accumulate in n years to $C - S$, the excess of the original cost of the asset over its salvage value after n years.

(a) For the sinking-fund method of depreciation, derive expressions for F, the depreciation fund and book value B_k at the end of year k, and the depreciation charge D_k for year k $(k = 1, 2, \cdots, n)$.

(b) Depreciate the car of Example 2.3 by the sinking-fund method with $j = .03$, construct a depreciation schedule containing B_k and D_k $(k = 0, 1, 2, \cdots, 5)$ and compare this schedule with those by the constant-percentage and straight-line methods of depreciation in Example 2.3.

(c) Repeat (a) for the case of continuous depreciation by the sinking-fund method, using (in place of F) f denoting the level annual rate of deposit into the fund.

(d) From List 2, Problem 66(c) we know that book values by the straight-line method exceed the corresponding ones by the constant-percentage method, except that they are equal when $k = 0$ or n. Prove that the book values by the sinking-fund method (with $j > 0$) exceed those by the straight-line method ($k \neq 0$ or n); and, assuming that book values are continuous functions of k, $0 \leq k \leq n$, prove that the excess is greatest when

$$k = \delta^{-1} \ln(\bar{s}_{\overline{n}|}/n).$$

75. (a) A debt of A is to be repaid in n periods by level payments R consisting of interest and principal, including interest as follows on the debt outstanding: at rate i'' on the first K_1, at rate i' on the next K_2 and at rate i on the balance, if any, where $i < i' < i''$. Work out a method for finding R when $A > K_1 + K_2$.

(b) If in (a), $A = \$1,000$, $n = 12$, $K_1 = \$200$, $K_2 = \$500$, $i'' = 2.5\%$, $i' = 1.5\%$ and $i = 1\%$, find R.

76. A loan is being repaid by level monthly payments, including interest on the outstanding principal payable as follows: 2% of the first \$300, 1% of the next \$700, 1/2% of the balance. If by the payment at the end of the hth month the principal is reduced by \$79.35 to \$842.13, find

(a) The monthly payment;

(b) The reduction in outstanding principal and amount of principal outstanding at the end of month $h + 4$.

77. A lends \$10,000 to B who promises to pay him a level amount at the end of every year for 3 years and to build up a sinking fund at 3% by annual deposits for 4 years to repay the balance. A will earn 5%, but B feels that he is essentially paying 6% when he considers the present value of all the payments he is to make. Determine the payments A receives, and draw up a schedule showing the progress of repayment of the debt and growth of the sinking fund.

78. (a) In amortization, for n a fixed positive integer independent of i, the need may arise to interpolate linearly for

(1) $a_{\overline{n}|i}$ (i untabulated) (2) i, given $a_{\overline{n}|i}$.

With reference to Example 1.6 and equation (3.50), determine in each case expressions which bracket the actual error and which show its sign.

(b) In (a), replace $a_{\overline{n}|i}$ by $s_{\overline{n}|i}$.

CHAPTER 5

BONDS

5.1. Introduction. One of the classical methods for a corporation or governmental unit to raise funds is by the issue of bonds. Thereby the organization borrows a substantial sum of money, possibly millions of dollars, but for ease of marketing, the loan is split into nominal units such as \$100, \$500, \$1,000, or more. For each such unit of the loan, the organization provides a bond which is a document setting forth the nominal amount of loan it represents and the promises of the organization in respect to the payment of interest and the redemption of the loan. Over the years many forms of bonds have developed, including some which do not pay interest periodically, but which provide for the payment of an accumulated value at redemption; others pay interest periodically but leave redemption to the option of the issuer, or permit the indefinite deferment of redemption; others may have a lottery element such as redemption based on drawing. For the various classifications of bonds the reader may consult a book on investments; here we shall concern ourselves with a mathematical model bond which conforms with the more usual kinds of bonds met in practice. For cases to which the model bond does not conform completely, it will often be easy to make whatever modifications are necessary in the theory.

The nominal amount of loan represented by the model bond, variously called its **denomination** or **face amount** or **par value**, will be denoted by F. One of the purposes of the amount F is to provide a base for the calculation of the periodic payments of bond interest. We shall assume the bond promises to pay interest at the rate r per period; that is, the periodic bond interest payments will be Fr.* In practice the bond interest rate is stated on an annual basis, but interest is usually payable semiannually, in which case r would represent the semiannual rate. Thus a \$1,000 6% bond with semiannual bond interest has $F = \$1,000$ and $r = .03$, and it pays a coupon of $Fr = \$30$ every six months.

*Some persons refer to bond interest payments as coupons. The term arises from certain bonds on which each sum Fr is payable upon presentation of a dated "coupon" clipped from the bond.

The other main promise of the bond is in regard to redemption, and we shall assume the model bond promises to pay the redemption amount $C \geq F$, at the end of n interest periods, to be referred to as the redemption date. If the amount payable on redemption is equal to F (that is, $C = F$), the bond is said to be redeemable at par. In practice, if the bond is not redeemed before a specified maturity date, the face amount F is payable at that date upon surrender of the bond. In other words, at the maturity date, the bond is redeemable at par. However, if redemption occurs before maturity, the redemption amount C may exceed F, as the option to redeem is usually exercised by the issuer of the bond who, under some circumstances, should compensate the bondholder for the premature termination of the investment.

Two other concepts, which are interrelated, are of importance in dealing with bonds. These are the yield rate and the price of the bond. The yield (or investor's) rate is the interest rate that a purchaser of the bond will earn on his investment. The price of a bond, in practical terms, is the amount an investor must pay to become holder or owner of the bond; in terms of theory, the price of the bond is defined as the amount an investor should pay for the bond, exclusive of acquisition costs, in order to earn a given yield rate. It is clear that, given one of these two quantities, yield rate or price, the other should be findable. In fact, the two main problems of bond theory are to determine the price given the yield rate, and to determine the yield rate given the price. The solution of the first problem provides the basis for the solution of the second.

For the model bond, the price will be denoted in general by P, but if the bond is transferred on an interest date, by A; the reasons for the double notation will become clear in Section 5.5. We denote the yield rate per period by i, and for the general development assume that the interest period for the yield rate coincides with the bond interest period. The formulas developed on the basis of this assumption can easily be generalized to the case where the bond interest and the yield rate have different periods. In practice, the yield rate is usually quoted as a nominal annual rate, compounded semiannually, so that i is equal to one half of the annual rate. As mentioned before, the bond interest is usually payable semiannually, so that in the ordinary case the bond interest period and the yield rate period are both a half year.

Bonds are bought and sold in the financial markets and a given bond may have several owners in the course of its term. The price of a bond at a specific time will depend on many factors, including the general level of interest rates and its relation to the bond interest rate, the likelihood that the payments promised by the bond will be made when due and in full, the demand for and supply of investment funds, the effect of income taxes, and so on. Usually, if the price of the bond is close to the face amount, the yield rate will approximate the bond interest rate; but when the price differs considerably from the face amount, the yield rate and the bond interest rate ordinarily also differ.

5.2. Price of a bond on an interest date. In this section there will be given a variety of formulas for finding the price of the model bond on a date n periods (n an integer) before redemption, at an assumed rate of i per period, immediately after payment of bond interest then due. To earn exactly this yield rate, a purchaser should pay the present value, at rate i, of the payments remaining to be made under the terms of the bond (and should hold the bond to the redemption date). Thus, the price A is given by

A = (the present value of the annuity of bond interest payments) plus (the present value of the redemption amount), at rate i. (5.1)

For the model bond,

$$A = Fr\, a_{\overline{n}|i} + C\, v^n. \qquad (5.2)$$

If, however, there are q yield interest periods in a bond interest period, and n represents the number of yield interest periods to redemption, then

$$A = Fr\, s^{-1}_{\overline{q}|i}\, a_{\overline{n}|i} + C\, v^n, \qquad (5.3)$$

where n/q, the term in bond interest periods, is an integer.

Formulas (5.1) to (5.3) are the basic ones for determining the price of a bond on an interest date. A number of rearrangements of these formulas are possible and, in some cases at least, are more convenient for the purpose of calculation. For example, one may substitute $1 - i\, a_{\overline{n}|i}$ for v^n in equation (5.2) to obtain

$$A = C + (Fr - Ci)\, a_{\overline{n}|i}. \qquad (5.4)$$

This formula might also have been gotten directly by considering that at yield rate i an investment of C now will produce interest of Ci per period and repayment of C at the end of n periods, while to yield rate i the investment of A in the bond produces income of Fr per period and a payment of C at the end of n periods. Hence, as indicated in Figure 5.1, $A - C$ must be equivalent at rate i to an annuity of $(Fr - Ci)$ for the n periods:

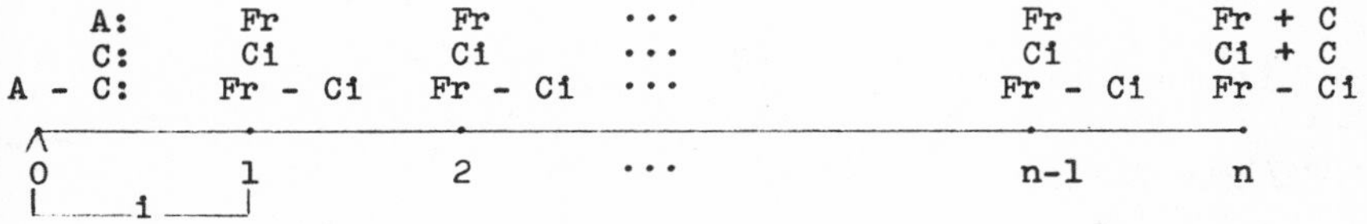
A: Fr Fr ... Fr Fr + C
C: Ci Ci ... Ci Ci + C
A - C: Fr - Ci Fr - Ci ... Fr - Ci Fr - Ci
0 1 2 ... n-1 n
i

Fig. 5.1

In words, the price A exceeds the redemption value C by the present value, at the yield rate, of an annuity of the excess of bond interest payments over periodic interest on C.

The amount $A - C$ is positive if $Fr > Ci$, zero if $Fr = Ci$, and negative if $Fr < Ci$. In the first case, the bond is often said to be bought (or sold) at a <u>premium</u> (particularly if $C = F$); in the last case, when $A < C$, the bond is said to be bought at a <u>discount</u>. In this terminology, the equation (5.4) is referred to as the premium-discount equation for the price of the bond, the amount $|A - C|$ representing the <u>premium</u> or the <u>discount</u>, as the case may be. Finally, if $C = F$ and $r = i$, then $A = F$ and one says that the bond is bought <u>at par</u>.

Another device for finding the price of a bond on an interest date is to determine the base amount G such that

$$Gi = Fr, \qquad i > 0. \tag{5.5}$$

In words, one determines the principal G which, if invested at rate i, would produce periodic interest equal to the bond interest. Then, from Figure 5.2

A: Gi Gi ... Gi Gi + C
G: Gi Gi ... Gi Gi + G
A - G: C - G
0 1 2 ... n-1 n
i

Fig. 5.2

we have $A - G = (C - G)v^n$, or

$$A = G + (C - G)v^n, \qquad i > 0. \tag{5.6}$$

Thus A equals the principal G (on which interest would equal bond interest) plus the present value of the excess of the redemption value C over G. The formula can be obtained also from the equation (5.2) by substituting $\frac{1 - v^n}{i}$ for $a_{\overline{n}|i}$, and rearranging. If G is a round number, formula (5.6) may be particularly convenient to use.

If we set

$$Cg = Fr, \tag{5.7}$$

that is, denote by g the rate of bond interest relative to the redemption value C, and if we denote by K the present value of C, namely,

$$K = C\,v^n, \tag{5.8}$$

then, for $i > 0$, equation (5.2) can be written

$$A = Cg\,\frac{1 - v^n}{i} + K.$$

On rearrangement this becomes

$$A = K + \frac{g}{i}(C - K) \tag{5.9}$$

which is well known to actuaries as Makeham's formula for the price of a bond on an interest date. Besides its use in valuing bonds the formula has wide applicability in valuing other kinds of loans; see Problems 46-48 in List 4 and Problem 46 in List 5.

It is interesting to obtain formula (5.9) by use of elementary analytic geometry. To do so, we must first concede, by considering equation (5.2) in the form $A = Cg\,a_{\overline{n}|i} + C\,v^n$, or directly, that A is a linear function of the rate g. Now, if $g = 0$, no bond interest would be payable, and A would have the value $C\,v^n = K$. Also, if $g = i$, A would have the value C. Thus the straight line representing A as a linear function of g passes through the points with co-ordinates (0, K) and (i, C) and has equation

$$A - K = \frac{C - K}{i - 0}(g - 0)$$

which is equivalent to equation (5.9).

Thus, there is a choice of four mathematical methods for valuing a bond on an interest date: the direct method of the basic formula (5.2) which uses the two interest functions $a_{\overline{n}|}$ and v^n, and three methods, each of which uses just one interest function;

TABLE 5.1

Price of a Bond by Various Methods

($F = \$1,000$; $r = 2\ 1/4\%$; $Fr = \$22.50$; $n = 20$; $C = \$1,050$; $g = \dfrac{22.50}{1,050} = 2\ 1/7\%$)

Formula number	(a) With $i = 2\%$, $G = \dfrac{22.50}{.02} = \$1,125$ and $K = 1,050v^{20} = \$706.6199$	(b) With $i = 2\ 1/2\%$, $G = \dfrac{22.50}{.025} = \$900$ and $K = 1,050v^{20} = \$640.7844$
(5.2)	$22.50\, a_{\overline{20}\rceil} + 1,050v^{20}$	$22.50\, a_{\overline{20}\rceil} + 1,050v^{20}$
(5.4)	$1,050 + [22.50 - 1,050(.02)]a_{\overline{20}\rceil}$	$1,050 + [22.50 - 1,050(.025)]\, a_{\overline{20}\rceil}$
(5.6)	$1,125 + (1,050 - 1,125)v^{20}$	$900 + (1,050 - 900)v^{20}$
(5.9)	$706.6199 + \dfrac{22.50}{1,050(.02)}(1,050 - 706.6199)$	$640.7844 + \dfrac{22.50}{1,050(.025)}(1,050 - 640.7844)$
	$A = \$1,074.53$	$A = \$991.54$

Formula (5.4) clearly brings out the fact that in (a) the bond is selling at a premium and in (b) at a discount. The amounts of premium and discount are, respectively, \$24.53 and \$58.46. Computational advantages of formulas (5.4) and (5.6) are evident here.

namely, the well-known premium-discount method of formula (5.4), the base amount (or G-) method of formula (5.6) and the Makeham (or rate g) method of formula (5.9). As an illustration of these methods, we have found the price of a \$1,000 bond which has bond interest at the rate of 4 1/2% per year, payable semiannually, and which is redeemable at 105 (meaning 105% of the face amount) at the end of 10 years, if the yield rate per year is (a) (4%, 2); (b) (5%, 2). The work appears in Table 5.1.

5.3. Bond tables. In practice, the price of an ordinary bond, redeemable at par and providing a specified yield rate, can be determined readily by use of a bond table. An extract from such a table is given in this section. Extensive tables of this

TABLE 5.2

Values of a \$1,000 Bond with Bond Interest at 4 1/2% per Year, Payable Semiannually

($F = C = \$1{,}000$, $r = 2\ 1/4\%$)

Nominal annual yield rate, convertible semi-annually	Years to redemption				
	8	8 1/2	9	9 1/2	10
4.00%	1,033.94	1,035.73	1,037.48	1,039.20	1,040.88
4.25	1,016.81	1,017.68	1,018.54	1,019.37	1,020.19
4.50	1,000.00	1,000.00	1,000.00	1,000.00	1,000.00
4.75	983.52	982.68	981.86	981.06	980.28
5.00	967.36	965.72	964.12	962.55	961.03

nature are available and may show values of A for each 0.05% step in the yield rate and for each month to redemption. It is to be noted that the tables are based on the assumption of redemption at par.

If redemption of a \$1,000 bond is not at par but at the value $C > 1{,}000$, then by setting $C - 1{,}000 = E$, one can obtain the value of the bond by

$$A = \text{value from table} + Ev^n.$$

Alternatively, one can write

$$A = Cg\, a_{\overline{n}|i} + Cv^n = \frac{C}{1{,}000}\left[1{,}000g\, a_{\overline{n}|i} + 1{,}000v^n\right]$$

$$= \frac{C}{1{,}000}\left[\text{Table value for bond with bond interest rate } 2g \text{ per year}\right].$$

In this latter procedure, 2g might not coincide with the rates for which values are tabulated, and interpolation would then be required. However, since A is a linear function of g, linear interpolation produces an exact result.

The first procedure applied to the previously considered \$1,000 4 1/2% bond, redeemable 10 years hence at 105%, produces at an annual yield rate of (.04, 2)

$$A = 1{,}040.88 + 50v^{20} = \$1{,}074.53$$

again, and at (.05, 2)

$$A = 961.03 + 50v^{20} = \$991.54,$$

as before. Even though our bond-table values are at the single rate $g = 2\ 1/4\%$, the second procedure can be illustrated by taking as the second rate $g = i$ in each instance, for then the price tabulated in the bond table would be \$1,000.00. The given rate g is $22.50/1{,}050 = 2\ 1/7\%$. Thus, to yield (.04, 2), we have by linear interpolation

$$A = \frac{1{,}050}{1{,}000}\left[1{,}000 + \frac{2\ 1/7 - 2}{2\ 1/4 - 2}(1{,}040.88 - 1{,}000)\right] = \$1{,}074.53,$$

while for an investor's rate of (.05, 2), linear extrapolation produces

$$A = \frac{1{,}050}{1{,}000}\left[1{,}000 - \frac{2\ 1/2 - 2\ 1/7}{2\ 1/2 - 2\ 1/4}(1{,}000 - 961.03)\right] = \$991.54.$$

5.4. Bond schedules. Generally when a bond is issued by a corporation or a government, or purchased by an investor, to provide a given yield rate, its value will differ from the redemption value, that is, the bond will be at a premium or at a discount. There then develop the problems of how the issuer can realistically value its liability from time to time during the term of the bond, and how the investor can value his asset. In other words, there is a need in the case of the issuer to determine its outstanding liability and, in the case of the investor, the outstanding principal or capital.

While there are several ways in which these values might be determined periodically, there is good accounting opinion that they should be calculated by a sort of partial amortization process. This procedure is most obvious in regard to bonds bought at a premium. In that case each bond interest payment is first applied to pay interest at the yield rate on the outstanding principal (as of the beginning of the interest period) and the balance of the bond interest payment is used to repay principal. In this way the value of the bond is "written down" from the amount originally invested to the amount available at redemption. The amount of outstanding principal so determined will be referred to as the book value of the bond. As we shall see later, for bonds bought at a discount, a mathematically identical procedure is applied, but the interpretation is different.

Let us consider the model bond purchased for price A on a date n periods (an integer) before redemption at the amount C, with bond interest of Fr to be paid at the end of each interest period, and yield interest to be at rate i; for the time being assume that $A > C$. From the relation

$$A = C + (A - C) = C + (Fr - Ci)\,a_{\overline{n}|\,i},$$

we see, as before, that the investment may be regarded as consisting of (1) a basic portion C on which interest will be paid periodically at rate i and which will be repaid at redemption date; (2) the premium portion $A - C$ which is to be amortized at rate i by payments of $Fr - Ci$, representing the excess of bond interest over the yield interest on C. Then the book value at the end of any interest period (immediately following the payment of bond interest) will equal C plus the outstanding premium. Denoting such a book value at the end of h integral interest periods after purchase by A_h, we have $A_0 = A$ and $A_n = C$.

The bond interest payment Fr for the first period can be split into three pieces:

(a) Ci, yield interest on C,

(b) $(A_0 - C)i = (Fr - Ci)(1 - v^n)$, yield interest on the outstanding premium, and

(c) $(Fr - Ci)v^n$, the portion of the premium-amortization payment $Fr - Ci$ that is applied on principal.

The sum of (a) and (b) is $A_0 i$, that is, interest on the book value at the beginning of the period. The amount (c) is available to reduce the book value which becomes

$$\begin{aligned} A_1 = A_0 - (Fr - Ci)v^n &= C + (Fr - Ci)\,a_{\overline{n}|\,i} - (Fr - Ci)v^n \\ &= C + (Fr - Ci)\,a_{\overline{n-1}|\,i}. \end{aligned}$$

Not unexpectedly, the book value A_1 equals the price an investor should pay in order to obtain a yield rate i by purchasing the bond $n - 1$ periods before redemption.

The process for the whole term of the bond is indicated in Table 5.3.

As in other amortization processes, the principal payments shown in column (4) for a premium bond form an increasing

TABLE 5.3

Investment Schedule for a Bond

(Term n periods; bond interest rate r; yield rate i)

(1) Interest period h	(2) Bond interest payment at end of period h Fr	(3) Yield interest (on book value at beginning of period h) $A_{h-1}\,i = (5)_{-1}\,i$	(4) Balance of bond interest used to decrease the book value (2)-(3)	(5) Book value at end of period h after payment of bond interest $A_h = (5)_{-1} - (4)$
0				$C + (Fr - Ci)\,a_{\overline{n}\rceil i}$
1	Fr	$Ci + (Fr - Ci)(1 - v^n)$	$(Fr - Ci)v^n$	$C + (Fr - Ci)\,a_{\overline{n-1}\rceil i}$
2	Fr	$Ci + (Fr - Ci)(1 - v^{n-1})$	$(Fr - Ci)v^{n-1}$	$C + (Fr - Ci)\,a_{\overline{n-2}\rceil i}$
⋮	⋮	⋮	⋮	⋮
h	Fr	$Ci + (Fr - Ci)(1 - v^{n-h+1})$	$(Fr - Ci)v^{n-h+1}$	$C + (Fr - Ci)\,a_{\overline{n-h}\rceil i}$
⋮	⋮	⋮	⋮	⋮
n - 1	Fr	$Ci + (Fr - Ci)(1 - v^2)$	$(Fr - Ci)v^2$	$C + (Fr - Ci)\,a_{\overline{1}\rceil i}$
n	Fr	$Ci + (Fr - Ci)(1 - v)$	$(Fr - Ci)v$	C
Totals	nFr	nFr - (A - C)	$(Fr - Ci)a_{\overline{n}\rceil} = A - C$	$(n + 1)C + (Fr - Ci)(n - a_{\overline{n}\rceil})/i$

geometric series. One notes that for period h the bond interest Fr provides (a) yield interest on A_{h-1} and (b) the amount $Fr - A_{h-1}\,i = (Fr - Ci)v^{n-h+1}$ for repayment of premium; that is, in all,

$$Fr = A_{h-1}\,i + (Fr - Ci)v^{n-h+1}, \qquad h = 1, 2, \cdots, n. \tag{5.10}$$

This can be rewritten as

$$Fr = A_{h-1}\,i + (A_{h-1} - A_h), \tag{5.11a}$$

or

$$A_h = A_{h-1}(1 + i) - Fr. \tag{5.11b}$$

It is instructive to make verbal interpretations of these last two formulas and to compare them with the amortization relation (4.1). On multiplying equation (5.11b) by v^h, one obtains

$$-\,\Delta(v^{h-1}\,A_{h-1}) = Fr\;v^h.$$

Changing h to k and summing over k = 1 to $k = h \le n$, we have after simplification

$$A_h = A(1 + i)^h - Fr\;s_{\overline{h}\rceil i}. \tag{5.11c}$$

Also, by summing over $k = h + 1$ to $k = n$, and taking account of $A_n = C$, we get

$$A_h = Fr\, a_{\overline{n-h}|i} + C\, v^{n-h} . \qquad (5.11d)$$

As indicated previously, for our bond bought at a premium the process can be considered as a partial amortization procedure with payments of Fr to pay interest on outstanding principal and to carry the investment down from its initial value A to the redemption value C, and this is borne out by the formulas (5.11). Alternatively, as indicated in Table 5.3, the process can be considered as complete amortization of the premium A - C by payments of Fr - Ci, the balance Ci of the bond interest payment Fr being utilized to pay interest on the redemption amount C. In practice, the amounts in column (4) are often labelled "For amortization of premium" while actually the amounts so applied are Fr - Ci, consisting of both interest on the outstanding premium and the amounts of column (4) for repayment of premium.

Let us construct the investment schedule for a $1,000 bond redeemable at par at the end of 3 years, bearing bond interest at 5% payable semiannually, and bought to yield an investor a rate of 4%, compounded semiannually. The price of this bond is given by the equation

$$A = 1,000 + (25 - 20)\, a_{\overline{6}|.02} = \$1,028.01;$$

the schedule appears in Table 5.4.

TABLE 5.4

Investment Schedule

For a $1,000 bond with annual bond interest rate (.05, 2), redeemable at par at the end of 3 years, and with annual yield rate (.04, 2).

(1) Interest period h	(2) Bond interest payment at end of period h .025 F	(3) Interest at 2% on book value at beginning of period h .02 A_{h-1}	(4) Balance of bond interest used to decrease book value (2) - (3)	(5) Book value at end of period h after payment of bond interest $A_h = (5)_{-1} - (4)$
0	$	$	$	$1,028.01
1	25.00	20.56	4.44	1,023.57
2	25.00	20.47	4.53	1,019.04
3	25.00	20.38	4.62	1,014.42
4	25.00	20.29	4.71	1,009.71
5	25.00	20.19	4.81	1,004.90
6	25.00	20.10	4.90	1,000.00
Totals	$150.00	$121.99	$28.01	$7,099.65

The totals are useful as check values to the corresponding totals as given in Table 5.3.

In the case of a bond bought at a discount, the items in the investment schedule have the same algebraic form, but now $C > A$ and $Fr - Ci$ is negative, and so the decreases in the book value shown in the schedule are negative, that is, are effectively increases. The relation (5.10) still holds, but can be rearranged as

$$A_{h-1}\, i = Fr + (Ci - Fr)v^{n-h+1}, \qquad h = 1, 2, \cdots, n \qquad (5.12)$$

which shows that only a portion of the yield interest is provided by the bond interest payment Fr, and the remainder is provided through the increase $(Ci - Fr)\, v^{n-h+1}$ in the book value. In this way the book value of the bond is "written up" from its initial value A to the redemption value C. In practice, this process is referred to as "accumulation of the discount."

To illustrate, we shall construct the investment schedule for the bond of the previous schedule but with yield rate at 6%, compounded semiannually. Now the price of the bond is

$$A = 1{,}000 + (25 - 30)\, a_{\overline{6}|.03} = \$972.91,$$

that is, the bond is at a discount of \$27.09. The accumulation of this discount is shown in Table 5.5. Headings of column (4) in Tables 5.5 and 5.4 might be compared.

TABLE 5.5

Investment Schedule

For a \$1,000 bond with annual bond interest rate (.05, 2), redeemable at par at the end of 3 years, and with annual yield rate (.06, 2).

(1) Interest period h	(2) Bond interest payment at end of period h $.025\,F$	(3) Interest at 3% on book value at beginning of period h $.03\,A_{h-1}$	(4) Excess of yield interest over bond interest to increase book value (3) - (2)	(5) Book value at end of period h after payment of bond interest $A_h = (5)_{-1} + (4)$
0	\$	\$	\$	\$ 972.91
1	25.00	29.19	4.19	977.10
2	25.00	29.31	4.31	981.41
3	25.00	29.44	4.44	985.85
4	25.00	29.58	4.58	990.43
5	25.00	29.71	4.71	995.14
6	25.00	29.85	4.85	999.99
Totals	\$150.00	\$177.08	\$27.08	\$6,902.83

The relations (5.11) are valid for both premium and discount cases. Also, in both cases, the book value at the end of any period is equal to the price of the bond as of that date on the basis of the given yield rate.

It is sometimes suggested that book values should be determined by uniform decreases of $\frac{A - C}{n}$ for a bond at a premium, and uniform increases of $\frac{C - A}{n}$ for a bond at a discount. Such constant adjustments would be greater at the beginning and smaller at the end than the absolute values of the geometric adjustments shown in column (4) of the investment schedule (Table 5.3). Hence for a bond bought at a premium the book values by the uniform method would be smaller than those by the amortization procedure, while for a bond bought at a discount they would exceed those provided by accumulating the discount. The uniform procedure would not keep interest payments up-to-date, and the book values would not coincide with the prices on interest dates. Despite these failings, the uniform method is useful for (1) affording estimates of the book values by the investment schedule method and (2) determining the average principal invested for purposes of estimating the yield rate when the price is given.

5.5. Price and book value between interest dates. In the preceding sections we have considered the price or book value of a bond on bond interest dates only. However, bonds are bought and sold throughout the year and, in most instances, will be purchased on a day which is not an interest date. Although the market price, as mentioned before, will be the resultant of many factors, not all of which are susceptible to mathematical formulation, there is both theoretical and practical interest in determining the price and book value of a given bond between interest dates on the assumption that a specified yield rate is to be earned if the bond is held to a specified redemption date.

When a bond is purchased between interest dates, the first bond interest payment after the purchase date has a special status. Part of that payment was earned or accrued in the interval from the previous interest date to the purchase date, and the balance in the interval since the purchase date. The first-named part of that bond interest payment is referred to as the accrued interest. The bond itself may be regarded as the combination of a short-term investment -- until the next interest date -- in the accrued interest, plus a basic investment providing bond interest from the purchase date and the redemption amount at the redemption date. For this basic investment, the initial bond interest payment is contained in the complement of the accrued interest, that is, in the difference between the regular bond interest payment and the accrued interest; thereafter, the full regular bond interest payments are available.

Let us consider consecutive interest dates 0, 1, 2, $\cdots$ and assume that 0 is n interest periods before redemption date. Let t, $0 \le t < 1$, denote a time (measured in interest periods) between the first two interest dates, or (in case $t = 0$) at the first interest date after interest then due has been paid. At time t, the price of the bond to provide a yield rate i will be denoted by P_t, the accrued interest by I_t, and the book, or investment, value by A_t. In general, A_t will equal or approximate the value of the basic investment, while P_t will take into account both the basic investment and the short-term investment in the accrued interest. We shall value these quantities in several ways, but in all cases there will be the relation

$$P_t = A_t + I_t \tag{5.13a}$$

which serves to define the book value of the bond at time t. Also, this equation indicates that the seller of the bond receives credit for the bond interest accrued from the preceding interest date.

For the second interest period, the price, accrued interest and book value will be denoted by P_{1+t}, I_{1+t} and A_{1+t}, $0 \le t < 1$; and so forth. The general relation is

$$P_{h+t} = A_{h+t} + I_{h+t}, \quad h = 0, 1, 2, \cdots, n-1 \text{ and } 0 \le t < 1, \text{ or } h = n, t = 0. \tag{5.13b}$$

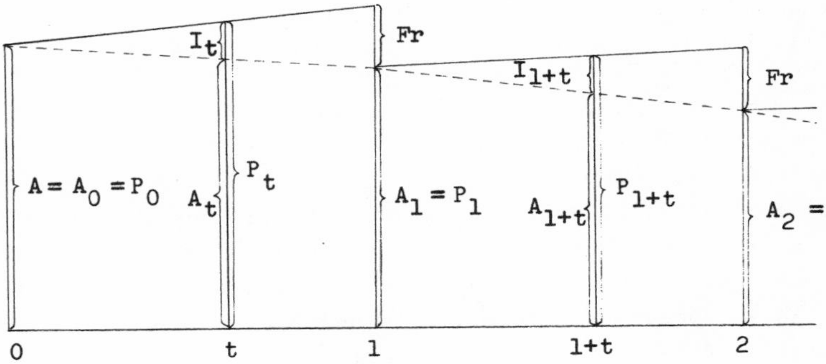

Fig. 5.3

Figure 5.3 illustrates equations (5.13) graphically. In this figure prices are illustrated by the upper solid segments and the book values by the dotted segments. On interest dates, after the bond interest has been paid, there is no accrued interest so at such times price and book value coincide. During an interest period, price and book value diverge by the amount of accrued interest which reaches its maximum, Fr, at the end of the period just before the bond interest is paid. On the interest date, the price breaks downward by the amount of the bond interest payment. To avoid such breaks in the market quotations of the price of a bond or in bond tables, it is customary to make the book value be the quoted price of the bond; the actual price (except for any acquisition costs) is the quoted price plus accrued interest.

Three methods will be used to value the quantities P_t, I_t and A_t. The first method uses compound interest consistently throughout, and will be called the theoretical method. The second, or semitheoretical method, uses compound interest to find P_t, but simple interest for I_t. The third method is the one commonly used in practice, and is called the practical method. As the name might suggest, the practical method employs simple interest for both P_t and I_t. A summary is given in Table 5.6.

TABLE 5.6

Formulas for Price, Accrued Interest and Book Value (At a time t interest periods since the last interest date, $0 \le t < 1$).

Method	Price, P_t	Accrued Interest, I_t	Book Value, A_t
I Theoretical	$A_0(1+i)^t$	$(Fr/s_{\overline{1}\rceil})s_{\overline{t}\rceil} = Fr\ s_{\overline{t}\rceil}$	$A_0(1+i)^t - Fr\ s_{\overline{t}\rceil}$
II Semi-theoretical	$A_0(1+i)^t$	Frt	$A_0(1+i)^t - Frt$
III Practical	$A_0(1+it)$	Frt	$A_0(1+it) - Frt$

The more general P_{h+t}, I_{h+t}, A_{h+t} for $h = 0, 1, 2, \cdots, n-1$ and $0 \le t < 1$ are obtained as in Table 5.6 with A_0 in P_t and A_t replaced by A_h. Note that $I_{h+t} = I_t$.

For a fixed yield rate, the price and the book value are functions of the term to redemption date; in particular, price and book value strictly between interest dates depend upon the book value on the previous interest date and the subsequent interval t, regardless of the method of valuation. Thus, a purchaser (or seller) has not only a price and book value for his bond at the time of the transaction but a whole set of corresponding prices and book values at all times from issue to redemption, based on the yield rate and any one of the three methods.

An additional remark, pertaining to all three methods of valuation is that, for $Fr > 0$ and i fixed, the price and accrued-interest functions have discontinuities (of Fr) at every interest date, but the book-value function is continuous wherever defined. Moreover, all three methods are identical if and only if $i = 0$. There follow a few remarks about the individual methods.

Since $A_h = Fr\, a_{\overline{n-h}|} + Cv^{n-h}$, the book value by the theoretical method can be expressed as $A_{h+t} = Fr\, a_{\overline{n-h-t}|} + Cv^{n-h-t}$ for $h = 0, 1, 2, \cdots, n - 1$; and $A_n = C$. This shows that the theoretical book value is given by the basic price formula (5.2) for all durations to redemption, whether integral or not.

The semitheoretical method, which has been used in some bond tables and elsewhere, has the anomaly that for bonds with $i = r$ and redeemable at par, it gives book values different from par value at any date which is not an interest date. This is a defect which the other methods do not have.

It is to be noted that under the practical method, P_t and A_t are linear functions of t and, more generally, for fixed h $(h = 0, 1, 2, \cdots, n - 1)$ so are P_{h+t} and A_{h+t}. Thus, their graphs (as in Figure 5.3) between any two consecutive interest dates are straight line segments. Since A_{h+t} is also continuous at $h + 1$, a consequence is that A_{h+t} for the practical method can be obtained by linear interpolation between A_h and A_{h+1}. In particular, when $h = 0$ we have

$$A_t = A_0 + t(A_1 - A_0) = (1 - t)A_0 + tA_1.$$

As an example, we will find the price and book value of a \$1,000 bond redeemable at par at the end of 9 months and bearing bond interest at an annual rate of 5% payable semiannually, next payment due at the end of 3 months. The yield rate is 6% per year, compounded semiannually.

This is the discount bond for which a schedule appears in Table 5.5, but it is considered at the middle of the second interest period before redemption. Now $A_0 = \$990.43$ from that schedule. The price, accrued interest and book value by the various methods, obtained by applying the formulas in Table 5.6, are given in Table 5.7. With the use of $A_1 = \$995.14$ from Table 5.5, the book value by the practical method can be checked by linear interpolation.

TABLE 5.7

Price, Accrued Interest and Book Value

For a \$1,000 bond with annual bond interest rate (.05, 2), redeemable at par at the end of 9 months, and with annual yield rate (.06, 2).

Method	Price	Accrued Interest	Book Value
Theoretical	\$1,005.18	\$12.41	\$992.77
Semitheoretical	1,005.18	12.50	992.68
Practical	1,005.29	12.50	992.79

It is wise to extend some definitions of Section 5.2; namely, that a bond is at a premium or at a discount on a date according as $A_t > C$ or $A_t < C$, where A_t is its book value on that date; the reader can supply the definition for a bond being at par. Thus the bond above is at a discount 9 months before redemption, although the actual price, including the accrued interest, is in excess of the \$1,000 par value.

Problem 25 in List 5 explores some relationships involving A_{h+t} and P_{h+t}. In particular, it provides the useful extension of formula (5.11c) to

$$A_{h+t} = A_t(1 + i)^h - Fr\, s_{\overline{h|}\, i}, \qquad (5.11c)'$$

valid for both the theoretical and practical methods. Note that formula (5.11c)' offers a way of calculating book values on anniversary dates of bond purchase.

It is of some practical interest to determine how the investment schedule would operate for the interval from purchase time t to time 1, the end of the interest period. This is indicated briefly for the three methods in Table 5.8.

A number of comments can be made concerning the items in Table 5.8.

(a) The schedules start off with A_t, the book value at time t. The accrued interest I_t is excluded and would require separate accounting.

(b) The schedules end up with A_1, the book value at time 1; from that point onward the bond schedule can proceed as in Section 5.4.

(c) In the theoretical and semitheoretical methods, the yield interest for the interval t to 1 is calculated on $P_t = A_0(1 + i)^t$ which is the total amount invested at time t, <u>including</u> the accrued interest. One of the purposes of the bond schedule is to show the total interest earned in the different

TABLE 5.8

Start of the Investment Schedule for a Bond Purchased between Interest Dates

(1) Interval	(2) Bond interest earned for interval	(3) Interest at yield rate for interval	(4) Balance of bond interest used to adjust book value	(5) Book value at end of interval (A_0, value at 0)
I Theoretical Method				
0 to t				$A_0(1+i)^t - Fr\, s_{\overline{t}\vert}$
t to 1	$Fr(1 - s_{\overline{t}\vert})$	$A_0\left[(1+i) - (1+i)^t\right]$ $= P_t\left[(1+i)^{1-t} - 1\right]$ $= A_0 i(1 - s_{\overline{t}\vert})$	$Fr(1 - s_{\overline{t}\vert}) - A_0\left[(1+i) - (1+i)^t\right]$ $= (Fr - A_0 i)(1 - s_{\overline{t}\vert})$	$A_0(1+i) - Fr = A_1$
II Semitheoretical Method. Same as above, except Frt everywhere replaces $Fr\, s_{\overline{t}\vert}$.				
III Practical Method				
0 to t				$A_0(1+it) - Frt$
t to 1	$Fr(1 - t)$	$A_0 i\,(1 - t)$	$(Fr - A_0 i)(1 - t)$	$A_0(1+i) - Fr = A_1$

intervals by the bond, and it is more realistic to show the total yield interest for the interval t to 1 rather than simply the yield interest on the book value A_t or A_0.

(d) In the practical method, consistent with the simple interest concept but inconsistent with the actual investment of $A_0(1 + it) = P_t$, the yield interest for the interval t to 1 has been calculated on a principal of A_0. One can argue, however, that $A_0i(1 - t)$ is a convenient approximation to the yield interest $A_0[(1 + i) - (1 + i)^t]$ determined by the theoretical method. In fact, the schedule for the practical method is a simplification of that for the theoretical method, with t replacing $s_{\overline{t|}}$ and with $(1 + it)$ replacing $(1 + i)^t$.

5.6. Determination of the yield rate. We turn now to what is perhaps the most important practical application of bond theory, namely the determination of the yield rate that would be earned by an investor who purchases a bond at a given price and holds it to redemption date. The yield rate is, of course, a major factor in the marketability of a bond. Also, it provides an important criterion for the comparison of bonds available for purchase by an investor.

We consider a bond that will be redeemed at the end of n interest periods and assume to begin with that n is an integer, that is, the bond is priced on an interest date. Then the actual price for the bond will agree with the quoted price or book value, and will be denoted by A. Many formulas and methods are available for the determination of the yield rate in such a case (see, for instance, Todhunter, Chapter VIII; Donald, Chapter 11; Hummel and Seebeck, Secs. 58, 77, 78; Sheppard and Baillie, Chapter VIII; and Kellison, Sec. 6.6). It is important to stress at the outset that, although various methods produce somewhat different answers, nevertheless for every bond with fixed redemption there is a unique, exact yield rate. The reader can convince himself of this fact by use, for example, of formula (5.2) in which the right member is a monotone decreasing function of i. The following five methods indicate some of the possible procedures.

(a) The method of averages. Here an estimate i_0 of the yield rate is obtained by taking the ratio of the average amount of yield interest per period to the average investment. As indicated in Table 5.3, the total yield interest for the n periods to redemption is $nFr - (A - C) = nFr + (C - A)$, that is, the total bond interest less the premium A - C in case the bond is bought at a premium, or the total bond interest plus the discount C - A, in the discount case. In either case, the average yield interest per period can be expressed as

$$[nFr - (A - C)]/n = Fr - (A - C)/n.$$

The average investment is estimated as the mean of the initial investment A and the redemption value C, that is, $\frac{1}{2}(A + C)$. (The exact average would be obtained by averaging the book values at the beginnings of the periods, but as can be seen from Table 5.3 the result would involve the unknown rate i.) Despite the rather rough estimate of the average investment, the formula

$$i_0 = \frac{Fr - (A - C)/n}{(A + C)/2} \tag{5.14}$$

usually provides a good initial estimate i_0 for the yield rate i per period. The formula is quick and easy to apply; in fact, it does not require the use of interest tables.

(b) Uniform-adjustment-of-book-values method. For this improvement on the method of averages the average investment is estimated by assuming that the book value is adjusted by the uniform amount (A - C)/n per period to carry it from its initial value A to the final value C. The successive book values at the beginnings of the n interest periods are then

$$A,\ A - \frac{1}{n}(A - C),\ A - \frac{2}{n}(A - C),\ \cdots,\ A - \frac{n-1}{n}(A - C),$$

and they have mean value

$$A - \frac{n-1}{2n}(A - C) = \frac{n+1}{2n}A + \frac{n-1}{2n}C.$$

Then, the estimated yield rate is

$$i_0 = \frac{Fr - (A - C)/n}{\frac{n+1}{2n}A + \frac{n-1}{2n}C} \tag{5.15}$$

which, unless n is small, does not differ greatly from the result of formula (5.14).

While for some purposes method (a) or (b) produces a satisfactory estimate of the true yield rate, in most cases it gives merely an initial estimate useful in obtaining a more reliable result from the more refined methods (c), (d) and (e) below.

(c) Interpolation method. After an approximate yield rate has been determined by formula (5.14) or (5.15), or otherwise, one can use linear interpolation to obtain a more accurate value i_1. By trying yield rates in the neighborhood of i_0, he can obtain rates i' and i'' where $i' < i''$, such that the corresponding prices A' and A'' for the bond will bracket the given price A. Then

$$i_1 = i' + \frac{A - A'}{A'' - A'}(i'' - i') \tag{5.16}$$

will provide a more refined approximation. If bond tables are available, the calculation will be facilitated. In fact, in that case, it may not be necessary to use formula (5.14) or (5.15) for a first approximation, as table inspection may be a sufficient guide for the selection of i' and i''.

By the theorem of Example 1.6 and its proof, it can be shown that i_1 exceeds the true value of i, but by not more than

$$\frac{1}{8}(i'' - i')^3 \frac{n(n + 1)A'}{A' - A''}.$$

To establish this, one must show that $\frac{d^2A}{di^2} < n(n + 1)A$. By writing $A = Fr(v + v^2 + \cdots + v^n) + Cv^n$ and then differentiating, we obtain the result.

With sufficiently powerful calculating equipment, the method can be repeated again and again until the bracketing, generally untabulated rates pinch in on the true yield rate and produce a rate as accurate as desired. However, the successive approximations by this method are more laborious than those of the iteration methods (d) and (e) which follow.

(d) First iteration method. In The Record of the American Institute of Actuaries, 1941, pp. 191-194, C.A. Spoerl indicated a useful iteration method and provided a table to facilitate its use. One starts with the formula

$$A = C + (Fr - Ci)a_{\overline{n}|i}$$

and solves for i to obtain

$$i = \frac{Fr - (A - C)a^{-1}_{\overline{n}|i}}{C}$$

or

$$i = g - k\,a^{-1}_{\overline{n}|i} \tag{5.17}$$

where $k = (A - C)/C$. As the factor $a^{-1}_{\overline{n}|i}$ changes slowly with change in i, a good estimate of i can be obtained by using an approximate value of i in the right member of (5.17). By starting with $i_0 = g + \Delta$ where $\Delta \doteq -k\, a^{-1}_{\overline{n}|i}$, or with an i_0 from (a) or (b), one obtains

$$i_1 = g - k\, a^{-1}_{\overline{n}|i_0}.$$

Further approximations are given by

$$i_m = g - k\, a^{-1}_{\overline{n}|i_{m-1}} \tag{5.18}$$

and the iteration can be continued within the limits of available or calculable values of $a^{-1}_{\overline{n}|}$. Two cranks in the process are usually enough to give a quite accurate value. The process produces i exactly if (and only if) $i_0 = i$.

By comparing formulas (5.17) and (5.18), one sees that

$$\begin{aligned} i - i_m &= k\, [a^{-1}_{\overline{n}|i_{m-1}} - a^{-1}_{\overline{n}|i}] \\ &= k\, [i_{m-1} - i + s^{-1}_{\overline{n}|i_{m-1}} - s^{-1}_{\overline{n}|i}] . \end{aligned}$$

From this it follows that if $i_0 \neq i$, then

$$|i - i_m| < |i - i_{m-1}|$$

whenever $|k| < 1$, which occurs if $A < 2C$. Thus, unless A is disproportionately large relative to C, we can conclude that the accuracy of the estimate for i is improved by each step in the iteration process, subject, of course, to the accuracy of the factors used.

If $i_0 \neq i$, it can be shown that for a discount bond the sequence $\{i_m\} = \{i_0, i_1, i_2, \cdots\}$ is strictly monotone in its convergence on i; but that for a premium bond, all consecutive values i_m and i_{m+1} are on opposite sides of i, and so in that case if i_m and i_{m+1} are equal up to a certain number of decimals, then the true rate i, to that degree of accuracy, is the common value. This is clearly an additional advantage of the method for premium bonds.

(e) Second iteration method. An alternative procedure is obtained by replacing $a^{-1}_{\overline{n}|i}$ in formula (5.17) by $i + s^{-1}_{\overline{n}|i}$ and solving for i to find

$$i = \frac{g - k\, s^{-1}_{\overline{n}|i}}{1 + k} . \tag{5.19}$$

Then

$$i_m = \frac{g - k\, s^{-1}_{\overline{n}|\,i_{m-1}}}{1 + k} \qquad (5.20)$$

can be used to give successive approximations for i. In the same way as for the first iteration method one can argue that, for $n \neq 1$, (1) the exact i is obtained if and only if $i_0 = i$ and (2) if $i_0 \neq i$, then each step improves the accuracy of estimate, provided that $|k/(1 + k)| \leq 1$ which implies $A \geq \frac{1}{2} C$. The procedure does not at first seem as convenient as (d) but has two useful properties for the typical case in which $i_0 \neq i$ and n is any integer larger than 1. The first of these is that if the same i_{m-1} is used for the two iteration processes, and i^{I}_m, i^{II}_m are the results, then

$$i - i^{II}_m = \frac{k}{1 + k}\left[s^{-1}_{\overline{n}|\,i_{m-1}} - s^{-1}_{\overline{n}|\,i}\right]$$

is of opposite sign to

$$i - i^{I}_m = k\left[a^{-1}_{\overline{n}|\,i_{m-1}} - a^{-1}_{\overline{n}|\,i}\right].$$

Hence, in such cases, i lies between i^{I}_m and i^{II}_m. Secondly, we note that the sequence $\{i^{II}_m\}$ has a strictly monotone convergence on i for a premium bond but for a discount bond its successive members leapfrog i. (Problem 30 in List 5 deals with the special case $n = 1$ with a result that $i^{II}_1 = i^{II}_2 = \cdots = i$.) Thus, the second iteration method efficiently produces i to any predetermined accuracy for discount bonds, just as the first iteration method does for premium bonds.

TABLE 5.9

Yield rate of a Bond by Various Methods
($F = 100$, $C = 110$, $n = 50$, $r = 2.75\%$, $A = 105$; then $g = 2.5\%$ and $k = -1/22$; to 6 decimal places, true value of the yield rate is .026656.)

	Method	Formula	Yield rate
(a)	Of averages	(5.14)	.026512
(b)	Uniform adjustment of book values	(5.15)	.026524
(c)	Interpolation with $i' = .025$, $i'' = .0275$ ($A' = 110$, $A'' = 102.575778$)	(5.16)	.026684
(d)	First iteration process with $i_0 = g$	(5.18)	i_1 = .026603 i_2 = .026654
(e)	Second iteration process with $i_0 = g$	(5.20)	i_1 = .026679 i_2 = .026656

In his Chapter VIII Todhunter gives an example which is summarized in Table 5.9 for the five methods of this section. Note that the true value lies between the first approximations given by the two iteration processes with $i_0 = g$. Also, for this discount bond observe the monotonic increasing nature of $\{i_m^I\}$ toward i and the fact that $i_0^{II} < i < i_1^{II}$, $i_2^{II} = i$ to six decimals. The excess of the approximation by interpolation over the true yield rate, .000028 to six decimals, is well within its upper limit, .000074, determined by the formula of subsection (c).

Up to now we have thought of n as an integer, that is, of the bond being purchased on an interest date. If, as often happens, n is nonintegral, say $n = n_0 - t$ where t, $0 < t < 1$, is the portion of an interest period elapsed since the last bond interest date, the quoted price or book value A_t of the bond will differ from the actual price P_t which includes the accrued bond interest. To adapt the preceding procedures to give the yield rate for such a case, it is most consistent with the theory to use the quoted price A_t for A in the yield rate formulas rather than to use P_t. As confirmation of this, we have seen from Table 5.6 and its discussion that, under the theoretical method of assigning book values, the quantity A_t is expressed by the same basic formulas

$$Fr\,a_{\overline{n_0-t}|} + Cv^{n_0-t} = Fr\,a_{\overline{n}|} + Cv^n = C + (Fr - Ci)\,a_{\overline{n}|i}$$

which were used in the development of the iteration procedures.

For all positive n, the sequence $\{i_m^I\}$ behaves as it did for positive integral n; and for all $n > 1$, the sequence $\{i_m^{II}\}$ behaves as for integral n exceeding 1. It follows from this, and the previous discussion of the iteration methods, that for $n \geq 1$ one can use the first iteration method for premium bonds and the second iteration method for discount bonds to be sure of obtaining the yield rate to a prescribed accuracy. For the case $n < 1$, it is natural to use simple direct methods such as those indicated in Problem 30 of List 5.

For an illustration of the computationally more laborious but nevertheless important practical case of nonintegral n, let us modify the example of Table 5.9 by taking $n = 49.75$ instead of $n = 50$. In Table 5.10 are the results, including, as the reader will note, the true six-decimal yield rate.

TABLE 5.10

Yield Rate of a Bond Bought between Interest Dates
(F = 100, C = 110, n = 49.75, r = 2.75%, A = 105, g = 2.5% and k = -1/22.)

	Method	Formula	Yield rate
(a)	Of averages, with n = 50	(5.14)	.026512
	n = 49.75		.026516
(b)	Uniform adjustment of book values, n = 50	(5.15)	.026524
	n = 49.75		.026529
(c)	Interpolation with $i' = .025$, $i'' = .0275$ and the practical method for A', A''	(5.16)	.026688
(d)	First iteration process with $i_0 = g$	(5.18)	i_1 = .026607
			i_2 = .026659
(e)	Second iteration process with $i_0 = g$	(5.20)	i_1 = .026683
			i_2 = .026660
			i_3 = .026660

When n is not small and method (a) or (b) is applied to estimate the yield rate, it suffices to take n to the nearer integer; but in the refined methods (c), (d) and (e) the true n should be used.

5.7. Callable bonds. In order to have a flexible financial position and, in particular, to be able to take advantage of decreases that may occur in the level of interest rates, the organization which issues a set of bonds may retain the option to redeem the bonds prior to the stated maturity date. The option usually provides that after a certain number of years from issue the bonds may be redeemed on stated interest dates for stated amounts not less than the par value. Bonds which have this option provision are said to be callable on the call dates, and the stated redemption values are referred to as the call prices.

Callable bonds, with redemption before maturity at the option of the issuer, introduce an element of uncertainty for the investor. To calculate the price or the yield of a callable bond, the investor must make some assumption concerning the date on which the bond will be redeemed. In choosing his assumption, the prudent investor will make sure that he will not suffer loss regardless of the redemption date exercised by the bond issuer. In other words, the book values that the investor would schedule for the bond, on the basis of his assumption, should not be more than the call prices at corresponding dates. If the bond is redeemed at a call price less than the investor's book value the investor incurs a capital loss and essentially receives less from the investment than he anticipated. If, however, the bond is called at a price in excess of the investor's book value, then a capital gain is made, and the investor has a greater return from the bond than he expected.

In order to choose the proper assumption for redemption date, it may be necessary to make several trial calculations to see which redemption date will produce the lowest price (if the yield rate is given) or the lowest yield rate (if the price is known). However, the following cases can be decided without calculations:

(1) If the bond is available at a discount, and is redeemable at par on its maturity date, it is prudent for the investor to assume that redemption will be at the maturity date. The investor's book values would then vary from the initial discounted value up to par value at the maturity date and would never exceed the call prices, each of which is at least par value.

(2) If the bond is available at a premium but is callable at par, then it is prudent to assume redemption on the earliest call date, as otherwise the book value would exceed the call price for that date.

For bonds purchased at a premium and callable at prices in excess of par, the relation of book values and call prices may not be obvious, and trial calculations, as indicated above, may be required. Sometimes a graph of approximate book values against time from purchase obviates some computation. For instance, if some redemption date is assumed and if any call price on an earlier date falls on or below the straight line joining the investor's initial book value to the final value on that assumed redemption date, then such a call price will definitely be less than the corresponding actual book value (see the closing paragraph of Section 5.4), and a different redemption date should be assumed. However, if any such price lies above such a straight line, it would be on the same side of the line as the book value, and further calculation would be required.

To illustrate, we consider a $1,000 bond with bond interest at 8%, payable semiannually, and redeemable at par at the end of 10 years. The issuer has the option to call the bond on any interest date on or after 5 years through 7 years from issue for

110 (that is, 110% of face amount) and for 105 on any interest date thereafter up to but excluding the maturity date. What approximate yield rate may be anticipated from this bond if it is quoted (a) at 90? (b) at 120? (c) at 117?

Let us analyze the whole problem before doing any computation.

(a) In this case the bond is at a discount. The prudent assumption is that it will run to maturity, for in only that case will redemption values be consistently never less than corresponding book values.

(b) Considering Figure 5.4, the graph of approximate book values if the bond is held to maturity, we see that the call prices, at the ends of 5 and 7 1/2 years, lie on the straight line joining the initial and final book values and consequently for these times are less than the corresponding book values. Thus, one must assume that the bond will not reach maturity but will be called. In like manner, redemption at the end of 7 1/2 years can be ruled out. Nor is assuming call after 7 1/2 years prudent, for under it a book loss would occur if call actually occurred at the end of 7 1/2 years. By such reasoning, one concludes that to be prudent he must assume that the bond is called at the end of 5 years.

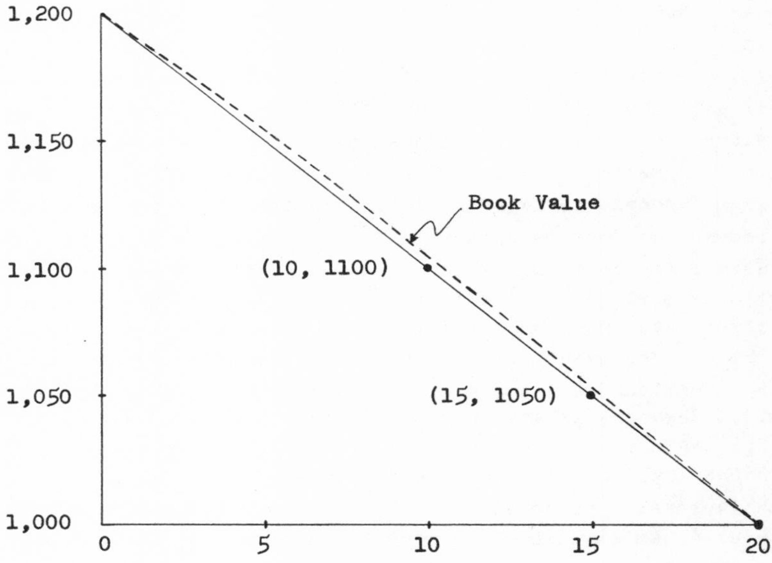

Fig. 5.4

(c) With reference to Figure 5.4, it is clear that the line segment joining (0, 1170) and (20, 1000) is below all the call points. This is the indecisive case, for on the assumption of redemption at maturity the actual book values lie above the line segment, and so do the call prices, but just how the book values compare with the call prices is unclear. One can argue, as in (b), that the assumption of call after 7 1/2 years would produce a loss if call occurred at 7 1/2 years, and similarly, the assumption of redemption between 5 and 7 1/2 years would produce a loss if call occurred at 5 years. By such thinking, we rule out redemption at all but n = 10, 15 or 20 but we must compute for those three possibilities to see which offers the minimum yield.

With this analysis, the amount of computation has been considerably reduced, since in both (a) and (b) the number of interest periods n has been fixed, while in (c) it has been confined to the three values n = 10, 15, 20. The computational results are given in Table 5.11, where i_0 is obtained by the method of averages and i is the true semiannual yield rate to the nearest 0.01%; in each case the answer is starred. Note that in (c) one surmises from the approximations i_0 that n = 15 is the

TABLE 5.11

Investor's Minimum Semiannual Yield Rate (*) in Call Bond Problem (F = 1,000, C = 1,100 (n = 10, 11, ···, 14), 1,050 (n = 15, 16, ···, 19), 1,000 (n = 20); r = 4%.)

	(a) A = 900 n = 20	(b) A = 1,200 n = 10	(c) A = 1,170 n = 10	n = 15	n = 20
i_0	4.74%	2.61%	2.91%	2.88%	2.90%
i	4.79*	2.59*	2.89	2.86*	2.87

conservative choice for the investor but the values are too close for assurance; the true rates here confirm the tentative conclusion. To give credence to the result in (b), we point out that the true yield rates if redemption is assumed at the ends of 15 and 20 periods are 2.64% and 2.69%, respectively, both greater than the 2.59% obtained.

5.8. Bond issues redeemable in installments.

Instead of redeeming a whole set of bonds on a single date, the issuing organization may prefer to spread the redemptions over a number of dates and, in effect, redeem the issue in installments. This may be accomplished by assigning a series of maturity dates to the bonds, as in the case of serial bond issues, or by arranging to call a certain portion of the bonds by lot each year, or possibly by other devices. In this section, we consider methods of calculating the price to be paid by the purchaser of a whole issue of bonds that is to be redeemed in installments.

Let us suppose that the issue consists of bonds of face amount F_h to be redeemed for the amount C_h at the end of n_h periods, $h = 1, 2, \cdots, m$. We denote the total face amount $\sum_{h=1}^{m} F_h$ by F^* and the total redemption amount $\sum_{h=1}^{m} C_h$ by C^*. It is assumed that the bond interest rate r is the same for all portions of the bond issue.

The price to provide a purchaser of the whole issue a yield rate of i per period can be obtained directly by applying any of the price formulas of Section 5.2 to each portion of the issue and then summing the results. This would involve m price calculations, one for each portion of the bond, and it is often simpler to work out a formula for the sum of the prices before proceeding to arithmetic calculations.

For instance, if

$$\frac{F_1 r}{C_1} = \frac{F_2 r}{C_2} = \cdots = \frac{F_m r}{C_m} = g \tag{5.21}$$

then from Makeham's formula (5.9), we have for the price A^* of the whole issue

$$A^* = \sum_{h=1}^{m} A_h = \sum_{h=1}^{m}\left[K_h + \frac{g}{i}(C_h - K_h)\right]$$

where $K_h = C_h v^{n_h}$. Setting $K^* = \sum_{h=1}^{m} K_h$, we obtain

$$A^* = K^* + \frac{g}{i}(C^* - K^*). \tag{5.22}$$

For this formula the principal calculation required is $K^* = \sum_{h=1}^{m} C_h v^{n_h}$, that is, the present value of the annuity of redemption amounts.

If condition (5.21) does not hold, one may split the redemption values C_h into $C_h' + C_h''$, $h = 1, 2, \cdots, m$, where the C_h' are chosen so that when substituted for the C_h in formula (5.21) the condition is satisfied. Then

$$A^* = K^{*\prime} + \frac{g}{i}(C^{*\prime} - K^{*\prime}) + K^{*\prime\prime}, \tag{5.23}$$

where $K^{*\prime} = \sum_h C_h' v^{n_h}$, $C^{*\prime} = \sum_h C_h'$ and $K^{*\prime\prime} = \sum_h C_h'' v^{n_h}$. The term $K^{*\prime\prime}$ introduces an additional annuity calculation but in many cases would not be difficult to handle.

Alternatively, when condition (5.21) does not hold, one may determine the base amounts G_h such that

$$G_h\, i = F_h\, r, \qquad h = 1, 2, \cdots, m$$

and apply formula (5.6) to obtain

$$A^* = \sum_h G_h + \sum_h (C_h - G_h) v^{n_h} \tag{5.24}$$

which involves just one annuity calculation.

The problem of determining the yield rate earned by the investor who buys the whole issue for a set price could, without a computer, be a fussy one. Fortunately, in practice such an issue is generally sold to the highest bidder. Each bidder can set his own yield rate and bid the price, or approximately the price, calculated at that rate.

<u>5.9. Summary.</u> This chapter has dealt with an important special form of investment at compound interest. In it, we have developed various methods for determining the price, book value and yield rate of a bond, both on and off bond interest dates. We have analyzed a bond through a bond schedule and otherwise. Finally, the theory has been extended to the callable bond and the serial bond issue. Our illustrative examples have been interspersed throughout the chapter.

Like Chapter 5 itself, Problem List 5 draws on many ideas and techniques of the earlier chapters, in addition to those developed in this chapter, so that the reader may feel that while he is learning new things through the problems he is also frequently reviewing and at the same time discerning the natural unity of the mathematics of compound interest. Besides Problems 46, 25 and 30 which have previously been cited, we call to the reader's attention the following problems from List 5:

Problems 8, 9, 10, 20 and 29 about bond tables;

Problems 14 and 63 dealing with relations between book values and with analysis of the coupon;

Problem 24 probing analytic behavior of the book-value function;

Problem 34 which investigates errors in the initial-estimate yield-rate methods, and Problems 66 and 67 which offer variations of our yield-rate methods;

Problems 58, 74 and 75 about the bond issuer preparing to meet his serial bond payments;

Problems 6 and 45 introducing -- apart from our model bonds -- accumulation, perpetual and annuity bonds;

Problem 49 pointing out that a loan being amortized can be considered as a special case of investment in a bond, with some interesting consequences; and

Problem 64 which asks an unusual question.

PROBLEM LIST 5

Basic List (Problems 1-49)

Sec. 5.1, 5.2

1. (a) Find by four methods the price of a \$1,000 bond which has bond interest at the rate of 5% per year, payable by means of semiannual coupons, and which is redeemable for 110% of the face amount at the end of 9 years, if the annual yield rate is (1) (4%, 2), (2) (6%, 2).

(b) Same as (a)(1), except that the bond interest is payable annually and the formulas are to be set up but not computed.

(c) Same as (b), except that the bond interest is payable quarterly.

(d) Same as (a)(1), except that the yield interest is compounded annually and the formulas are to be set up but not computed.

2. Determine the price of each bond below without using interest tables. Each bond has face value of \$1,000 and semiannual coupons.

(a) The bond is redeemable at par at the end of n years. To provide a certain yield rate, the price would be \$1,042 if the coupons were at 4% per year, but if they were at 6% per year the price would be \$1,209. Find the price to provide this yield rate if coupons are at (1) 4 1/2% per year, (2) 3% per year.

(b) The bond is redeemable at 125% at the end of n years. Its price to yield an annual rate (.04, 2) would be \$455.30 if the annual coupon rate were zero. Find its price if the annual coupon rate is 6%, but the yield rate is still (.04, 2).

(c) Same as (b), but with an effective annual yield rate of 4% and price of \$417 when the coupon rate is zero. Given $s^{(2)}_{\overline{1}|.04} = 1.0099$.

(d) The bond has coupons at 5% per year and is redeemable at the end of a certain number of years. If the bond were redeemable at 110, its price to yield (.05, 2) would be \$1,026. Find the price to yield (.05, 2) if the bond is redeemable at 102.

3. (a) A \$1,000 bond has coupons at 4% per year payable semiannually for a given term. If at the end of the term the bond is redeemable at 110%, the price to yield an effective

annual rate of 4% is $1,028. Find the price at the same yield rate if the bond is redeemable at par.

(b) A $1,000 bond has annual coupons at 5% for a given term. If at the end of the term the bond is redeemable at 110%, the price to yield an annual rate (.05, 2) is $990. Find the price at the same yield rate, if the bond is redeemable at 101%.

4. What price should an investor pay for a $1,000 6% bond with annual coupons, redeemable at par in 10 years, if he seeks a yield of 5% per year on his whole investment and will set up a sinking fund earning 4% compounded annually to repay the premium he will pay for the bond?

5. A $100 4% bond with coupons payable semiannually was bought, 10 years before redemption at par, at a price yielding 5% per year compounded semiannually. Four years later the investor sold the bond for $97.50, after the coupon then due had been paid. What were his total earnings from the bond?

6. What price should an investor pay for each of the following bonds, if he wants to earn an effective annual rate of 7%?

(a) The bond has denomination $1,000, provides no payments before maturity and promises at maturity in 10 years to pay face value together with accumulated interest at (.05, 2). (Such a security is called an <u>accumulation bond</u>.)

(b) The security, a $1,000 5% bond with semiannual bond interest payable in perpetuity, has no redemption date. (Such a security is called a <u>perpetual bond</u>.)

7. For a bond, the term n is a positive integer.

(a) Show that if (1) $r = i > 0$ and (2) not all of A, C and F are equal, then $F < A < C$.

(b) If instead $r = i = 0$, what conclusions can you draw?

(c) Show that if (1) $r = i \geq 0$ and (2) a pair of A, C and F are equal, then $A = C = F$ except for one special case.

<u>Sec. 5.3</u>

8. (a) By use of the portion of the bond table in Section 5.3 but without interest tables, obtain the price of a $1,000 bond having semiannual coupons of $30, maturing at par in 9 years and yielding (.05, 2) per year.

(b) Same as (a) but by a different method, given also that a bond which is identical except for having $20 coupons has bond-table value of $928.23.

9. Find the price of a $1,000 9% bond with quarterly coupons, to yield a purchaser (8 1/2%, 4), if the bond will be redeemed at 102 in 5 years.

10. Let $A(n)$ denote the price of a bond having bond interest Fr and redeemable at C in n interest periods. Show that at yield rate i

(a) $A(h + k) = A(h) + v^h\left[A(k) - C\right]$

(b) $v^h = \dfrac{Fr - A(h)\,i}{Fr - Ci}$.

Thus, without interest tables, use of a bond table can be extended to bonds redeemable beyond the range of its tabulated "years to redemption."

Sec. 5.4

11. If the price of a 6% bond with half-yearly coupons is \$118.70 per \$100 of face amount on a given coupon date, find the price 5 years later, if the yield rate is 5% per year compounded (a) semiannually, (b) annually.

12. A \$1,000 5% bond with semiannual coupons and redeemable at par is purchased 10 years before maturity to yield (1) 6% per year, compounded semiannually, (2) 4% per year, compounded semiannually. For both cases find

(a) The total amount of yield interest the purchaser will earn;

(b) The book value of the bond one year after purchase;

(c) The book value of the bond six years after purchase;

(d) The yield interest earned in the 13th coupon period;

(e) The yield interest earned in the 5th year after purchase.

13. (a) The price of a \$1,000 6% bond with semiannual coupons, yielding (.04, 2) per year, is \$1,120 on a given coupon date (ex coupon). Find the price on

(i) The preceding coupon date;

(ii) The next coupon date.

(b) Same as (a) except the yield rate is the effective rate of 4% per year.

14. Let $A = A_0$ denote the price of a bond n periods before it is redeemed at the amount C, with bond interest of Fr to be paid at the end of each interest period and yield interest to be at the effective rate i per period. Assume each bond interest payment is first applied to pay yield interest on the outstanding principal and the balance, if positive, is used to repay principal and, if negative, to accumulate principal. The amount of outstanding principal at the end of h periods, i.e., the book value of the bond then, is denoted by A_h. Show the following relations and interpret them for (1) $A_0 > C$, (2) $A_0 < C$.

(a) $A_{h-1} - A_h = Fr - A_{h-1}\, i = (Fr - Ci)v^{n-h+1}$

(b) $A_h = A_0(1 + i)^h - Fr\, s_{\overline{h}|i}$

(c) $A_h - C = (A_0 - C)(1 + i)^h - (Fr - Ci)s_{\overline{h}|i}$
$= (Fr - Ci)a_{\overline{n-h}|i}$

(d) $A_h = A_0 - (Fr - A_0\, i)\, s_{\overline{h}|i}$

(e) $A_{h+k} = A_h - (Fr - A_h\, i)s_{\overline{k}|i}$

(f) $A_{h-1} = v(Fr + A_h)$

(g) $A_{h-k} = Fr\, a_{\overline{k}|i} + v^k A_h$.

15. (a) Given that $F = C = \$1,000$, $r = 2\ 1/2\%$, $i = 2\%$, and that the book value on a certain interest date is \$1,023.57, find the book value 4 periods later. Also find the total yield interest earned during the 4 periods.

(b) Given that $F = C = \$1,000$, $r = 2\ 1/2\%$, $i = 3\%$, and that the book value on a certain interest date is \$990.43, find the book value 4 periods earlier. Also find the total yield interest earned during the 4 periods.

16. Semiannual bond interest has just been paid, resulting at the investor's yield rate of (.06, 2) in a $10 write-up in the book value to $900. What price did the investor pay for the bond 5 years ago, and what will its value be 5 years from now? Given that F = $1,000, what is the semiannual bond interest rate?

17. Suppose, for a premium bond bought on a bond interest date, that a sinking fund earning the yield rate i is established at purchase date to contain the premium, $A_0 - C$, n periods later at redemption date. Show that

(a) The sinking-fund payment is the reduction in book value of the bond in the first period after purchase;

(b) The increase in the sinking fund in the hth period equals the reduction in book value of the bond in the hth period ($h = 1, 2, \cdots, n$);

(c) The purchase price reduced by the sinking-fund accumulation at the end of the hth period equals the book value at the end of the hth period;

(d) The interest earned by the sinking fund in the hth period equals the excess of yield interest on the book value in the first period over that in the hth period.

Sec. 5.5

18. For the bond of Problem 15(a), assume semiannual coupons and find by three methods the price, accrued interest and book value 1 1/2 months after the date on which the book value is $1,023.57.

19. How many years before redemption will a bond, bought to yield (.10, 2) per year and having semiannual bond interest of $35 and redemption at $1,100, have a book value of $1,000? Use the practical method.

20. (a) From the bond-table excerpt and without interest tables, find the book value 9 years, 2 months before maturity of a bond having F = $1,000, r = 2.25%, semiannual coupons, and

(i) $i = .025$, C = F;

(ii) $i = .025$, C = $1,030;

(iii) $i = .024$, C = $1,030.

Indicate any approximate methods used.

(b) Check (a)(ii) and (iii) using interest tables but not a bond table.

21. Prove that by the theoretical and semitheoretical methods

$$P_t = (A_1 + Fr)v^{1-t},$$

and that by the practical method

$$P_t = (A_1 + Fr)[1 - d(1 - t)] = (1 - t)P_0 + t(P_1 + Fr).$$

22. For the bond of Problem 18,

(a) Construct the bond schedule for the time from purchase to the end of the second bond interest date thereafter, using three methods for the first full line of your schedule;

(b) Find the total yield interest earned by the bond if it was purchased through regular market channels and held until maturity.

23. A, the owner of a bond bought to yield the rate i if held to maturity, sells the bond t periods ($0 < t < 1$) after

he has cashed his hth coupon. For convenience let integral time h denote that coupon date, with purchase having occurred $h - k$ $(0 \leq k < 1)$ periods earlier. What entries would A's schedule show for the interval h to $h + t$, according to each of the three methods of interim valuation? What would his capital gain (or loss) on sale be?

24. For a given bond purchased to yield a fixed rate i to redemption, prove that

(a) The book-value function is continuous at $t = 1$ (and hence everywhere) according to all three methods of interim valuation;

(b) The book-value function has a derivative at $t = 1$ (assumed to occur before redemption date), if and only if among text methods the theoretical method of valuation is used;

(c) For h a fixed nonnegative integer less than $n - 1$ and for $0 < t < 1$, by the practical method $\frac{d}{dt} A_{h+t}$ is constant but

$$\frac{d}{dt} A_{h+1+t} = (1 + i) \frac{d}{dt} A_{h+t} .$$

What do these results imply for the graph of the book value, according to the practical method, as a function of time?

25. For h a positive integer and $0 < t < 1$, prove or disprove each of the following for each of the three methods (I, II, III) for interim bond purchase:

(a) $(A_{h+t} - A_t)/(A_h - A_0) = (1 + i)^t$

(b) $(A_{h+t} - A_h)/(A_t - A_0) = (A_{h+1} - A_h)/(A_1 - A_0)$

(c) $A_{h+t} = A_t(1 + i)^h - Fr\, s_{\overline{h}|i}$

(d) $(P_{h+t} - P_t)/(P_h - P_0) = (1 + i)^t$

(e) $(P_{h+t} - P_h)/(P_t - P_0) = P_h/P_0$

(f) $P_{h+t} = P_t(1 + i)^h - Fr(s_{\overline{h+t}|i} - s_{\overline{t}|i})$.

Sec. 5.6

26. An 8% bond with semiannual coupons is redeemable at par at the end of 10 years. If the quoted price (per hundred of face) is 120, find the annual yield rate, convertible semiannually, by the five methods of Section 5.6, including (to the nearest .01%) the true rate.

27. Suppose that $C \leq 2A < 4C$, so that the accuracy of the approximation for i is improved by each step in each iteration process.

(a) Show that if, for either iteration method,

(i) $i_{m-1} < i$, then $i_m > i_{m-1}$ and $i > (i_{m-1} + i_m)/2$;

(ii) $i_{m-1} = i$, then $i_m = i_{m-1}$;

(iii) $i_{m-1} > i$, then $i_m < i_{m-1}$ and $i < (i_{m-1} + i_m)/2$.

(b) Suppose one starts each iteration method with i_0. How can one decide whether $i_0 < i$, $i_0 = i$ or $i_0 > i$?

28. Find to the nearest .001% the annual yield rate, convertible semiannually, on a $1,000 5% bond with semiannual coupons, redeemable at par at the end of 5 years, if the purchase price is $1,045. Prove your answer.

29. (a) By use of the bond-table excerpt, find the annual yield rate, compounded semiannually, earned on a bond held for 9 years, 2 months to maturity at par and having actual price $992.96 and bond interest at 4 1/2% per year payable semiannually. (See Problem 20.)

(b) Describe a bond-table process for obtaining an approximate nominal annual yield rate of a bond, given its book value on a bond interest date, at a tabulated bond interest rate but with $C \neq F$. Assume interest tables are not available.

(c) Same as (b) except purchase is on an interim date rather than a bond interest date.

30. (a) If $n = 1$ for a bond, show that the exact yield rate can be found directly, as follows:

(i) $i = (C + Fr)/A - 1$

(ii) $i = (C - A)/(A - G)$

(iii) By the second iteration method, which produces $i_1 = i$ and hence $i_1 = i_2 = \cdots = i$.

(In Problem 34 the initial-estimate methods are considered.)

(b) If $n < 1$ for a bond, say $n = 1 - t$, show that

(i) By the practical method,

$$i = (C + Fr - P_t)/[P_t - t(C + Fr)];$$

(ii) By the theoretical method

$$(1 + i)^{1-t} = (C + Fr)/P_t$$

determines i.

31. (a) A certain bond carries annual coupons at 4% for the first 5 years and at 5% for the remaining 10 years to maturity. Find the annual yield rate to the nearest .1% if the bond is sold at par and is redeemable at par.

(b) If the bond in (a) were priced at 80, what would the annual yield rate be?

32. A $100 bond with semiannual coupons is redeemable at par at the end of 15 years. At a purchase price of $80 the semiannual yield rate is exactly 1% more than the semiannual coupon rate. By linear interpolation find the annual yield rate, compounded semiannually.

Note that the following iteration methods are available for solving for i the equation $a_{\overline{n}|i} = c$ (n and c constants):

(1) $i_m = [1 - (1 + i_{m-1})^{-n}]/c$

(2) $i_m = 1/c - s^{-1}_{\overline{n}|i_{m-1}}$.

Convergence is fairly slow but is faster by (2) and for the foregoing data substantiates a yield rate of (.0569, 2).

33. A 5% bond with semiannual coupons was sold for 105, 5 years after purchase at 107. Find to the nearest .1% the effective annual yield rate earned by the investor. Prove your answer. (Assume purchase occurred on a coupon date.)

34. (a) Prove that for a bond bought on an interest date but with $n \neq 1$, the estimated yield rate by the uniform-adjustment-of-book-values method is too low for a discount bond and too high for a premium bond.

(b) By comparison with (a), what can be inferred about the estimate of the yield rate by the method of averages?

Remark. Note that if $n = 1$ the method of (a) is exact, but that of (b) is not.

Sec. 5.7

35. A \$1,000 5% bond with semiannual coupons matures at par at the end of 20 years. The bond is callable at par at the end of 15 years and every coupon date thereafter up through 19 1/2 years. What price should an investor pay for this bond if he wishes an annual yield rate of (a) (.06, 2), (b) (.05, 2), (c) (.04, 2)?

36. Same as Problem 35 except that the bond is callable at 105%.

37. Same as Problem 35, but with the bond callable at 110% at the end of 5 years, there being no further call privilege before redemption at 105% at the end of 20 years.

38. (a) What semiannual yield rate would the bondholder actually earn if the bond in Problem 36(c) were purchased for \$1,136.78 and

(i) Called at the end of 19 1/2 years?

(ii) Redeemed at maturity date?

(b) Argue that the yield rates in (a) bracket the yields obtained if redemption occurred at any of the other call dates.

39. A \$1,000 4% bond with semiannual bond interest is purchased at 102 1/2, 3 years before maturity at par and 1 1/2 years before it is callable at 101. The purchaser plans to hold the bond until redemption.

(a) By use of the basic formula of one of the iteration methods, show that he can consider that he has earned a semiannual yield rate of 1.4705% if the bond is called, and of 1.4705% to call date and of 1.6556% thereafter if the bond matures.

(b) Check the rates in (a) with a bond schedule.

40. True or false? Give your reasoning.

(a) If a callable discount bond has no stated maturity date, the prudent investor would assume that the bond would never be redeemed.

(b) An investor seeking to earn rate i (or more) on a callable premium bond can determine the price he is willing to pay by cost comparison based on the assumption that, for each fixed redemption value, the earliest possible redemption date will be used.

(c) The purchaser of a callable premium bond can determine the minimum yield rate he will earn if he holds the bond until it is redeemed, by rate comparison based on the assumption that, for each fixed redemption value, the earliest possible redemption date will be used.

(d) If an investor pays A for a bond on the assumption that it will be called at C_h in h periods and so yield him rate i, his capital gain is

$$F - A + (Fr - Ai)s_{\overline{n}|i}$$

if, in fact, the bond matures at par in n integral periods and the investor has carried it on his books at rate i up to maturity.

Sec. 5.8

41. A $1,000,000 issue of bonds bearing interest at 6% per year payable semiannually is to be redeemed over 10 years by 5 biennial redemptions of $200,000 each. Find an expression for the price to yield a purchaser of the whole issue a nominal annual rate of (.05, 2) if

(a) The biennial redemptions are at par;

(b) The biennial redemptions are at 105, 104, 103, 102 and 101, respectively.

42. Ten $100 bonds bearing annual coupons of 6% are redeemable at $125 each, the first at the end of 6 years, and one at the end of each succeeding year until all are redeemed.

(a) Find the total price that should be paid for the bonds, to yield 5% effective per year.

(b) What is the present value at (.05, 1) of the coupon payments?

(c) Construct the three lines of the investor's schedule covering the 5th through 7th years.

43. A serial bond issue having semiannual bond interest is purchased for $90,000 to yield an effective annual rate of 5%. It is redeemable in fixed installments at fixed times. The present value at the yield rate of the redemption values is $10,000. Find the price of a bond issue which is identical except that the bond interest of the same amount each year as that of the first issue is payable annually.

44. A company has just purchased at 95 a set of 5% bonds having semiannual bond interest and redemption at 105. The bonds will be redeemed in equal installments by 24 annual drawings, the first redemption being at the end of 6 years. What proportion of the bonds will earn at least (6%, 2)?

45. A 5%, 20-year <u>annuity bond</u> for $10,000 is the promise of the issuer to make equal payments at the end of each year for 20 years, each payment to consist of (1) bond interest at 5% on the remainder of the $10,000 of face amount outstanding at the beginning of the year and (2) redemption of some of the face amount.

(a) What is the price of the annuity bond to yield a purchaser an effective annual rate of 6%?

(b) Construct the first two lines of the schedule of the purchaser in (a), and find what amount of reduction in capital investment his schedule would show (i) for the 15th year, (ii) in total for the first 15 years.

46. (a) Problem 46 in List 4 showed that Makeham's formula is applicable to one class of amortization problem when the value of

future payments is sought. More generally, consider amortization by a set of (possibly varying) payments (used to pay interest on the outstanding principal and reduce that principal) as equivalent to a bond redeemable in installments. Thus, show that Makeham's formula expresses the present value of the payments on a loan being amortized, at a rate of interest not necessarily equal to the amortization rate of interest. Define all your symbols.

(b) When a loan is repaid by the sinking-fund method with the borrower each period making interest payments to the lender and sinking-fund payments elsewhere, show that, at any positive rate of interest,

(1) The present value of all the borrower's payments can be expressed by Makeham's formula plus an additional term;

(2) The present value of all the payments the lender receives (including the return of his capital) can be expressed by Makeham's formula.

Sec. 5.9

47. A bond bought at time t_1 $(0 \leq t_1 < 1)$ is sold at time $h + t_2$ $(0 \leq t_2 < 1$, h a nonnegative integer), where time is measured in interest periods from the coupon date preceding purchase. Find an expression useful in obtaining

(a) The quoted price of the bond, to yield the seller rate i;

(b) The yield rate earned by the seller.

48. (a) A $1,000 5% bond with semiannual bond interest is bought at par 10 years before maturity at par. After 10 years what total interest has the investment produced if bond interest is reinvested immediately at (.05, 2) per annum?

(b) Same as (a), except that the bond is bought for $900.

(c) Same as (b), except that the reinvestment rate is (.04, 2).

(d) For each case above compare the investor's nominal annual yield rate compounded semiannually, determined in a traditional manner for bonds, with that determined by taking into account the reinvestment of the bond interest.

49. Consider a loan of A to be amortized by level payments R as a special case of investment in a bond (namely, R replaces the bond interest and the redemption value is zero). Apply the formulas and schedules of Sections 5.2-5.6 to the amortization case, and show that the essential formulas and schedule of Section 4.2 emerge and also some additional ideas, in particular with reference to purchase between payment dates of an existent amortization agreement and to determination of the yield rate earned by a person who purchases an amortization contract. The counterparts of formulas (5.14) and (5.15) are in everyday use, especially for short-term loans and installment purchases. For example, the 1967 Connecticut "Act concerning the disclosure of finance charges in connection with extensions of credit" specifies the counterpart of (5.15), adjusted to be a nominal annual rate, as the charge for credit (but makes exceptions, for example, for mortgages*).

*Although (5.14) and (5.15) produce reasonably accurate estimates of the yield rate for most bonds, even long-term ones, they are much less accurate in a long-term ordinary amortization case. For example, for a 20-year mortgage actually financed at (.07, 12), formula (5.15) produces (.0857, 12).

Supplementary List (Problems 50-75)

50. Two $1,000 bonds which will mature at par at the same time bear semiannual coupons of $20 and $30, respectively. The semiannual yield rate is the same for both bonds, and the discount on the first bond is twice the premium on the second bond. Find the semiannual yield rate.

51. A $100 bond with semiannual coupons is redeemable at par. Its price at a certain yield rate convertible semiannually is $102.98 six years before redemption. Given $v^{12} = .8615$, without using interest tables find the price of this bond twelve years before redemption.

52. What are the possible redemption values and redemption dates for a $1,000 6% bond with annual coupons, selling on a coupon date at 120 to yield (.05, 1) per year?

53. Show how, without interest or bond tables, you could obtain the book value of a bond at purchase (not necessarily on a coupon date) and at every coupon date thereafter until redemption. Assume known just F, C, r, i, t and n; the practical method applies.

54. (a) Show that

(1) $(g - k/n)/[1 + k(n+1)/(2n)]$

(2) $[Fr - (A - C)\, s^{-1}_{\overline{n}|\,i}]/A$

(3) $g - \dfrac{A - C}{C - K}\, i$

are essentially methods of the chapter for finding the yield rate i of a bond.

(b) Show that

$$i = \frac{C - K}{A - K}\, g\ .$$

Considering that K is a function of i, of what use would this formula be in finding i?

Note that the methods in (a)(3) and (b) may be suitable for approximating the yield rate of a serial bond issue.

55. A corporation has outstanding a $1,000,000 10% bond issue with semiannual bond interest. The bonds mature at par in 15 years but can be called now at 105. If the corporation can sell at par a new issue of 8% bonds with semiannual bond interest, to mature at par in 15 years, and if it ignores costs of redemption and issue, what is the present value at (.08, 2) of the savings that it can obtain by exercising immediate call rather than letting the old issue mature?

56. A $100 5% bond with semiannual bond interest is selling on a coupon date to yield (.10, 2) per year. If, on that basis, the increase in book value in the 5th semiannual period after purchase is $1.28, find the price.

57. Two $100 bonds which mature at par at the same time and have semiannual coupons are selling on a coupon date at the same yield rate. The quoted price of the 4% bond is $120 and of the 5% bond is $140. Without tables, find

(a) The nominal annual yield rate compounded semiannually and the portion of the price of each bond paid for the maturity value;

(b) The price of a bond identical in all respects to the 4% bond except for having annual 4% coupons.

58. A $1,000,000 issue of 6% bonds with semiannual bond interest is redeemable at par in 4 equal amounts at the ends of 10, 12, 14 and 16 years. A special account is set up to receive equal deposits at the end of each half year during the 16-year period, to pay semiannual bond interest on the bonds outstanding and to redeem the bonds as they fall due; balances in the account are credited with interest at (.05, 2) per year. Give an expression for the semiannual deposit.

59. True or false?

(a) $A_t = A_0 + 4t(A_{1/4} - A_0), \quad 0 \leq t < 1.$

(b) If P_t, P_t' and P_t'' are prices of bonds having the same face amount, yield rate, term and redemption value but different coupon rates r, r' and r'' respectively, then

$$(P_t - P_t')/(P_t'' - P_t') = (r - r')/(r'' - r'), \quad 0 \leq t < 1.$$

(c) For a bond bought between interest dates to yield $i > 0$, the adjustment in book value in the initial partial interest period is greatest if, of the 3 methods of the text, the practical method is used.

(d) If $i = r > 0$, $C = F$ and $0 < t < 1$, then $A_{h+t} < F$ by the semitheoretical method but $A_{h+t} = F$ by the theoretical and practical methods.

60. A $1,000 6% bond with semiannual bond interest, scheduled to be redeemed at par 8 years hence, is being replaced right now by a new $1,000 5% bond with semiannual bond interest. To make the exchange equitable on the basis of money currently being worth (.05, 2),

(a) At what premium (to the nearest dollar) should the new bond mature in 15 years?

(b) What face amount (to the nearest dollar) should the new bond have if it is to mature at 102% in 15 years?

(c) For what possible terms (i.e., integral numbers of half years) could the new bond be issued so as to mature at 110% and assure the bondholder of a yield of at least (.05, 2) from exchange date to maturity date?

61. An issue of 5% bonds maturing at par in 10 years is callable now at 102. The issuer has the funds to call. Should he (a) retire the issue now or (b) buy at 95 4% bonds also maturing at par in 10 years? Assume all bond interest is payable semiannually.

62. (a) A 6% bond with semiannual bond interest will mature in 14 years at 105. It is bought at 110.5 by a purchaser who plans to set up a sinking fund at (.03, 2) per year to replace the premium. Sinking fund payments are to be made on bond interest dates. After taking the sinking fund into consideration, what nominal annual yield rate (j, 2) does the purchaser earn?

(b) How would you proceed in (a) if the bond were quoted at 110.5 on a date 13 years, 10 months before maturity?

63. Prove algebraically and verbally:

(a) $Fr = Ai + (A - C)\, s^{-1}_{\overline{n}|i}$

(b) $Fr = Ai + C(g - i)/(1 + i)^n$

(c) $Fr = Ci + (A - C)\, a^{-1}_{\overline{n}|i}$

(d) $A_0 - A_h = (Fr - A_h\, i)\, a_{\overline{n}|i} + (C - A_h)v^n$

(e) $A_0 - A_h = (Fr - Ci)\;{}_{n-h|}a_{\overline{h}|i}$.

Note also the expression for $A_0 - A_h$ in Problem 14(d).

64. Is it possible for a bond at a fixed yield rate and having a set redemption date to be at a premium on one date and at a discount on another? Explain. Consider all three interim methods.

65. Consider two \$1,000 bonds with semiannual coupons which are bought 30 years before maturity to yield (.06, 2) per year.

(a) Find the price and coupon of the first bond if it is to mature at 102 and if in the 25th coupon period the book value is to increase \$1.

(b) Find the maturity value and coupon of the second bond if its price is \$1,040 and if the interest in the 25th coupon is \$31.

66. (a) For a bond bought on an interest date n periods before redemption, show that the average of the beginning-of-period book values is

$$C + (A - C)\,\frac{1}{i}\,\left(a^{-1}_{\overline{n}|i} - \frac{1}{n}\right).$$

(b) By series expansion in i for $a^{-1}_{\overline{n}|i}$, or otherwise, show that approximations to the book value in (a) are

$$(1)\quad C + (A - C)\,\frac{n + 1}{2n} = \frac{n + 1}{2n}\,A + \frac{n - 1}{2n}\,C,$$

as used in formula (5.15) to estimate the yield rate of a bond, and

$$(2)\quad C + (A - C)\left(\frac{n + 1}{2n} + \frac{n^2 - 1}{12n}\,i\right).$$

(c) For the bond of Table 5.9, use (b)(2) as approximate average book value in obtaining an estimate of the yield rate; for the value of i in (2) use the estimate given by the uniform-adjustment-of-book-values method.

67. Suppose that in approximating the yield rate of a bond, one combines linear interpolation and one of the iteration methods of Section 5.6, as follows:

(1) Determine the tabulated rates i', i'' closest to i, such that $i' < i < i''$.

(2) In the iteration method set i_0 in turn equal to i', i''; convince yourself that the resulting i_1's bracket i, and more closely than i', i'' do.

(3) Use linear interpolation for i based on i', i, i'' and i_1', i, i_1''.

(a) Show algebraically that the same approximation to the yield rate is obtained regardless of which iteration method is used.

(b) For the data of Table 5.9, obtain the yield-rate approximation by this method using $i' = .025$ and $i'' = .0275$, given $a^{-1}_{\overline{50}|.0275} = .03704092$.

68. An issue of 5% bonds with semiannual coupons is to have \$10,000 of the bonds redeemed at the end of 5 years, \$11,000 at the end of 6 years, \$12,000 at the end of 7 years, and so on, with a final redemption of \$25,000 at the end of 20 years. All redemptions are to be at par. Give formulas for the price to yield a purchaser of the whole issue

(a) 4% per year, compounded semiannually;
(b) 4% effective per year.

69. A \$1,000 bond, redeemable at par on January 1, year N + 9, bears semiannual coupons of \$25 each, payable on January 1 and July 1. It is callable at \$1,080 on any interest date from January 1, N + 1 to December 31, N + 4, and at \$1,040 on any interest date from January 1, N + 5 to December 31, N + 8. It is bought for \$1,090 (including accrued interest) on April 1, N by an investor who uses the practical method. What is the greatest nominal annual rate of interest, compounded semiannually, which he can earn if he holds this bond to redemption?

70. On a certain date Company A purchased at par 6% bonds of \$1,000,000 par value maturing in 10 years. On the same date Company B purchased at 99.409 3 1/2% bonds of \$1,000,000 par value maturing in 2 1/2 years; when those bonds matured, the principal was then invested in 7 1/2-year bonds at par. Assuming that all the bonds bear quarterly coupons,

(a) What coupon rate must the 7 1/2-year bonds have if both companies are to get the same yield over the 10-year period?

(b) If each company is able to reinvest coupons received to accumulate at a rate of only (.02, 4) per year, show which company has done better at the end of the 10-year period.

71. Seventeen years ago an investor bought at 80 bonds paying semiannual bond interest at 2%. After 12 years when these bonds matured at par, he invested the maturity value in stock at 90. For each \$90 invested in the stock, he received semiannually cash dividends of \$2.50 on the bond interest dates, and he has just sold the stock for \$105, per \$90 invested. To the nearest 1/4%, what nominal annual yield rate converted semiannually did he earn over the entire 17-year period?

72. For $0 < t < 1$, arrange in increasing order of magnitude for the three interim-purchase methods:

(a) Price (b) Book value.

73. (a) For a bond purchased t interest periods $(0 < t < 1)$ after an interest date and valued by the theoretical method, devise a bond schedule to cover investment progress over intervals of length one bond interest period, i.e., t to $t + 1$, $t + 1$ to $t + 2$, $\cdots$, $t + k - 1$ to $t + k = n - (1 - t)$, and complete the schedule to a book value C at time n, with entries as analogous as possible to those in Table 5.3.

(b) Same as (a), except that the practical method is used.

74. On January 1, year N there are issued 200 $1,000 bonds which will pay 5% bond interest once a year. They are to be redeemed by call in 5 annual payments beginning January 1, year N + 16. Fractions of a bond cannot be retired. Level annual payments to retire the bonds and to pay interest on the bonds are to be made at the end of each year. The first 15 payments, after payment of the $10,000 of interest, are to be accumulated in a sinking fund earning 3% effective, but the remaining payments are to be applied directly to the redemption of bonds and payment of interest on the outstanding bonds. The sinking fund is to be used to provide 5 as nearly as possible equal payments, which are to help retire the bonds. Find the level annual payment and prepare a schedule for the redemption of the bonds. Work to the nearest dollar.

75. An issue of 1,000 4% bonds, each having par value of $1,000 and semiannual bond interest, is to be redeemed at 105 by quinquennial drawings. As many bonds will be redeemed each 5 years as a sinking fund earning (.03, 2) per year can support. The bond issuer will apply $30,000 at the end of each half year to the service of the loan, the balance above the required bond interest being put into the sinking fund.

(a) By waiving the restriction that the bonds must be redeemed in $1,000 units, determine how many regular redemptions there will be. The final redemption is to occur on the bond interest date as soon after the last regular redemption as the sinking fund can provide, by means of its interest earnings, regular deposits and (if needed) a final deposit smaller than the regular one would be on that date.

(b) Trace the actual redemptions. When does the final sinking-fund deposit occur, and what is its size?

(c) What price should a potential purchaser, who wants to earn an effective annual rate of 5%, offer for the whole issue? Answer to the nearest dollar.

CHAPTER 6

RECENT DEVELOPMENTS

6.1. Introduction. While the preceding chapters have included some new approaches and techniques, in the main they have presented the classical American course in mathematics of finance which reached a zenith in the 1940's. The present chapter aims to give some introduction to more recent developments in the theory and application of compound interest. A number of external factors have influenced these developments.

The most significant external factor has been the advent of electronic computers. In large measure, the new ideas and applications are tied up in some way with computers, and have been facilitated by their increasing utilization. In the next section, we shall explore the potential impact of computer methods on the classical theory, and this will lead into the problem of finding the rate of interest in a given transaction. An application of the latter yields the methods and tables developed in connection with the Federal Reserve Regulation Z for Truth in Lending legislation. In a somewhat different context, British actuaries have developed the notion of immunized funding and we shall note some relations of this to the interest rate problem.

Another factor that has influenced the study and application of compound interest theory has been the extensive progress in applying mathematical and statistical ideas to business operations. This surge of new ideas has tended to shift attention away from compound interest theory which has been considered elementary and closed. On the other hand, there has been considerable inquiry into the problems of evaluating capital projects and the rate of return thereon. A difficulty encountered here has been the possibility of more than one real positive solution. This has stimulated new thinking concerning compound interest models.

The inflation of the 1960's, and the concurrent high rates of interest, have led banks and other savings institutions to compete on the rate of interest paid to their depositors. They are now exploiting the fact that the maximum effective annual rate corresponding to a fixed nominal annual rate is obtained by compounding the rate continuously, that is, by applying the rate as a force of interest. As yet, the possibility of obtaining an even higher effective rate by payment of interest-in-advance has not occurred to many, and may not be possible under operating regulations. At any rate, the financial environment of the 1960's has promoted new variations in the application of basic compound interest concepts.

A number of papers related to the various topics in this chapter are listed at the end and will be referred to by name of author and year in parentheses.

6.2. The impact of computers. The mathematical theory we have set out in the previous chapters was developed prior to the computer revolution. It will continue to exist in the computer age as the simplest and most commonly understood model of financial transactions but there may well be considerable elaboration of it. There may also be a drift away from application of some of the more specialized mathematical techniques in favor of powerful and general computer methods.

In Chapters 1 and 2 various rates of interest were defined but it was almost uniformly assumed that such rates were constant, that is, did not vary with time. One exception was the variable force of interest δ_t but in most cases we considered a constant force. A direct consequence of the assumption of constant rates of compound interest is that the equivalence of the various rates does not depend on the particular interval of time over which the rates operate. Further, the assumption has the consequence, very useful in practice, that the basic functions for accumulating and discounting are the simple exponential function $(1 + i)^n$ and its reciprocal. If, however, the effective rate of interest varies with the interest period, and is i_k, say, in period k, $k = 1, 2, \cdots, n$, then the accumulation function is

$$(1 + i_1)(1 + i_2) \cdots (1 + i_n) \tag{6.1}$$

and the discounting function is the corresponding reciprocal.

It is quite feasible for computers to evaluate such functions as given in (6.1) even for large values of n, e.g., n = 360. In fact, more complex functions may be defined and calculated wherein the rate of interest depends not only on the current period but also on the period in which the investment was originally made. Such an approach is now utilized by some life insurance companies which allocate investment income by investment generations [see, for instance, Turoff (1963)]. In the simpler case where the interest rate depends only on the current period, it would still be true that the equivalence of two sets of payments would not depend on the particular comparison date chosen, which is one of the significant properties of the usual compound interest model based on the assumption of a constant rate of interest. However, it will likely remain easier for a lender to offer, and a borrower to accept, a mortgage loan based on a constant rate of interest than on a rate that varies according to some pattern.

This brings us to another point. In the past, for transactions based on constant rate models, much of the work could be accomplished by looking up values in standard tables of the basic interest functions, or by interpolating thereon. At first, the advent of computers tended to further this practice as more extensive tables of the basic functions could be prepared readily [see, for instance, Malta (1963) and (1965)]. In many situations now it may be easier to compute the desired function value rather than to use tables, particularly if the rate of interest is not one for which tabular values are available and interpolation or compounding would be required. While tables may still be the most efficient for isolated calculations, for production work direct computation of values is likely to take over. For models involving varying rates of interest there are no standard tables and it is unlikely that such will be produced as there is an uncountable number of patterns for varying the interest rate and none has general recognition.

There are instances when a financial institution, such as a life insurance company, in establishing premiums for long-term insurance contracts or in projecting the growth of the institution's funds, may choose to assume varying rates of interest; or it may want to compare the results of assuming various levels of constant rates of interest. Such calculations, projections and comparisons are made feasible by the availability of computers. It is comparatively easy, for instance, after a computation has been programmed and carried through with one rate of interest, to successively change the rate parameter and repeat the computation, thereby securing a range of results.

A still further elaboration of the basic assumptions is to consider future rates of interest as random variables with probability distributions assigned in some way. A computer may then be used to simulate the growth of funds under these circumstances. A simple illustration of this is given in Appendix 5 of Benjamin's paper (1966). Such elaboration of the basic assumptions would be even less acceptable than varying rates of interest for a single transaction between a lender and a borrower but may be useful for projecting the growth of a financial institution or, as in Benjamin's case, in attempting to value an equity investment, where the future returns on the investment are uncertain.

Alternatively, or in conjunction, one might consider that the future payments for a transaction are random variables, each with its own probability distribution. In the theory up to now, it has been considered that payments were of fixed size and certain to be made. If payments are considered as random variables, a new dimension is added to the model and the need of extensive computer facilities becomes evident. An overview of some of the ideas in this approach is given by Hodges and Moore (1968). Beyond this brief mention, we shall not pursue this possibility, and turn now to consider computer possibilities for annuity, amortization and bond calculations.

<u>6.3. Annuity valuation by computers.</u> One immediate simplification that is gained in valuing annuities by computers is that the interest period may be taken equal to the payment period with the interest rate changed if necessary to the equivalent effective rate i per payment period. This may result in a rate of interest for which tabular values of the interest function are not available but this is immaterial as the computer can easily iterate to the values required. To include both ordinary and annuity-due cases, we consider an annuity with payments W_h at time h, $h = 0, 1, 2, \cdots, n$. Note that the time unit is the payment period, and that for an ordinary annuity $W_0 = 0$ and for an annuity-due $W_n = 0$.

A direct approach to the present value of this annuity would be by means of the formula

$$A = \sum_{h=0}^{n} v^h W_h \tag{6.2}$$

but this would involve the prior computation of the powers v^h, then calculation of the products $v^h W_h$ and finally the sum. In place of this, for ordinary annuities the following iterative calculation might be followed:

$$
\begin{aligned}
A_n &= 0 \\
A_{n-1} &= v(A_n + W_n) \\
&\vdots \\
A_h &= v(A_{h+1} + W_{h+1}) \\
&\vdots \\
A_0 &= v(A_1 + W_1).
\end{aligned}
\tag{6.3}
$$

For ordinary annuities, $W_0 = 0$, and $A_0 = A$, the present value. At any time h, A_h represents the present value of the remaining payments, excluding, however, the payment W_h due at time h. The process yields not only the value at 0, but the residual values at 1, 2, $\cdots$, n - 1.

For annuities-due, with $W_n = 0$, we can utilize the function $\ddot{A}_h$ which represents the present value at time h of the remaining payments including the payment W_h then due. This function might be calculated directly from the iterative formula

$$\ddot{A}_h = v\,\ddot{A}_{h+1} + W_h \tag{6.4}$$

or indirectly from A_h by the formula

$$\ddot{A}_h = A_h + W_h\ . \tag{6.5}$$

For some purposes, it may be useful to have iterative methods for calculating accumulated values. Let S_h represent the accumulated value at time h of the preceding payments including the payment W_h. Then

$$
\begin{aligned}
S_0 &= W_0 \\
S_1 &= S_0(1 + i) + W_1 \\
&\vdots \\
S_h &= S_{h-1}(1 + i) + W_h \\
&\vdots \\
S_n &= S_{n-1}(1 + i) + W_n\ .
\end{aligned}
\tag{6.6}
$$

For an ordinary annuity, $W_0 = 0$, and S_n represents the accumulated value of the annuity at the end of its term. One might calculate S_h indirectly by

$$S_h = \ddot{A}_0(1 + i)^h - A_h\ . \tag{6.7}$$

Note that for an ordinary annuity $\ddot{A}_0 = A_0$, so that A_0 could be substituted for $\ddot{A}_0$ in formula (6.7).

The accumulation function $\ddot{S}_h$ that is useful for annuities-due represents the accumulated value at time h of the preceding payments, excluding W_h. Then

$$\ddot{S}_h = (\ddot{S}_{h-1} + W_{h-1})(1 + i) \tag{6.8}$$

and

$$\ddot{S}_h = S_h - W_h \,. \tag{6.9}$$

To indicate the application of these processes, let us consider how they might be applied to solve illustrative Examples 3.2, 3.4, 3.5 and 3.6.

Example 3.2. To compute W, we first calculate A_0 by formulas (6.3), with $n = 30$, $W_h = 1$ $(h = 1, 2, \cdots, 30)$ and $v = (1.005)^{-6}$. Then $W = 10{,}000/A_0$. The total payment to be made *to* B is $A_0 + W$ where now A_0 is calculated by formulas (6.3) with $n = 10$, $W_h = W$ $(h = 1, 2, \cdots, 10)$ and $v = (1.05)^{-1/2}$.

Example 3.4. The computation for A might be carried out by formulas (6.3) with $n = 30$, $W_h = 50$ $(h = 1, 2, \cdots, 12)$, $W_h = 100$ $(h = 13, \cdots, 20)$ and $W_h = 10$ $(h = 21, \cdots, 30)$; $i = .005$. For S, one might employ formulas (6.6), or $A(1 + i)^{30}$.

Example 3.5. For the computation here take $i = (1.06)^{1/4} - 1$. Next, one may utilize formulas (6.6) with $W_0 = 1{,}100$, $W_h = -50$ $(h = 1, 2, \cdots)$ to find the first n such that $S_n < 0$. Then $W_n = S_{n-1}(1 + i)$ or $50 + S_n$.

Example 3.6. Here one would take $i = (1.025)^2 - 1$ and employ formulas (6.4) with $W_h = (h + 1)^2$ $(h = 0, 1, \cdots, 10)$. The starting value would be $\ddot{A}_{10} = 121$. For S, use A, or (6.8), $\ddot{S}_0 = 0$.

These examples indicate that by choosing the time unit to be the payment period and utilizing the effective rate of interest per payment period, the valuation by computer of annuities is a relatively simple iterative process. It is almost immaterial whether the annuity payments are level or varying. Do these findings mean that the mathematical formulas for annuity valuation are obsolete? In our opinion, no. For isolated calculations, the mathematical methods may still be more convenient and, in fact, the computer methods may not be available for ready use by the person wishing to make the calculation. In a production situation, however, the computer methods will definitely prevail. Even there the basic mathematics has a role. For example, the iterative processes (6.3) and (6.4) cannot be applied for the valuation of a perpetuity while, on the other hand, the mathematical formula for the value is normally simple. Also, computers work with numbers truncated to a fixed number of decimals and in some processes, especially iterative ones, errors may accumulate. Mathematical formulas may be needed to test for error development. A combination of both mathematical and computer techniques would seem to be the best equipment for annuity valuations.

6.4. Application of computers to amortization and sinking funds. Computers have a natural application here, particularly to the production of amortization schedules. To illustrate, consider the amortization case discussed in Section 4.2. To determine R, one might first use formulas (6.3) with $W_0 = 0$, $W_h = 1$ $(h = 1, 2, \cdots, n)$ to obtain the values of $a_{\overline{1|}}, \cdots, a_{\overline{n|}}$. Then $R = A/a_{\overline{n|}}$, and by multiplying R into the previously computed values of $a_{\overline{h|}}$, one would obtain the outstanding-principal column of the amortization schedule (see Table 4.1). Alternatively, once R is determined, one might use formula (4.1) rearranged as

$$A_h = (1 + i)A_{h-1} - R \ , \qquad (6.10)$$

with $A_0 = A$, to compute the outstanding-principal column. Note that the process indicated by formula (6.10) is equivalent to the process (6.6) with $W_0 = A$, $W_h = -R$ $(h = 1, 2, \cdots, n)$. If the full schedule is required the process (6.10) may be broken into steps of computing $i\ A_{h-1}$, $R - i\ A_{h-1}$, and $A_{h-1} - (R - i\ A_{h-1})$.

The amortization in Section 4.4 may be computed by use of the process (6.10) to find the first n such that $A_n < 0$; then the final payment is $A_{n-1}(1 + i)$ or $A_n + R$.

For sinking-fund calculations, the values of $s_{\overline{h|}\,j}$ can be obtained by the process (6.6) with $W_0 = 0$, $W_h = 1$ $(h=1, 2,\cdots, n)$. Then $F = A/s_{\overline{n|}\,j}$, and the accumulated sinking fund is given by $F\ s_{\overline{h|}\,j}$ $(h = 1, 2, \cdots, n)$.

Despite these ready applications of computer methods to amortization and sinking-fund schedules, one finds that computers would not be particularly helpful for the illustrative examples at the end of Chapter 4, although as we shall discuss later, a computer method could be used to find the interest rate from the relation $a^{-1}_{\overline{10|}\,i} = .118825$ in Example 4.1. The reader might consider how in more extensive transactions of the types of Examples 4.4 and 4.5, it might be worthwhile to set up a computer process for the calculation.

6.5. Bond values by computer. Sections 5.2 to 5.4 are concerned with the values, at a given yield rate i, of a given bond on various interest dates prior to maturity. These values can be obtained readily by a computer process. One can start with formula (5.2) for the price of a bond and adapt it to a process similar to (6.3) with $W_h = Fr$ $(h = 1, 2, \cdots, n)$ but $A_n = C$ instead of 0. One obtains the book-value column of the investment schedule [see column (5) of Tables 5.3-5.5]. From the book-value column the other columns can be obtained easily. For $F = C$, the A_h provide bond-table values on interest dates.

An alternative process would be to calculate values of $a_{\overline{h|}}$ and apply formula (5.4).

The iterative methods, indicated in formulas (5.18) and (5.20), for finding the yield rate, given the price of a bond, also lend themselves to computer processes. One specifies A, C, F, r and n, and computes $g = Fr/C$, $k = (A - C)/C$. In the next stage, one might set $i_0 = g$ and compute $a_{\overline{n|}\,i_0}$ by a (6.3) process, then $i_1 = g - k/a_{\overline{n|}\,i_0}$. The process is repeated using $i_1, i_2, \cdots$. Note that no table look-up is required, and that the process can be repeated easily until desired accuracy is obtained.

Computer processes may also be useful for calculating the yield rates corresponding to the various redemption dates for a callable bond quoted at a given price, or for calculating the value of a serial bond issue by formula (5.22) or (5.24).

In this and the preceding three sections, we have considered how a number of the main problems of the classical mathematics of finance could be solved by computer processes applied within the classical compound interest model, and have made brief mention of how the model itself might be generalized. We have suggested that computer processes will supersede mathematical methods for production work but that for isolated calculations, for error testing of the computer processes, and for general understanding, much of the mathematical formulation will remain of value. A combination of both the mathematical view and the computer-directed approach is suggested as ideal. We shall try to illustrate this in the following sections where we discuss the problem of finding the rate of interest implied by the terms of a transaction. We shall first discuss the general mathematical setting of the problem, then indicate a general computer process for finding the rate, and later note some special mathematical devices.

6.6. The mathematical setting of the interest rate problem. We shall look at the problem from the lender's or investor's point of view and shall consider as positive the payments from the lender to the borrower, as well as the outstanding principal while the borrower is in a debtor position. Payments by the borrower to the lender will be considered negative and if it should happen that the borrower at some stage more than pays off the outstanding principal and acquires a credit with the lender, then the outstanding principal will be negative. In normal investment situations, the investor could see to it that the outstanding principal is nonnegative. However, the negative possibility will not be excluded initially in our discussion, and the complications resulting therefrom will be touched upon briefly.

We think of an investment extending over n interest periods and involving a stream of net payments $W_0, W_1, \cdots, W_n$ at the ends of the respective periods. We shall assume $W_0 > 0$, that is, the initial payment is an investment. Other payments W_h may also be positive, particularly for the early periods. For some periods, there may be both an investment and a repayment, in which case W_h represents the net balance of the two.

The interest rate problem is usually presented as that of solving for $v = (1 + i)^{-1}$ the equation

$$W_0 + W_1 v + W_2 v^2 + \cdots + W_n v^n = 0. \tag{6.11}$$

Note this is simply an equation of value of the form (1.37) with all nonzero terms collected on one side and netted where necessary.

The hyperbolic relationship $v = (1 + i)^{-1}$ is somewhat complicated, and there are some advantages, for purposes of mathematical interpretation, in using the simpler relation $u = 1 + i$, and rewriting the equation as

$$W_0 u^n + W_1 u^{n-1} + W_2 u^{n-2} + \cdots + W_n = 0. \tag{6.12}$$

In this form, the equation states that the accumulated fund (outstanding principal) at the end of the n periods is zero. The interest rate problem is to solve (6.12) for u and hence obtain $i = u - 1$. This is one of the main problems of the mathematics of finance and special cases have been touched upon from time to time in previous chapters. Now we propose to take a more general look at the problem.

We observe first that the left member of equation (6.12) is a polynomial of degree n with real coefficients. This implies the existence of n solutions, real or complex. Also, with proper choice of the coefficients W_h, the polynomial may be made to pass through any choice of n real roots, so that solving the equation may be as nasty as one cares to imagine it to be. This could be quite disturbing to the financial world were it not that the practical terms of a transaction will normally ensure that there is a unique positive solution for i.

Before identifying investment cases which do have unique positive solutions for i, we consider the outstanding principal at the end of each period, namely,

$$\begin{aligned} S_0(u) &= W_0 \\ S_1(u) &= W_0u + W_1 \\ S_2(u) &= W_0u^2 + W_1u + W_2 \\ &\vdots \\ S_{n-1}(u) &= W_0u^{n-1} + W_1u^{n-2} + \cdots + W_{n-1} \\ S_n(u) &= W_0u^n + W_1u^{n-1} + \cdots + W_n . \end{aligned} \tag{6.13}$$

If we multiply the first n of these equations through by $i = u - 1$ and add, we obtain

$$i \sum_{h=0}^{n-1} S_h(u) = W_0(u^n - 1) + W_1(u^{n-1} - 1) + \cdots + W_{n-1}(u - 1)$$

which can be rearranged as

$$i \sum_{h=0}^{n-1} S_h(u) = S_n(u) - \sum_{h=0}^{n} W_h. \tag{6.14}$$

Now if u is a solution of equation (6.12), we have $S_n(u) = 0$ and

$$i \sum_{h=0}^{n-1} S_h(u) = - \sum_{h=0}^{n} W_h . \tag{6.15}$$

Both members here represent the total interest at rate i on the successive principals outstanding. The investor will wish a positive rate of return i, and the normal way to achieve this will be to have $\sum_{h=0}^{n-1} S_h(u) > 0$, that is, the sum of the principals outstanding shall be positive (in fact, ordinarily we shall seek to have each principal $S_h(u)$ $(h = 0, 1, \cdots, n-1)$ be positive), and concurrently have $\sum_{h=0}^{n} W_h < 0$. The latter means that the borrower pays to the lender more than the latter has loaned to the borrower. To be still more explicit,

$$- \sum_{h=0}^{n} W_h = \sum(\text{payments by borrower to lender}) - \sum(\text{payments by lender to borrower})$$

and since it represents the total interest, it is known as the finance charge.

We note there is the recurrence relation

$$S_{h+1}(u) = S_h(u)\cdot u + W_{h+1}. \qquad (6.16)$$

Now, if we think of dividing $S_n(u)$ by $u - u_*$ using synthetic division, and take account of formulas (6.13) and (6.16), we find

$$S_n(u) = (u - u_*)[S_0(u_*)u^{n-1} + S_1(u_*)u^{n-2} + \cdots + S_{n-1}(u_*)] + S_n(u_*). \qquad (6.17)$$

Thus, at interest rate $i_* = u_* - 1$, the outstanding principals $S_h(u_*)$ $(h = 0, 1, \cdots, n - 1)$ appear as the coefficients of the quotient when $S_n(u)$ is divided by $u - u_*$, and $S_n(u_*)$ itself is the remainder. In particular, for $u_* = 1$, we obtain

$$S_n(u) = (u - 1)[S_0(1)u^{n-1} + S_1(1)u^{n-2} + \cdots + S_{n-1}(1)] + S_n(1). \qquad (6.18)$$

This can be rewritten as

$$S_n(u) = i[W_0u^{n-1} + (W_0 + W_1)u^{n-2} + \cdots + (W_0 + W_1 + \cdots + W_{n-1})] + \textstyle\sum_{h=0}^{n} W_h$$

and rearranged to give formula (6.14) again. The reader may be interested in trying to interpret

$$i[S_0(1)u^{n-1} + S_1(1)u^{n-2} + \cdots + S_{n-1}(1)]$$

as the total interest.

A general discussion of the interest rate problem is given by Teichroew, Robichek and Montalbano (Jan., 1965) and we shall not attempt to duplicate their effort here. We do point out their work is in the framework of capital budgeting, and they look at the problem of determining the internal rate of return provided by a capital project. We, on our part, have been looking at an analogous financial problem involving a loan or loans repaid by a series of payments. We shall stick to situations where $S_h(u) \geq 0$ for $h = 0, 1, \cdots, n - 1$ which the cited authors call pure investments (at interest rate i). If $S_h(u) < 0$ for some h, the problem comes up as to whether the lender should credit the borrower with interest on $S_h(u)$ at the lender's full rate i or at some other presumably lower rate. If such lower rate is introduced, then the polynomial equation (6.12) is replaced by one in two variables. The reader may also wish to refer to the paper by Jean (1968) which is restricted to somewhat the same limits as our discussion.

As previously indicated, we shall assume throughout that:

A. $W_0 > 0$,
B. $W_n \neq 0$ and
C. $\sum_{h=0}^{n} W_h < 0$.

Condition A implies that the transaction starts off as an investment. Condition B indicates the transaction extends to the end of period n. Condition C requires the total interest, or finance charge, to be positive. We shall now systematically consider the various cases that can arise under these conditions. For each case, we first state a theorem and then proceed to its proof. We note that conditions A and C together imply that there must be at least one change of sign among the W_h $(h = 0, 1, \cdots, n)$.

<u>Case 1.</u> If conditions A, B and C hold, and there is only one change of sign among the W_h $(h = 0, 1, \cdots, n)$, then $S_n(u) = 0$ has a unique solution $u_1 > 1$, and hence the interest rate problem has a unique solution. Further, for this solution u_1 the outstanding principals $S_h(u_1)$ $(h = 0, 1, \cdots, n - 1)$ are all positive; that is, the transaction is a pure investment at interest rate $i_1 = u_1 - 1$.

Since $W_0 > 0$, $W_n \neq 0$ and there is only one change of sign, there is some $m \leq n - 1$ such that $W_1 \geq 0$, $W_2 \geq 0$, $\cdots$, $W_m \geq 0$, $W_{m+1} < 0$, $W_{m+2} \leq 0$, $\cdots$, $W_{n-1} \leq 0$, $W_n < 0$. Because of the single change of sign of the coefficients W_h, there is by Descartes' Rule of Signs exactly one real positive solution of the equation $S_n(u) = 0$. Further, since $S_n(1) = \sum_{h=0}^{n} W_h < 0$, and $S_n(u) \to +\infty$ for $u \to +\infty$, the solution > 1.

If u_1 is the unique solution, then $S_h(u_1) > 0$ $(h = 0, 1, \cdots, n - 1)$. Certainly for $h \leq m$ this holds. If for some $h > m$, $S_h(u_1) \leq 0$, then $S_{h+1}(u_1) = S_h(u_1)u_1 + W_{h+1}$ is also ≤ 0 (since $W_{h+1} \leq 0$), and one may argue successively till one reaches $S_n(u_1) = S_{n-1}(u_1)u_1 + W_n < 0$ (since $W_n < 0$), contrary to $S_n(u_1) = 0$. This proves our assertion, and it follows that the transaction is a pure investment at rate $i_1 = u_1 - 1$.

A frequent and simple subcase is that in which $W_0 > 0$, $W_h \leq 0$ $(h = 1, 2, \cdots, n - 1)$, $W_n < 0$. For this subcase in effect only a single advance W_0 is made by the lender to the borrower, and the remaining W_h represent repayments by the borrower. Both the usual amortization and the usual bond transactions fall into this subcase.

Case 2. If conditions A, B and C hold, and there is an even number (>0) of changes of sign among the W_h ($h = 0, 1, \cdots, n$), then no solution $u_1 > 1$ of the equation $S_n(u) = 0$ exists such that the transaction is a pure investment at rate $i_1 = u_1 - 1$.

It follows from conditions A and B, and the even number of changes of sign among the W_h, that in this case $W_n > 0$.

If a solution $u_1 > 1$ exists, we have from the relation $S_n(u_1) = S_{n-1}(u_1)u_1 + W_n = 0$ that $S_{n-1}(u_1) = -W_n/u_1 < 0$, so that the transaction is not a pure investment at $i_1 = u_1 - 1$.

If we restrict ourselves to pure investments, Case 2 transactions are to be excluded.

We preface Case 3 by noting that since $W_0 > 0$, then for some sufficiently large positive u the $S_h(u)$ ($h = 0, 1, \cdots, n - 1$) of formulas (6.13) are all nonnegative, that is, the transaction is a pure investment at interest rate $i = u - 1$. Let u_0 denote a positive u for which this is true.

Case 3. If conditions A, B and C hold, and there is an odd number (>1) of changes of sign among the W_h ($h = 0, 1, \cdots, n$), then the $S_h(u)$ ($h = 1, 2, \cdots, n$) are strictly increasing functions of u for $u > u_0$, and the transaction is a pure investment for all $u \geq u_0$. Further, the equation $S_n(u) = 0$ has at most one solution u_1 with $u_1 \geq u_0$ and $u_1 > 1$, $i_1 = u_1 - 1 > 0$.

It follows from conditions A and B, and the odd number of changes of sign among the W_h, that in this case $W_n < 0$.

From formula (6.17) with $u_* = u_0$ we could find easily that $S_n(u)$ is a strictly increasing function for $u > u_0$. However, we want to show that all $S_h(u)$, $h \geq 1$, are strictly increasing for $u > u_0$. For this purpose we note that if $u > u_0$, then

$$S_1(u) = S_0(u)u + W_1 = W_0u + W_1 > W_0u_0 + W_1 = S_1(u_0) \geq 0$$

which imply $S_1(u) > 0$ and is a strictly increasing function of u. We may now argue recursively that if $S_h(u)$ is positive and strictly increasing for $u > u_0$, then

$$S_{h+1}(u) = S_h(u)u + W_{h+1} > S_h(u_0)u_0 + W_{h+1} = S_{h+1}(u_0) \geq 0;$$

that is, $S_{h+1}(u)$ is positive and strictly increasing for $u > u_0$. We finally reach

$$S_n(u) = S_{n-1}(u)u + W_n$$

and conclude that $S_n(u)$ is strictly increasing for $u > u_0$. As no assumption has been made yet about the sign of $S_n(u_0)$, we have no conclusion about the sign of $S_n(u)$. However, from the strictly increasing character of the $S_h(u)$ ($h = 1, 2, \cdots, n - 1$)

and condition A, we may conclude the transaction is a pure investment for all $u \geq u_0$.

We now consider three subcases:

(a) $u_0 \leq 1$. Since $S_n(1) = \sum_{h=0}^{n} W_h < 0$ and $S_n(u)$ is strictly increasing here for $u > 1$ with $S_n(u) \to +\infty$ for $u \to +\infty$, there is one and only one solution of $S_n(u) = 0$ in the domain $u > 1$. There may, however, exist other solutions in the interval $0 \leq u < u_0$; these are of no practical interest since $i = u - 1 < u_0 - 1$ would be negative.

(b) $u_0 > 1$, $S_n(u_0) \leq 0$. Again, from the strictly increasing property of $S_n(u)$, $u > u_0$, we conclude there is one and only one solution in the domain $u \geq u_0$ and for this solution $i > 0$.

(c) $u_0 > 1$, $S_n(u_0) > 0$. Since $S_n(u)$ is strictly increasing, this implies no solution exists for $u \geq u_0$.

In both subcases (b) and (c), there may exist other solutions of $S_n(u) = 0$ with $1 < u < u_0$. If now we choose for u_0 the smallest value, u_{min} say, such that $S_h(u_0) \geq 0$ $(h = 0, 1, \cdots, n - 1)$, it follows that for these other solutions some of the outstanding principals $S_h(u)$ $(h = 0, \cdots, n - 1)$ are less than zero. This means that at some stage the original lender is no longer investing but is borrowing instead. We have purposely excluded this situation as it brings up the question of what rate of interest should be credited when the investor becomes a borrower. Case 1 and subcases (a) and (b) of Case 3 (with $u_0 = u_{min}$) are the only situations which offer a solution with pure-investment status and with a positive rate of interest.

Although it is clear from equation (6.12) that the interest rate problem may easily have more than one solution, it is only recently that this fact has been commented on in print. An early paper was that by Lorie and Savage (1955); the papers by Teichroew, Robichek and Montalbano (Jan., Nov., 1965) give extensive analysis and illustration. The paper by Jean (1968) has a considerable bibliography. The February, 1968 and several later issues of The Actuary had a number of amusing examples and discussions. See, in particular, the article by James C. Hickman on "The Health of the Math of Finance" in the October, 1968 issue, as it had considerable influence on our writing of this chapter. Most of the examples involve mixed investment and borrowing situations. One can easily construct examples; for instance, take $W_0 = -72$, $W_1 = 170$, $W_2 = -100$ involving a loan of 170 at time 1 balanced by payments of 72 immediately and 100 at time 2. The equation $S_2(u) = 0$ for this case has solutions $u = 5/4$ and $u = 10/9$. Since $W_0 < 0$, this is not a pure investment at any rate of interest.

6.7. Algorithms for computing the rate of interest. Assuming that we have isolated an interval containing a solution of the interest rate problem, how do we proceed to compute the rate? For this purpose, some of the standard methods might be used such as the secant method or the Newton-Raphson method [see Ralston (1965), pp. 371-373]. A direct application of the Newton-Raphson method to an equation such as (6.11) is given in Appendix I of the paper by Hodges and Moore (1968); note that in this appendix $c_r = c_{r+1}x + b_r$ not $c_{r+1}x + a_r$ as given. In our notation, one would iterate to a solution v of the equation (6.11) by the formula

$$v_{k+1} = v_k - f(v_k)/f'(v_k) \qquad (6.19)$$

where $f(v) = W_n v^n + W_{n-1}v^{n-1} + \cdots + W_1 v + W_0$. For this purpose, one may use the algorithm indicated by equation (6.4) to compute $f(v_k) = \ddot{A}_0$ where $\ddot{A}_n = W_n$ ($\neq 0$ here) and $\ddot{A}_h = v_k\ddot{A}_{h+1} + W_h$ ($h = n - 1, n - 2, \cdots, 0$). One may then think of the polynomial

$$\ddot{A}_n v^{n-1} + \ddot{A}_{n-1}v^{n-2} + \cdots + \ddot{A}_2 v + \ddot{A}_1 \qquad (6.20)$$

and reapply the process to find $f'(v_k) = \ddot{B}_1$ where $\ddot{B}_n = \ddot{A}_n$ and $\ddot{B}_h = v_k\ddot{B}_{h+1} + \ddot{A}_h$ ($h = n - 1, n - 2, \cdots, 1$). As pointed out in different notation by Ralston, formula (6.20) is the quotient on dividing $f(v)$ by $v - v_k$, and the remainder is $\ddot{A}_0 = f(v_k)$ by the Remainder Theorem. From Taylor's series applied to the polynomial $f(v)$, we see that the quotient (6.20) is expressible as

$$f'(v_k) + \frac{f''(v_k)}{2!}(v - v_k) + \cdots + \frac{f^{(n)}(v_k)}{n!}(v - v_k)^{n-1}. \qquad (6.20a)$$

If now we divide the quotient (6.20) by $v - v_k$ by means of the analogous $\ddot{B}$-process, the remainder $\ddot{B}_1$ is $f'(v_k)$. Calculation of the right member of (6.19) yields v_{k+1} and one can proceed by iteration.

This algorithm is applied in a slightly different way by Fisher (1966) who chose to solve for δ where $v = e^{-\delta}$. Kaplan (1967) points out that the algorithm may be slow to converge particularly in the neighborhood of a local maximum or minimum of the function. He illustrates some of the difficulties, and suggests modifications of the algorithm to obviate them. This provides a warning that algorithms cannot be used blindly but may require adaptation in particular cases. The reader may refer to Weisner (1938), Sec. 41, for an elementary discussion of the convergence of the Newton-Raphson process.

How formulas may be developed on a minimax principle for finding the rate of interest in standardized loan cases is indicated in an article by Good (1968). Information about the minimax technique may be obtained from the reference in the article, or from Ralston (1965), Chapter 7.

6.8. Special devices for computing the rate of interest. In the computer age, with extensive tables and various general algorithms available, special devices for finding the rate of interest are probably of less significance than formerly. We shall give here only a brief summary of some of the more useful formulas or methods for finding the rate of interest in an annuity transaction. For the full discussion of the methods, including how they are derived, how they are applied, what the author claims for them, and what their limitations are, the reader is referred to the original papers. A convenient summary of some of the methods is given by Karpin (1967).

We consider the simple case where from the terms of an annuity transaction with level payments the value of $a_{\overline{n|}i}$ is obtained and it is desired to find i. For this purpose, it is useful to introduce the notation

$$p = \frac{n - a_{\overline{n|}}}{a_{\overline{n|}}} \tag{6.21}$$

which in case of a loan repaid by n level installments is the ratio of the total interest to the amount loaned. A formula by Evans (1946) is expressible as

$$i = \frac{2}{(n + 1)q}\left[(1 + p)^q - 1\right] \tag{6.22}$$

where $q = \frac{1}{5} + \frac{4}{3}\left[\frac{1}{n + 1} + \frac{1}{10}(1 + p)^{1/2}\right]$. It is effective over a wide range of loan durations and interest rates but involves rather complicated calculation, and there is no indication of the magnitude or direction of the error.

Bizley (1962) presents an alternating infinite series

$$i = \sum_{t=1}^{\infty} f_t p^t \tag{6.23}$$

where the f_t are obtained by inverting the series

$$p = \frac{n}{a_{\overline{n}|}} - 1$$

$$= \frac{n+1}{2} i + \frac{n^2-1}{12} i^2 - \frac{n^2-1}{24} i^3 - \frac{(n^2-1)(n^2-19)}{720} i^4 + \cdots. \qquad (6.24)$$

The coefficients f_t are functions of n alone and the f_t $(t = 1, 2, \cdots, 6)$ are tabulated by Bizley for $n = 1, 2, \cdots, 30$. He states the method is suitable either when n is not large or when the rate of interest is low. For rapid convergence, p should not exceed 0.6.

Karpin (1967), by appropriate manipulation, arrived at the simple formula

$$i = \frac{2p(3 + p)}{2np + 3(n + 1)} \qquad (6.25)$$

which does not require any special tables. He compares results obtained by his formula with those found by using Evans' and Bizley's formulas, for a wide range of values of n and i.

In his paper, Worger (1967) gives some iterative processes and methods which converge quickly to the exact rate i, and which, in his opinion, leave little room for further improvements in accuracy. As it is difficult to summarize briefly his various methods, we refer the interested reader to his paper.

One should note that the algorithms indicated in Section 6.7 have wide application and, in particular, are not limited to the case of level payments, while the methods discussed in this section are applicable to level annuities only. However, in the next sections on Truth in Lending, we shall find that tables developed on the basis of level annuities may, with adjustments or by means of supplementary tables, be adapted to yield the interest rate for many irregular cases.

6.9. Truth in Lending Regulation Z. In 1968 Congress enacted a Consumer Credit Protection Act of which Title I is widely known as the Truth in Lending Act. The main purpose of the Act was to assure a meaningful disclosure of credit terms so that the uninformed use of credit might be avoided. The Board of Governors of the Federal Reserve System was authorized and required to prescribe regulations to carry out the purposes of the Act. Regulation Z, Supplement I, and Volumes I and II of the Annual Percentage Rate Tables were issued by the Board in 1969.

The Regulation requires the disclosure of the finance charge and the annual percentage rate so that a credit customer may tell at a glance how much he is paying for his credit and its relative cost in percentage terms. We shall discuss the annual percentage rate first, and to do so shall follow notations and some of the discussion in Supplement I to Regulation Z. Paragraph (a) thereof gives the general rule for credit other than open end accounts such as charge accounts or credit cards:

> "The annual percentage rate shall be that nominal annual percentage rate determined by multiplying the unit-period rate by the number of unit-periods in a year and shall be computed so that it may be disclosed with an accuracy at least equal to the nearest quarter of 1 per cent. The unit-period rate shall be determined as that percentage rate which will yield a sum equal to the amount of the finance charge when it is applied in accordance with the actuarial method under which payments made on a debt are allocated between the amount of the finance charge and the amount financed, so that each payment is applied first to the accumulated finance charge and any remainder is subtracted from, or any deficiency is added to, the unpaid balance of the amount financed."

If we compare this with the definition of amortization of a loan in Section 4.1, we see that under the so-called actuarial method the payments are applied to amortize the amount financed. In effect then the "unit-period rate" can be determined by setting up an equation of value between the advance(s) made by the creditor and the repayments by the borrower, and solving for the rate of interest. The mathematical background and procedures for doing this have been discussed in the previous three sections. Supplement I gives some of the mathematical background, while Volumes I and II of the Annual Percentage Rate Tables give values whereby for almost all regular or irregular transactions the rate of interest or the finance charge can be determined by inspection, or by simplified computations. These materials provide what might be called "financial engineering" for the disclosure process.

Paragraph (b) of Supplement I defines the unit-period which, in general, is the common period, not to exceed 1 year, which occurs most frequently in the transaction. Paragraph (c) permits either the simple interest approximation or the exact compound value for fractional periods. Paragraph (d) sets up the following notations:

U_k = The amount of credit advanced directly or indirectly in the kth advance.

q_k = The number of unit-periods from the date the finance charge begins to accrue to the kth advance.*

m = The number of advances to be made by the creditor.

P_j = The amount of the jth payment.

t_j = The number of unit-periods from the date the finance charge begins to accrue to the jth payment.

n = The number of payments to be made by the borrower.

w = The number of unit-periods in a year.

i = The rate of finance charge per unit-period (expressed as a decimal number).

R = The nominal annual rate expressed as a decimal number and to be converted into a percentage rate.

The basic equations then are:

$$U_1 v^{q_1} + U_2 v^{q_2} + \cdots + U_m v^{q_m} = P_1 v^{t_1} + P_2 v^{t_2} + \cdots + P_n v^{t_n}, \qquad (6.26)$$

where v as usual is $(1 + i)^{-1}$, and

$$R = wi. \qquad (6.27)$$

We observe that (6.26) could be rearranged in the form (6.11) or (6.12) so that all our previous discussion applies. Also, observe that R is the nominal annual rate, not the effective annual rate. The total interest or finance charge, namely,

$$\sum_{j=1}^{n} P_j - \sum_{k=1}^{m} U_k \qquad (6.28)$$

according to formula (6.15) represents the total interest at rate i per unit-period on the outstanding principals. In other words, it is the total interest at rate i paid by the borrower on the unpaid balances. There is advantage in dealing with the nominal annual rate (or the equivalent effective rate per unit-period) rather than the effective annual rate as the former is applied in a simple fashion to calculate the interest on the unpaid balance at the beginning of the unit-period while the latter would require use of expressions such as $(1 + r)^{1/w} - 1$. Of course, if payments are not made regularly at the end of each

---

*Supplement I reads "from the date of consummation or the date the finance charge begins to accrue, as applicable," but only the latter is mentioned in the definition of t_j. The definitions should be consistent in order that the equation of value make sense. The reasonable choice for the time origin is the date that the finance charge begins to accrue. Of course, this date may also be the date of consummation of the transaction. (See (b) of Supplement.)

unit-period, then some compounding of the rate per unit-period will occur. Also, if there are payments occurring between the ends of unit-periods, the interest based on the rate per unit-period requires an expression such as $(1 + i)^f - 1$, or a simple interest approximation. But, in general, interest based on the rate per unit-period is more easily understood than interest expressed by the equivalent effective annual rate.

While we have considered the finance charge (6.28) from the mathematical point of view as total interest paid by the borrower on unpaid balances, from the practical point of view the finance charge and the payments P_j may have been arrived at on the basis of a number of cost factors including interest, loan fee, service charge, points, premiums for credit life insurance if this is a condition of the loan, and investigation fees. However, once the payments P_j have been determined, one calculates the interest rate per unit-period that would produce total interest equal to the finance charge (6.28).

The Supplement goes on to illustrate the application of the rules and formulas (6.26) and (6.27) for a number of transactions. Most of these are straightforward and will not be presented here. However, the transactions (i) and (iii) on pages 10 and 12 invoke questions similar in nature. We consider just

"(iii) Transaction where customer is required to make periodic deposits into a restricted account.

"Assume creditor advances \$1,000, and customer is to make 12 equal monthly payments of \$110, \$90 of which is to be applied to repayment of the advance and the finance charge and \$20 of which is to be deposited into an account. The account will be released to the customer upon final payment of the advance."

The solution presented follows.

"Unit-period is 1 month.

$$
\begin{array}{ll}
U_1 = \$1{,}000 & q_1 = 0 \\
U_2 = \$240 & q_2 = 12 \\
P_1 = \$110 & t_1 = 1 \\
P_2 = \$110 & t_2 = 2 \\
\ldots & \ldots \\
P_{12} = \$110 & t_{12} = 12
\end{array}
$$

"The equations are adapted as follows:

$$1{,}000 + \frac{240}{(1 + i)^{12}} = \frac{110}{(1 + i)^1} + \frac{110}{(1 + i)^2} + \cdots + \frac{110}{(1 + i)^{12}}$$

$w = 12$.
$i = 0.01482$.
$R = wi = 12 \times 0.01482 = 0.1778$ or 17.78%."

If the equation is rearranged in the form (6.12), we have

$$1{,}000\ u^{12} - 110\ u^{11} - 110\ u^{10} - \cdots - 110\ u^{1} + 130 = 0.$$

There are exactly two changes of sign and as one positive root has been found already there exists a second one but it lies between $u = 0$ and $u = 1$, so that the corresponding i is negative. But W_n (= 130 here) is positive, so that the transaction falls under Case 2 discussed in Section 6.6, and we find that the outstanding principals at the ends of the 11th and 10th periods are at $u = 1.01482$

$$S_{11} = -130/1.01482 = -128.10,$$
$$S_{10} = (S_{11} + 110)/1.01482 = -17.84.$$

This implies that the creditor, instead of being in an investing position in the last two months, is in a borrowing position and paying interest at the annual rate of 17.78%! The creditor probably thinks he is paying interest at rate zero on the $20 deposits and earning interest at the monthly rate i_1 determined by

$$1{,}000 = 90\ a_{\overline{12|}\,i_1}\ .$$

The finance charge per $100 is then $[12(90) - 1{,}000]/10 = 8$, and from Table FRB-104-M of Volume I, $12i_1 = 14.50\%$. Nevertheless, according to the illustration of Supplement I, he would be required to take account of the full payments of $110 and to disclose an annual percentage rate of 17.75% to the nearest 1/4%, which the creditor earns on positive unpaid balances in the first 10 months and then pays on the negative balances in the last two months. In either case, the total net interest earned is $80.

6.10. Truth in Lending, Annual Percentage Rate Tables, Volume I.

These tables are based on a standard amount financed of $100 to be repaid by n level payments $100/a_{\overline{n|}\,i}$ at the ends of the n unit-periods following consummation of the loan. The finance charge per $100 is then

$$100\left(\frac{n}{a_{\overline{n|}\,i}} - 1\right)\ . \qquad (6.29)$$

The main tables give the values of the finance charge (6.29) for a wide range of values of n and $12i$ or $52i$. The scope of the tables is indicated in Table 6.1.

TABLE 6.1

Truth in Lending, Regulation Z, Annual Percentage Rate Tables
Volume I, Finance Charge per $100 of Amount Financed

Table Codes	Number of Unit-Periods per Year w	Range for Number of Payments n (interval 1)	Range for Annual Percentage Rate wi (interval 1/4%)
FRB-101-M to FRB-115-M	12	1 to 60	2% to 61 3/4%
FRB-201-M to FRB-210-M	12	61 to 120	2% to 41 3/4%
FRB-301-M to FRB-330-M	12	121 to 480	2% to 21 3/4%
FRB-101-W to FRB-130-W	52	1 to 104	2% to 61 3/4%

For a regular transaction, involving a single advance and equal payments at the ends of n equal periods following the date of the advance, the finance charge is computed as the sum of the payments less the single advance, and is converted into a finance charge per $100 of advance (amount financed). If the unit-period is a month, the annual percentage rate can be found to the nearest 1/4% by inspection in the -M tables. If the unit-period is m months ($m \leq 12$), the annual percentage rate is $1/m$ times the rate found in the -M tables. If the unit-period is a week, or a multiple thereof, a similar procedure is used with the -W tables.

In Appendix A there are given adjustments to be used for finding the rate in certain single advance transactions with an odd first period, odd first payment and/or odd final payment. These adjustments have a Procrustean flavor; the given transaction does not fit the tables; therefore, we stretch out and level the payments so that the revised transaction does fit a table. There are several steps, but in the preliminary adjustments we proceed so that the finance charge per $100 remains unchanged, and also a first-order estimate of the interest rate is not altered.

For a regular transaction over n periods with level payment P and standard advance of $100, we have

$$100 = P a_{\overline{n}|i} = P[1 - (1 + i)^{-n}]/i$$

$$= P[n - \frac{n(n + 1)}{2} i + \dots]$$

so that

$$i \doteq \frac{nP - 100}{P \frac{n(n + 1)}{2}} \qquad (6.30)$$

where the numerator is the finance charge per $100, and the denominator is an overestimate, $P \sum_{h=0}^{n-1} (n - h)$, of the sum of the successive outstanding principals, $P \sum_{h=0}^{n-1} a_{\overline{n-h}|}$.

An irregular transaction of the type considered in Appendix A may have data as in Figure 6.1.

Payments				P_{h+1}	P	...	P	P_{h+n}
Advance	100							
Unit-periods	0	...	h	h+1	h+2	...	h+n-1	h+n

Fig. 6.1

The equation for i is now

$$100 = P_{h+1}(1 + i)^{-h-1} + P\left[(1 + i)^{-h-2} + \cdots + (1 + i)^{-h-n+1}\right]$$
$$+ P_{h+n}(1 + i)^{-h-n}.$$

If we expand this to linear terms in i, and solve as in (6.30) we obtain for the numerator, the finance charge

$$P_{h+1} + (n - 2)P + P_{h+n} - 100, \tag{6.31}$$

and for the denominator, the expression

$$(h + 1)P_{h+1} + \frac{(n - 2)(n + 2h + 1)}{2} P + (h + n)P_{h+n}. \tag{6.32}$$

We now seek a regular transaction for n' periods and with payment P' so that the finance charge $n'P' - 100$ equals the expression (6.31), and the approximation (6.30) for this revised series equals the approximate interest rate that would be obtained from the ratio of (6.31) to (6.32). The requirements are thus

$$n'P' = P_{h+1} + (n - 2)P + P_{h+n} \tag{6.33}$$

and

$$\frac{n'(n' + 1)}{2} P' = (h + 1)P_{h+1} + \frac{(n - 2)(n + 2h + 1)}{2} P$$
$$+ (h + n)P_{h+n}. \tag{6.34}$$

On substitution from (6.33) into (6.34), we have

$$\left[P_{h+1} + (n - 2)P + P_{h+n}\right](n' + 1)$$
$$= (2h + 2)P_{h+1} + (n - 2)(n + 2h + 1)P + (2h + 2n)P_{h+n}$$

or, on rearrangement,

$$\left[P_{h+1} + (n - 2)P + P_{h+n}\right]n'$$
$$= (n + 2h)\left[P_{h+1} + (n - 2)P + P_{h+n}\right] + (P_{h+n} - P_{h+1})(n - 1)$$

from which

$$n' = n + 2h + (P_{h+n} - P_{h+1})(n-1)/[P_{h+1} + (n-2)P + P_{h+n}]. \qquad (6.35)$$

If $P_{h+n} = P_{h+1}$, the adjusted set of payments P' extend over a term of n + 2h, that is, have been stretched to cover the deferment period h and an equal term beyond n + h, the time of the last payment. The third term on the right side of (6.35) is a special adjustment to allow for possible asymmetry of the original set of payments. For n' an integer, one can interpret the n' payments P' as a set of level payments with the same total amount as the original payments [cf. (6.33)] and with the same approximate equated time (see List 1, Problem 87) as the original set. Here the equated time t of a set of payments P_j at times t_j is given by $\left(\sum_{j=1}^{n} P_j\right) v^t = \sum_{j=1}^{n} P_j v^{t_j}$.

The adjustments indicated by formula (6.35) are those shown as the bases for the adjustment tables on pages A2 and A3. But h may not be integral, nor indeed n', and this brings up another adjustment needed if we are to be able to obtain reasonably accurate results by using the annual percentage rate tables. One first notes that the finance charge for repaying a loan of $100 over n periods with interest at rate i is, by formulas (6.29) and (6.24),

$$100\left(\frac{n+1}{2}\, i + \frac{n^2-1}{12}\, i^2 - \cdots\right),$$

and hence the ratio of the finance charge for the case $n = n_1$ to that for $n = n_2$ is approximately

$$\frac{1+n_1}{1+n_2}\ . \qquad (6.36)$$

Now if $1 \le n' < 60$, Appendix A indicates the rate tables should be entered at $\bar{n}'$, where $\bar{n}'$ is the greatest integer in n', and the finance charge per $100 should be adjusted by the approximation (6.36) to

$$\frac{1+\bar{n}'}{1+n'} \cdot \text{(original finance charge per 100)}. \qquad (6.37)$$

If $n' \ge 60$, the rate tables are to be entered at the integer nearest to n', and the finance charge is not adjusted.

Appendix B indicates how to find the finance charge for regular transactions by direct use of the -M or -W tables. (Recall that these tables give the finance charge (6.29) for the tabulated number of payments and annual interest rate.) Appendix C discusses some special transactions and, in particular, how to determine the unearned finance charge after a transaction has been in progress for some time. (Problem for the reader: How would you find from the tables the unearned finance charge at the end of h months of a loan to be discharged by n monthly payments?)

Appendix D gives some notes on accuracy. In using the tables for transactions with payments which are uniform in period and amount it is generally possible to read the rate to the nearest 1/4% directly, and to determine it to a greater precision by interpolation, if desired. For rates determined after adjustment for certain irregularities by the methods of Appendix A there may be an error of 1/4% or more. Error illustrations are presented.

6.11. Truth in Lending, Annual Percentage Rate Tables, Volume II. The last section of Appendix C in Volume I states somewhat optimistically: "The rates for irregular transactions of all types can be found by using the factor tables contained in Volume II in conjunction with the rate tables in this volume. By the use of these two volumes all combinations of highly irregular advances and payments (within the range of the tables) can be solved with reasonable accuracy by the actuarial method, and the results so obtained shall be considered to comply with the requirements of Regulation Z."

If one has computer facilities available, he could for any transaction start with equations (6.26) and (6.27) and employ some solution algorithm as outlined in Section 6.7. Volume II seeks to obviate this process by setting up procedures for finding the percentage rate by use of the factor tables in Volume II and the tables of Volume I.

The main tables in Volume II are indicated in Table 6.2 .

Each of these tables gives values for three factors A, B and C for computing the theoretical finance charges in various subsequences of payments in a transaction.

The A factor represents the number of regular (monthly or weekly) payments.

The B factor represents the equated time for A regular payments of 1, thus

$$Av^B = a_{\overline{A|}} . \qquad (6.38)$$

TABLE 6.2

Truth in Lending, Regulation Z, Annual Percentage Rate Tables
Volume II, Factor Tables for Irregular Transactions

Table Codes	Number of Unit-Periods per Year	Range for Number of Payments	Range for Annual Percentage Rate (interval 5%)
FRB-101MF to FRB-146MF	12	0 to 480	5% to 20 %
FRB-147MF to FRB-158MF	12	0 to 120	25% to 40 %
FRB-159MF to FRB-166MF	12	0 to 60	45% to 60 %
FRB-101WF to FRB-112WF	52	0 to 104	5% to 60 %

Observe that the total payment at B equals the total of A regular payments of 1, and that whether one considers the single payment of A at B, or the set of A regular payments of 1, the finance charge is the same, namely,

$$A - Av^B = A - a_{\overline{A}|} . \tag{6.39}$$

The C factor represents the finance charge per $1,000 of payment at the equated time B, or per $1,000 of total payments made in A regular installments. Therefore,

$$C = (A - a_{\overline{A}|}) \frac{1,000}{A}$$

$$= 1,000\,(1 - a_{\overline{A}|}/A) . \tag{6.40}$$

Alternatively, we have

$$C = (A - Av^B) \frac{1,000}{A}$$

$$= 1,000(1 - v^B)$$

so that

$$v^B = 1 - C/1,000. \tag{6.41}$$

Formulas (6.40) and (6.41) were utilized in the calculation of the tables by computer.

To find the finance charge contained in a deferred sequence of payments indicated in Figure 6.2, we first find the factor B_1

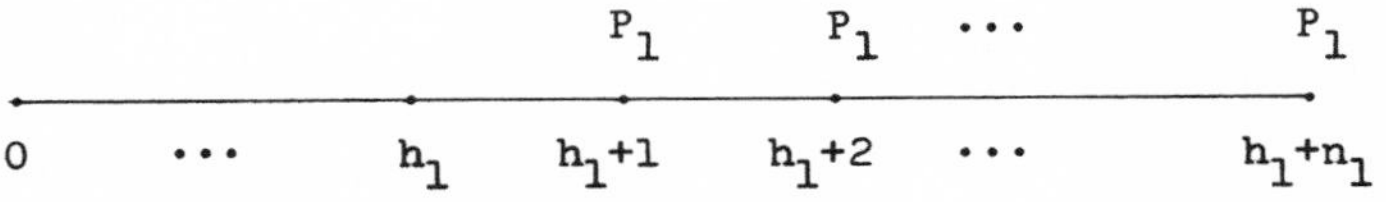

Fig. 6.2

corresponding to n_1 level payments P_1, and have

$$P_1 a_{\overline{n_1}|} = (n_1 P_1) v^{B_1} .$$

Then

$$P_1 v^{h_1} a_{\overline{n_1}|} = (n_1 P_1) v^{B_1+h_1}$$

and the finance charge for these n_1 payments is expressible as

$$n_1 P_1 [1 - v^{B_1+h_1}] . \qquad (6.42)$$

This can be calculated as $\frac{n_1 P_1}{1,000}$ times the C factor at $B_1 + h_1$.

Now suppose, as before, that there are m advances $U_1, \cdots, U_m$ at times $q_1, \cdots, q_m$ and that there are r sequences of equal payments, the first as indicated in Figure 6.2; the second consisting of n_2 regular payments of P_2, deferred h_2 periods; etc. The total finance charge [cf. formula (6.28)] is

$$n_1 P_1 + n_2 P_2 + \cdots + n_r P_r - \sum_{k=1}^{m} U_k . \qquad (6.43)$$

But the equation of value between payments and advances can be written

$$n_1 P_1 v^{B_1+h_1} + n_2 P_2 v^{B_2+h_2} + \cdots + n_r P_r v^{B_r+h_r} - \sum_{k=1}^{m} U_k v^{q_k} = 0.$$

Subtracting this from (6.43), we get the total finance charge as

$$n_1 P_1 (1 - v^{B_1+h_1}) + n_2 P_2 (1 - v^{B_2+h_2}) + \cdots$$

$$+ n_r P_r (1 - v^{B_r+h_r}) - \sum_{k=1}^{m} U_k (1 - v^{q_k}). \qquad (6.44)$$

All of the terms of (6.44) can be calculated from C factors. The formula displays the finance charge for the whole transaction as the sum of component charges for the r sequences of payments less a finance charge calculated with respect to the m advances. If there were only a single advance U made at time 0 then the $\sum_{k=1}^{m} U_k (1 - v^{q_k})$ term vanishes, and the total finance charge is simply

$$n_1 P_1 (1 - v^{B_1+h_1}) + n_2 P_2 (1 - v^{B_2+h_2}) + \cdots + n_r P_r (1 - v^{B_r+h_r}). \qquad (6.45)$$

Does the reader now see the essence of the idea underlying use of the tables in Volume II to obtain the annual percentage rate in a transaction? In effect, any credit transaction, no matter how irregular, can be expressed as a combination of sequences of level advances and level payments. A trial annual percentage rate (perhaps based on an estimate) can be chosen from those for which there are tables in Volume II and the total finance charge for the transaction calculated by formula (6.44) using the factors A, B and C at the trial rate. One compares the result with the actual total finance charge for the transaction [see formula (6.43)], and recalculates (6.44) at a second trial rate chosen so that the two results will bracket the actual finance charge. Then interpolation yields the annual percentage rate of the transaction. Example 1 (Schoolteacher loan) on p. 6 of the volume illustrates the process:

Advances: 1 advance of $2,000 on 7/1/70.
Payments: 9 monthly payments of $90.09 each beginning 10/1/70,
9 monthly payments of $90.09 each beginning 10/1/71,
9 monthly payments of $90.09 each beginning 10/1/72.

Finance charge: Payments minus advances = $432.43.

The central payment is at 19 months after consummation on 7/1/70 and we consider an equivalent set of 2(19) - 1 = 37 level payments without gaps. For n = 37, and finance charge per $100 of 432.43/20 = 21.62, the estimated annual percentage rate is 12 3/4%. This preliminary estimate turns out to be very good.

For each set of 9 payments, the B factor at 10% is 5.0. To this must be added the deferment terms of 2, 14 and 26 months, respectively, to get the finance charges [see formula (6.42)] from the corresponding C factors. The result is a total finance charge of $348.65, while the actual charge is $432.43. Repetition of the calculation using 15% factors produces a finance charge of $497.84 and an interpolation process yields 12.75% as the annual percentage rate to the nearest 1/4%.

The inverse problem, given the annual percentage rate, the advances and the arrangements for the payments, to determine the finance charge and hence the payments, can also be handled by means of the tables of factors in Volume II. The reader is referred to the examples presented there, and the suggested computation forms. Some notes on accuracy are included. The so-called double-run method indicated above appears to give rates well within the 1/4% tolerance except for very short transactions for which more direct methods may be available.

In the case of unusual sequences such as uniformly increasing or decreasing payments, it is suggested in Volume II that auxiliary tables be developed for specific situations to convert such unusual sequences to their single payment equivalents.

We conclude that the two volumes of tables represent a well-executed effort to make it feasible and practical for creditors to provide the disclosures required by the Truth in Lending Act.

6.12. Immunization. It is perhaps fitting that in this last section of text we explore an idea developed by British actuaries to gain an insight into the over-all financial position of a long-term financial institution such as a life insurance company or pension fund. As contrasted with most of the preceding text, we here consider a whole group of transactions rather than a single one. Thus, for instance, a life insurance company has on the one hand a collection of insurance contracts which will require future outgo for claims payments and will produce negative outgo (or income) from premiums. We assume that the net of such positive and negative liability outgo has been projected over the future duration of the existing insurance contracts to be equivalent to a series of payments $L_0, L_1, L_2, \cdots$ at times $0, 1, 2, \cdots$ in regard to some appropriate time unit. On the other hand, the company has a collection of investments which conceivably could be projected to produce asset income of $A_0, A_1, A_2, \cdots$ at times $0, 1, 2, \cdots$. Here, asset income includes maturity values as well as interest income. A major problem for the company is to achieve a safe balance between the flow of asset income and the flow of liability outgo.

We note first that the projection of these flows is made only in regard to the present insurance contracts and present investment securities of the institution. In other words, the projections are limited to the closed groups of existing insurances and securities. If equilibrium is achieved for these, and if future insurance contracts are self-supporting, it is reasonable to suppose that the equilibrium will be maintained or improved. It is obviously difficult to project the flows for the existing liabilities and assets, and projection of flows for insurances to be issued and securities to be purchased in the future involves additional hazards. One notable situation in which open groups are considered is that of the Social Security system where benefit and tax flows are projected for the total insured group including both existing and future new participants.

A second observation is that if the flow of asset income exactly matched the flow of liability outgo, i.e., $A_h = L_h$, $h = 0, 1, 2, \cdots$, then equilibrium is established irrespective of what interest rate is effective in the future. Such complete matching is achieved rarely, and there arises the question of the equivalence of the two flows under a rate of interest i which the institution regards as a reasonable assumption for the accrual of the balances,

$$W_h = A_h - L_h \qquad (h = 0, 1, 2, \cdots). \tag{6.46}$$

There is also the important question as to how secure this equivalence is under variation of the interest rate i.

To relate the discussion here to previous developments in this chapter, we shall limit the term over which the flows are projected to n units (where n may be quite large) and we shall assume that at a selected rate i_0 sufficient assets have been allocated to balance exactly the liabilities, that is we assume

$$\sum_{h=0}^{n} A_h v_0^{\,h} = \sum_{h=0}^{n} L_h v_0^{\,h} \tag{6.47}$$

where $v_0 = (1 + i_0)^{-1} = u_0^{-1}$. Equation (6.47), rewritten as

$$\sum_{h=0}^{n} W_h u_0^{n-h} = 0 \tag{6.48}$$

is now in the form of equation (6.12). As before, denoting the left member of (6.48) by $S_n(u_0)$, we inquire how secure this balance is in the neighborhood of u_0. From Taylor's series,

$$S_n(u) = S_n(u_0) + S_n'(u_0)(u - u_0) + S_n''(u_0)\,\frac{(u - u_0)^2}{2!} + \cdots \tag{6.49a}$$

$$= S_n'(u_0)(u - u_0) + S_n''(u_0)\,\frac{(u - u_0)^2}{2!} + \cdots, \tag{6.49b}$$

since we are assuming $S_n(u_0) = 0$. If $S_n'(u_0) = 0$ and $S_n''(u_0) > 0$, then $S_n(u)$ has a local minimum at $u = u_0$. There is in this case some measure of security, for if the interest rate i is near i_0 (either somewhat less or more than i_0), the variation from $S_n(u_0) = 0$ is fairly small and favorable since $S_n(u) > 0$; that is, some surplus will emerge.

This is the essence of the immunization idea. The insurance fund is "immunized" against variation in the actual interest rate available in the future for investing the balances W_h if the assumed rate i_0 corresponds to a local minimum of $S_n(u)$. If the fund is not in an immunized position, one may try to rearrange the investment portfolio so that immunization is approximated. Note that there is little the fund can do about the liability outgo L_h, and its only lever is provided by the flow of asset income.

A practical test of the immunization position of the fund can be provided by calculating $S_n(u)$ at several rates of interest in the neighborhood of $i_0 = u_0 - 1$, and thereby finding the shape of the graph of $S_n(u)$ in this neighborhood.

As noted in formulas (6.16) and (6.17), the values of $S_h(u_*)$ can be calculated recursively, and appear as the coefficients of $S_n(u)$ divided by $(u - u_*)$, with $S_n(u_*)$ equal to the remainder. Similarly, but with reference also to (6.49a), the value of $S_n'(u_*)$ is the remainder on dividing the first quotient by a second factor $u - u_*$, and the coefficients in this new quotient are the successive accumulations at u_* of the $S_h(u_*)$, $h = 0, 1, \cdots, n - 2$. If these coefficients are all positive, then $S_n''(u_*)$, which would be twice the remainder on dividing the second quotient by $(u - u_*)$, is necessarily positive.

A test provided by Redington (1952), can be obtained by writing

$$S_n'(u_0) = \sum_{h=0}^{n} (A_h - L_h)(n - h)u_0^{n-h-1}. \tag{6.50}$$

For (6.50) to be zero in the presence of (6.47) or (6.48), we require

$$\sum_{h=0}^{n}(A_h - L_h)hu_0^{n-h-1} = 0$$

or

$$\sum_{h=0}^{n} hA_h v_0^h = \sum_{h=0}^{n} hL_h v_0^h \ . \tag{6.51}$$

Denoting the weighted mean term of the asset income $\sum_{h=0}^{n} hA_h v_0^h \Big/ \sum_{h=0}^{n} A_h v_0^h$ by τ_A, and using a similar notation τ_L for the mean term of the liability outgo, and dividing the members of (6.51) by the corresponding members of equation (6.47), we obtain the condition

$$\tau_A = \tau_L \ . \tag{6.52}$$

Similarly, the condition $S_n''(u_0) > 0$ can, in the presence of (6.47) and (6.51), be reduced to

$$\sum_{h=0}^{n} h^2 A_h v_0^h > \sum_{h=0}^{n} h^2 L_h v_0^h \; . \tag{6.53}$$

For further interpretation of these ideas see Wallas (1959). Both Redington and Wallas define immunization in terms of the single condition $S_n'(u_0) = 0$, which provides a stationary point at u_0 for $S_n(u)$, but we have gone further to require a local minimum (which they consider but do not require).

Further readings on immunization are indicated in the references. In summary, in the computer age it is becoming more feasible to project the flows of asset income and liability outgo for an insurance or pension fund and to test the security of the equivalence of these flows by computing the accumulation of the fund at various rates of interest. If the fund is in an immunized position, the variation will be smaller than it would be otherwise, and it will be favorable to the fund.

6.13. References for this chapter. Readers who wish to follow up in more detail some of the recent developments outlined in this chapter may find it useful to consult the following references. These have been assembled under six headings with topics arranged in the same general order as in the chapter. For ease of indicating references the following abbreviations are used:

JIA: Journal of the Institute of Actuaries, London.
JIASS: Journal of the Institute of Actuaries Students' Society, London.
TFA: Transactions of the Faculty of Actuaries, Edinburgh.
TSA: Transactions of the Society of Actuaries, Chicago.

(1) Impact of Computers.

Benjamin, S. (1966): Putting Computers on to Actuarial Work, JIA 92, pp. 134-171.

Malta, A. (1963): Nouvelles Tables Financières (établies par un ordinateur électronique), v. 1 (1963), v. 2 (1965), Dunod, Paris.

Turoff, J.H. (1963): Investment Generations and Asset Accumulations, TSA 15, pp. 366-395.

(2) Interest Rate Problem. Analysis of Capital Projects.

The Actuary: Feb., June, Sept., Oct., Nov. and Dec., 1968; Jan., April, May, Sept. and Nov., 1969. Newsletter published by the Society of Actuaries.

Hodges, S.D. and Moore, P.G. (1968): The Consideration of Risk in Project Selection, JIA 94, pp. 355-378.

Jean, W.H. (1968): On Multiple Rates of Return, J. of Finance 23, pp. 187-191.

Lewin, C.G. (1967): The Appraisal of Capital Projects, JIASS 18, pp. 150-176.

Lorie, J.H. and Savage, L.J. (1955): Three Problems in Rationing Capital, J. of Business 28, pp. 229-239.

Teichroew, D., Robichek, A.A. and Montalbano, M. (Jan., 1965): Mathematical Analysis of Rates of Return under Certainty, Management Sci. 11 (Ser. A), pp. 395-403.

____________ (Nov., 1965): An Analysis of Criteria for Investment and Financing Decisions under Certainty, Management Sci. 12 (Ser. A), pp. 151-179.

(3) Algorithms for Computing the Rate of Interest.

Fisher, L. (1966): An Algorithm for Finding Exact Rates of Return, J. of Business 39, pp. 111-118.

Good, D.M. (1968): The Problem of the Installment Loan, The Actuary, June, 1968.

Kaplan, S. (1967): Computer Algorithms for Finding Exact Rates of Return, J. of Business 40, pp. 389-392.

Ralston, A. (1965): A First Course in Numerical Analysis, McGraw-Hill, New York.

Weisner, L. (1938): Introduction to the Theory of Equations, Macmillan, New York.

(See also Hodges and Moore cited in (2), Appendix I.)

(4) Special Devices for Computing the Rate of Interest.

Bizley, M.T.L. (1962): Determination of Yields on Annuities-Certain, JIA 88, pp. 95-99.

Evans, A.W. (1946): Further Remarks on the Relationship between the Values of Life Annuities at Different Rates of Interest, Including a Description of a Method of First-Difference Interpolation and a Reference to Annuities-Certain, JIA 72, pp. 447-454.

Karpin, H. (1967): Simple Algebraic Formulae for Estimating the Rate of Interest, JIA 93, pp. 297-309.

Worger, H.O. (1967): On Finding the Rate of Interest of an Annuity Certain, JIA 93, pp. 279-295.

(5) Truth in Lending.

Federal Trade Commission; Washington, D.C. (Mar., 1969): What you ought to know about Federal Reserve Regulation Z. Pamphlet. (Includes Regulation Z.)

Board of Governors, Federal Reserve System (1969): Supplement I to Regulation Z.

______________ (1969): Truth in Lending Regulation Z, Annual Percentage Rate Tables, v. I and II.

(6) Immunization.

Cavaye, C. M. and Springbett, T.M. (1964): Actuarial Note on the Calculation of Premium Rates Using a Decreasing Rate of Interest and Allowing for the Benefits of Immunisation, TFA 28, pp. 308-322.

Haynes, A.T. and Kirton, R.J. (1953): The Financial Structure of a Life Office, TFA 21, pp. 141-195.

Redington, F.M. (1952): Review of the Principles of Life-Office Valuations, JIA 78, pp. 286-315.

Rose, D.S. (1968): The Interdependence of Funding and Investment in Life Assurance Funds, Trans. 18th Int. Cong. Actuaries, Munich, v. 2, pp. 283-292.

Sutherland, J.W. (1954): Modern Ideas on Choosing the Maturity Dates of Life Office Investments, Trans. 14th Int. Cong. Actuaries, Madrid, v. 2, pp. 304-314.

Wallas, G. E. (1959): Immunization, JIASS 15, pp. 345-357.

APPENDIX

A.1. A brief introduction to finite differences. The reader is familiar with calculus which defines and treats derivatives

$$D_x f(x) = df(x)/dx = f'(x)$$

$$D_x^2 f(x) = D_x f'(x) = f''(x), \text{ etc.}$$

and integrals

$$\int_a^b f'(x)\, dx = \int_a^b df(x) = \left[f(x)\right]_a^b .$$

Somewhat analogous is the subject called finite differences, based on differences instead of derivatives and summation instead of integration.

For a function f(x) one defines

(First) Difference	$\Delta f(x) = f(x + 1) - f(x)$	(A.1)
Second Difference	$\Delta^2 f(x) = \Delta[\Delta f(x)]$	(A.2)
Third Difference	$\Delta^3 f(x) = \Delta[\Delta^2 f(x)]$,	(A.3)

etc. One consequence is that if $g(x) = \Delta f(x)$, then

$$\Delta^2 f(x) = \Delta g(x) = g(x + 1) - g(x) = \Delta f(x + 1) - \Delta f(x)$$
$$= \left[f(x + 2) - f(x + 1)\right] - \left[f(x + 1) - f(x)\right] .$$

That is,

$$\Delta^2 f(x) = f(x + 2) - 2\, f(x + 1) + f(x). \qquad \text{(A.4)}$$

An illustration from compound interest is given by v^t (a function of t when i is fixed), with

$$\Delta v^t = v^{t+1} - v^t = v^t(v - 1) \qquad \text{(A.5)}$$

$$\Delta^2 v^t = \Delta\left[v^t(v - 1)\right] = (v - 1)(v^{t+1} - v^t)$$
$$= (v - 1)^2 v^t$$

$$\Delta^3 v^t = (v - 1)^3 v^t, \text{ etc.}$$

and

$$\Delta^2 v^t = (v - 1)^2\, v^t = v^{t+2} - 2\, v^{t+1} + v^t$$

which is (A.4) for $f(t) = v^t$.

More general definitions of differences are

$$\underset{q}{\Delta} f(x) = f(x + q) - f(x) \tag{A.1a}$$

$$\underset{q}{\Delta^2} f(x) = \underset{q}{\Delta}\left[\underset{q}{\Delta} f(x)\right], \tag{A.2a}$$

etc., where q, a nonzero real number, is called the interval of differencing. In this notation the derivative of f(x) is defined to be

$$\lim_{q\to 0}\left[\underset{q}{\Delta} f(x)/\underset{q}{\Delta} x\right]$$

(provided this limit exists), the familiar "limit of the difference quotient." The definite integral is definable as a limit of a sum. One is thus led to think of calculus as "infinitesimal calculus" (for $q \to 0$, so q is infinitesimal) and of finite differences as "finite calculus" (for q is finite).

Some equations involve a function f at a finite number of uniformly spaced values of its variable and are expressible in terms of differences of f; such equations are called difference equations. (Cf. differential equations.) Examples of difference equations are

$$S_k = S_{k-1} + i\, S_{k-1} \tag{1.1}$$

$$R = iA_{h-1} + A_{h-1} - A_h \tag{4.1}$$

$$-\Delta(v^{h-1} A_{h-1}) = Rv^h \tag{4.2}$$

and also the generalizations (4.9) and (4.10) of (4.1) and (4.2), with R_h replacing the constant R. The text develops the solutions

$$S_k = A(1 + i)^k \tag{1.3}$$

of (1.1), with A denoting S_0, and

$$A_h = A(1 + i)^h - R\, s_{\overline{h}|i}\,, \tag{4.5}$$

where $A = A_0$, and

$$A_h = R\, a_{\overline{n-h}|i} \tag{4.6}$$

of both (4.1) and (4.2). The boundary condition $A_n = 0$, attached to equations (4.1) and (4.2), is essential in obtaining the solution (4.6).

In the solution of difference equations and in other problems, summation of series by finite difference methods is often a valuable device. To get a brief look at summation, let us assume that f and g are functions such that

$$g(x) = \Delta f(x) \tag{A.6}$$

for all x-values in the domain of g, including x = a, a + 1, a + 2, ···, a + n. Then

$$\sum_{x=a}^{a+n} g(x) = \sum_{x=a}^{a+n} \Delta f(x)$$

$$= [f(a+1) - f(a)] + [f(a+2) - f(a+1)] + [f(a+3) - f(a+2)]$$
$$+ \cdots + [f(a+n) - f(a+n-1)] + [f(a+n+1) - f(a+n)]$$

or

$$\sum_{x=a}^{a+n} g(x) = f(a+n+1) - f(a). \tag{A.7}$$

This result is often denoted by

$$\sum_{x=a}^{a+n} \Delta f(x) = [f(x)]_a^{a+n+1}. \tag{A.8}$$

To illustrate:

$$a_{\overline{n}|i} = \sum_{t=1}^{n} v^t = \sum_{t=1}^{n} \Delta v^t/(v-1) \text{ by (A.5)}$$

$$= \frac{1}{v-1} \sum_{t=1}^{n} \Delta v^t, \text{ since } 1/(v-1) \text{ is a constant,}$$

$$= \frac{1}{v-1} [v^t]_1^{n+1} = \frac{v^{n+1} - v}{v-1} = (1 - v^n)/i$$

which is (3.2).

In a more complicated situation one may have to simplify $\sum_{x=a}^{a+n} [u(x)\Delta v(x)]$. It may help him to use

$$u(x)\Delta v(x) = \Delta[u(x)v(x)] - v(x+1)\Delta u(x) \tag{A.9}$$

derived from

$$\begin{aligned} \Delta[u(x)v(x)] &= u(x+1)v(x+1) - u(x)v(x) \\ &= v(x+1)[u(x+1) - u(x)] + u(x)[v(x+1) - v(x)] \\ &= v(x+1)\Delta u(x) + u(x)\Delta v(x). \end{aligned}$$

Thus,

$$\sum_{x=a}^{a+n} [u(x)\Delta v(x)] = \sum_{x=a}^{a+n} \{\Delta[u(x)v(x)] - v(x+1)\Delta u(x)\} \text{ by (A.9)}$$

$$= \sum_{x=a}^{a+n} \Delta[u(x)v(x)] - \sum_{x=a}^{a+n} v(x+1)\Delta u(x)$$

so that from (A.8)

$$\sum_{x=a}^{a+n} [u(x)\Delta v(x)] = [u(x)v(x)]_a^{a+n+1} - \sum_{x=a}^{a+n} v(x+1)\Delta u(x). \quad (A.10)$$

Equation (A.10) is called the formula for "summation by parts." Its infinitesimal calculus counterpart, the formula for "integration by parts,"

$$\int_a^b u(x)\ dv(x) = [u(x)v(x)]_a^b - \int_a^b v(x)\ du(x)$$

is more symmetric and therefore less tricky to apply.

The problems which follow offer practice in the finite calculus approach to interest theory.

Problems 1-6. By finite differences show that when i is fixed

1. $\Delta(1+i)^t = i(1+i)^t$, $\quad \Delta^n(1+i)^t = i^n(1+i)^t$.
2. $\Delta s_{\overline{n}|i} = (1+i)^n$, $\quad \Delta a_{\overline{n}|i} = v^{n+1}$.
3. $\Delta(Is)_{\overline{n}|i} = s_{\overline{n+1}|i}$, $\quad \Delta(Da)_{\overline{n}|i} = a_{\overline{n+1}|i}$.
4. $s_{\overline{n}|i} = [(1+i)^n - 1]/i$, $\quad \ddot{s}_{\overline{n}|i} = [(1+i)^n - 1]/d$.
5. $(Is)_{\overline{n}|i} = (\ddot{s}_{\overline{n}|i} - n)/i$.
6. $(Da)_{\overline{n}|i} = (n - a_{\overline{n}|i})/i$.

Problem 7. Show that

(a) Equation (3.48) can be derived by summation by parts.

(b) Equation (3.48) implies equation (3.47). (Hint: Replace i in (3.48) by $i' = (1+i)^q - 1$.)

(c) Equation (3.48) implies equation (3.50), and thus (3.47) implies (3.49).

Problems 8-10.

(a) Verbally interpret and classify each of the following difference equations in terms of interest theory.

(b) Solve the difference equation for the case $h = n$, and name the result.

8. $S_h = S_{h-1} + i\ S_0$, $\quad h = 1, 2, \cdots, n$.

Cf. equation (1.1).

9. $A_h = (1+i)A_{h-1} + R$, $\quad h = 1, 2, \cdots, n;\ A_0 = 0$.

Cf. equation (4.1). (Hint for (b): Show that equations (4.1) and (4.2) are equivalent; then find a corresponding equivalent equation for this problem; solve that equation for A_n.)

10. $A_h = (1+i)A_{h-1} + hR$, $\quad h = 1, 2, \cdots, n;\ A_0 = 0$.

Problem 11. In the light of the solution $Rs_{\overline{n}|}$ to the difference equation in Problem 9, surmise the solution

(a) A_n of $A_h = (1 + i)(A_{h-1} + R)$, $h = 1, 2, \cdots, n$; $A_0 = 0$

(b) A_0 of $A_h = (1 + i)A_{h-1} - R$, $h = 1, 2, \cdots, n$; $A_n = 0$

(c) A_0 of $A_h = (1 + i)(A_{h-1} - R)$, $h = 1, 2, \cdots, n$; $A_n = 0$.

Problem 12. Write down difference equations, including boundary conditions, the solutions (A_n or A_0 as the case may be) of which produce in turn (a) $R(I\ddot{s})_{\overline{n}|}$, (b) $R(Ia)_{\overline{n}|}$, (c) $R(I\ddot{a})_{\overline{n}|}$. (Hint: See Problems 10 and 11.)

A.2. References to books. The following books on compound interest are on a level more or less comparable to that of the present book:

Donald, D.W.A. (1953): Compound Interest and Annuities-Certain, Cambridge University Press, London (2nd ed., 1970).

Kellison, S.G. (1970): The Theory of Interest, Richard D. Irwin, Inc., Homewood, Illinois.

Sheppard, N.E. and Baillie, D.C. (1960): Compound Interest, University of Toronto Press, Toronto.

Todhunter, R. (1937): The Institute of Actuaries' Text-Book on Compound Interest and Annuities-Certain, 4th ed., Cambridge University Press, London.

From among the large number of more elementary books on the mathematics of finance, we cite three:

Hummel, P.M. and Seebeck, C.L. (1956): Mathematics of Finance, 2nd ed., McGraw-Hill, New York (3rd ed., 1971).

Rider, P.R. and Fischer, C.H. (1951): Mathematics of Investment, Ulrich's Books, Inc., Ann Arbor, Michigan.

Smith, F.C. (1951): The Matnematics of Finance, Appleton-Century-Crofts, New York.

A.3. References to tables. The following have extensive tabulations of values of compound interest functions:

Financial Publishing Company (1970): Financial Compound Interest and Annuity Tables, 5th ed., Financial Publishing Company, Boston.

Glover, J.W. (1948): Compound Interest and Insurance Tables and Seven Place Logarithms, George Wahr, Publisher, Ann Arbor, Michigan.

Kent, F.C. and Kent, M.E. (1926): Compound Interest and Annuity Tables, McGraw-Hill, New York. Available in paperback.

Malta, A. (1963): Nouvelles Tables Financières (établies par un ordinateur électronique), v. 1 (1963), v. 2 (1965), Dunod, Paris.

A useful working set of compound interest tables is given in The Handbook of Tables for Mathematics (4th edition, 1970) published by The Chemical Rubber Co., Cleveland. This edition contains tables of six-place mantissas for common logarithms as used in our computations for problems in this book. The Chemical Rubber Co. also publishes a smaller compilation containing interest tables, namely, Standard Mathematical Tables. A few editions of it [e.g., the 16th (1968)] contain tables of six-place mantissas for common logarithms, but most [e.g., the 18th (1970)] have instead the ordinary five-place mantissas.

A.4. Tables.

I. Interest functions: $(1 + i)^n$, v^n, $s_{\overline{n}|i}$, $a_{\overline{n}|i}$, $s^{-1}_{\overline{n}|i}$.

II. Rates: i, d, δ , i/δ , $100\, i^{(m)}$, $100\, d^{(m)}$, $i/i^{(m)}$.

III. Seven-place mantissas for 10,000 to 11,009 for obtaining $\log (1 + i)$, $0 \le i \le 0.1009$.

IV. The number of each day of the year.

Acknowledgments

Tables I and II were computed by Allen L. Mayerson, Professor of Insurance and Mathematics, and his graduate student assistant, Donald Gieffers, at the Computing Center, University of Michigan. The tables are taken directly from the computer print-out so that a great deal of laborious table preparation was obviated. The assistance of Professor Mayerson and Mr. Gieffers in this matter is greatly appreciated by the authors.

Tables III and IV are by courtesy of Carl H. Fischer, Professor of Insurance and Actuarial Mathematics, University of Michigan, from Mathematics of Investment by P.R. Rider and C.H. Fischer (see A.2). Again, the authors are grateful for this assistance.

n	$(1+i)^n$	v^n	$s_{\overline{n}\rvert}$	$a_{\overline{n}\rvert}$	$s_{\overline{n}\rvert}^{-1}$
1/12	1.0002081	0.9997919	0.083238	0.083221	12.01374380
1/ 6	1.0004162	0.9995839	0.166493	0.166424	6.00624697
1/ 4	1.0006244	0.9993760	0.249766	0.249610	4.00374805
1/ 3	1.0008326	0.9991681	0.333056	0.332779	3.00249861
1/ 2	1.0012492	0.9987523	0.499688	0.499064	2.00124922
1	1.0025000	0.9975062	1.000000	0.997506	1.00000000
2	1.0050062	0.9950187	2.002500	1.992525	0.49937578
3	1.0075188	0.9925373	3.007506	2.985062	0.33250139
4	1.0100376	0.9900622	4.015025	3.975124	0.24906445
5	1.0125627	0.9875932	5.025063	4.962718	0.19900250
6	1.0150941	0.9851304	6.037625	5.947848	0.16562803
7	1.0176318	0.9826737	7.052719	6.930522	0.14178928
8	1.0201759	0.9802231	8.070351	7.910745	0.12391035
9	1.0227263	0.9777787	9.090527	8.888524	0.11000462
10	1.0252831	0.9753403	10.113253	9.863864	0.09888015
11	1.0278463	0.9729081	11.138536	10.836772	0.08977840
12	1.0304160	0.9704819	12.166383	11.807254	0.08219370
13	1.0329920	0.9680617	13.196799	12.775316	0.07577595
14	1.0355745	0.9656476	14.229791	13.740963	0.07027510
15	1.0381634	0.9632395	15.265365	14.704203	0.06550777
16	1.0407588	0.9608374	16.303529	15.665040	0.06133642
17	1.0433607	0.9584413	17.344287	16.623481	0.05765587
18	1.0459691	0.9560512	18.387648	17.579533	0.05438433
19	1.0485840	0.9536670	19.433617	18.533200	0.05145722
20	1.0512055	0.9512888	20.482201	19.484488	0.04882288
21	1.0538335	0.9489165	21.533407	20.433405	0.04643947
22	1.0564681	0.9465501	22.587240	21.379955	0.04427278
23	1.0591093	0.9441896	23.643708	22.324145	0.04229455
24	1.0617570	0.9418351	24.702818	23.265980	0.04048121
25	1.0644114	0.9394863	25.764575	24.205466	0.03881298
26	1.0670725	0.9371435	26.828986	25.142609	0.03727312
27	1.0697401	0.9348065	27.896059	26.077416	0.03584736
28	1.0724145	0.9324753	28.965799	27.009891	0.03452347
29	1.0750955	0.9301499	30.038213	27.940041	0.03329093
30	1.0777833	0.9278303	31.113309	28.867871	0.03214059
31	1.0804777	0.9255165	32.191092	29.793388	0.03106449
32	1.0831789	0.9232085	33.271570	30.716596	0.03005569
33	1.0858869	0.9209062	34.354749	31.637503	0.02910806
34	1.0886016	0.9186097	35.440636	32.556112	0.02821620
35	1.0913231	0.9163189	36.529237	33.472431	0.02737533
36	1.0940514	0.9140338	37.620560	34.386465	0.02658121
37	1.0967865	0.9117545	38.714612	35.298220	0.02583004
38	1.0995285	0.9094807	39.811398	36.207700	0.02511843
39	1.1022773	0.9072127	40.910927	37.114913	0.02444335
40	1.1050330	0.9049503	42.013204	38.019863	0.02380204
50	1.1329717	0.8826346	53.188683	46.946170	0.01880099
60	1.1616168	0.8608691	64.646713	55.652358	0.01546869
70	1.1909861	0.8396404	76.394437	64.143853	0.01308996
80	1.2210980	0.8189351	88.439181	72.425952	0.01130721
90	1.2519711	0.7987405	100.788454	80.503816	0.00992177
100	1.2836249	0.7790438	113.449955	88.382483	0.00881446

II: RATES: $i=0.0025$, $d=0.002493766$, $\delta=0.002496880$, $i/\delta=1.0012495$

m	2	3	4	6	12
100 $i^{(m)}$	0.2498439	0.2497920	0.2497660	0.2497400	0.2497140
100 $d^{(m)}$	0.2495322	0.2495841	0.2496101	0.2496361	0.2496620
$i / i^{(m)}$	1.0006246	1.0008329	1.0009370	1.0010412	1.0011453

I: INTEREST FUNCTIONS; i=0.0050

n	$(1+i)^n$	v^n	$s_{\overline{n}\rceil}$	$a_{\overline{n}\rceil}$	$s_{\overline{n}\rceil}^{-1}$
1/12	1.0004157	0.9995845	0.083143	0.083108	12.02747524
1/ 6	1.0008316	0.9991691	0.166321	0.166182	6.01248788
1/ 4	1.0012477	0.9987539	0.249533	0.249222	4.00749221
1/ 3	1.0016639	0.9983389	0.332779	0.332227	3.00499446
1/ 2	1.0024969	0.9975093	0.499377	0.498133	2.00249688
1	1.0050000	0.9950249	1.000000	0.995025	1.00000000
2	1.0100250	0.9900745	2.005000	1.985099	0.49875312
3	1.0150751	0.9851488	3.015025	2.970248	0.33167221
4	1.0201505	0.9802475	4.030100	3.950496	0.24813279
5	1.0252513	0.9753707	5.050251	4.925866	0.19800997
6	1.0303775	0.9705181	6.075502	5.896384	0.16459546
7	1.0355294	0.9656896	7.105879	6.862074	0.14072854
8	1.0407070	0.9608852	8.141409	7.822959	0.12282886
9	1.0459106	0.9561047	9.182116	8.779064	0.10890736
10	1.0511401	0.9513479	10.228026	9.730412	0.09777057
11	1.0563958	0.9466149	11.279167	10.677027	0.08865903
12	1.0616778	0.9419053	12.335562	11.618932	0.08106643
13	1.0669862	0.9372192	13.397240	12.556151	0.07464224
14	1.0723211	0.9325565	14.464226	13.488708	0.06913609
15	1.0776827	0.9279169	15.536548	14.416625	0.06436436
16	1.0830712	0.9233004	16.614230	15.339925	0.06018937
17	1.0884865	0.9187068	17.697301	16.258632	0.05650579
18	1.0939289	0.9141362	18.785788	17.172768	0.05323173
19	1.0993986	0.9095882	19.879717	18.082356	0.05030253
20	1.1048956	0.9050629	20.979115	18.987419	0.04766645
21	1.1104201	0.9005601	22.084011	19.887979	0.04528163
22	1.1159722	0.8960797	23.194431	20.784059	0.04311380
23	1.1215520	0.8916216	24.310403	21.675681	0.04113465
24	1.1271598	0.8871857	25.431955	22.562866	0.03932061
25	1.1327956	0.8827718	26.559115	23.445638	0.03765186
26	1.1384596	0.8783799	27.691911	24.324018	0.03611163
27	1.1441519	0.8740099	28.830370	25.198028	0.03468565
28	1.1498726	0.8696616	29.974522	26.067689	0.03336167
29	1.1556220	0.8653349	31.124395	26.933024	0.03212914
30	1.1614001	0.8610297	32.280017	27.794054	0.03097892
31	1.1672071	0.8567460	33.441417	28.650800	0.02990304
32	1.1730431	0.8524836	34.608624	29.503284	0.02889453
33	1.1789083	0.8482424	35.781667	30.351526	0.02794727
34	1.1848029	0.8440223	36.960575	31.195548	0.02705586
35	1.1907269	0.8398231	38.145378	32.035371	0.02621550
36	1.1966805	0.8356449	39.336105	32.871016	0.02542194
37	1.2026639	0.8314875	40.532785	33.702504	0.02467139
38	1.2086772	0.8273507	41.735449	34.529854	0.02396045
39	1.2147206	0.8232346	42.944127	35.353089	0.02328607
40	1.2207942	0.8191389	44.158847	36.172228	0.02264552
50	1.2832258	0.7792861	56.645163	44.142786	0.01765376
60	1.3488502	0.7413722	69.770031	51.725561	0.01433280
70	1.4178305	0.7053029	83.566105	58.939418	0.01196657
80	1.4903386	0.6709885	98.067714	65.802305	0.01019704
90	1.5665547	0.6383435	113.310936	72.331300	0.00882527
100	1.6466685	0.6072868	129.333698	78.542645	0.00773194

II: RATES; i =0.0050, d=0.004975124, δ =0.004987542, i/δ = 1.0024979

m	2	3	4	6	12
100 i(m)	0.4993766	0.4991690	0.4990652	0.4989615	0.4988578
100 d(m)	0.4981328	0.4983398	0.4984433	0.4985469	0.4986505
i / i(m)	1.0012484	1.0016648	1.0018731	1.0020813	1.0022896

n	$(1+i)^n$	v^n	$s_{\overline{n}\rceil}$	$a_{\overline{n}\rceil}$	$s_{\overline{n}\rceil}^{-1}$
1/12	1.0006229	0.9993775	0.083048	0.082997	12.04119435
1/ 6	1.0012461	0.9987554	0.166148	0.165941	6.01872276
1/ 4	1.0018697	0.9981337	0.249300	0.248835	4.01123249
1/ 3	1.0024938	0.9975124	0.332503	0.331676	3.00748755
1/ 2	1.0037430	0.9962710	0.499066	0.497205	2.00374299
1	1.0075000	0.9925558	1.000000	0.992556	1.00000000
2	1.0150562	0.9851671	2.007500	1.977723	0.49813200
3	1.0226692	0.9778333	3.022556	2.955556	0.33084579
4	1.0303392	0.9705542	4.045225	3.926110	0.24720501
5	1.0380667	0.9633292	5.075565	4.889440	0.19702242
6	1.0458522	0.9561580	6.113631	5.845598	0.16356891
7	1.0536961	0.9490402	7.159484	6.794638	0.13967488
8	1.0615988	0.9419754	8.213180	7.736613	0.12175552
9	1.0695608	0.9349632	9.274779	8.671576	0.10781929
10	1.0775825	0.9280032	10.344339	9.599580	0.09667123
11	1.0856644	0.9210949	11.421922	10.520675	0.08755094
12	1.0938069	0.9142382	12.507586	11.434913	0.07995148
13	1.1020104	0.9074324	13.601393	12.342345	0.07352188
14	1.1102755	0.9006773	14.703404	13.243022	0.06801146
15	1.1186026	0.8939725	15.813679	14.136995	0.06323639
16	1.1269921	0.8873177	16.932282	15.024313	0.05905879
17	1.1354446	0.8807123	18.059274	15.905025	0.05537321
18	1.1439604	0.8741561	19.194718	16.779181	0.05209766
19	1.1525401	0.8676488	20.338679	17.646830	0.04916740
20	1.1611841	0.8611899	21.491219	18.508020	0.04653063
21	1.1698930	0.8547790	22.652403	19.362799	0.04414543
22	1.1786672	0.8484159	23.822296	20.211215	0.04197748
23	1.1875072	0.8421001	25.000963	21.053315	0.03999846
24	1.1964135	0.8358314	26.188471	21.889146	0.03818474
25	1.2053866	0.8296093	27.384884	22.718755	0.03651650
26	1.2144270	0.8234336	28.590271	23.542189	0.03497693
27	1.2235352	0.8173038	29.804698	24.359493	0.03355176
28	1.2327117	0.8112197	31.028233	25.170713	0.03222871
29	1.2419571	0.8051808	32.260945	25.975893	0.03099723
30	1.2512718	0.7991869	33.502902	26.775080	0.02984816
31	1.2606563	0.7932376	34.754174	27.568318	0.02877352
32	1.2701112	0.7873326	36.014830	28.355650	0.02776634
33	1.2796371	0.7814716	37.284941	29.137122	0.02682048
34	1.2892343	0.7756542	38.564578	29.912776	0.02593053
35	1.2989036	0.7698801	39.853813	30.682656	0.02509170
36	1.3086454	0.7641490	41.152716	31.446805	0.02429973
37	1.3184602	0.7584605	42.461361	32.205266	0.02355082
38	1.3283487	0.7528144	43.779822	32.958080	0.02284157
39	1.3383113	0.7472103	45.108170	33.705290	0.02216893
40	1.3483486	0.7416480	46.446482	34.446938	0.02153016
50	1.4529569	0.6882516	60.394257	41.566447	0.01655787
60	1.5656810	0.6386997	75.424137	48.173374	0.01325836
70	1.6871505	0.5927153	91.620073	54.304622	0.01091464
80	1.8180440	0.5500417	109.072531	59.994440	0.00916821
90	1.9590925	0.5104404	127.878995	65.274609	0.00781989
100	2.1110838	0.4736903	148.144512	70.174623	0.00675017

II: RATES; $i = 0.0075$, $d = 0.007444169$, $\delta = 0.007472015$, $i/\delta = 1.0037453$

m	2	3	4	6	12
$100\, i^{(m)}$	0.7485990	0.7481328	0.7478998	0.7476669	0.7474342
$100\, d^{(m)}$	0.7458074	0.7462717	0.7465040	0.7467364	0.7469689
$i / i^{(m)}$	1.0018715	1.0024958	1.0028081	1.0031205	1.0034329

I: INTEREST FUNCTIONS; i = 0.0100

n	$(1+i)^n$	v^n	$s_{\overline{n}\rceil}$	$a_{\overline{n}\rceil}$	$s^{-1}_{\overline{n}\rceil}$
1/12	1.0008295	0.9991711	0.082954	0.082885	12.05490119
1/ 6	1.0016598	0.9983430	0.165976	0.165701	6.02495163
1/ 4	1.0024907	0.9975155	0.249068	0.248449	4.01496891
1/ 3	1.0033223	0.9966887	0.332228	0.331128	3.00997789
1/ 2	1.0049876	0.9950372	0.498756	0.496281	2.00498756
1	1.0100000	0.9900990	1.000000	0.990099	1.00000000
2	1.0201000	0.9802960	2.010000	1.970395	0.49751244
3	1.0303010	0.9705901	3.030100	2.940985	0.33002211
4	1.0406040	0.9609803	4.060401	3.901966	0.24628109
5	1.0510101	0.9514657	5.101005	4.853431	0.19603980
6	1.0615202	0.9420452	6.152015	5.795476	0.16254837
7	1.0721354	0.9327181	7.213535	6.728195	0.13862828
8	1.0828567	0.9234832	8.285671	7.651678	0.12069029
9	1.0936853	0.9143398	9.368527	8.566018	0.10674036
10	1.1046221	0.9052870	10.462213	9.471305	0.09558208
11	1.1156683	0.8963237	11.566835	10.367628	0.08645408
12	1.1268250	0.8874492	12.682503	11.255077	0.07884879
13	1.1380933	0.8786626	13.809328	12.133740	0.07241482
14	1.1494742	0.8699630	14.947421	13.003703	0.06690117
15	1.1609690	0.8613495	16.096896	13.865053	0.06212378
16	1.1725786	0.8528213	17.257864	14.717874	0.05794460
17	1.1843044	0.8443775	18.430443	15.562251	0.05425806
18	1.1961475	0.8360173	19.614748	16.398269	0.05098205
19	1.2081090	0.8277399	20.810895	17.226008	0.04805175
20	1.2201900	0.8195445	22.019004	18.045553	0.04541531
21	1.2323919	0.8114302	23.239194	18.856983	0.04303075
22	1.2447159	0.8033962	24.471586	19.660379	0.04086372
23	1.2571630	0.7954418	25.716302	20.455821	0.03888584
24	1.2697346	0.7875661	26.973465	21.243387	0.03707347
25	1.2824320	0.7797684	28.243200	22.023156	0.03540675
26	1.2952563	0.7720480	29.525631	22.795204	0.03386888
27	1.3082089	0.7644039	30.820888	23.559608	0.03244553
28	1.3212910	0.7568356	32.129097	24.316443	0.03112444
29	1.3345039	0.7493421	33.450388	25.065785	0.02989502
30	1.3478489	0.7419229	34.784892	25.807708	0.02874811
31	1.3613274	0.7345771	36.132740	26.542285	0.02767573
32	1.3749407	0.7273041	37.494068	27.269589	0.02667089
33	1.3886901	0.7201031	38.869009	27.989693	0.02572744
34	1.4025770	0.7129733	40.257699	28.702666	0.02483997
35	1.4166028	0.7059142	41.660276	29.408580	0.02400368
36	1.4307688	0.6989249	43.076878	30.107505	0.02321431
37	1.4450765	0.6920049	44.507647	30.799510	0.02246805
38	1.4595272	0.6851534	45.952724	31.484663	0.02176150
39	1.4741225	0.6783697	47.412251	32.163033	0.02109160
40	1.4888637	0.6716531	48.886373	32.834686	0.02045560
50	1.6446318	0.6080388	64.463182	39.196118	0.01551273
60	1.8166967	0.5504496	81.669670	44.955038	0.01224445
70	2.0067634	0.4983149	100.676337	50.168514	0.00993282
80	2.2167152	0.4511179	121.671522	54.888206	0.00821885
90	2.4486327	0.4083912	144.863267	59.160881	0.00690306
100	2.7048138	0.3697112	170.481383	63.028879	0.00586574

II: RATES; i = 0.0100, d = 0.00990099, δ = 0.00995033, i/δ = 1.0049917

m	2	3	4	6	12
$100\ i^{(m)}$	0.9975124	0.9966851	0.9962717	0.9958586	0.9954457
$100\ d^{(m)}$	0.9925620	0.9933848	0.9937965	0.9942085	0.9946207
$i\ /\ i^{(m)}$	1.0024938	1.0033260	1.0037422	1.0041586	1.0045751

I: INTEREST FUNCTIONS; i =0.0125

n	$(1 + i)^n$	v^n	$s_{\overline{n}\rceil}$	$a_{\overline{n}\rceil}$	$s_{\overline{n}\rceil}^{-1}$
1/12	1.0010357	0.9989653	0.082860	0.082774	12.06859580
1/ 6	1.0020726	0.9979317	0.165805	0.165462	6.03117452
1/ 4	1.0031105	0.9968992	0.248837	0.248065	4.01870147
1/ 3	1.0041494	0.9958677	0.331954	0.330582	3.01246549
1/ 2	1.0062306	0.9938080	0.498447	0.495361	2.00623059
1	1.0125000	0.9876543	1.000000	0.987654	1.00000000
2	1.0251562	0.9754611	2.012500	1.963115	0.49689441
3	1.0379707	0.9634183	3.037656	2.926534	0.32920117
4	1.0509453	0.9515243	4.075627	3.878058	0.24536102
5	1.0640822	0.9397771	5.126572	4.817835	0.19506211
6	1.0773832	0.9281749	6.190654	5.746010	0.16153381
7	1.0908505	0.9167159	7.268038	6.662726	0.13758872
8	1.1044861	0.9053984	8.358888	7.568124	0.11963314
9	1.1182922	0.8942207	9.463374	8.462345	0.10567055
10	1.1322708	0.8831809	10.581666	9.345526	0.09450307
11	1.1464242	0.8722775	11.713937	10.217803	0.08536839
12	1.1607545	0.8615086	12.860361	11.079312	0.07775831
13	1.1752639	0.8508727	14.021116	11.930185	0.07132100
14	1.1899547	0.8403681	15.196380	12.770553	0.06580515
15	1.2048292	0.8299932	16.386335	13.600546	0.06102646
16	1.2198895	0.8197463	17.591164	14.420292	0.05684672
17	1.2351382	0.8096260	18.811053	15.229918	0.05316023
18	1.2505774	0.7996306	20.046192	16.029549	0.04988479
19	1.2662096	0.7897587	21.296769	16.819308	0.04695548
20	1.2820372	0.7800085	22.562979	17.599316	0.04432039
21	1.2980627	0.7703788	23.845016	18.369695	0.04193749
22	1.3142885	0.7608680	25.143078	19.130563	0.03977238
23	1.3307171	0.7514745	26.457367	19.882037	0.03779666
24	1.3473511	0.7421971	27.788084	20.624235	0.03598665
25	1.3641929	0.7330341	29.135435	21.357269	0.03432247
26	1.3812454	0.7239843	30.499628	22.081253	0.03278729
27	1.3985109	0.7150463	31.880873	22.796299	0.03136677
28	1.4159923	0.7062185	33.279384	23.502518	0.03004863
29	1.4336922	0.6974998	34.695377	24.200018	0.02882228
30	1.4516134	0.6888887	36.129069	24.888906	0.02767854
31	1.4697585	0.6803839	37.580682	25.569290	0.02660942
32	1.4881305	0.6719841	39.050441	26.241274	0.02560791
33	1.5067321	0.6636880	40.538571	26.904962	0.02466786
34	1.5255663	0.6554943	42.045303	27.560456	0.02378387
35	1.5446359	0.6474018	43.570870	28.207858	0.02295111
36	1.5639438	0.6394092	45.115505	28.847267	0.02216533
37	1.5834931	0.6315152	46.679449	29.478783	0.02142270
38	1.6032868	0.6237187	48.262942	30.102501	0.02071983
39	1.6233279	0.6160185	49.866229	30.718520	0.02005365
40	1.6436195	0.6084133	51.489557	31.326933	0.01942141
50	1.8610224	0.5373391	68.881790	37.012876	0.01451763
60	2.1071813	0.4745676	88.574508	42.034592	0.01128993
70	2.3859000	0.4191291	110.871998	46.469676	0.00901941
80	2.7014849	0.3701668	136.118795	50.386657	0.00734652
90	3.0588126	0.3269242	164.705008	53.846060	0.00607146
100	3.4634043	0.2887333	197.072342	56.901339	0.00507428

II: RATES; i =0.0125, d =0.012345679, δ=0.012422520, i/δ =1.0062371

m	2	3	4	6	12
$100\ i^{(m)}$	1.2461180	1.2448275	1.2441830	1.2435389	1.2428952
$100\ d^{(m)}$	1.2384020	1.2396836	1.2403250	1.2409669	1.2416092
$i / i^{(m)}$	1.0031153	1.0041552	1.0046754	1.0051958	1.0057163

I: INTEREST FUNCTIONS; i =0.0150

n	$(1 + i)^n$	v^n	$s_{\overline{n}\rceil}$	$a_{\overline{n}\rceil}$	$s_{\overline{n}\rceil}^{-1}$
1/12	1.0012415	0.9987601	0.082766	0.082663	12.08227822
1/ 6	1.0024845	0.9975216	0.165634	0.165224	6.03739144
1/ 4	1.0037291	0.9962848	0.248606	0.247682	4.02243021
1/ 3	1.0049752	0.9950494	0.331680	0.330038	3.01495037
1/ 2	1.0074721	0.9925833	0.498139	0.494444	2.00747208
1	1.0150000	0.9852217	1.000000	0.985222	1.00000000
2	1.0302250	0.9706617	2.015000	1.955883	0.49627792
3	1.0456784	0.9563170	3.045225	2.912200	0.32838296
4	1.0613636	0.9421842	4.090903	3.854385	0.24444479
5	1.0772840	0.9282603	5.152267	4.782645	0.19408932
6	1.0934433	0.9145422	6.229551	5.697187	0.16052521
7	1.1098449	0.9010268	7.322994	6.598214	0.13655616
8	1.1264926	0.8877111	8.432839	7.485925	0.11858402
9	1.1433900	0.8745922	9.559332	8.360517	0.10460982
10	1.1605408	0.8616672	10.702722	9.222185	0.09343418
11	1.1779489	0.8489332	11.863262	10.071118	0.08429384
12	1.1956182	0.8363874	13.041211	10.907505	0.07667999
13	1.2135524	0.8240270	14.236830	11.731532	0.07024036
14	1.2317557	0.8118493	15.450382	12.543382	0.06472332
15	1.2502321	0.7998515	16.682138	13.343233	0.05994436
16	1.2689855	0.7880310	17.932370	14.131264	0.05576508
17	1.2880203	0.7763853	19.201355	14.907649	0.05207966
18	1.3073406	0.7649116	20.489376	15.672561	0.04880578
19	1.3269507	0.7536075	21.796716	16.426168	0.04587847
20	1.3468550	0.7424704	23.123667	17.168639	0.04324574
21	1.3670578	0.7314979	24.470522	17.900137	0.04086550
22	1.3875637	0.7206876	25.837580	18.620824	0.03870332
23	1.4083772	0.7100371	27.225144	19.330861	0.03673075
24	1.4295028	0.6995439	28.633521	20.030405	0.03492410
25	1.4509454	0.6892058	30.063024	20.719611	0.03326345
26	1.4727095	0.6790205	31.513969	21.398632	0.03173196
27	1.4948002	0.6689857	32.986678	22.067617	0.03031527
28	1.5172222	0.6590992	34.481479	22.726717	0.02900108
29	1.5399805	0.6493589	35.998701	23.376076	0.02777878
30	1.5630802	0.6397624	37.538681	24.015838	0.02663919
31	1.5865264	0.6303078	39.101762	24.646146	0.02557430
32	1.6103243	0.6209929	40.688288	25.267139	0.02457710
33	1.6344792	0.6118157	42.298612	25.878954	0.02364144
34	1.6589964	0.6027741	43.933092	26.481728	0.02276189
35	1.6838813	0.5938661	45.592088	27.075595	0.02193363
36	1.7091395	0.5850897	47.275969	27.660684	0.02115240
37	1.7347766	0.5764431	48.985109	28.237127	0.02041437
38	1.7607983	0.5679242	50.719885	28.805052	0.01971613
39	1.7872103	0.5595313	52.480684	29.364583	0.01905463
40	1.8140184	0.5512623	54.267894	29.915845	0.01842710
50	2.1052424	0.4750047	73.682828	34.999688	0.01357168
60	2.4432198	0.4092960	96.214652	39.380269	0.01039343
70	2.8354563	0.3526769	122.363753	43.154872	0.00817235
80	3.2906628	0.3038901	152.710852	46.407323	0.00654832
90	3.8189485	0.2618522	187.929900	49.209855	0.00532113
100	4.4320456	0.2256294	228.803043	51.624704	0.00437057

II: RATES; i =0.0150, d =0.014778325, δ =0.014888612, i/δ =1.0074814

m	2	3	4	6	12
$100\ i^{(m)}$	1.4944168	1.4925619	1.4916356	1.4907100	1.4897853
$100\ d^{(m)}$	1.4833332	1.4851728	1.4860938	1.4870155	1.4879380
$i / i^{(m)}$	1.0037360	1.0049835	1.0056076	1.0062319	1.0068565

n	$(1+i)^n$	v^n	$s_{\overline{n}\vert}$	$a_{\overline{n}\vert}$	$s_{\overline{n}\vert}^{-1}$
1/12	1.0014468	0.9985553	0.082672	0.082553	12.09594851
1/ 6	1.0028956	0.9971127	0.165464	0.164986	6.04360242
1/ 4	1.0043466	0.9956722	0.248376	0.247301	4.02615513
1/ 3	1.0057996	0.9942338	0.331408	0.329497	3.01743253
1/ 2	1.0087121	0.9913632	0.497831	0.493532	2.00871205
1	1.0175000	0.9828010	1.000000	0.982801	1.00000000
2	1.0353062	0.9658978	2.017500	1.948699	0.49566295
3	1.0534241	0.9492853	3.052806	2.897984	0.32756746
4	1.0718590	0.9329585	4.106230	3.830943	0.24353237
5	1.0906166	0.9169125	5.178089	4.747855	0.19312142
6	1.1097024	0.9011425	6.268706	5.648998	0.15952256
7	1.1291221	0.8856438	7.378408	6.534641	0.13553059
8	1.1488818	0.8704116	8.507530	7.405053	0.11754292
9	1.1689872	0.8554413	9.656412	8.260494	0.10355813
10	1.1894445	0.8407286	10.825399	9.101223	0.09237534
11	1.2102598	0.8262689	12.014844	9.927492	0.08323038
12	1.2314393	0.8120579	13.225104	10.739550	0.07561377
13	1.2529895	0.7980913	14.456543	11.537641	0.06917283
14	1.2749168	0.7843649	15.709533	12.322006	0.06365562
15	1.2972279	0.7708746	16.984449	13.092880	0.05887739
16	1.3199294	0.7576163	18.281677	13.850497	0.05469958
17	1.3430281	0.7445861	19.601607	14.595083	0.05101623
18	1.3665311	0.7317799	20.944635	15.326863	0.04774492
19	1.3904454	0.7191940	22.311166	16.046057	0.04482061
20	1.4147782	0.7068246	23.701611	16.752881	0.04219122
21	1.4395368	0.6946679	25.116389	17.447549	0.03981464
22	1.4647287	0.6827203	26.555926	18.130269	0.03765638
23	1.4903615	0.6709782	28.020655	18.801248	0.03568796
24	1.5164428	0.6594380	29.511016	19.460686	0.03388565
25	1.5429805	0.6480963	31.027459	20.108782	0.03222952
26	1.5699827	0.6369497	32.570440	20.745732	0.03070269
27	1.5974574	0.6259948	34.140422	21.371726	0.02929079
28	1.6254129	0.6152283	35.737880	21.986955	0.02798151
29	1.6538576	0.6046470	37.363293	22.591602	0.02676424
30	1.6828001	0.5942476	39.017150	23.185849	0.02562975
31	1.7122491	0.5840272	40.699950	23.769877	0.02457005
32	1.7422135	0.5739825	42.412200	24.343859	0.02357812
33	1.7727022	0.5641105	44.154413	24.907970	0.02264779
34	1.8037245	0.5544084	45.927115	25.462378	0.02177363
35	1.8352897	0.5448731	47.730840	26.007251	0.02095082
36	1.8674073	0.5355018	49.566129	26.542753	0.02017507
37	1.9000869	0.5262917	51.433537	27.069045	0.01944257
38	1.9333384	0.5172400	53.333624	27.586285	0.01874990
39	1.9671718	0.5083440	55.266962	28.094629	0.01809399
40	2.0015973	0.4996010	57.234134	28.594230	0.01747209
50	2.3807889	0.4200288	78.902225	33.141209	0.01267391
60	2.8318163	0.3531303	104.675216	36.963986	0.00955336
70	3.3682883	0.2968867	135.330758	40.177903	0.00738930
80	4.0063919	0.2496011	171.793824	42.879935	0.00582093
90	4.7653808	0.2098468	215.164617	45.151610	0.00464760
100	5.6681559	0.1764242	266.751768	47.061473	0.00374880

II: RATES; i =0.0175, d =0.017199017, δ =0.017348638, i/δ =1.0087247

m	2	3	4	6	12
100 $i^{(m)}$	1.7424100	1.7398898	1.7386315	1.7373744	1.7361185
100 $d^{(m)}$	1.7273612	1.7298572	1.7311071	1.7323581	1.7336104
$i / i^{(m)}$	1.0043560	1.0058108	1.0065388	1.0072671	1.0079957

I: INTEREST FUNCTIONS; i = 0.0200

n	$(1+i)^n$	v^n	$s_{\overline{n}\rceil}$	$a_{\overline{n}\rceil}$	$s_{\overline{n}\rceil}^{-1}$
1/12	1.0016516	0.9983511	0.082579	0.082443	12.10960670
1/ 6	1.0033059	0.9967050	0.165295	0.164750	6.04980748
1/ 4	1.0049629	0.9950616	0.248147	0.246921	4.02987623
1/ 3	1.0066227	0.9934209	0.331135	0.328957	3.01991199
1/ 2	1.0099505	0.9901475	0.497525	0.492623	2.00995049
1	1.0200000	0.9803922	1.000000	0.980392	1.00000000
2	1.0404000	0.9611688	2.020000	1.941561	0.49504950
3	1.0612080	0.9423223	3.060400	2.883883	0.32675467
4	1.0824322	0.9238454	4.121608	3.807729	0.24262375
5	1.1040808	0.9057308	5.204040	4.713460	0.19215839
6	1.1261624	0.8879714	6.308121	5.601431	0.15852581
7	1.1486857	0.8705602	7.434283	6.471991	0.13451196
8	1.1716594	0.8534904	8.582969	7.325481	0.11650980
9	1.1950926	0.8367553	9.754628	8.162237	0.10251544
10	1.2189944	0.8203483	10.949721	8.982585	0.09132653
11	1.2433743	0.8042630	12.168715	9.786848	0.08217794
12	1.2682418	0.7884932	13.412090	10.575341	0.07455960
13	1.2936066	0.7730325	14.680332	11.348374	0.06811835
14	1.3194788	0.7578750	15.973938	12.106249	0.06260197
15	1.3458683	0.7430147	17.293417	12.849264	0.05782547
16	1.3727857	0.7284458	18.639285	13.577709	0.05365013
17	1.4002414	0.7141626	20.012071	14.291872	0.04996984
18	1.4282462	0.7001594	21.412312	14.992031	0.04670210
19	1.4568112	0.6864308	22.840559	15.678462	0.04378177
20	1.4859474	0.6729713	24.297370	16.351433	0.04115672
21	1.5156663	0.6597758	25.783317	17.011209	0.03878477
22	1.5459797	0.6468390	27.298984	17.658048	0.03663140
23	1.5768993	0.6341559	28.844963	18.292204	0.03466810
24	1.6084372	0.6217215	30.421862	18.913926	0.03287110
25	1.6406060	0.6095309	32.030300	19.523456	0.03122044
26	1.6734181	0.5975793	33.670906	20.121036	0.02969923
27	1.7068865	0.5858620	35.344324	20.706898	0.02829309
28	1.7410242	0.5743746	37.051210	21.281272	0.02698967
29	1.7758447	0.5631123	38.792235	21.844385	0.02577836
30	1.8113616	0.5520709	40.568079	22.396456	0.02464992
31	1.8475888	0.5412460	42.379441	22.937702	0.02359635
32	1.8845406	0.5306333	44.227030	23.468335	0.02261061
33	1.9222314	0.5202287	46.111570	23.988564	0.02168653
34	1.9606760	0.5100282	48.033802	24.498592	0.02081867
35	1.9998896	0.5000276	49.994478	24.998619	0.02000221
36	2.0398873	0.4902232	51.994367	25.488842	0.01923285
37	2.0806851	0.4806109	54.034255	25.969453	0.01850678
38	2.1222988	0.4711872	56.114940	26.440641	0.01782057
39	2.1647448	0.4619482	58.237238	26.902589	0.01717114
40	2.2080397	0.4528904	60.401983	27.355479	0.01655575
50	2.6915880	0.3715279	84.579401	31.423606	0.01182321
60	3.2810308	0.3047823	114.051539	34.760887	0.00876797
70	3.9995582	0.2500276	149.977911	37.498619	0.00666765
80	4.8754392	0.2051097	193.771958	39.744514	0.00516071
90	5.9431331	0.1682614	247.156656	41.586929	0.00404602
100	7.2446461	0.1380330	312.232306	43.098352	0.00320274

II: RATES; $i = 0.0200$, $d = 0.01960784 3$, $\delta = 0.01980262 7$, $i/\delta = 1.0099670$

m	2	3	4	6	12
$100\, i^{(m)}$	1.9900988	1.9868129	1.9851726	1.9835342	1.9818976
$100\, d^{(m)}$	1.9704914	1.9737414	1.9753690	1.9769985	1.9786297
$i / i^{(m)}$	1.0049752	1.0066373	1.0074691	1.0083012	1.0091339

I: INTEREST FUNCTIONS; i = 0.0250

n	$(1+i)^n$	v^n	$s_{\overline{n\vert}}$	$a_{\overline{n\vert}}$	$s_{\overline{n\vert}}^{-1}$
1/12	1.0020598	0.9979444	0.082393	0.082224	12.13688698
1/6	1.0041239	0.9958930	0.164957	0.164279	6.06219992
1/4	1.0061922	0.9938459	0.247690	0.246166	4.03730709
1/3	1.0082648	0.9918029	0.330594	0.327884	3.02486282
1/2	1.0124228	0.9877296	0.496913	0.490816	2.01242284
1	1.0250000	0.9756098	1.000000	0.975610	1.00000000
2	1.0506250	0.9518144	2.025000	1.927424	0.49382716
3	1.0768906	0.9285994	3.075625	2.856024	0.32513717
4	1.1038129	0.9059506	4.152516	3.761974	0.24081788
5	1.1314082	0.8838543	5.256329	4.645828	0.19024686
6	1.1596934	0.8622969	6.387737	5.508125	0.15654997
7	1.1886858	0.8412652	7.547430	6.349391	0.13249543
8	1.2184029	0.8207466	8.736116	7.170137	0.11446735
9	1.2488630	0.8007284	9.954519	7.970866	0.10045689
10	1.2800845	0.7811984	11.203382	8.752064	0.08925876
11	1.3120867	0.7621448	12.483466	9.514209	0.08010596
12	1.3448888	0.7435559	13.795553	10.257765	0.07248713
13	1.3785110	0.7254204	15.140442	10.983185	0.06604827
14	1.4129738	0.7077272	16.518953	11.690912	0.06053652
15	1.4482982	0.6904656	17.931927	12.381378	0.05576646
16	1.4845056	0.6736249	19.380225	13.055003	0.05159899
17	1.5216183	0.6571951	20.864730	13.712198	0.04792777
18	1.5596587	0.6411659	22.386349	14.353364	0.04467008
19	1.5986502	0.6255277	23.946007	14.978891	0.04176062
20	1.6386164	0.6102709	25.544658	15.589162	0.03914713
21	1.6795819	0.5953863	27.183274	16.184549	0.03678733
22	1.7215714	0.5808647	28.862856	16.765413	0.03464661
23	1.7646107	0.5666972	30.584427	17.332110	0.03269638
24	1.8087259	0.5528754	32.349038	17.884986	0.03091282
25	1.8539441	0.5393906	34.157764	18.424376	0.02927592
26	1.9002927	0.5262347	36.011708	18.950611	0.02776875
27	1.9478000	0.5133997	37.912001	19.464011	0.02637687
28	1.9964950	0.5008778	39.859801	19.964889	0.02508793
29	2.0464074	0.4886613	41.856296	20.453550	0.02389127
30	2.0975676	0.4767427	43.902703	20.930293	0.02277764
31	2.1500068	0.4651148	46.000271	21.395407	0.02173900
32	2.2037569	0.4537706	48.150278	21.849178	0.02076831
33	2.2588509	0.4427030	50.354034	22.291881	0.01985938
34	2.3153221	0.4319053	52.612885	22.723786	0.01900675
35	2.3732052	0.4213711	54.928207	23.145157	0.01820558
36	2.4325353	0.4110937	57.301413	23.556251	0.01745158
37	2.4933487	0.4010670	59.733948	23.957318	0.01674090
38	2.5556824	0.3912849	62.227297	24.348603	0.01607012
39	2.6195745	0.3817414	64.782979	24.730344	0.01543615
40	2.6850638	0.3724306	67.402554	25.102775	0.01483623
50	3.4371087	0.2909422	97.484349	28.362312	0.01025806
60	4.3997897	0.2272836	135.991590	30.908656	0.00735340
70	5.6321029	0.1775536	185.284114	32.897857	0.00539712
80	7.2095678	0.1387046	248.382713	34.451817	0.00402605
90	9.2288563	0.1083558	329.154253	35.665768	0.00303809
100	11.8137164	0.0846474	432.548654	36.614105	0.00231188

II: RATES; i = 0.0250, d = 0.024390244, δ = 0.024692613, i/δ = 1.0124486

m	2	3	4	6	12
$100\, i^{(m)}$	2.4845673	2.4794513	2.4768985	2.4743493	2.4718035
$100\, d^{(m)}$	2.4540807	2.4591270	2.4616554	2.4641872	2.4667225
$i / i^{(m)}$	1.0062114	1.0082876	1.0093268	1.0103667	1.0114072

I: INTEREST FUNCTIONS; i = 0.0300

n	$(1+i)^n$	v^n	$s_{\overline{n}\rceil}$	$a_{\overline{n}\rceil}$	$s_{\overline{n}\rceil}^{-1}$
1/12	1.0024663	0.9975398	0.082209	0.082007	12.16411941
1/ 6	1.0049386	0.9950856	0.164621	0.163812	6.07456894
1/ 4	1.0074171	0.9926375	0.247236	0.245415	4.04472289
1/ 3	1.0099016	0.9901954	0.330054	0.326818	3.02980294
1/ 2	1.0148892	0.9853293	0.496305	0.489024	2.01488916
1	1.0300000	0.9708738	1.000000	0.970874	1.00000000
2	1.0609000	0.9425959	2.030000	1.913470	0.49261084
3	1.0927270	0.9151417	3.090900	2.828611	0.32353036
4	1.1255088	0.8884870	4.183627	3.717098	0.23902705
5	1.1592741	0.8626088	5.309136	4.579707	0.18835457
6	1.1940523	0.8374843	6.468410	5.417191	0.15459750
7	1.2298739	0.8130915	7.662462	6.230283	0.13050635
8	1.2667701	0.7894092	8.892336	7.019692	0.11245639
9	1.3047732	0.7664167	10.159106	7.786109	0.09843386
10	1.3439164	0.7440939	11.463879	8.530203	0.08723051
11	1.3842339	0.7224213	12.807796	9.252624	0.07807745
12	1.4257609	0.7013799	14.192030	9.954004	0.07046209
13	1.4685337	0.6809513	15.617790	10.634955	0.06402954
14	1.5125897	0.6611178	17.086324	11.296073	0.05852634
15	1.5579674	0.6418619	18.598914	11.937935	0.05376658
16	1.6047064	0.6231669	20.156881	12.561102	0.04961085
17	1.6528476	0.6050164	21.761588	13.166118	0.04595253
18	1.7024331	0.5873946	23.414435	13.753513	0.04270870
19	1.7535061	0.5702860	25.116868	14.323799	0.03981388
20	1.8061112	0.5536758	26.870374	14.877475	0.03721571
21	1.8602946	0.5375493	28.676486	15.415024	0.03487178
22	1.9161034	0.5218925	30.536780	15.936917	0.03274739
23	1.9735865	0.5066917	32.452884	16.443608	0.03081390
24	2.0327941	0.4919337	34.426470	16.935542	0.02904742
25	2.0937779	0.4776056	36.459264	17.413148	0.02742787
26	2.1565913	0.4636947	38.553042	17.876842	0.02593829
27	2.2212890	0.4501891	40.709634	18.327031	0.02456421
28	2.2879277	0.4370768	42.930923	18.764108	0.02329323
29	2.3565655	0.4243464	45.218850	19.188455	0.02211467
30	2.4272625	0.4119868	47.575416	19.600441	0.02101926
31	2.5000803	0.3999871	50.002678	20.000428	0.01999893
32	2.5750828	0.3883370	52.502759	20.388766	0.01904662
33	2.6523352	0.3770262	55.077841	20.765792	0.01815612
34	2.7319053	0.3660449	57.730177	21.131837	0.01732196
35	2.8138625	0.3553834	60.462082	21.487220	0.01653929
36	2.8982783	0.3450324	63.275944	21.832252	0.01580379
37	2.9852267	0.3349829	66.174223	22.167235	0.01511162
38	3.0747835	0.3252262	69.159449	22.492462	0.01445934
39	3.1670270	0.3157535	72.234233	22.808215	0.01384385
40	3.2620378	0.3065568	75.401260	23.114772	0.01326238
50	4.3839060	0.2281071	112.796867	25.729764	0.00886549
60	5.8916031	0.1697331	163.053437	27.675564	0.00613296
70	7.9178219	0.1262974	230.594064	29.123421	0.00433663
80	10.6408906	0.0939771	321.363019	30.200763	0.00311175
90	14.3004671	0.0699278	443.348904	31.002407	0.00225556
100	19.2186320	0.0520328	607.287733	31.598905	0.00164667

II: RATES; i = 0.0300, d = 0.029126214, δ = 0.029558802, i/δ = 1.0149261

m	2	3	4	6	12
$100\ i^{(m)}$	2.9778313	2.9704902	2.9668287	2.9631732	2.9595237
$100\ d^{(m)}$	2.9341444	2.9413659	2.9449855	2.9486111	2.9522427
$i\ /\ i^{(m)}$	1.0074446	1.0099343	1.0111807	1.0124282	1.0136766

n	$(1+i)^n$	v^n	$s_{\overline{n\rceil}}$	$a_{\overline{n\rceil}}$	$s_{\overline{n\rceil}}^{-1}$
1/12	1.0028709	0.9971373	0.082026	0.081791	12.19130434
1/ 6	1.0057500	0.9942828	0.164287	0.163348	6.08691471
1/ 4	1.0086374	0.9914365	0.246784	0.244671	4.05212374
1/ 3	1.0115331	0.9885984	0.329518	0.325761	3.03473244
1/ 2	1.0173495	0.9829464	0.495700	0.487246	2.01734950
1	1.0350000	0.9661836	1.000000	0.966184	1.00000000
2	1.0712250	0.9335107	2.035000	1.899694	0.49140049
3	1.1087179	0.9019427	3.106225	2.801637	0.32193418
4	1.1475230	0.8714422	4.214943	3.673079	0.23725114
5	1.1876863	0.8419732	5.362466	4.515052	0.18648137
6	1.2292553	0.8135006	6.550152	5.328553	0.15266821
7	1.2722793	0.7859910	7.779408	6.114544	0.12854449
8	1.3168090	0.7594116	9.051687	6.873956	0.11047665
9	1.3628974	0.7337310	10.368496	7.607687	0.09644601
10	1.4105988	0.7089188	11.731393	8.316605	0.08524137
11	1.4599697	0.6849457	13.141992	9.001551	0.07609197
12	1.5110687	0.6617833	14.601962	9.663334	0.06848395
13	1.5639561	0.6394042	16.113030	10.302738	0.06206157
14	1.6186945	0.6177818	17.676986	10.920520	0.05657073
15	1.6753488	0.5968906	19.295681	11.517411	0.05182507
16	1.7339860	0.5767059	20.971030	12.094117	0.04768483
17	1.7946756	0.5572038	22.705016	12.651321	0.04404313
18	1.8574892	0.5383611	24.499691	13.189682	0.04081684
19	1.9225013	0.5201557	26.357180	13.709837	0.03794033
20	1.9897889	0.5025659	28.279682	14.212403	0.03536108
21	2.0594315	0.4855709	30.269471	14.697974	0.03303659
22	2.1315116	0.4691506	32.328902	15.167125	0.03093207
23	2.2061145	0.4532856	34.460414	15.620410	0.02901880
24	2.2833285	0.4379571	36.666528	16.058368	0.02727283
25	2.3632450	0.4231470	38.949857	16.481515	0.02567404
26	2.4459586	0.4088377	41.313102	16.890352	0.02420540
27	2.5315671	0.3950122	43.759060	17.285365	0.02285241
28	2.6201720	0.3816543	46.290627	17.667019	0.02160265
29	2.7118780	0.3687482	48.910799	18.035767	0.02044538
30	2.8067937	0.3562784	51.622677	18.392045	0.01937133
31	2.9050315	0.3442303	54.429471	18.736276	0.01837240
32	3.0067076	0.3325897	57.334502	19.068865	0.01744150
33	3.1119424	0.3213427	60.341210	19.390208	0.01657242
34	3.2208603	0.3104761	63.453152	19.700684	0.01575966
35	3.3335904	0.2999769	66.674013	20.000661	0.01499835
36	3.4502661	0.2898327	70.007603	20.290494	0.01428416
37	3.5710254	0.2800316	73.457869	20.570525	0.01361325
38	3.6960113	0.2705619	77.028895	20.841087	0.01298214
39	3.8253717	0.2614125	80.724906	21.102500	0.01238775
40	3.9592597	0.2525725	84.550278	21.355072	0.01182728
50	5.5849269	0.1790534	130.997910	23.455618	0.00763371
60	7.8780909	0.1269343	196.516883	24.944734	0.00508862
70	11.1128253	0.0899861	288.937865	26.000397	0.00346095
80	15.6757375	0.0637929	419.306787	26.748776	0.00238489
90	22.1121759	0.0452240	603.205027	27.279316	0.00165781
100	31.1914080	0.0320601	862.611657	27.655425	0.00115927

II: RATES; i=0.0350, d=0.033816425, δ=0.034401427, i/δ =1.0173997

m	2	3	4	6	12
100 $i^{(m)}$	3.4698995	3.4599426	3.4549784	3.4500237	3.4450785
100 $d^{(m)}$	3.4107251	3.4204935	3.4253918	3.4302993	3.4352163
$i / i^{(m)}$	1.0086747	1.0115775	1.0130309	1.0144858	1.0159420

I: INTEREST FUNCTIONS; i = 0.0400

n	$(1+i)^n$	v^n	$s_{\overline{n}\rceil}$	$a_{\overline{n}\rceil}$	$s_{\overline{n}\rceil}^{-1}$
1/12	1.0032737	0.9967369	0.081843	0.081576	12.21844211
1/ 6	1.0065582	0.9934845	0.163955	0.162887	6.09923740
1/ 4	1.0098534	0.9902427	0.246335	0.243932	4.05950975
1/ 3	1.0131594	0.9870115	0.328985	0.324712	3.03965138
1/ 2	1.0198039	0.9805807	0.495098	0.485483	2.01980390
1	1.0400000	0.9615385	1.000000	0.961538	1.00000000
2	1.0816000	0.9245562	2.040000	1.886095	0.49019608
3	1.1248640	0.8889964	3.121600	2.775091	0.32034854
4	1.1698586	0.8548042	4.246464	3.629895	0.23549005
5	1.2166529	0.8219271	5.416323	4.451822	0.18462711
6	1.2653190	0.7903145	6.632975	5.242137	0.15076190
7	1.3159318	0.7599178	7.898294	6.002055	0.12660961
8	1.3685691	0.7306902	9.214226	6.732745	0.10852783
9	1.4233118	0.7025867	10.582795	7.435332	0.09449299
10	1.4802443	0.6755642	12.006107	8.110896	0.08329094
11	1.5394541	0.6495809	13.486351	8.760477	0.07414904
12	1.6010322	0.6245970	15.025805	9.385074	0.06655217
13	1.6650735	0.6005741	16.626838	9.985648	0.06014373
14	1.7316764	0.5774751	18.291911	10.563123	0.05466897
15	1.8009435	0.5552645	20.023588	11.118387	0.04994110
16	1.8729812	0.5339082	21.824531	11.652296	0.04582000
17	1.9479005	0.5133732	23.697512	12.165669	0.04219852
18	2.0258165	0.4936281	25.645413	12.659297	0.03899333
19	2.1068492	0.4746424	27.671229	13.133939	0.03613862
20	2.1911231	0.4563869	29.778079	13.590326	0.03358175
21	2.2787681	0.4388336	31.969202	14.029160	0.03128011
22	2.3699188	0.4219554	34.247970	14.451115	0.02919881
23	2.4647155	0.4057263	36.617889	14.856842	0.02730906
24	2.5633042	0.3901215	39.082604	15.246963	0.02558683
25	2.6658363	0.3751168	41.645908	15.622080	0.02401196
26	2.7724698	0.3606892	44.311745	15.982769	0.02256738
27	2.8833686	0.3468166	47.084214	16.329586	0.02123854
28	2.9987033	0.3334775	49.967583	16.663063	0.02001298
29	3.1186515	0.3206514	52.966286	16.983715	0.01887993
30	3.2433975	0.3083187	56.084938	17.292033	0.01783010
31	3.3731334	0.2964603	59.328335	17.588494	0.01685535
32	3.5080587	0.2850579	62.701469	17.873551	0.01594859
33	3.6483811	0.2740942	66.209527	18.147646	0.01510357
34	3.7943163	0.2635521	69.857909	18.411198	0.01431477
35	3.9460890	0.2534155	73.652225	18.664613	0.01357732
36	4.1039326	0.2436687	77.598314	18.908282	0.01288688
37	4.2680899	0.2342968	81.702246	19.142579	0.01223957
38	4.4388135	0.2252854	85.970336	19.367864	0.01163192
39	4.6163660	0.2166206	90.409150	19.584485	0.01106083
40	4.8010206	0.2082890	95.025516	19.792774	0.01052349
50	7.1066833	0.1407126	152.667084	21.482185	0.00655020
60	10.5196274	0.0950604	237.990685	22.623490	0.00420185
70	15.5716184	0.0642194	364.290459	23.394515	0.00274506
80	23.0497991	0.0433843	551.244977	23.915392	0.00181408
90	34.1193333	0.0293089	827.983334	24.267278	0.00120775
100	50.5049482	0.0198000	1237.623705	24.504999	0.00080800

II: RATES; i = 0.0400, d = 0.038461538, δ = 0.039220713, i/δ = 1.0198693

m	2	3	4	6	12
100 $i^{(m)}$	3.9607805	3.9478211	3.9413626	3.9349182	3.9284877
100 $d^{(m)}$	3.8838649	3.8965449	3.9029057	3.9092803	3.9156689
$i / i^{(m)}$	1.0099020	1.0132171	1.0148774	1.0165396	1.0182035

n	$(1+i)^n$	v^n	$s_{\overline{n}\vert}$	$a_{\overline{n}\vert}$	$s_{\overline{n}\vert}^{-1}$
1/12	1.0040741	0.9959424	0.081482	0.081152	12.27257753
1/ 6	1.0081648	0.9919013	0.163297	0.161974	6.12381418
1/ 4	1.0122722	0.9878765	0.245445	0.242469	4.07423769
1/ 3	1.0163964	0.9838681	0.327927	0.322637	3.04945791
1/ 2	1.0246951	0.9759001	0.493902	0.481999	2.02469508
1	1.0500000	0.9523810	1.000000	0.952381	1.00000000
2	1.1025000	0.9070295	2.050000	1.859410	0.48780488
3	1.1576250	0.8638376	3.152500	2.723248	0.31720856
4	1.2155062	0.8227025	4.310125	3.545951	0.23201183
5	1.2762816	0.7835262	5.525631	4.329477	0.18097480
6	1.3400956	0.7462154	6.801913	5.075692	0.14701747
7	1.4071004	0.7106813	8.142008	5.786373	0.12281982
8	1.4774554	0.6768394	9.549109	6.463213	0.10472181
9	1.5513282	0.6446089	11.026564	7.107822	0.09069008
10	1.6288946	0.6139133	12.577893	7.721735	0.07950457
11	1.7103394	0.5846793	14.206787	8.306414	0.07038889
12	1.7958563	0.5568374	15.917127	8.863252	0.06282541
13	1.8856491	0.5303214	17.712983	9.393573	0.05645577
14	1.9799316	0.5050680	19.598632	9.898641	0.05102397
15	2.0789282	0.4810171	21.578564	10.379658	0.04634229
16	2.1828746	0.4581115	23.657492	10.837770	0.04226991
17	2.2920183	0.4362967	25.840366	11.274066	0.03869914
18	2.4066192	0.4155207	28.132385	11.689587	0.03554622
19	2.5269502	0.3957340	30.539004	12.085321	0.03274501
20	2.6532977	0.3768895	33.065954	12.462210	0.03024259
21	2.7859626	0.3589424	35.719252	12.821153	0.02799611
22	2.9252607	0.3418499	38.505214	13.163003	0.02597051
23	3.0715238	0.3255713	41.430475	13.488574	0.02413682
24	3.2250999	0.3100679	44.501999	13.798642	0.02247090
25	3.3863549	0.2953028	47.727099	14.093945	0.02095246
26	3.5556727	0.2812407	51.113454	14.375185	0.01956432
27	3.7334563	0.2678483	54.669126	14.643034	0.01829186
28	3.9201291	0.2550936	58.402583	14.898127	0.01712253
29	4.1161356	0.2429463	62.322712	15.141074	0.01604551
30	4.3219424	0.2313774	66.438848	15.372451	0.01505144
31	4.5380395	0.2203595	70.760790	15.592811	0.01413212
32	4.7649415	0.2098662	75.298829	15.802677	0.01328042
33	5.0031885	0.1998725	80.063771	16.002549	0.01249004
34	5.2533480	0.1903548	85.066959	16.192904	0.01175545
35	5.5160154	0.1812903	90.320307	16.374194	0.01107171
36	5.7918161	0.1726574	95.836323	16.546852	0.01043446
37	6.0814069	0.1644356	101.628139	16.711287	0.00983979
38	6.3854773	0.1566054	107.709546	16.867893	0.00928423
39	6.7047512	0.1491480	114.095023	17.017041	0.00876462
40	7.0399887	0.1420457	120.799774	17.159086	0.00827816
50	11.4673998	0.0872037	209.347996	18.255925	0.00477674
60	18.6791859	0.0535355	353.583718	18.929290	0.00282818
70	30.4264255	0.0328662	588.528511	19.342677	0.00169915
80	49.5614411	0.0201770	971.228821	19.596460	0.00102962
90	80.7303650	0.0123869	1594.607301	19.752262	0.00062711
100	131.5012578	0.0076045	2610.025157	19.847910	0.00038314

II: RATES; $i = 0.0500$, $d = 0.047619048$, $\delta = 0.048790164$, $i/\delta = 1.0247967$

m	2	3	4	6	12
$100\, i^{(m)}$	4.9390153	4.9189070	4.9088938	4.8989076	4.8889485
$100\, d^{(m)}$	4.8199854	4.8395560	4.8493810	4.8592327	4.8691112
$i / i^{(m)}$	1.0123475	1.0164860	1.0185594	1.0206357	1.0227148

I: INTEREST FUNCTIONS; i = 0.0600

n	$(1+i)^n$	v^n	$s_{\overline{n}\rceil}$	$a_{\overline{n}\rceil}$	$s_{\overline{n}\rceil}^{-1}$
1/12	1.0048676	0.9951560	0.081126	0.080733	12.32652834
1/ 6	1.0097588	0.9903355	0.162647	0.161075	6.14830059
1/ 4	1.0146738	0.9855384	0.244564	0.241027	4.08890752
1/ 3	1.0196128	0.9807644	0.326880	0.320593	3.05922313
1/ 2	1.0295630	0.9712859	0.492717	0.478569	2.02956301
1	1.0600000	0.9433962	1.000000	0.943396	1.00000000
2	1.1236000	0.8899964	2.060000	1.833393	0.48543689
3	1.1910160	0.8396193	3.183600	2.673012	0.31410981
4	1.2624770	0.7920937	4.374616	3.465106	0.22859149
5	1.3382256	0.7472582	5.637093	4.212364	0.17739640
6	1.4185191	0.7049605	6.975319	4.917324	0.14336263
7	1.5036303	0.6650571	8.393838	5.582381	0.11913502
8	1.5938481	0.6274124	9.897468	6.209794	0.10103594
9	1.6894790	0.5918985	11.491316	6.801692	0.08702224
10	1.7908477	0.5583948	13.180795	7.360087	0.07586796
11	1.8982986	0.5267875	14.971643	7.886875	0.06679294
12	2.0121965	0.4969694	16.869941	8.383844	0.05927703
13	2.1329283	0.4688390	18.882138	8.852683	0.05296011
14	2.2609040	0.4423010	21.015066	9.294984	0.04758491
15	2.3965582	0.4172651	23.275970	9.712249	0.04296276
16	2.5403517	0.3936463	25.672528	10.105895	0.03895214
17	2.6927728	0.3713644	28.212880	10.477260	0.03544480
18	2.8543392	0.3503438	30.905653	10.827603	0.03235654
19	3.0255995	0.3305130	33.759992	11.158116	0.02962086
20	3.2071355	0.3118047	36.785591	11.469921	0.02718456
21	3.3995636	0.2941554	39.992727	11.764077	0.02500455
22	3.6035374	0.2775051	43.392290	12.041582	0.02304557
23	3.8197497	0.2617973	46.995828	12.303379	0.02127848
24	4.0489346	0.2469785	50.815577	12.550358	0.01967900
25	4.2918707	0.2329986	54.864512	12.783356	0.01822672
26	4.5493830	0.2198100	59.156383	13.003166	0.01690435
27	4.8223459	0.2073680	63.705766	13.210534	0.01569717
28	5.1116867	0.1956301	68.528112	13.406164	0.01459255
29	5.4183879	0.1845567	73.639798	13.590721	0.01357961
30	5.7434912	0.1741101	79.058186	13.764831	0.01264891
31	6.0881006	0.1642548	84.801677	13.929086	0.01179222
32	6.4533867	0.1549574	90.889778	14.084043	0.01100234
33	6.8405899	0.1461862	97.343165	14.230230	0.01027293
34	7.2510253	0.1379115	104.183755	14.368141	0.00959843
35	7.6860868	0.1301052	111.434780	14.498246	0.00897386
36	8.1472520	0.1227408	119.120867	14.620987	0.00839483
37	8.6360871	0.1157932	127.268119	14.736780	0.00785743
38	9.1542523	0.1092389	135.904206	14.846019	0.00735812
39	9.7035075	0.1030555	145.058458	14.949075	0.00689377
40	10.2857179	0.0972222	154.761966	15.046297	0.00646154
50	18.4201543	0.0542884	290.335905	15.761861	0.00344429
60	32.9876909	0.0303143	533.128181	16.161428	0.00187572
70	59.0759302	0.0169274	967.932170	16.384544	0.00103313
80	105.7959935	0.0094522	1746.599891	16.509131	0.00057254
90	189.4645112	0.0052780	3141.075187	16.578699	0.00031836
100	339.3020835	0.0029472	5638.368059	16.617546	0.00017736

II: RATES; i = 0.0600, d = 0.056603774, δ = 0.058268908, i/δ = 1.0297087

m	2	3	4	6	12
$100\, i^{(m)}$	5.9126028	5.8838467	5.8695385	5.8552765	5.8410607
$100\, d^{(m)}$	5.7428275	5.7706676	5.7846553	5.7986883	5.8127667
$i / i^{(m)}$	1.0147815	1.0197410	1.0222269	1.0247168	1.0272107

I: INTEREST FUNCTIONS; i = 0.0700

n	$(1+i)^n$	v^n	$s_{\overline{n}\vert}$	$a_{\overline{n}\vert}$	$s_{\overline{n}\vert}^{-1}$
1/12	1.0056541	0.9943776	0.080774	0.080319	12.38029715
1/ 6	1.0113403	0.9887869	0.162004	0.160187	6.17269791
1/ 4	1.0170585	0.9832276	0.243693	0.239606	4.10352009
1/ 3	1.0228091	0.9776995	0.325845	0.318578	3.06894762
1/ 2	1.0344080	0.9667365	0.491543	0.475193	2.03440804
1	1.0700000	0.9345794	1.000000	0.934579	1.00000000
2	1.1449000	0.8734387	2.070000	1.808018	0.48309179
3	1.2250430	0.8162979	3.214900	2.624316	0.31105167
4	1.3107960	0.7628952	4.439943	3.387211	0.22522812
5	1.4025517	0.7129862	5.750739	4.100197	0.17389069
6	1.5007304	0.6663422	7.153291	4.766540	0.13979580
7	1.6057815	0.6227497	8.654021	5.389289	0.11555322
8	1.7181862	0.5820091	10.259803	5.971299	0.09746776
9	1.8384592	0.5439337	11.977989	6.515232	0.08348647
10	1.9671514	0.5083493	13.816448	7.023582	0.07237750
11	2.1048520	0.4750928	15.783599	7.498674	0.06335690
12	2.2521916	0.4440120	17.888451	7.942686	0.05590199
13	2.4098450	0.4149644	20.140643	8.357651	0.04965085
14	2.5785342	0.3878172	22.550488	8.745468	0.04434494
15	2.7590315	0.3624460	25.129022	9.107914	0.03979462
16	2.9521637	0.3387346	27.888054	9.446649	0.03585765
17	3.1588152	0.3165744	30.840217	9.763223	0.03242519
18	3.3799323	0.2958639	33.999033	10.059087	0.02941260
19	3.6165275	0.2765083	37.378965	10.335595	0.02675301
20	3.8696845	0.2584190	40.995492	10.594014	0.02439293
21	4.1405624	0.2415131	44.865177	10.835527	0.02228900
22	4.4304017	0.2257132	49.005739	11.061240	0.02040577
23	4.7405299	0.2109469	53.436141	11.272187	0.01871393
24	5.0723670	0.1971466	58.176671	11.469334	0.01718902
25	5.4274326	0.1842492	63.249038	11.653583	0.01581052
26	5.8073529	0.1721955	68.676470	11.825779	0.01456103
27	6.2138676	0.1609304	74.483823	11.986709	0.01342573
28	6.6488384	0.1504022	80.697691	12.137111	0.01239193
29	7.1142570	0.1405628	87.346529	12.277674	0.01144865
30	7.6122550	0.1313671	94.460786	12.409041	0.01058640
31	8.1451129	0.1227730	102.073041	12.531814	0.00979691
32	8.7152708	0.1147411	110.218154	12.646555	0.00907292
33	9.3253398	0.1072347	118.933425	12.753790	0.00840807
34	9.9781135	0.1002193	128.258765	12.854009	0.00779674
35	10.6765815	0.0936629	138.236878	12.947672	0.00723396
36	11.4239422	0.0875355	148.913460	13.035208	0.00671531
37	12.2236181	0.0818088	160.337402	13.117017	0.00623685
38	13.0792714	0.0764569	172.561020	13.193473	0.00579505
39	13.9948204	0.0714550	185.640292	13.264928	0.00538676
40	14.9744578	0.0667804	199.635112	13.331709	0.00500914
50	29.4570251	0.0339478	406.528929	13.800746	0.00245985
60	57.9464268	0.0172573	813.520383	14.039181	0.00122923
70	113.9893922	0.0087727	1614.134174	14.160389	0.00061953
80	224.2343876	0.0044596	3189.062680	14.222005	0.00031357
90	441.1029799	0.0022670	6287.185427	14.253328	0.00015905
100	867.7163256	0.0011525	12381.661794	14.269251	0.00008076

II: RATES; i = 0.0700, d = 0.065420561, δ = 0.067658648, i/δ = 1.0346054

m	2	3	4	6	12
$100\ i^{(m)}$	6.8816087	6.8427365	6.8234100	6.8041561	6.7849745
$100\ d^{(m)}$	6.6527022	6.6901403	6.7089650	6.7278604	6.7468269
$i\ /\ i^{(m)}$	1.0172040	1.0229825	1.0258800	1.0287830	1.0316914

I: INTEREST FUNCTIONS; i = 0.0800

n	$(1+i)^n$	v^n	$s_{\overline{n}\rceil}$	$a_{\overline{n}\rceil}$	$s_{\overline{n}\rceil}^{-1}$
1/12	1.0064340	0.9936071	0.080425	0.079911	12.43388648
1/ 6	1.0129095	0.9872551	0.161368	0.159312	6.19700737
1/ 4	1.0194265	0.9809437	0.242832	0.238204	4.11807618
1/ 3	1.0259856	0.9746726	0.324820	0.316593	3.07863195
1/ 2	1.0392305	0.9622504	0.490381	0.471869	2.03923048
1	1.0800000	0.9259259	1.000000	0.925926	1.00000000
2	1.1664000	0.8573388	2.080000	1.783265	0.48076923
3	1.2597120	0.7938322	3.246400	2.577097	0.30803351
4	1.3604890	0.7350299	4.506112	3.312127	0.22192080
5	1.4693281	0.6805832	5.866601	3.992710	0.17045645
6	1.5868743	0.6301696	7.335929	4.622880	0.13631539
7	1.7138243	0.5834904	8.922803	5.206370	0.11207240
8	1.8509302	0.5402689	10.636628	5.746639	0.09401476
9	1.9990046	0.5002490	12.487558	6.246888	0.08007971
10	2.1589250	0.4631935	14.486562	6.710081	0.06902949
11	2.3316390	0.4288829	16.645487	7.138964	0.06007634
12	2.5181701	0.3971138	18.977126	7.536078	0.05269502
13	2.7196237	0.3676979	21.495297	7.903776	0.04652181
14	2.9371936	0.3404610	24.214920	8.244237	0.04129685
15	3.1721691	0.3152417	27.152114	8.559479	0.03682954
16	3.4259426	0.2918905	30.324283	8.851369	0.03297687
17	3.7000181	0.2702690	33.750226	9.121638	0.02962943
18	3.9960195	0.2502490	37.450244	9.371887	0.02670210
19	4.3157011	0.2317121	41.446263	9.603599	0.02412763
20	4.6609571	0.2145482	45.761964	9.818147	0.02185221
21	5.0338337	0.1986557	50.422921	10.016803	0.01983225
22	5.4365404	0.1839405	55.456755	10.200744	0.01803207
23	5.8714636	0.1703153	60.893296	10.371059	0.01642217
24	6.3411807	0.1576993	66.764759	10.528758	0.01497796
25	6.8484752	0.1460179	73.105940	10.674776	0.01367878
26	7.3963532	0.1352018	79.954415	10.809978	0.01250713
27	7.9880615	0.1251868	87.350768	10.935165	0.01144810
28	8.6271064	0.1159137	95.338830	11.051078	0.01048891
29	9.3172749	0.1073275	103.965936	11.158406	0.00961854
30	10.0626569	0.0993773	113.283211	11.257783	0.00882743
31	10.8676694	0.0920160	123.345868	11.349799	0.00810728
32	11.7370830	0.0852000	134.213537	11.434999	0.00745081
33	12.6760496	0.0788889	145.950620	11.513888	0.00685163
34	13.6901336	0.0730453	158.626670	11.586934	0.00630411
35	14.7853443	0.0676345	172.316804	11.654568	0.00580326
36	15.9681718	0.0626246	187.102148	11.717193	0.00534467
37	17.2456256	0.0579857	203.070320	11.775179	0.00492440
38	18.6252756	0.0536905	220.315945	11.828869	0.00453894
39	20.1152977	0.0497134	238.941221	11.878582	0.00418513
40	21.7245215	0.0460309	259.056519	11.924613	0.00386016
50	46.9016125	0.0213212	573.770156	12.233485	0.00174286
60	101.2570637	0.0098759	1253.213296	12.376552	0.00079795
70	218.6064059	0.0045744	2720.080074	12.442820	0.00036764
80	471.9548343	0.0021188	5886.935428	12.473514	0.00016987
90	1018.9150893	0.0009814	12723.938616	12.487732	0.00007859
100	2199.7612563	0.0004546	27484.515704	12.494318	0.00003638

II: RATES; i = 0.0800, d = 0.07407407, δ = 0.07696104, i/δ = 1.0394870

m	2	3	4	6	12
$100\ i^{(m)}$	7.8460969	7.7956704	7.7706188	7.7456742	7.7208361
$100\ d^{(m)}$	7.5499103	7.5982262	7.6225391	7.6469561	7.6714776
$i / i^{(m)}$	1.0196152	1.0262107	1.0295190	1.0328346	1.0361572

III: SEVEN-PLACE MANTISSAS FOR 10,000 TO 11,009

N.	0	1	2	3	4	5	6	7	8	9
1000	000 0000	0434	0869	1303	1737	2171	2605	3039	3473	3907
01	4341	4775	5208	5642	6076	6510	6943	7377	7810	8244
02	8677	9111	9544	9977	*0411	*0844	*1277	*1710	*2143	*2576
03	001 3009	3442	3875	4308	4741	5174	5607	6039	6472	6905
04	7337	7770	8202	8635	9067	9499	9932	*0364	*0796	*1228
05	002 1661	2093	2525	2957	3389	3821	4253	4685	5116	5548
06	5980	6411	6843	7275	7706	8138	8569	9001	9432	9863
07	003 0295	0726	1157	1588	2019	2451	2882	3313	3744	4174
08	4605	5036	5467	5898	6328	6759	7190	7620	8051	8481
09	8912	9342	9772	*0203	*0633	*1063	*1493	*1924	*2354	*2784
1010	004 3214	3644	4074	4504	4933	5363	5793	6223	6652	7082
11	7512	7941	8371	8800	9229	9659	*0088	*0517	*0947	*1376
12	005 1805	2234	2663	3092	3521	3950	4379	4808	5237	5666
13	6094	6523	6952	7380	7809	8238	8666	9094	9523	9951
14	006 0380	0808	1236	1664	2092	2521	2949	3377	3805	4233
15	4660	5088	5516	5944	6372	6799	7227	7655	8082	8510
16	8937	9365	9792	*0219	*0647	*1074	*1501	*1928	*2355	*2782
17	007 3210	3637	4064	4490	4917	5344	5771	6198	6624	7051
18	7478	7904	8331	8757	9184	9610	*0037	*0463	*0889	*1316
19	008 1742	2168	2594	3020	3446	3872	4298	4724	5150	5576
1020	6002	6427	6853	7279	7704	8130	8556	8981	9407	9832
21	009 0257	0683	1108	1533	1959	2384	2809	3234	3659	4084
22	4509	4934	5359	5784	6208	6633	7058	7483	7907	8332
23	8756	9181	9605	*0030	*0454	*0878	*1303	*1727	*2151	*2575
24	010 3000	3424	3848	4272	4696	5120	5544	5967	6391	6815
25	7239	7662	8086	8510	8933	9357	9780	*0204	*0627	*1050
26	011 1474	1897	2320	2743	3166	3590	4013	4436	4859	5282
27	5704	6127	6550	6973	7396	7818	8241	8664	9086	9509
28	9931	*0354	*0776	*1198	*1621	*2043	*2465	*2887	*3310	*3732
29	012 4154	4576	4998	5420	5842	6264	6685	7107	7529	7951
1030	8372	8794	9215	9637	*0059	*0480	*0901	*1323	*1744	*2165
31	013 2587	3008	3429	3850	4271	4692	5113	5534	5955	6376
32	6797	7218	7639	8059	8480	8901	9321	9742	*0162	*0583
33	014 1003	1424	1844	2264	2685	3105	3525	3945	4365	4785
34	5205	5625	6045	6465	6885	7305	7725	8144	8564	8984
35	9403	9823	*0243	*0662	*1082	*1501	*1920	*2340	*2759	*3178
36	015 3598	4017	4436	4855	5274	5693	6112	6531	6950	7369
37	7788	8206	8625	9044	9462	9881	*0300	*0718	*1137	*1555
38	016 1974	2392	2810	3229	3647	4065	4483	4901	5319	5737
39	6155	6573	6991	7409	7827	8245	8663	9080	9498	9916
1040	017 0333	0751	1168	1586	2003	2421	2838	3256	3673	4090
41	4507	4924	5342	5759	6176	6593	7010	7427	7844	8260
42	8677	9094	9511	9927	*0344	*0761	*1177	*1594	*2010	*2427
43	018 2843	3259	3676	4092	4508	4925	5341	5757	6173	6589
44	7005	7421	7837	8253	8669	9084	9500	9916	*0332	*0747
45	019 1163	1578	1994	2410	2825	3240	3656	4071	4486	4902
46	5317	5732	6147	6562	6977	7392	7807	8222	8637	9052
47	9467	9882	*0296	*0711	*1126	*1540	*1955	*2369	*2784	*3198
48	020 3613	4027	4442	4856	5270	5684	6099	6513	6927	7341
49	7755	8169	8583	8997	9411	9824	*0238	*0652	*1066	*1479
1050	021 1893	2307	2720	3134	3547	3961	4374	4787	5201	5614
N.	0	1	2	3	4	5	6	7	8	9

FOR OBTAINING LOG(1 + i), $0 \le i \le 0.1009$

N.	0	1	2	3	4	5	6	7	8	9
1050	021 1893	2307	2720	3134	3547	3961	4374	4787	5201	5614
51	6027	6440	6854	7267	7680	8093	8506	8919	9332	9745
52	022 0157	0570	0983	1396	1808	2221	2634	3046	3459	3871
53	4284	4696	5109	5521	5933	6345	6758	7170	7582	7994
54	8406	8818	9230	9642	*0054	*0466	*0878	*1289	*1701	*2113
55	023 2525	2936	3348	3759	4171	4582	4994	5405	5817	6228
56	6639	7050	7462	7873	8284	8695	9106	9517	9928	*0339
57	024 0750	1161	1572	1982	2393	2804	3214	3625	4036	4446
58	4857	5267	5678	6088	6498	6909	7319	7729	8139	8549
59	8960	9370	9780	*0190	*0600	*1010	*1419	*1829	*2239	*2649
1060	025 3059	3468	3878	4288	4697	5107	5516	5926	6335	6744
61	7154	7563	7972	8382	8791	9200	9609	*0018	*0427	*0836
62	026 1245	1654	2063	2472	2881	3289	3698	4107	4515	4924
63	5333	5741	6150	6558	6967	7375	7783	8192	8600	9008
64	9416	9824	*0233	*0641	*1049	*1457	*1865	*2273	*2680	*3088
65	027 3496	3904	4312	4719	5127	5535	5942	6350	6757	7165
66	7572	7979	8387	8794	9201	9609	*0016	*0423	*0830	*1237
67	028 1644	2051	2458	2865	3272	3679	4086	4492	4899	5306
68	5713	6119	6526	6932	7339	7745	8152	8558	8964	9371
69	9777	*0183	*0590	*0996	*1402	*1808	*2214	*2620	*3026	*3432
1070	029 3838	4244	4649	5055	5461	5867	6272	6678	7084	7489
71	7895	8300	8706	9111	9516	9922	*0327	*0732	*1138	*1543
72	030 1948	2353	2758	3163	3568	3973	4378	4783	5188	5592
73	5997	6402	6807	7211	7616	8020	8425	8830	9234	9638
74	031 0043	0447	0851	1256	1660	2064	2468	2872	3277	3681
75	4085	4489	4893	5296	5700	6104	6508	6912	7315	7719
76	8123	8526	8930	9333	9737	*0140	*0544	*0947	*1350	*1754
77	032 2157	2560	2963	3367	3770	4173	4576	4979	5382	5785
78	6188	6590	6993	7396	7799	8201	8604	9007	9409	9812
79	033 0214	0617	1019	1422	1824	2226	2629	3031	3433	3835
1080	4238	4640	5042	5444	5846	6248	6650	7052	7453	7855
81	8257	8659	9060	9462	9864	*0265	*0667	*1068	*1470	*1871
82	034 2273	2674	3075	3477	3878	4279	4680	5081	5482	5884
83	6285	6686	7087	7487	7888	8289	8690	9091	9491	9892
84	035 0293	0693	1094	1495	1895	2296	2696	3096	3497	3897
85	4297	4698	5098	5498	5898	6298	6698	7098	7498	7898
86	8298	8698	9098	9498	9898	*0297	*0697	*1097	*1496	*1896
87	036 2295	2695	3094	3494	3893	4293	4692	5091	5491	5890
88	6289	6688	7087	7486	7885	8284	8683	9082	9481	9880
89	037 0279	0678	1076	1475	1874	2272	2671	3070	3468	3867
1090	4265	4663	5062	5460	5858	6257	6655	7053	7451	7849
91	8248	8646	9044	9442	9839	*0237	*0635	*1033	*1431	*1829
92	038 2226	2624	3022	3419	3817	4214	4612	5009	5407	5804
93	6202	6599	6996	7393	7791	8188	8585	8982	9379	9776
94	039 0173	0570	0967	1364	1761	2158	2554	2951	3348	3745
95	4141	4538	4934	5331	5727	6124	6520	6917	7313	7709
96	8106	8502	8898	9294	9690	*0086	*0482	*0878	*1274	*1670
97	040 2066	2462	2858	3254	3650	4045	4441	4837	5232	5628
98	6023	6419	6814	7210	7605	8001	8396	8791	9187	9582
99	9977	*0372	*0767	*1162	*1557	*1952	*2347	*2742	*3137	*3532
1100	041 3927	4322	4716	5111	5506	5900	6295	6690	7084	7479
N.	0	1	2	3	4	5	6	7	8	9

IV: The Number of Each Day of the Year

For *leap years* the number of the day is *one greater* than the tabular number after February 28.

Day of Month	January	February	March	April	May	June	July	August	September	October	November	December	Day of Month
1	1	32	60	91	121	152	182	213	244	274	305	335	1
2	2	33	61	92	122	153	183	214	245	275	306	336	2
3	3	34	62	93	123	154	184	215	246	276	307	337	3
4	4	35	63	94	124	155	185	216	247	277	308	338	4
5	5	36	64	95	125	156	186	217	248	278	309	339	5
6	6	37	65	96	126	157	187	218	249	279	310	340	6
7	7	38	66	97	127	158	188	219	250	280	311	341	7
8	8	39	67	98	128	159	189	220	251	281	312	342	8
9	9	40	68	99	129	160	190	221	252	282	313	343	9
10	10	41	69	100	130	161	191	222	253	283	314	344	10
11	11	42	70	101	131	162	192	223	254	284	315	345	11
12	12	43	71	102	132	163	193	224	255	285	316	346	12
13	13	44	72	103	133	164	194	225	256	286	317	347	13
14	14	45	73	104	134	165	195	226	257	287	318	348	14
15	15	46	74	105	135	166	196	227	258	288	319	349	15
16	16	47	75	106	136	167	197	228	259	289	320	350	16
17	17	48	76	107	137	168	198	229	260	290	321	351	17
18	18	49	77	108	138	169	199	230	261	291	322	352	18
19	19	50	78	109	139	170	200	231	262	292	323	353	19
20	20	51	79	110	140	171	201	232	263	293	324	354	20
21	21	52	80	111	141	172	202	233	264	294	325	355	21
22	22	53	81	112	142	173	203	234	265	295	326	356	22
23	23	54	82	113	143	174	204	235	266	296	327	357	23
24	24	55	83	114	144	175	205	236	267	297	328	358	24
25	25	56	84	115	145	176	206	237	268	298	329	359	25
26	26	57	85	116	146	177	207	238	269	299	330	360	26
27	27	58	86	117	147	178	208	239	270	300	331	361	27
28	28	59	87	118	148	179	209	240	271	301	332	362	28
29	29		88	119	149	180	210	241	272	302	333	363	29
30	30		89	120	150	181	211	242	273	303	334	364	30
31	31		90		151		212	243		304		365	31

ANSWERS TO BASIC PROBLEMS

(Determined from the tables of the text supplemented by a table of six-place common logarithms.)

Problem List 1

1. Immaterial, mathematically
2. (a) \$1,000; (b) \$850
3. (a) \$223.97; (b) \$227.57. Note: Ex. 1.6 leads one to expect that the interpolation method would give an unsatisfactory result, which it does (\$228.12).
4. No
5. \$45.04
6. \$815.75
7. (a) \$759.38; (b) (i) S^2/A, (ii) S^{m+1}/A^m
8. No
9. (a) 3.42%; (b) 10.84%
10. 0% or 5%
11. \$5,896.53
12. (a) No; (b) No; (c) Yes; (d) No
13. (a) \$3,281.03; (b) \$3,243.40; (c) \$3,172.17; (d) \$3,243.40
14. (a) \$549.63; (b) \$549.63; (c) \$551.26
15. \$1,120.64
16. (a) \$3,046.91
17. 3
18. (a) 4.91%; (b) 5.09%; (c) (i) 1.23%, (ii) 1.25%
19. (a) \$1,681.20; (b) 3.74% (interpolation), 3.73% (logarithms); (d) 3.72%
20. (a) 5.99%; (b) 6.28%
21. (a) 2.040%; (b) 1.961%
22. (a) 12.68%; (b) \$5.75
23. (c) 6.152%, 6.060%, 6.015%, 6.000%, 5.985%
24. (a) 0.009954; (b) 1.000829538
25. 0.1
26. 0.0824
27. (a) 3.004%; (b) 11.9404%; (c) 4.08%; (d) 4.16%; (e) 12.00%
28. 64, $\sqrt{2}$

29. (a) 3 1/3%; (b) 2 1/2%
30. (a) 2; (b) $746.92
31. (a) $1,067.16; (b) $722.53
32. (.051, 4)
33. (a) 31/600; (b) $24 < t < 30$
34. 24
35. 8%
36. 66.67%
37. $509.80
38. (a)
39. $558.66
40. (a) 16.67%; (b) 17.01%
41. (a) 5.71%; (b) 6.03%
42. No; lost $12.46 or (approximate method) $12.45
43. $56,441.32; $56,451.88; $56,430.79
44. (a) $3,415.39; (b) $3,765.46
45. (a) True; (b) True
46. (a) 16.231 yr.; (b) Simple interest for the 0.231 year
47. At compound interest obtaining n by linear interpolation in that table is exact.
48. (c) No; $(1 + i)^{\overline{n}+1}/[1 + i(1 - t)]$
49. (c), $31.67
50. $2,666.67, No
51. (a) $|t(t - 1)(t - 2)\cdots(t - k + 1)i^k/k!|$; (c) .00005, .0000495
52. (a) $(-1)^p\, n(n + 1)(n + 2)\cdots(n + p - 1)v^{n+p}$;
    (b) $(-\delta)^p\, v^n$; (c) $v^{n+1}(n\delta - 1)$
53. $1,131.27
54. (a) $1,000; end of 7 yrs.; (b) $1,200; Yes
55. $1/9 = 0.111\cdots$
56. (a) $335.00; (b) $334.95
57. $6,599.05
58. (a) $746.59; (b) 7.46%
59. $835.50
60. $8,382.43
61. $2,524.26
62. At end of: (a) 0.985 yr.; (b) 0.981 yr., 0.990 yr.; (c) 0.971 yr., when (in (b) and (c)) valuation date is the present
63. 247.06
64. (a) 3%; (b) 1.00002
65. (a) $1,024 based on doubling in approximately .7/.07 yrs.; (b) $868

66. (a) Annual force of interest, annual rate of simple interest; (b) True

67. (a) 3.203858, 4.925795; (b) 0.774533

Problem List 2

1. \$729.00
2. (a) $\frac{.693}{d} - .35$; (b) 18
3. (a) A; (b) $A + d(S - A)$; (c) $A - \frac{d}{1-d}(S - A)$; (d) A
4. (a) (i) \$300.00, (ii) \$8,100.00; (b) (i) \$11.11, (ii) \$33.33, (iii) \$1.23
5. \$942.42 gain
6. At end of 36 yrs., \$944
7. \$941.48
8. Bond
9. $(1 - f)^{-1}$ is larger.
11. (1) 8.42%, (2) 7.76%
12. 15.06 yrs. after date of loan
13. (a) 5.49%; (b) 5.21%
14. $A(1 + i)$
15. $2A + d(S - A)$
16. (a) $(k - 1)^{-1}$, $(k + 1)^{-1}$
17. (a) $(1 + i)^2$; (b) 1.331
18. (a) 5.87%; (b) 6.03%; (c) 6.09%; (d) 6.06%; (e) 6.23%; (f) 6.05%
19 (a) 5.78%; (b) 5.94%; (c) 5.91%; (d) 5.97%; (e) 6.14%; (f) 5.96%
21. (a) 10%; (b) $1 - x$. Zero is a trivial solution.
22. (a) 4.06%; (b) 3.97%
23. (a) 5.28%; (b) 8%; (c) 0.98, 3.96%; (d) 3.94%; (e) 8.87% or 8.88%
24. (c) $i^{(m)} = i^{(2m)}[1 + i^{(2m)}/4m]$
25. (a) 0.0953102; (b) 0.0975803; (c) 0.105361; (d) 0.210721
26. (a) 3.92%, 3.98%, 4.02%, 4.08%; (b) 1.49%
28. (a) $(\ln 2)/\delta$ (exact) $\doteq .693/\delta$; (b) 11.55
29. (a) $1/m$; (b) 4.94%; (c) 3; (d) 0
31. (a) 11.76%; (b) 11.88%
32. 5.94%
33. (a) 18.00%; (b) 18.18%; (c) 17.95%; (d) 18.51%; over a 20-day term, yes
34. July 11
35. (a) \$0.67; (b) 12.24%

36. \$800.00

37. (a) 8.25%; (b) 8.33%;
(c) 8.51%

38. (a) (i) $[1 - (1 + j/m)^{-mN}]/N$, (ii) $[1 - (1 - f/m)^{mN}]/N$,
(iii) $(1 - e^{-\delta N})/N$

39. \$0.80

40. (b) (iii), (i)

41. (f), (b), (d), (e), (a), (c)

Problem List 3

3. $s_{\overline{25}|i}$

4.

	$(1+i)^n$	v^n	$s_{\overline{n}|}$	$a_{\overline{n}|}$
$(1+i)^n$	——	$1/v^n$	$1+is_{\overline{n}|}$	$1/(1-ia_{\overline{n}|})$
v^n	$1/(1+i)^n$	——	$1/(1+is_{\overline{n}|})$	$1-ia_{\overline{n}|}$
$s_{\overline{n}|}$	$[(1+i)^n-1]/i$	$[(1/v^n)-1]/i$	——	$a_{\overline{n}|}/(1-ia_{\overline{n}|})$
$a_{\overline{n}|}$	$[1-1/(1+i)^n]/i$	$[1-v^n]/i$	$s_{\overline{n}|}/(1+is_{\overline{n}|})$	——

5. (a) 175.0; (b) 31.20; (c) 52.50; (d) 20.39

6. 20

7. (a) 1; (b) 0

8. (a) 32; (b) 108

9. (a) 10.00%; (b) 6.00%: (c) 2, 350, 2.00%, 25;
(d) 1.728; (e) 0.10; (f) 1.5

11. 8.00%, 20, 259.05

12. $a_{\overline{0}|i} = s_{\overline{0}|i} = 0$

13. (a) \$14,669.59; (b) \$14,714.69; (c) \$14,724.98

14. (a) \$13,590.33; (b) \$13,542.32; (c) \$13,517.93

15. $1{,}000\ (1.015)^{40} + 400\ s^{-1}_{\overline{4}|.015}\ s_{\overline{40}|.015} - 1{,}300\ (1.015)^8$

16. (a) $100\, a^{(2)}_{\overline{n}|i}$, where i is equivalent to δ; (b) $a^{(4)}_{\overline{20}|.03}$

17. (a) (i) \$24.63, (ii) \$301.00, (iii) \$199.76;
(b) (i) \$24.63, (ii) \$300.99, (iii) \$199.76

18. $600(1 - v^6 v^{1/2})/i^{(6)}$ at $i = .03$

19. 177

20. \$47,893.88

21. 9.38%

22. (a) 1; (b) $i^{(p)}$

23. (a) \$14,717.62; (b) \$14,763.58; (c) \$14,774.06

24. (a) \$14,133.94; (b) \$14,089.43; (c) \$14,066.81

25. \$10,097.67

26. (a) (i) \$81.07, (ii) \$86.07 = $81.07\,(1.005)^{12}$;
(b) (i) \$80.66, (ii) \$85.64 = $80.66\,(1.005)^{12}$;
(c) Availability of tables of $s^{-1}_{\overline{n|}}$ but not $\ddot{s}^{-1}_{\overline{n|}}$ makes computation easier by (a) than by (b).

27. (a) (i) \$1,232.65, (ii) \$1,238.65;
(b) (i) \$1,162.88, (ii) \$1,168.54

28. (a) $a_{\overline{n|}}$; (b) $\ddot{s}_{\overline{n|}}$; (c) 2; (d) $\ddot{s}^{(m)}_{\overline{n|}}$; (e) $\ddot{a}^{-1}_{\overline{n|}}$; (f) $\ddot{a}^{(m)}_{\overline{n|}}$;
(g) $\ddot{s}_{\overline{n|}}$

30. (3.9') $\ddot{a}_{\overline{n|}i}\,(1 + i) = (1 + i) + \ddot{a}_{\overline{n-1|}i}$,
(3.10') $\ddot{s}_{\overline{n|}i}\,(1 + i) + (1 + i) = \ddot{s}_{\overline{n+1|}i}$,
(3.11') $1 = d\,\ddot{a}_{\overline{n|}i} + v^n$, (3.12') $(1 + i)^n = d\ddot{s}_{\overline{n|}i} + 1$,
(3.13') $\ddot{a}^{-1}_{\overline{n|}i} = d + \ddot{s}^{-1}_{\overline{n|}i}$

32. \$297.04

33. (a) 16; (b) \$7.33

34. (a) (i) \$495.10, (ii) \$485.48, (iii) \$490.27;
(b) (i) \$154.69, (ii) \$467.13, (iii) \$310.14

35. At .01, $1{,}000 s^{-1}_{\overline{4|}i}\,(a_{\overline{38|}i} - a_{\overline{6|}i})$ or
$1{,}000\, a^{-1}_{\overline{4|}i}\,(a_{\overline{42|}i} - a_{\overline{10|}i})$

36. At .01, $100(a_{\overline{100|}i} - a_{\overline{20|}i})/a_{\overline{8|}i}$ or
$100\, a_{\overline{80|}i}(1 - .01\, a_{\overline{20|}i})/a_{\overline{8|}i}$

37. $1{,}000\, a^{-1}_{\overline{12|}i}\, s_{\overline{60|}i}/(1 + a_{\overline{119|}i})$ at $i = 1/3\%$

38. (a) \$74.41; (b) $1{,}000\, v^{10}\, s_{\overline{176|}.03}/s_{\overline{2|}.03}$

39. \$1,609.02

40. $500\, a_{\overline{90|}}\,(1 + i)^2/s_{\overline{6|}}$ at $i = .005$, or $500(a_{\overline{94|}} - a_{\overline{4|}})/a_{\overline{6|}}$

41. \$11.12

42. (a) $a_{\overline{88|}i}$; (b) $\ddot{a}^{(2)}_{\overline{88|}i}$

43. n

44. (a) \$56,244.99; (b) \$65,992.35

45. $(10 + 3\,a_{\overline{29|}i} - a_{\overline{19|}i} - a_{\overline{9|}i} - 69v^{30})/i$

46. (a) $(n - a_{\overline{n|}i})/i$; (b) $(\ddot{s}_{\overline{n|}i} - n)/i$;
(c) $(n - a_{\overline{2n|}i}\, s^{-1}_{\overline{2|}i})/i$

48. $2\, s^{-1}_{\overline{1/12|}}[16\, s_{\overline{30|}} + (s_{\overline{30|}} - 30)/i]$

50. (a) $1{,}000(s_{\overline{29|}} + 3s_{\overline{17|}} - 4)$ at .015;
(b) $1{,}000[4\, s_{\overline{48|}} + s_{\overline{36|}}\,(1 + i)^{48}]/a_{\overline{3|}}$ at .005, etc.

52. (a) 16.76; (b) 52.50

53. (a) $(I\ddot{s})_{\overline{n|}}$; (b) $\ddot{a}_{\overline{n+1|}}$; (c) $(I\ddot{s})_{\overline{k|}}$; (d) $s^{(p)}_{\overline{1|}}$;
(e) $(Ia)_{\overline{n|}}$; (f) $(Da)_{\overline{10|}}$

54. All

55. All but (d)

56. (2) $s_{\overline{1|}} = 1$, $s_{\overline{t|}} = s_{\overline{t-1|}}(1 + i) + 1$ or $s_{\overline{t-1|}} + (1 + i)^{t-1}$,
$(Is)_{\overline{n|}} = [s_{\overline{n|}}(1 + i) - n]/i$;
(4) $(Da)_{\overline{1|}} = v$, $(Da)_{\overline{t|}} = (Da)_{\overline{t-1|}} + a_{\overline{t|}}$,
$[.5n(n + 1) - (Da)_{\overline{n|}}]/i$;
(6) $(Ds)_{\overline{1|}} = 1$, $(Ds)_{\overline{t|}} = (Ds)_{\overline{t-1|}} + t(1 + i)^{t-1}$,
$[(1 + i)(Ds)_{\overline{n|}} - (Is)_{\overline{n|}}]/i$

57. \$1,130.98

58. $(\bar{a}_{\overline{n|}})^2$

60. (a) (1) $-v(\bar{I}\,\bar{a})_{\overline{n|}}$, (2) $v(\bar{D}\,\bar{s})_{\overline{n|}}$, (3) $v[(\bar{D}\,\bar{s})_{\overline{n|}} - (\bar{I}\,\bar{s})_{\overline{n|}}]/\delta$,
(4) $v[(\bar{I}\,\bar{a})_{\overline{n|}} - (\bar{D}\,\bar{a})_{\overline{n|}}]/\delta$;
(b) (1) v^n, (2) $(1 + i)^n$, (3) $\bar{s}_{\overline{n|}}$, (4) $\bar{a}_{\overline{n|}}$

61. 27.47 yrs.

62. (a)-(c) True; (d), (e) False

63. $(\bar{I}\,\bar{a})_{\overline{n|}} < (\bar{a}_{\overline{n|}})^2$

65. (a) $A = [1 - (1 + r)^n v^n]/[\ln(1 + i) - \ln(1 + r)]$,
if $r \neq i$, $r > -1$; n if $r = i$;
(b) $A = [2(\bar{I}\,\bar{a})_{\overline{n|}} - n^2v^n]/\delta$

66. (a) 7/6; (b) $2 \ln 2 \doteq 1.39$; (c) $4(1 - \ln 2) \doteq 1.23$

67. (a) (1) $\bar{s}_{\overline{1|}}$, (2) $\lim_{p\to\infty} s^{(p)}_{\overline{1|}}$; (b) (1) $\lim_{p\to\infty} s^{(p)}_{\overline{n|}}$,
(2) $\lim_{p\to\infty} \ddot{s}^{(p)}_{\overline{n|}}$; (c) (1) $\bar{s}_{\overline{1|}}(Is)_{\overline{n|}}$, (2) $\lim_{p\to\infty} (Is)^{(p)}_{\overline{n|}}$

68. (a) Payments $1/p^2$, $2/p^2$, $3/p^2$, ... , np/p^2

69. (a) \$1,980.13; (b) \$2,000.00; (c) \$2,029.56

70. 30; \$1,161.36

71. \$550.87

72. $100\,\bar{a}_{\overline{25|}}/\delta$

73. 16,020.00

76. (a) (1) $1/d^2$, (2) $1/[i^{(p)}d]$, (3) $1/[d^{(p)}d]$,
(4) $1/[i^{(p)}d^{(p)}]$, (5) $[1/d^{(p)}]^2$;
(b) (i) (1) 100, (2) 101, (3) 100.4992, (4) 100.4575,
(5) 100.5408, (6) 10,100, (7) 10,150.42, (8) 10,100.09;
(ii) (1) 10,201, (2) 10,146.21, (3) 10,154.62,
(4) 10,100.08, (5) 10,108.45

77. 105; \$0.84 to A

78. (a) \$28.00; (b) \$26.93; (c) \$14.99; (d) \$27.27;
(e) \$67.84; (f) \$21.75

79. At $i = .02$: (a) $100\, a_{\overline{10}|} v^3 = 100(a_{\overline{13}|} - a_{\overline{3}|})$;
(b) $100\, a_{\overline{20}|} / a_{\overline{2}|}$; (c) $100 + 200\, s_{\overline{1}|}^{(2)} a_{\overline{4}|}$;
(d) $600\, s_{\overline{1}|}^{(6)}\, s_{\overline{20}|}$; (e) $100\, s_{\overline{60}|} [1 + (1+i)^{60}]$;
(f) $50(i/\delta)(s_{\overline{10}|} + a_{\overline{20}|})$; (g) $50(1.02)^{10}/\delta$;
(h) $90\, a_{\overline{40}|} - 20\, a_{\overline{30}|} + 30\, a_{\overline{16}|}$

80. (a) $20{,}000(5\, s_{\overline{1}|}^{(2)} + 6\, \bar{s}_{\overline{1}|} + 4\, s_{\overline{3}|}^{-1} + 2\, a_{\overline{5}|}^{-1}) v^{1/2}$;
(b) Buy \$100 article

81. (a) \$365.63; (b) \$515.75

82. (a) 17 payments of \$50 and an 18th of \$25.03;
(b) 17 payments of \$50 and at the end of 9 yrs. no payment but a refund of \$4.97

83. (a) $A(1 + i' s_{\overline{n}|i})$, $S/(1 + i' s_{\overline{n}|i})$;
(b) $\sum_{t=1}^{n} B_t (1 + i' s_{\overline{n-t}|i})$,
$R[n + \frac{i'}{i}(s_{\overline{n}|i} - n)] = R[n + i'(Is)_{\overline{n-1}|i}]$;

(d)

	$i = i'$	$i = 0$
(a)	$A(1+i)^n$, $S v^n$	$A(1 + i'n)$, $S/(1 + i'n)$
(b)	$\sum_1^n B_t (1+i)^{n-t}$, $R s_{\overline{n}|}$	$\sum_1^n B_t [1+i'(n-t)]$, $nR[1+i'(n-1)/2]$
(c)	$\sum_1^n B_t v^t$, $R\, a_{\overline{n}|}$	$\sum_1^n B_t/(1+i'n)$, $nR/(1+i'n)$

(e) (i) (1) \$2,200.61, (2) \$2,202.84; (ii) \$754.58;
(iii) \$18,616.64; (v) \$7,695.79; (vi) \$7,704.59

Problem List 4

1. (a) 0.6 A; (b) 0.4 A; (c) 1.2 Ai; (d) 0.9 A
2. (a) 9.00%; (b) 6.09%
3. (a) 2.23; (b) 1.7413722; (d) \$6,394
4. (a) \$513.96; (b) \$13,325; (c) $R(5 - a_{\overline{40}|} + a_{\overline{35}|})$;
(d) \$58.59; (e) (1) $R(2\, a_{\overline{n}|} - a_{\overline{2n}|})$,
(2) $R(1 - v^{2n})/s_{\overline{2}|}$
5. (a) 16th, after 31 periods; (b) (i) 13, (ii) 33
6. A_{42} = \$3,647.64, $\sum$ Interest = 120.41 = $R(3 - a_{\overline{21}|} + a_{\overline{18}|})$

7. $1,232.48; $5,264.70

8. (1) $A/(p\,a^{(p)}_{\overline{n}|})$, (2) $A(1 - v^{n-(h-1)/p})/(p\,a^{(p)}_{\overline{n}|})$,

(3) $Av^{n-(h-1)/p}/(p\,a^{(p)}_{\overline{n}|})$,

(4) $A\,a^{(p)}_{\overline{n-(h/p)}|} / a^{(p)}_{\overline{n}|}$, (5) $A(1 - a^{(p)}_{\overline{n-k+1}|} + a^{(p)}_{\overline{n-k}|}) / a^{(p)}_{\overline{n}|}$,

(6) $A(a^{(p)}_{\overline{n-k+1}|} - a^{(p)}_{\overline{n-k}|}) / a^{(p)}_{\overline{n}|}$

9. (a) (1) $3.96, (2) $188.09, (3) $35.34;

(b) (1) $1{,}000\,[(1.06)^{1/12} - 1]\,a_{\overline{4-1/6}|.06} / a_{\overline{5}|.06}$,

(2) $1{,}000\,a_{\overline{1-1/6}|.06} / a_{\overline{5}|.06}$,

(3) $1{,}000\,\{[5/(6s^{(12)}_{\overline{1}|.06})] - a_{\overline{4-1/4}|.06} + a_{\overline{3-1/12}|.06}\}/a_{\overline{5}|.06}$

10. $1,000.00; 6.09%; $79.61

11. (a) (1) $nR\,v^{n+1}$, $R(v_j^n - v_i^n)/(i - j)$;

(2) $R(a_{\overline{n}|} - nv^{n+1})$, $R[a_{\overline{n}|j} + (v_j^n - v_i^n)/(j - i)]$

or $Ri[a_{\overline{n}|i} + (v_j^n - v_i^n)/(j - i)]/j$

12. $A_h < A'_h$ $(h = 1, 2, \cdots, n - 1)$,

$i\,A_h < i'A'_h$ $(h = 0, 1, 2, \cdots, n - 1)$

13. $10{,}000\,i/(1 + a_{\overline{9}|} - 10v^{10})$, $R(h + 1 + a_{\overline{9-h}|} - 10v^{10-h})/i$

or $10{,}000(1+i)^h - R(s_{\overline{h+1}|} - h - 1)/i$, $R(h + 1 + a_{\overline{9-h}|} - 10v^{10-h})$

14. (a) (1) $21v^{11} - a_{\overline{11}|}$, (2) $(21 + \frac{1}{i})v^{11}(1 - v^9)$;

(b) $0 \le i \le 1/2\%$

15. (a) $A(1 + i)^t - [(Ds)_{\overline{t}|} + (n - t)s_{\overline{t}|}]$, $(Da)_{\overline{n-t}|} + {}_{n-t|}a_{\overline{m}|}$;

(b) $A(1 + i)^t - [(Ds)_{\overline{n}|}(1 + i)^{t-n} + s_{\overline{t-n}|}]$, $a_{\overline{n+m-t}|}$

16. $544.90, $714.96, $6,222.50

17. (a) $2{,}000\,a^{-1}_{\overline{30}|}[7 + 18\,a_{\overline{23}|}(1 + i)^5/a_{\overline{18}|} - a_{\overline{30}|}]$ at .035;

(b) $2{,}000(a_{\overline{23}|} - a_{\overline{18}|})/a_{\overline{30}|}$ at .035

18. (a) $940; (b) $2,457

19. (a) (1) $254.29, (2) $58.98; (b) $58.67

20. (a) $10.09 at end of 78 months;

(b) At .005, $1{,}000(1 + i)^{30} - 100\,s_{\overline{24}|}/a_{\overline{6}|}$,

$10.09\,v^{48} + 100\,a_{\overline{48}|}/a_{\overline{6}|}$

21. $967.59; $6,282.54

22. (a) 59

24. (a) $1,144.61; (b) $4,114.40;

(c) (1) $380.36, (2) $864.09

27. (a) $10{,}000(15 - \bar{s}_{\overline{1}|}\, a_{\overline{15}|})/(20 - \bar{s}_{\overline{1}|}\, a_{\overline{20}|})$;

(b) $10{,}000(14.5\delta + \bar{s}_{\overline{1}|}\, v^{15} - 1)/(20 - \bar{s}_{\overline{1}|}\, a_{\overline{20}|})$

28. $A_{10} = \$10{,}135.34$

29. $159.12

30. (a) $R(1 - i/i')(k - a'_{\overline{n-h}|} + a'_{\overline{n-h-k}|})$;

(b) $R(a_{\overline{k}|} - a'_{\overline{n-h}|} + v^k a'_{\overline{n-h-k}|})$

31. (a) $935.82; (b) $6,048.40, Yes

32. (a) $5,162.77; (b) $36,000

33. (a) $40.19; (b) $118.17

34. (a) (1) $6,269.41, (2) $36,995.26; see Example 4.4;

(b) $$\frac{1000\left[(10s_{\overline{10}|.05} - 2s_{\overline{2}|.05})(1.04)^{10} + 8s_{\overline{10}|.04} - 3s_{\overline{5}|.04}\right]}{1 + .07\left[s_{\overline{10}|.05}(1.04)^{10} + s_{\overline{10}|.04}\right]}$$

35. (a) $432.91; (b) $1,761; (c) $1,892

36. (b) 5.66%; (c) 6.76%

37. (b) $(1 + i')^{1/p} - (1 + i)^{1/p}$

38. (a) $700/(.05 + s^{-1}_{\overline{5}|.04})$;

(b) $25\, a_{\overline{2}|.05} + 1{,}150(1.05)^{-2}/(.05 + s^{-1}_{\overline{3}|.04})$;

(c) $500(2\, s_{\overline{5}|.04} - s_{\overline{3}|.04})/(1 + .05\, s_{\overline{5}|.04})$

39. (a) (1) $458.37, (2) $91.72; (b) $30.87; (c) (2) No

42. $3,839.96

43. (b) $86.89

44. $90.20, at the end of 11 quarters; $A_5 = \$556.21$, $A_{10} = \$88.43$

45. (a) $(i' - i)K(1 + i)^h$; (b) $(R - iA)(1 + i)^h - Rv'^{\,n-h}$

46. (b) $36,838.87;

(c)(1) $2000s^{(2)}_{\overline{1}|.04}a_{\overline{20}|.04} + \dfrac{.03}{.04^{(2)}}(40000 - 2000s^{(2)}_{\overline{1}|.04}a_{\overline{20}|.04})$,

(2) $1000s^{-1}_{\overline{2}|.01}a_{\overline{80}|.01} + \dfrac{.0150}{.0201}(40000 - 1000s^{-1}_{\overline{2}|.01}a_{\overline{80}|.01})$

47. (a) 4.50%; (b)(1) $4,158.06, (2) $3,657.76;

(c) $3,691.68

49. (c) $i = (nR - A)/\{n[A - (n - 1)R/2]\}$

50. (a) (1) $10{,}000\, a_{\overline{6}|.06} / a_{\overline{10}|.05}$,

(2) $(10{,}000\, s^{-1}_{\overline{10}|.05} + 500)/(s^{-1}_{\overline{6}|.04} + .06)$;

(b) (1) $5{,}000 + 1{,}000\, a_{\overline{6|}.06} / 6$,

(2) $(7{,}500 + 50\, s_{\overline{6|}.04}) / (1 + .06\, s_{\overline{6|}.04})$

Problem List 5

1. (a) (1) \$1,144.98, (2) \$989.97;

(b) At .02, $A = 50\, s_{\overline{2|}}^{-1}\, a_{\overline{18|}} + 1{,}100\, v^{18}$

$= 1{,}100 + (50\, s_{\overline{2|}}^{-1} - 22)\, a_{\overline{18|}}$

$= 2{,}500\, s_{\overline{2|}}^{-1} + (1{,}100 - 2{,}500\, s_{\overline{2|}}^{-1})\, v^{18}$

$= K + \frac{25}{11}\, s_{\overline{2|}}^{-1}\, (1{,}100 - K)$, where $K = 1{,}100\, v^{18}$;

(c) $25\, s_{\overline{1|}}^{(2)}\, a_{\overline{18|}} + 1{,}100\, v^{18}$ at .02, etc.;

(d) $50\, s_{\overline{1|}}^{(2)}\, a_{\overline{9|}} + 1{,}100\, v^{9}$, etc.

2. (a) (1) \$1,083.75, (2) \$958.50; (b) \$1,408.94; (c) \$1,426.50; (d) \$1,005.20
3. (a) \$1,007.91; (b) \$988.12
4. \$1,075.02
5. \$21.29
6. (a) \$832.99; (b) \$726.57
8. (a) \$1,071.76; (b) \$1,071.79
9. \$1,033.33
11. (a) \$118.34; (b) \$117.93
12. (1) (a) \$574.39; (b) \$931.23; (c) \$964.90; (d) \$28.95; (e) \$57.12;
    (2) (a) \$418.24; (b) \$1,074.96; (c) \$1,036.63; (d) \$20.73; (e) \$42.04
13. (a) (i) \$1,127.45, (ii) \$1,112.40;
    (b) (i) \$1,127.67, (ii) \$1,112.18
15. (a) \$1,004.90, \$81.33; (b) \$972.91, \$117.52
16. \$812.14, \$1,018.08, 1.67%
18. Theoretical I: \$1,028.65, \$6.20, \$1,022.45;
    Semitheoretical II: \$1,028.65, \$6.25, \$1,022.40;
    Practical III: \$1,028.69, \$6.25, \$1,022.44
19. 2.95 yrs.
20. By the practical method: (a) (i) \$963.60 (exact), (ii) \$982.68 (exact), (iii) \$997.42 (approx.)
22. (a) $A_2 = \$1{,}014.42$; (b) \$96.31
23. Bond interest for interval: $Frs_{\overline{t|}\,i}$ for I, Frt for II, III;
    Interest at yield rate for interval: $A_h\,[(1 + i)^t - 1]$ for I, II, $A_h it$ for III; Etc.;
    Capital gain (loss) = $|\text{Quoted price} - A_{h+t}|$
25. (a) True for I, II only; (b) I, III; (c) I, III; (d) I, II; (e) All; (f) I, II

26. 5.45%, 5.43%, 5.40%; for $i_0 = 2.5\%$, $2i_3^{I} = 2i_4^{I} = 2i = 5.39\% = 2i_2^{II}$

27. (b) Calculate i_1; if $i_1 \gtreqless i_0$, then $i_0 \lesseqgtr i$.

28. 3.998%

29. (a) 4.80%

31. (a) 4.6%; (b) 6.7%

32. 5.69% based on $a_{\overline{30|}}^{-1}$; 5.70%, on $a_{\overline{30|}}$

33. 4.4%

34. (b) Errs in the same direction as in (a), but worse.

35. (a) \$884.43; (b) \$1,000.00; (c) \$1,111.98

36. (a) \$884.43; (b) \$1,000.00; (c) \$1,136.78

37. (a) \$899.75; (b) \$1,018.62; (c) \$1,126.95

38. (a) (i) 2.07%, (ii) 2.00%

40. All true

41. (a) $A^* = 40{,}000\,(30 - a_{\overline{20|}.025} / s_{\overline{4|}.025})$;

(b) $A^* + 80{,}000\ s_{\overline{4|}}^{-1}\ (5 - a_{\overline{20|}} / s_{\overline{4|}})$

or $A^* + 2{,}000\ \sum_{k=1}^{5} k\ v^{4(6-k)}$ at .025

42. (a) \$1,230.25; (b) \$473.98; (c) $A_7^* = \$992.32$

43. \$89,024.25

44. 5/24

45. (a) \$9,203.81; (b) $A_2 = \$8{,}688.40$, (i) \$565.68, (ii) \$5,823.68

47. (a) $A_h + (A_h i - Fr)t_2$, where A_h is the book value at time h, to yield rate i if the bond were held to redemption;
(b) Use an iteration method, with $g = Fr/A_{h+t_2}$,

$k = (A_{t_1} - A_{h+t_2}) / A_{h+t_2}$, $n = h + t_2 - t_1$

48. (a) \$638.62; (b) \$738.62; (c) \$707.43;
(d) Case (a): Both 5%, Case (b): 6.37% vs. 6.08%;
Case (c): 6.37% vs. 5.88%

Problems in A.1

8. (b) $S_n = S_0(1 + in)$

9. (b) $A_n = Rs_{\overline{n|}}$

10. (b) $A_n = R(Is)_{\overline{n|}}$

11. (a) $A_n = R\ddot{s}_{\overline{n|}}$; (b) $A_0 = R\,a_{\overline{n|}}$; (c) $A_0 = R\,\ddot{a}_{\overline{n|}}$

12. If h = 1, 2, 3, ⋯, n, (a) $A_h = (1 + i)(A_{h-1} + hR)$, $A_0 = 0$; (b) $A_h = (1 + i)A_{h-1} - hR$, $A_n = 0$;
(c) $A_h = (1 + i)(A_{h-1} - hR)$, $A_n = 0$

INDEX

(Numbers refer to pages, except numbers in parentheses are problem numbers.)